S0-BQY-537

A volume in the

DOUGLASS SERIES IN EDUCATION,

edited by HARL R. DOUGLASS, Ph.D.,

DIRECTOR OF THE COLLEGE OF EDUCATION,
UNIVERSITY OF COLORADO

TECHNIQUES OF SECONDARY SCHOOL TEACHING

RALPH K. WATKINS

PROFESSOR OF EDUCATION
THE UNIVERSITY OF MISSOURI

THE RONALD PRESS COMPANY · NEW YORK

Preface

This is a book on ways of teaching secondary school pupils. The emphasis throughout is on how the operations involved in good teaching are performed. The book should be useful as a text in courses for prospective secondary school teachers and as a reference for the improvement of teaching procedures for teachers in service.

It is probable that during the lifetime of this book there will not be enough adequately prepared teachers to meet the pressures brought about by the increasing numbers of pupils entering our secondary schools. Even now these pressures are producing countless expedients proposed as partial substitutes for the well-educated teachers who are needed but not available. These expedients range from the use of motion pictures, the televising of expert lecturing and demonstration, and the use of closed-circuit television so that one teacher can serve many classrooms, to the use of partially trained teachers' aides—in the pattern of nurses' aides—who relieve teachers of routine duties and thereby enable the teachers to extend their services to these increasing numbers of pupils. Some of these proposals may have merit, but in the main they are inadequate substitutes for a classroom teacher who knows what he is about and how he should proceed.

There has always been controversy about the value of courses on "methods of teaching." Some maintain that teachers are born, not made. The implication is that the "born teacher" needs no indoctrination in methods. Others claim that anyone who knows enough subject matter can teach it. The implication is that all methodology is nonsense, that any scholar can teach. This book is written from the point of view that intelligent, well-adjusted, mature people can *learn to teach,* and that even experienced teachers can improve their teaching. There is no claim that personality factors do not affect teaching, and there is certainly no claim that the teacher can teach something of which he is ignorant. Teaching method is not a crutch for inadequate scholarship—but neither is scholarship a substitute for teaching competency.

In a course on methods of teaching, the prospective teacher should be made aware of the limitations under which teaching operates. No teacher can establish learning in pupils; learning is the changed behavior which results from the experiences of the learners. The teacher cannot substitute his experiences for those of the pupils. Effective learning requires a degree of willingness on the part of the learners. At best, the teacher can stimulate and guide, or direct, the learning experiences of pupils. The football coach agonizing on the bench cannot run plays for the players. He may send in a substitute with directions, but finally what happens on the field develops out of the experiences of the boys on the team. Effective coaching provides these experiences in the weeks preceding the game. What is said here of the coach and his team applies equally well to the classroom teacher and his pupils in English, algebra, Spanish, music, speech, art, home economics, shop, chemistry, or typewriting.

The prospective teacher should be reminded that effective teaching is a closely interwoven process the operations of which are exceedingly difficult to separate, although it is useful to attempt such a separation in order to see more clearly how the operations can be performed well. He should be reminded that in this book the various teaching operations are pulled out from the complex of the total process and are presented in sequence—even though in practice the operations are often carried out simultaneously—in order to describe the methods involved. The fabric is pulled apart until the web is apparent, in order to see how the fabric is put together.

The order of presentation, built around a series of major questions (see Contents), corresponds to the steps a teacher would employ in planning and carrying out his work: determining what objectives are to be accomplished; selecting the subject matter needed to accomplish the objectives; organizing the subject matter and the experiences of pupils to accomplish the objectives with a minimum of waste; organizing for learning to insure a maximum of retention and of efficiency in use; implementing the learning processes through the selection of experiences and activities; stimulating and directing the learning experiences (this is the problem of method); and, finally, determining how much has been learned and how well.

Each of these major questions which must be raised in teaching finally comes back to the question of what the teacher is trying to accomplish in terms of changes produced in pupils.

Throughout the book, large-unit organization in planning has been emphasized. For this reason the book itself has been arranged in six units. Each of these units takes as its title one of the major questions which confront the reader. The chapters in Units IV, V, and VI may be regarded as subunits.

The units and subunits have a definite structure. At the beginning of each unit there is an introduction addressed directly to the reader. Then, at the beginning of each unit or subunit, there is a list of questions (WHAT TO LOOK FOR) to be used as guides in reading and as possible centers for discussion.

At the close of each unit or subunit will be found a section titled "Unit Implementation" or "Subunit Implementation." Each of these sections begins with a sentence-statement outline of the content (UNIT ORGANIZATION or SUBUNIT ORGANIZATION). Students should be reminded that this is a summary and an aid in organization, not a set of statements to be memorized for passing tests. Readers are invited to make their own statements in summary, using those in the text for purposes of comparison. Following the sentence-statement outline will be found a set of exercises (THINGS TO DO). It is hoped that these will be valuable, but others will doubtless occur to the teacher and to the student. Finally, there will be found a selected reading list (HELPFUL READINGS) which includes pertinent parallel reading and also source materials which amplify the text.

The concept of unit planning is introduced in the first unit and is then used throughout the rest of the book. It is expected that in addition to reading and discussing what is in the text, the student will participate in a variety of accompanying experiences in planning. Such experiences may range from writing course and unit introductions, and developing unit tests and evaluative devices, to planning a layout for an entire high school course and then developing the content for selected units of the course.

The organization and content of the book have been tested and developed with college students over a period of many years. The exercises recommended have actually been carried out by students and by selected teachers in the field. In the illustrative applications an attempt has been made to keep in mind the range of subject-matter interests of teachers and pupils in present-day secondary schools. Applications have been drawn from shop, art, music, typewriting, home economics, agriculture, and physical education, as well as from English, literature, mathematics, natural science, social studies, and foreign languages.

It is my hope that this book will contribute to the teaching competency of its readers and therefore to the very great and real need for the kind of teaching which can reach the pupils of our rapidly expanding secondary schools.

I wish to acknowledge my indebtedness to the many people who have contributed to the development of my professional thinking. These include famous teachers of a previous generation, many of my colleagues in the professional education of teachers, and a host of students, undergraduate and graduate, who over the years have furnished stimulation, suggestion, and criticism.

R. K. W.

Columbia, Missouri
    January, 1958

Contents

TECHNIQUES OF SECONDARY SCHOOL TEACHING

Unit I

What Are the School and the Teacher Trying to Accomplish?

Suppose that you were placed in a group of new high school pupils for the first time this morning. What do you believe these young people should be learning? How can you justify your own belief about what young people of secondary school age should learn?

What can be accomplished with young people in your teaching field? Perhaps better, what is there to offer from your teaching field that is valuable to young people in our present world?

To what extent do you agree with published statements of purposes for secondary education? What are your reactions to current statements of objectives in your own teaching field?

The material of this unit is presented in the hope that it will help in formulating answers to questions such as these. It is not intended that the reader must accept solutions to such problems as presented here. Rather, the content of the unit should help him in formulating his own ideas concerning his place in directing the growth of the pupils in his classes.

What to look for in this unit

1. Which of the several recently published sets of institutional aims for the secondary school are you most willing to accept?

2. Why should the modern secondary school teacher be concerned with Herbert Spencer's analysis of "complete living" made in 1859? Why should the modern teacher be concerned with the statement of the "Cardinal Principles" made in 1918?

3. What difficulties are involved in trying to build workable teaching procedures for a high school course in your major field, using a set of institutional aims as the basis?

4. Where can you find satisfactory statements of teaching objectives for courses in your field?

5. How do unit objectives differ from course objectives?

6. How can the teacher evaluate the statements of objectives that he may work out for his own pupils?

7. What is to be done when the teacher drifts into traditional statements of disciplinary objectives to justify practices in a teaching field?

8. What do people outside the school do with principles, ideals, ideas, or skills found in your teaching field?

9. Do young people of high school age have any real need for the subject matter of your courses?

Formulation of Teaching
Objectives

The teacher with a new group of pupils is always confronted with questions of what is best for them. Are their needs the same as those of the young folk with whom the teacher went to school? How do their problems differ from those of the boys and girls in last year's class? Are the demands of society upon its members the same as they were a year or ten years ago?

Many teachers still tend to respond to queries such as these by such statements as the following: "I am employed to teach English. What else should I do?" "Boys and girls come to school to learn what the school offers. Why waste time discussing the obvious?" "I teach algebra. Algebra is always the same. I expect every pupil who comes into my class to learn algebra." "All pupils should learn to think. I expect everyone who comes into my chemistry class to learn to reason."

Professional educators have stressed the importance of statements of educational objectives until teachers have grown weary of the reiteration. Yet the problem of direction of the educative process is fundamental. In order to do any planning at all, both pupil and teacher must face the issue, "What are we trying to accomplish?" Even the statements quoted in the preceding paragraph, which seem to avoid the issue, do in themselves commit the teacher to a certain policy.

3

The question of direction is as fundamental to all of life's other basic enterprises as it is to learning and teaching. People talk about vacation trips during which they wander from day to day. Few make such trips. Most frequently, travel means a definite objective and a plan for getting more out of the experience. The man who enters merchandising must determine certain policies in purchasing and selling before the business can be organized and the stock purchased. So the teacher, in determining the direction of a given course, must establish goals, fix policies, and define the centers about which the course can be planned.

Traditionally, teachers say: "I teach music," or "I teach English." Actually, teachers do not teach *subjects,* such as literature, geometry, and physical education. Nor do they teach the various forms of reorganized *curricula*—core curriculum, social living, and general education. Rather they teach *people.* Even more appropriately, teachers attempt to direct the experiences and activities of young people toward the achievement of certain projected outcomes. The subject matter and the activities are a means to the accomplishment of the desired goals, not the goals themselves.

In educational literature there are many discussions of the ultimate goals of education, such as the famous pronouncement of Herbert Spencer, the proposal of the Educational Policies Commission of the National Education Association in 1938, and the statement of the National Association of Secondary School Principals in *Planning for American Youth* in 1951.

Most teachers readily agree upon the desirability of improved citizenship or the appreciation of the family as a social institution. A difficulty arises, however, from the gap between lip service to high ideals of education and the practical need for planning this week's work in the classroom. The teacher who sees the obvious need for good citizenship too often thinks of himself as, say, a teacher of American history, but in requiring pupils to memorize a chronology of events he forgets the immediate issues of citizenship occurring in the evolving history of the pupil's own world.

This gap between a defined philosophy of education and daily school practices seems to grow out of confusion concerning the relationship of school processes to the size of the goals to be attained. It is proposed that objectives for secondary schools can be classified in terms of the school units involved. Such a classification is suggested below.

1. Institutional objectives
2. Course objectives
3. Unit objectives

Institutional objectives

Institutional purposes are the broad, general objectives set up for the whole of education, for such an institution as the public high school, or for some one particular high school. The primary source of institutional objectives is found in a philosophy of education.

It is not expected that all institutional objectives are to be served at the same time by a single high school course. On the other hand, the objectives for any one high school course must be consistent with the accepted purposes of the school as a whole.

Illustrations of institutional objectives can be found in the well-known pronouncements mentioned above. Other illustrative statements are in *The Functions of Secondary Education* of the Department of Secondary School Principals of the National Education Association, and in the proposals of Harl Douglass for the report of the American Youth Commission of the American Council on Education, *Secondary Education for Youth in Modern America.*

Others can be found in the publications of state departments of education of the various states and in those of several city school systems. Sometimes very effective statements of institutional purposes are produced by local committees of teachers and administrators. For the prospective teacher, a collection of institutional objectives from the various sources will serve as a means of making the function of institutional purposes more evident.

One illustration of a modern statement of institutional objectives follows. It is reprinted from *Planning for American Youth*, National Association of Secondary School Principals.

The Ten Imperative Needs of Youth

1. All youth need to develop saleable skills and those understandings and attitudes that make the worker an intelligent and productive participant in economic life.

2. All youth need to develop and maintain good health and physical fitness and mental health.

3. All youth need to understand the rights and duties of the citizen of a democratic society, and to be diligent and competent in the performance of their obligations as members of the community and citizens of the state and nation, and to have an understanding of the nations and peoples of the world.

4. All youth need to understand the significance of the family for the individual and society and the conditions conducive to successful family life.

5. All youth need to know how to purchase and use goods and services intelligently, understanding both the values received by the consumer and the economic consequences of their acts.

6. All youth need to understand the methods of science, the influence of science on human life, and the main scientific facts concerning the nature of the world and man.

7. All youth need opportunities to develop their capacities to appreciate beauty, in literature, art, music, and nature.

8. All youth need to be able to use their leisure time well and budget it wisely, balancing activities that yield satisfaction to the individual with those that are socially useful.

9. All youth need to develop respect for other persons . . . to be able to live and work co-operatively with others, and to grow in the moral and spiritual values of life.

10. All youth need to grow in their ability to think rationally, to express their thoughts clearly, and to read and listen with understanding.

FUNCTION OF INSTITUTIONAL OBJECTIVES. The function of institutional objectives is to aid school people in determining the direction of the school as a whole. Such objectives should sketch in broad outlines the important educational policies of the school. They should serve as the primary determiners of the nature and content of the school program. For example, if the staff of a school in an industrial area says that the most important goal of the school is to provide young people with vocational skills, it is clear that the program of the school is to be vocational and that the next step is to determine which vocations are to be stressed.

On the other hand, if the staff of a small rural high school says that, within its physical and financial limitations, the most important goal is a well-rounded general education, all vocational courses as such should be questioned immediately. The next step is to determine the more crucial common educational needs of all young people attending the school.

THE TEACHER AND INSTITUTIONAL OBJECTIVES. Often a teacher feels that institutional objectives are of little concern to him. This is likely to be the attitude of a teacher in a school system where teachers have had nothing to do with the development of the goals.

Examine the effect of such an attitude upon the teacher himself. Suppose a teacher is considering a position in a new school, or suppose an inexperienced teacher is applying for a first teaching position. Would it not be wise to ask some questions of policy concerning the new school before making a final decision? Suppose the school in question is in a privileged residential area of a city. It is committed to a policy of academic training, chiefly for purposes of college preparation. If the teacher is a teacher of vocational home economics, is it probable that she will be professionally happy in a narrowly academic school?

Or again, the school is a relatively large school in a rural area. It is committed to a program of terminal vocational education with a major emphasis upon vocational agriculture and vocational home economics. The teacher is trained in English. She believes in high standards of literary appreciation of classic selections from famous literature. She also believes that young people should attempt polished written compositions through an analytic study of language structure. Can she be happy in the school under consideration? Questions of this kind should always arise with teachers seeking employment.

Teachers of long tenure who find themselves out of step with established school policies have similar problems. Sometimes, the inquiring teacher can find no trace of announced institutional policies. Possibly a school such as this is the least desirable from the point of view of the professional worker.

Course objectives

Most classroom teachers will be more concerned with details of planning the courses they teach than with large-scale planning of school programs. Intelligent determination of what to do within the limits of a particular course depends upon the purposes to be attained by the pupils. What are the sources of course objectives? Where does the teacher get his course objectives? How are these formulated? How are they presented to the pupils?

Before attempting to arrive at answers to such questions it may be wise to clarify the definitions of a few terms. A school "course" is usually defined as a *school year's work* in a given field or curricular area. Customarily, it is assumed that if the pupils meet five days per week for at least 36 weeks, they will receive one credit. This seems to be a satisfactory administrative definition. The relatively few courses that continue for 18 weeks rather than 36 may be defined as half courses. Courses continuing for 36 weeks and meeting for only two or three days per week receive fractional credit.

Sometimes there is confusion in making a distinction between courses and subjects. For example, algebra is a subject, but Algebra I taught to ninth-grade pupils for a school year is a course in algebra. Physical education is a subject, but Physical Education II taught to second-year girls for the school year is a course.

In many schools, at least a part of the school program is organized in *broad* areas which are often complexes of previous subjects or attempts to draw materials directly from the lives of pupils. A few such areas are those of health, citizenship, homemaking, and diversified occupations. Courses may be developed directly within the areas, so that there are such courses as Health I, Citizenship II, or Homemaking III.

Some schools organize the basic requirements of the program

into a *core curriculum* which occupies half the time of the pupils each year and most often carries two credits for the year's work. In terms of the original definition, a school year's work within the core may be thought of as a course. Administratively, since the work receives two credits, it may be considered as a double course.

FUNCTIONS OF COURSE OBJECTIVES. Course objectives, then, are the statements of purpose for a school year's work within a single course. The functions of the course objectives are:

1. To help teachers and pupils in clarifying the nature and direction of a particular course
2. To help in selecting the instructional units that are to compose the content of the course
3. To offer suggestions in determining the types of pupil activities that may be of value in attaining goals
4. To aid in determining the appropriateness of tests and evaluative devices

In other words, course objectives become the guide lines about which the content and work of a course are planned.

A few illustrations will show the difference in courses in the same field with changed objectives. Consider the difference between Spanish I intended to help pupils acquire a knowledge of Spanish grammar to pass college entrance examinations and Spanish I intended to help pupils learn to read Spanish newspapers at sight. Or, consider physical education for physical conditioning as contrasted with physical education to improve basic skills in popular sports. What would be the difference in literature courses to accomplish these objectives—"to become acquainted with a few of the greatest English classics" or "to improve standards of selection in personal reading through contact with a relatively wide range of popular literature"?

SOURCES OF COURSE OBJECTIVES. Many of the published statements of objectives for courses within particular fields are the work of committees of experienced teachers. Some of the reports have been made by local committees for a particular high school and some by national groups of teachers for their particular organizations. Materials from city and state systems are usually published as city and state courses of study.

They can be obtained from the city superintendent of schools or from the state department of education. Many teacher-training institutions have collections of such courses of study in their libraries and curriculum laboratories.

National organizations of teachers interested in instruction in particular fields or subjects publish both magazines and yearbooks. Some of these are the National Council of Teachers of English, National Council of Teachers of Mathematics, National Council for the Social Studies, American Science Teachers Association, National Commercial Teachers Federation, American Vocational Association, and College Physical Education Association.

Publications of these organizations are in professional libraries and often in special libraries for teachers provided by local school systems. These publications furnish the most stimulating and suggestive sources of course objectives for the teachers interested in the field covered. Two cautions need to be observed in the use of such published statements. First, organized teachers of such fields as mathematics, English, foreign languages, home economics, industrial arts, and physical education are always enthusiasts concerning the values to be found in their own courses. Second, published statements of objectives for fields and courses tend to be general in nature. Always there needs to be an attempt to modify them in terms of the immediate needs of the local groups of pupils.

It is highly desirable that course objectives be developed by the teacher who is actually attempting to direct the learning of the pupils. In this sense, the sources of the ultimate course objectives are to be found in an analysis of the needs of the young people in the courses and in the educational philosophy of the teacher. Published statements of course objectives should be considered as suggestive samples of the work of others rather than as finally established goals to be slavishly followed.

In schools large enough to employ more than one teacher in a given field, teachers plan objectives cooperatively. The professional give-and-take involved in arriving at a tentative agreement among the teachers will do much to clarify the thinking of all concerned. There is always the possibility of certain peculiarities in the pupils in one class, making it necessary that the objectives set up for these pupils differ from those set up for other courses in the same field.

FORMS OF EXPRESSION FOR COURSE OBJECTIVES. Styles of expression used in stating course objectives change with shifting pedagogical movements. For this reason the form of statement does not seem to be as important as the thinking of the teachers behind the verbal expressions.

Infinitive statements. A currently popular form of expression for course objectives begins with an infinitive. Samples of objectives so expressed follow:

To develop an understanding and appreciation of the movements that have made the United States unique in the story of mankind

To develop in citizens a reasoned patriotism

To develop an appreciation and understanding of the dependence of one quantity upon another

To develop in pupils an appreciation and understanding of the language of algebra

To encourage good taste in music

To help students develop the ability, based on their knowledge of listening, to analyze music

To promote wide and discriminative reading of current periodicals and newspapers

To develop in students an appreciation of the fine ideals of the culture as exemplified in its literature

To assist pupils in using intelligently the services and facilities needed in conducting the business activities of a citizen

To help the pupil to understand and use his natural environment more effectively

To develop in each pupil elementary skills in the use of the more common tools and machines, and a knowledge of the methods of procedure in tasks frequently encountered by the average man

A careful examination of these typical samples of this form of statement will uncover some difficulties for the teacher. In the first place there is a sameness of expression that tends to make the statements of objectives a mere routine. Secondly, these expressions are often rather pointlessly vague. They say very little. Thirdly, they are addressed to other teachers and to other school workers. They tend toward what some critic of professional education has called *pedaguese*. Certainly, objectives should be so formulated that those people most concerned with their attainment—the pupils and the school patrons—can interpret them. A fourth criticism, not evident from the samples presented, is that sets of such expressions of objectives often include too many statements so that the primary attainments proposed are covered up by the mere number of objectives. Both teacher and pupils are confused in the detail of the design for the course.

Informal course introductions. A simpler approach to the formulation of course objectives is incorporation of the purposes in an informal introduction to the course presented orally to the pupils. Have in mind that a good course introduction is addressed to the young people concerned—not to fellow teachers, principals, and professional pedagogues. The course introduction has a dual function. It should make it possible for the members of the class and the *dual function of course objectives.*

teacher to see clearly the values to be attained from the work that follows. It should also attract. In some ways a good course introduction is a sales talk in which the teacher is the salesman and the pupils are the buyers. A good course introduction should make pupils want what the course has to offer and make them eager to get at the work proposed.

A few excerpts of statements of objectives taken from informal course introductions follow:

As you read literature primarily for enjoyment, you will be able to escape into the fascinating and adventurous realms of the past. You will be able to get an emotional and stimulating satisfaction from reading such stories as *Sir Gawain and the Green Knight.* You will be able to see that adventurous tales of the past are not so far removed from the *Superman* and the *Buck Rogers* stories of today.

We are going to study various forms of living organisms that affect you. Some of these you already know. But we shall acquire some new information, how these living organisms affect your health, your food, and your daily environment.

Our main objective in this class will be skill and speed in the writing of shorthand. I think that you will be able to write shorthand at the rate of 60 words per minute, possibly more, when this course is completed. Your vocabulary will be enlarged and enriched because you will come in contact with new words which you will want to know how to spell and use. We shall try to develop those desirable personal traits and qualities which will help you fit into life in the business world.

In our first-year course we shall not waste time by making samples of bound buttonholes or other specialized skills, but we shall study these skills in relationship to an entire garment. You will learn to make whole garments. We may make a simple house dress, and, if a need arises to have bound buttonholes in the garment, we shall make them. In home economics you will not make very complicated garments, but you will strive to make simple garments well.

Unit objectives

Almost all modern course planning assumes the "unit" as the center of organization for the work to be done most immediately. The old hand-to-mouth daily lesson planning has either passed from the scene or is rapidly passing. Obviously the first stage in a unit plan is that of agreeing upon the immediate goals.

NATURE OF A UNIT. The task of arriving at a statement of unit objectives will be much more definite if the nature of the unit is clarified. In the first place the unit has wholeness. It deals with a particular theme, problem, or project. Teacher and pupils try to see the implications of the whole enterprise to be undertaken in the next few weeks. The unit is built around something of immediate concern to the young people who are to work with it. It must have some center about which it can be organized. It should have some fundamental human or social worth, not be a temporary whim.

The unit often takes from three to twelve weeks for completion. Units which require less than three weeks are often so short as to be almost completely superficial. Very long units present the problem of the retention of sustained interest of pupils over many weeks. In practice, typical short units run three or four weeks; long ones, six, eight, or nine.

In most schools, courses are broken down into a pattern of units. In terms of time limits, six to twelve units will constitute a course.

A few teachers and a few schools think of the unit as the all-important center of planning and disregard the course structure. A relatively few units are selected for the year's work. These need not be the same from year to year but may vary with the particular pupils at hand. Obviously such units tend to be long, sometimes taking up a whole school term. At least two, three, or four units may make the school year's work. Often there seems to be little relationship between the units taught to a given group in a particular school year.

There is a tendency in some schools for the teacher and pupils to plan units together. Such cooperative planning may take place either with units which constitute a course or with units which seem to have sufficient worth to stand alone.

Whatever the relationship between the units used with the same group of pupils in a given school year, the units must be planned, and the planning involves a consideration of the objectives to be reached.

FORMS OF EXPRESSION FOR UNIT OBJECTIVES. Following are a few samples of statements of unit objectives which may be compared with the course objectives in the previous section.

Infinitive statements. As with course objectives, statements of unit objectives beginning with an infinitive are currently popular. Some samples follow:

> To learn to comprehend common idiomatic French expressions such as "Comment allez vous" and "Je suis tres bien "
> To arouse interests in planning and cooking meals at home
> To get pupils to form the habit of reading a worthwhile newspaper every day
> To help pupils select wholesome magazine stories for leisure reading
> To attempt to understand the economic and industrial conditions

affecting immigration, such as wages satisfying the immigrant and those satisfying the native

To develop ability to solve first degree equations involving one unknown, e.g., $14 - x = 27$; $x = 14 - 27$, etc.

To develop the abilities to analyze and present in outline form the gist of a lecture or a piece of literature and to write an expansion of such an outline

To learn to interpret different kinds of graphs such as temperature, population, and statistical graphs

Informal unit introductions. A more modern approach to the formulation of unit objectives is to include the unit objectives in an informal unit introduction addressed to the pupils. Again, such an introduction has a dual function. It should help set the specific goals of the immediate work for both teacher and pupils. It should include some of the elements of a sales talk, so that pupils will see more clearly the values of the new unit and be willing to work to attain them. In cooperative planning of units by teacher and pupils, the unit introduction may be developed by discussion techniques and summarized for the group by one of the pupils or by a committee.

Following are brief excerpts from sample unit introductions:

The objectives in the unit on improving everyday speech are: to learn to meet and to introduce people easily; to learn to converse readily; to learn to discuss problems interestingly and effectively; to learn social courtesies in public conversations, entertaining, and talking over the telephone; to be able to tell a story effectively. These objectives might be summed up by saying that we should like to develop the sort of person John Dryden was speaking of when he said, "Whatever he did was done with so much ease."

When you are through with this unit, I will be very happy if when you buy a drug, a fertilizer, a paint, a disinfectant, or a fly spray, you have some idea of what these things are chemically, what they will do, and how they will do it. I should like to think that you will buy such things with these ideas in mind rather than because father, grandfather, or the druggist tells you to buy them.

Perhaps some of you will have an opportunity to visit Mexico. If you do, what would you like to see? Think how much more satisfaction you will get out of the trip if you are able to understand and speak the language and have some knowledge of the country and people. The object of this unit is to learn something of the geography, history, art, entertainment, customs, and people of our nearest Spanish-speaking neighbor.

This is to be a nine-weeks unit, at the end of which we shall have our annual Christmas vespers. You have selected the songs which you wish to sing for this program. We have eleven songs to learn well in this short time. We shall read through the music this morning so that you will be able to see the difficult places.

Sources of Unit Objectives.   Published unit introductions can be found often in state and city courses of study. Many modern textbooks now present introductions to units. Some of the most useful samples can be found in the working manuscripts of units in use by teachers in the field. If there is an opportunity to examine the work of such teachers, the inexperienced teacher will find it quite worthwhile to take time to read carefully the introduction to the pupils. Often the teacher's introduction to a unit is not written but developed on the spot with the pupils and built around the teacher's ideas of relative values and his experiences in working with a particular group. Such introductions might be caught by means of a tape recorder and used as effective illustrations. Previews to some of the better motion pictures may well be studied by the teacher from the point of view of how to set the stage for something to come.

A Formula for Unit Objectives.   Crude analysis can contribute much to the thinking of a teacher in planning a unit. This analysis can be done by attempting to identify the more important potential outcomes of work of the pupils with the unit and to classify the projected outcomes as attitudes, ideals, interests, habits and skills, and important items of information.

In the initial stages of unit planning, the teacher may well raise with himself such questions as the following:

What significant attitudes can be developed as an outcome of the work in this unit?

What interests can be left with the pupils?

What important skills should pupils form or perfect?

What items of information are of enough importance that pupils should retain them over long periods of time?

Are there important generalizations to be formed, interpreted, and remembered?

Note: For Unit I (chapters 1 and 2), the Unit Implementation (summary, exercises, and recommended readings) will be found at the end of Chapter 2.

2

Criteria for Course
and Unit Objectives

In addition to the analysis formula for developing objectives recommended at the end of the preceding chapter, another possible aid to the teacher in formulating his thinking about objectives might be a working set of criteria for judging expressions of purpose. Such criteria can be useful either for criticizing the teacher's own thinking or for judging the appropriateness of objectives borrowed from published sources.

The following are suggested as criteria for judging course or unit objectives:

1. Can high school pupils interpret the objectives for themselves?
2. Does each objective fit the course or unit for which it is stated better than it fits any other course or unit?
3. Does each objective indicate some value other than an appeal to general discipline?
4. Can each objective be reached within reasonable time limits?
5. Does each objective indicate some definite value other than preparation for later school work?
6. Is each objective consistent with the intrinsic function of the subject matter?
7. Are objectives stated in terms of the effect upon the learner?

Pupil interpretation

If course and unit objectives are to serve the functions designated earlier in this chapter, pupils obviously must be able to understand what is proposed for them to achieve. Learning will be accomplished more readily if goals are approached by pupils with willingness and drive. The sales function of statements of objectives can be accomplished only as pupils can make their own interpretations of objectives and accept them.

There is an advantage if teacher and pupils arrive at a common understanding of a single brief set of objectives. Such an understanding will tend to wipe out an ancient dualism in which the teacher worked out one set of goals and presented another set to the pupils. This outworn attitude assumed that teacher always knows best, that pupils are unwilling to work toward the true goals of any particular school enterprise, and that the pupils are too young and immature to understand what they are trying to do.

The modern approach to learning and teaching assumes that there is greater efficiency when pupils and teacher pull together rather than in opposite directions as implied in the notion of dual objectives. If a given objective is suitable for the maturity of the pupils, the pupils are capable of seeing the values implied in the attainment of the objectives.

In a subject-centered secondary school curriculum, there is a tendency for the teacher, expert in his subject field, to express objectives in the technical terms of the subject which are unfamiliar to beginning pupils. For example, the mathematics teacher can easily say, "In the coming unit we are going to learn the trigonometric functions of the angles of a right triangle." If pupils have little experience with geometric terms and none with trigonometry, what will they expect to be able to do when the unit is completed?

Suppose the teacher said, "We sometimes have a right triangle in which only one dimension of the triangle is known and where it is relatively difficult to find the other dimensions by actual measurement. If we knew the angles included in the triangle we could determine the unknown dimensions of the triangle itself. In trigonometry we shall try to learn the mathematical thinking and the processes by means of which we can arrive at solutions to such problems." Obviously the pupils might be able to get a better glimpse of at least one phase of trigonometry. Of course, the statement given can be improved by illustrative blackboard diagrams and a description of concrete situations in which problems requiring solutions of triangles arise.

Specific definition

The second criterion for stated objectives involves the difficulties found in the generality of many presentations by teachers. For example, a teacher has said to a group of girls, "For the next several weeks we are going to strive to help the girls in the class develop pleasing personalities." As a reader, try to guess whether these girls are in a class in home economics, physical education, elementary psychology, secretarial practice, school orientation, elementary citizenship, or a core on personal living. Is the unit personal grooming, emotions, group adjustment, physical conditioning, or posture?

Certainly the teacher has been hazy in her analysis of the learning situation and has by implication promised the girls far more than might be achieved within any such course or unit.

In simplest terms, the objective needs much better definition and much more specific limits. If the girls are in Home Economics I of a four-year high school and the unit is defined as personal grooming, how should the objectives be stated?

Positive values

The third criterion for stated objectives presents the problem of values inherent in the outworn doctrine of general discipline or mental discipline. In spite of the fact that most reputable psychologists have long since given up theories of general mental discipline, many teachers have clung to its implications in the statement of objectives to their pupils.

Illustrations of disciplinary objectives are:

To train pupils in accurate reasoning
To train pupils in neatness
To train pupils to use scientific method
To develop general all-round mental and muscular coordination

Note that such statements of objectives also violate the first and second criteria described above. In addition to being based upon a false interpretation of the psychology of learning, these objectives tend to be confusing to pupils and to lack specific definition.

Suppose a teacher of plane geometry says that the primary purpose of his course is to develop reasoning power in the pupils. If he accepts the proposal that the objective violates an important criterion for good teaching objectives, what is he to do about it?

It is possible that he might abandon all reference to such an objective as psychologically unsound. Then he must find some other goals to present to the pupils. What should these be? He might consider the possibilities included in the common out-of-school applications of geometry in art, architecture, building construction, and simple farm engineering. He might say, "In our course in plane geometry we are going to learn to make accurate constructions of the common plane figures such as the circle, the square, a perpendicular to a line, and the right triangle. We are going to learn to compute dimensions and areas of such figures."

But the teacher still believes that there is some value to be derived from learning to prove a theorem in plane geometry. How is he to express his belief in such a value for the pupils? It is possible that he can come within the limits of the criteria by much more specific definition and by bringing the claims to improved reasoning within the range of what seems possible to accomplish in a geometry class. He might propose the following to the pupils: "Over many years the workers in geometry have been concerned with how it is possible to prove some of our accepted rules in geometry. For example, if the area of a rectangle is found by multiplying its two dimensions, how is it proved that this rule will work for all rectangles? Geometricians have developed a system of proof for geometry. The principles to be proved are called theorems. The geometry textbooks present the systems of proof that can be used for each theorem. Since the system of proof can often be used to prove the solutions to other kinds of problems, it would seem useful for us to learn something of geometric proof and the ways in which such proof can be applied to other problems that we may have outside the field of geometry."

The statement given is not intended to be a perfect statement of an objective for plane geometry, but it does illustrate an attempt to redefine a disciplinary objective and to keep it within the bounds of what might be taught within the limits of the described learning situation.

Reasonable time limits

One added difficulty with general disciplinary objectives is that their accomplishment can never be completely defined and that the time limits for accomplishment can never be set, even approximately.

Another of the criteria proposed for objectives suggests that goals set for secondary school pupils should be possible of accomplishment within reasonable time limits. Practically all disciplinary objectives violate this criterion. There are other types of objectives which violate this criterion too.

Young people live very much in the present, and objectives with no time limits at all, or objectives expressed in terms of reaching adult status, seem as remote to adolescents as the hope of reaching heaven. For example, most young people are not strongly motivated by such expressions as "when you are able to vote," "when you have a family of your own," "by the time you are thirty," "when you are old enough to make your own living," "if you should become an engineer." If this limitation is recognized in dealing with young people, it is necessary to learn to state objectives for schoolwork so that their achievement will seem to fall within the realm of immediate possibility.

Again, it is easier to illustrate objectives having "reasonable time limits" than to define them. Suggestive examples of improved phrasing of objectives follow:

By the end of the next six weeks you should be able to have mastered the typewriter keyboard well enough to begin to write some of your shorter school papers.

We shall expect to be able to sing the songs that we have just selected for our Christmas program for parents.

We shall be able to spend the last six weeks of the school year on softball. In this time we can expect that every member of our squad can raise his batting average above what it now is.

Apparently most of us know only eight or ten of the commonest birds, such as the English sparrow, the robin, and the cardinal. During the spring migration season from the first of March to the middle of May, most of us should be able to learn to recognize thirty birds. Some of us can learn to identify fifty or sixty.

There are two frequent violations of reasonable time limits. Many teachers of citizenship and history attempt to motivate the work of pupils by appeals to "when you become a citizen." This attitude ignores the fact that all of the pupils are *now* citizens. The fact that most high school pupils are not old enough to vote in the city, state, and federal elections does not keep them from being citizens and having civic rights, duties, privileges, and obligations. It would be much better for the teacher of citizenship to express objectives for citizens in terms of these present civic relationships rather than in terms of long-deferred values.

The second type of violation of this criterion frequently occurs with teachers of the fine arts. The English teacher says, "We are going to learn to appreciate the world's greatest literature." The music teacher says, "You should learn to enjoy the finest classical music." The art teacher expresses the major objective as "becoming acquainted with the great masters of painting and sculpture." The pupils might well ask, "How long does it take to learn to appreciate the world's finest literature? The teachers that we have had for the last two years said the same thing. How do we know when we have some appreciation?"

Is it impossible to set reasonable time limits for appreciation objectives? Suppose that the music teacher tries a statement such as: "I have observed the records that you like to play on the juke box in the recreation room downstairs. Most musicians would consider such music rather cheap. We should like to improve our taste for music as we listen. Certainly we could hope to raise the level of our listening as high as the music played by the Boston Pops Orchestra on its radio programs. Do you suppose that we can get far enough along with our improved appreciation to be regular and willing listeners to the Boston Pops radio programs by this coming Christmas vacation?" There is no argument here that a Strauss waltz played by the Boston Pops Orchestra is the ultimate in music appreciation. However, the difference between this and the juke box tunes is obvious and understandable to the pupils. The standard of achievement is reasonably defined and possible of attainment within less than the time of the existing school year.

Immediate values

The fifth criterion for judging objectives may be considered as a corollary of the fourth. Another of the indefinite deferments of accomplishment from the point of view of many secondary school pupils is that of preparation for some future school course. The situation becomes particularly acute with the statement of values for a tenth-grade group in terms of preparation for a college course some years ahead. A positive statement of the criterion is that values presented for a secondary school course should be inherent in the course as presently taught. It has been said that any high school course should be useful in so far as it is pursued. That is, there should be something of immediate value at each stage of the development of a course so that, if a pupil should drop out before completion, he could carry away something of value to him. The teacher needs to be acutely aware that only approximately 150–200 pupils out of 1,000 who were in the fifth grade ever reach college and that only 30–40 per cent of high school graduates enter college. Certainly objectives for courses must include suggestions of values to be attained by the great majority of pupils for whom college may be as remote as the hope of becoming a corporation president.

The motivation of pupils in almost any high school course will be better if the pupils can see something that can be accomplished within the limits of the course itself, rather than having to postpone attainment for one or more years. Another way of presenting this same issue is to say that, at the high school level, prerequisite or background courses with little justification other than that of building up to the next course are of doubtful value. There should be something attainable within each course, and it should be presented in the course objectives or the course introduction.

Teachers of first-year courses that fall in a sequence of courses within the same field or area are always confronted with the problem just presented. Is it possible to reach some definite control of language proficiency in Spanish I other than preparation for admission into Spanish II? Is there any other value for second-year algebra other than preparation of a few for success in college algebra? The problem here is also reversible. Is the first course always essential to success in the second? Is it possible that for many pupils maturity factors may outweigh mere exposure to the content of the first course? In the typical secondary school it is entirely probable that a normal tenth-grade pupil who missed ninth-grade English might better proceed with tenth-grade English rather than be turned back to a prerequisite ninth-grade English. As courses are now organized, it is often difficult to make a case for Physical Education I, Home Economics I, Shop I, or Core Curriculum I as prerequisites to Physical Education II, Home Economics II, Shop II, or Core Curriculum II. If the case cannot be made, it becomes obvious that objectives for both courses I and II must stand on their own merits and be limited largely to the particular year's work for each course.

Perhaps a few positive illustrations will serve as further clarification of criterion five. It would be better for the teacher of Spanish I to say that this year we can hope to learn to read the front page of a Spanish newspaper at sight, rather than to say that this year we are going to attempt to lay the foundations for Spanish grammar that you will need next year in Spanish II. It would be better for the teacher of Home Economics I to say that we are going to try to improve our present eating habits through the immediate application of what we can learn about sound principles of diet, rather than to say that we are going to try to fix the "basic seven" rules of diet this year so that we can be able to plan meals better next year in Home Economics II.

Consistency with intrinsic function

These questions of the nature of the values of the present course in relationship to the pressing needs of the boys and girls now in the class raise questions of the usefulness of the items of subject matter included in the content of the course. The sixth criterion for objectives states that course objectives should be consistent with the *intrinsic function* of the subject matter involved. By subject matter is meant any accepted practice developed by human beings as a solution to a human problem. These solutions are transmitted from one person to another and most frequently from one generation to the next. Subject matter need not be contained in published books. Language is perhaps the most important means of transmission, but not the only one. By way of illustration, a fountain pen is a bit of subject matter. So also is a custom or convention, one of the mores of the people. A great painting is subject matter. So also is a song, a march, or a dance. The binomial theorem is a bit of subject matter. The "Bill of Rights" in the Constitution of the United States forms a most important collection of items of subject matter for us.

The *intrinsic function* of any bit of subject matter is the use which that subject matter has for the majority of people. To avoid uses which may be limited to the temporary artificialities of the schoolroom, let us say that the intrinsic function is the use that a bit of subject matter has for the majority of people *outside of schools*.

A few simple illustrations may serve to clarify this definition. Obviously the intrinsic function of a watch is to mark the passage of time. Note there are other possible functions for watches, such as the decorative function. Nonetheless, few of us would purchase or carry watches that did not mark the passage of time. The intrinsic function of the electric fan is that of cooling by circulating air in such a way as to hasten evaporation. For ordinary cooling, the fan evaporates the moisture of perspiration to cool the too warm individual. Such fans are also used as hair driers. Perhaps few large fans would be purchased for hair drying only. From these illustrations it may be seen also that it is possible to make a second catch-all classification of all those functions other than the intrinsic function. We can call all of these other functions *indirect functions*.

To carry the notion of intrinsic function into the school, spelling will serve as a good illustration. The intrinsic function of spelling is that of making written words intelligible to the reader through a uniformity of the same combination of symbols (letters) for the same meaning (word). If this interpretation of the intrinsic function of spelling is accepted, other possible functions become indirect and probably of less general value.

What has just been said implies that spelling to impress a neighbor with one's learning, or spelling to beat someone else, are indirect functions.

Note what this change in thinking has done to the teaching of spelling in our schools. The older schools taught oral spelling. Today, in good schools, pupils write their spelling. Words are chosen from those which the pupils need in writing. Special drills are given upon words that frequently cause trouble for individual pupils. Most often the words to be spelled are dictated in sentences, so that the learner may form habits of spelling in continuous context.

Suppose that the question of function is raised in relationship to some parts of the present secondary school program. What is the function of baseball or of softball? What uses does the game have for the majority of people? To what extent do the players of softball in twilight leagues play to improve health? Are sandlot players of baseball conscious of an effort to improve "general all-round muscular coordination"? Why do people listen to or watch a world series by radio or television? What changes would be made in teaching baseball if the teacher maintained a clear vision of its intrinsic function?

What are possible intrinsic functions of literature? Why do most people out of school read? Should the teaching of literature be modified so that what is done with literature in school is more nearly consistent with its normal function? If such changes were made, would the pupils be damaged? Would the literature be damaged?

To return to the original statement of criteria for course and unit objectives, it can now be repeated that such objectives should be consistent with the intrinsic function of the subject matter used. To arrive at the function, the teacher needs always to be sensitive to what people outside of school are doing with the content of what may be learned in the school course. Careful consideration of much school practice will indicate that many things learned in school are learned for school purposes only and that, since these tend to be relatively artificial, the functions served are indirect. A complete consistency with desirable out-of-school uses of subject matter would help each pupil to attain what educators now define as a functional education.

One further caution in the application of this criterion needs to be considered. Uses of subject matter are not always those that are sometimes characterized as bread-and-butter, concrete, or money-making. Listening to fine music, enjoyment of the beauty of a great painting, mathematical speculation are all uses. One does not have to compute the cubical contents of a silo to use geometry. He may use geometry in an awareness of the nature of the design in a stained glass window.

Pupil change

The final criterion for objectives seems indeed to include all the others. Certainly what has been said about a functional education implies a final criterion that objectives should be stated in terms of the effect of the school experiences upon the pupils rather than in terms of covering a given body of subject matter. Teachers will no longer say, "The purpose of this course is to cover the field of algebra up to quadratic equations." Rather they will say, "This year in our mathematics course we shall try to learn to use mathematical symbols in order to simplify our processes of calculation. We shall try to learn how to form equations from descriptive data given in statements of problems. We shall try to improve our skills in the resolution of such equations after they are formed." The idea of the importance of the effect of experiences with a body of subject matter upon the behavior of the pupils is an essentially important one in all of modern education. The subject matter has value insofar as it affects the behavior of the learner. Otherwise it becomes merely an interesting record of past behavior of other people and of little consequence to those who form our present society. At least the school teacher of the present is much safer in expressing the goals for pupils in his courses in terms of expected changes in their behavior rather than in terms of a body of subject matter to be covered.

Unit implementation

Unit Organization

1. Secondary school aims may be classified into institutional aims, course objectives, and unit objectives.

2. Institutional aims are the broad general purposes set up for the whole of secondary education, for such an institution as the public high school, or for some one secondary school as an institution.

3. Course objectives are those ends to be attained by the pupils within the limits of a single high school course.

4. Unit objectives are those immediate attainments expected of pupils as a result of experiences developed within a teaching unit.

5. It is not expected that all institutional objectives are to be served at the same time by a single high school course, but the objectives for any high school course must be consistent with the accepted objectives of the institution.

6. Specific objectives for the teaching units within a course must be consistent with the objectives for the course.

7. A simple formula indicating desired skills or habits, needed information, and desirable interests and ideals is useful in determining the immediate unit objectives.

✗ 8. School objectives at all levels must be adapted continually to meet changing social conditions.

9. Secondary school pupils must know what attainments are expected of them. In many cases pupils can participate in the formulation of the more immediate objectives.

10. Each high school course should have certain values that are peculiar to that course and not found in other courses.

✗ 11. It is reasonable for high school pupils to expect to be able to see some of the results of experiences in a high school course within the time limits of the course itself.

12. Secondary school courses may no longer be justified on the basis of disciplinary values alone.

13. High school teachers must learn to think of secondary school work in terms of the effect of the work upon the young learners now in school rather than in terms of blocks or sections of subject matter per se.

THINGS TO DO

1. List by title the courses which you had as a high school pupil. Using a published statement of purposes for high schools, with the different purposes as headings for columns in a table, place each of these courses in the column under that aim in the heading which you consider the course in question best serves.

From your table, which of the purposes chosen did your own high school education best serve?

Where are the gaps?

2. Find out when, how, and why the subject in which you have a major interest became a part of the secondary school program of studies. Write a half-page summary of your findings.

3. What are the present-day justifications for the continued inclusion of your subject in the program of studies of the modern high school?

Write out a summary of these claims in not more than six numbered sentence statements.

4. Select some part of the subject matter commonly included in a high school course in your major field.

Write out a clear statement of the intrinsic function of this selected bit of subject matter.

5. Select a relatively small unit from one course in your major field, e.g., two, three, or four weeks' work. State the title of the course and the unit of work chosen.

Write out a list of the specific objectives to be accomplished with pupils by means of this unit of work.

In making this list of objectives, the application of the following formula will be found useful:

What specific habits or skills are to be formed?
What bits of information or ideas are to be retained?
What interests may be formed?
What ideals should be developed?
What attitudes should be formed?

Apply the criteria suggested for judging objectives to your own list. Revise the original statements in terms of these criteria. Ask the teacher to examine both the original and the revised list.

6. List those high school courses which retain their hold in the high school program largely through claims to disciplinary values.

From the best available evidence, summarize the validity of claims to general disciplinary value.

7. Characterize briefly in contrasting paragraphs the type of high school population found in the high schools of 1893, 1930, 1950, and 1960. How do changes in the nature of the high school population affect the aims of secondary education?

8. Set up your own carefully evaluated aims for high school courses in your major field. Check these by the criteria proposed for course objectives.

9. What changes in teaching in your field are likely to take place in the next generation? Why do you think that each of these changes is probable?

10. Write a course introduction for one high school course which you expect to teach. Address this introduction to the pupils in the class. What needs do the pupils have which you will expect to meet with the proposed course?

HELPFUL READINGS

ASSOCIATION FOR SUPERVISION AND CURRICULUM DEVELOPMENT. *What Shall the High Schools Teach?* Washington, D.C.: National Education Association, 1956. Pp. 104–21.

Purposes as a guide to the selection of content for the school program.

ALEXANDER, WILLIAM M. and SAYLOR, J. GALEN. *Secondary Education.* New York: Rinehart & Co., Inc., 1950. Chap. 4.

Treats the school as a social agency and presents institutional purposes within this frame of reference.

BAYLES, ERNEST E. *The Theory and Practice of Teaching.* New York: Harper & Bros., 1950. Chap. 8, pp. 116–23.

The schools as a means of implementation of social purposes. May be interpreted as a defense of a subject-centered curriculum.

BRIGGS, THOMAS H., LEONARD, J. PAUL, and JUSTMAN, JOSEPH. *Secondary Education.* Rev. ed. New York: The Macmillan Co., 1950. Chap. 7, pp. 168–95.

Gives historical résumé of institutional purposes for the secondary school.

CHARTERS, W. W. *Methods of Teaching.* Rev. ed. Evanston, Ill.: Row, Peterson & Co., 1912. Pp. 59–81.

Defines the intrinsic function of subject matter and suggests the use of the function as a criterion for judging objectives and selecting subject-matter items.

COMMISSION ON THE REORGANIZATION OF SECONDARY EDUCATION. *The Cardinal Principles of Secondary Education.* Bul. 35. Washington, D.C.: U.S. Office of Education, 1918.

Original source of the statement of the best known set of institutional purposes for the American secondary school.

DOUGLASS, HARL R. *Secondary Education for Youth in Modern America.* Washington, D.C.: American Council on Education, 1938.

Read, by all means. A clear-cut concise statement of institutional purposes in a social setting.

EDUCATIONAL POLICIES COMMISSION. *The Purposes of Education in American Democracy.* Washington, D.C.: National Education Association, 1938.

Title and source indicate content.

FRENCH, WILLIAM MARSHALL. *American Secondary Education.* New York: Odyssey Press, 1957.

See chap. 7 on "Mr. Spencer and His Descendants" and chap. 20 on "The Future of Secondary Education."

GWYNN, J. M. *Curriculum Principles and Social Trends.* Rev. ed. New York: The Macmillan Co., 1950. Chap. 12.

A good source for a summary of changing statements of institutional purposes from 1930 to 1950.

NATIONAL ASSOCIATION OF SECONDARY-SCHOOL PRINCIPALS. *Planning for American Youth.* Rev. ed. Washington, D.C.: National Association of Secondary-School Principals. 1951.

Contains a statement of institutional purposes expressed as the ten imperative needs of youth, plus curricular patterns to implement them.

NATIONAL SOCIETY FOR THE STUDY OF EDUCATION. *52d Yearbook. Part I. Adapting the Secondary-School Program to the Needs of Youth.* Chicago: University of Chicago Press, 1953. Chaps. 1 and 2.

Institutional purposes stated in terms of the needs of youth. Chap. 2 on the determination of youth needs.

———. *54th Yearbook. Part I. Modern Philosophies of Education.* Chicago: University of Chicago Press, 1955. Chaps. 1, 2, 8, and 9.

Chap. 1 on traditional vs. progressive aims. Chap. 2 on educational aims and values in human society. Chap. 8 deals with linguistic aims and Chap. 9 with aims in an age of science.

SMITH, B. OTHANEL, STANLEY, WILLIAM C., and SHORES, J. HARLAN. *Fundamentals of Curriculum Development.* Rev. ed. Yonkers, N.Y.: World Book Co., 1957. Chaps. 1 and 7.

Extensive treatment of the development of institutional purposes as they have affected curriculum development in secondary schools.

SPEARS, HAROLD. *The High School for Today.* New York: American Book Co., 1950. Chap. 3, pp. 24–44.

Quotes statements of the institutional purposes of secondary schools from the *Cardinal Principles* to the *Prosser Resolution.* A useful source for getting the pronouncements of various commissions all in one short chapter.

SPENCER, HERBERT. *Education.* New York: A. S. Burt Co., 1859. Chap. 1.

Contains the famous and often-quoted analysis of "complete living" from which most of the later statements of institutional purposes for schools have been developed.

WILLIAMS, L. A. *Secondary Schools for American Youth.* New York: American Book Co., 1948. Chaps. 5 and 6, pp. 161–213.

Chap. 5 quotes statements of institutional purposes from Spencer to the American Council on Education. Read especially chap. 6 which deals with the derivation of immediate course objectives and the teacher's responsibility in the determination of objectives.

Unit II

What Is Worth Learning?

In any field of human knowledge more things are known than can be learned by one person within reasonable time limits. The need for learning varies considerably with different people. How can you determine what the people in a particular class need to learn?

Some things are learned in school, and many others are learned outside of school. What is the school's obligation in selecting what is most important for in-school learning?

Suppose that a pupil does not want to learn what the school has to offer. What is to be done with him? Are there some things which each person *must* try to learn? If so, how is it possible to determine what these things are?

In this unit the problems of the teacher that have to do with the selection of the subject matter to be taught will be considered. This involves, first, the content of courses as a whole and, second, the nature of the content of each unit as it is developed and learned. The point of view throughout will be that the problems of selection are primarily problems for the teacher rather than being solved beforehand by the administrator, the textbook maker, or the curriculum expert.

What to look for in this unit

1. How does the principle of social integration apply to the selection of the details of content for both required and elective high school courses?

2. How does the principle of individual adaptation apply to the selection of content for high school courses?

3. Upon what bases are required courses within a high school program determined?

4. How does a teacher go about planning the general layout for a high school course?

5. What use does the secondary school teacher make of an adopted textbook in planning the layout for a high school course?

6. What relationship does the teacher's layout have to city and state courses of study?

7. What is the relationship of the high school program to the institutional purposes?

8. What is the relationship of the pattern of units for a high school course to the course objectives?

9. How many units should a high school course in a given field contain?

10. How can the allotment of time for units be determined?

11. How can provision for individual differences be made in planning a high school course?

12. What is to be done with text material which does not fit the layout planned?

3

Selection of Subject Matter

As previously noted, the teacher always faces the immediate problem of the selection and adaptation of course content to the needs of his pupils. There is, however, the larger problem of what the school as a whole is to offer in the way of opportunities for learning. There is, also, the obligation of the school to attempt to insure certain learnings in order that society may function with a minimum of friction.

The school program

The total offerings of a school constitute the *program* of that school. The program includes the subjects offered, the courses taught, and the activities engaged in by the pupils and their organizations. Plane geometry, the core in social living, home economics, and physical education for boys are all probable parts of the total program of a school. So also are basketball, the candid camera club, the student council, the dramatics club, the school band, and the school assembly program. Any activities of a school which purport to have educational values are parts of the school's program.

Most school programs have grown up within the framework of the local community with its particular organization, customs, and traditions. The community in turn has been influenced by state, regional, and national customs and traditions, and by shifting economic forces. In general, school programs have changed quite slowly. In many cases, the school program has remained relatively

31

constant while the society within which it operates has changed rapidly.

Like a house long occupied by succeeding generations of the same family, the great majority of local school programs have been changed by patching or remodeling. Is there any way to reduce the amount of mere curricular patching in the school program, or at least to carry out a more intelligent program of remodeling? Is it possible that we should wreck the old structure and begin anew? Within another generation the new structure of this year may have become considerably patched and begin to appear dilapidated. How often do we need to wreck the old completely and begin all over? With the school program, is this ever wholly desirable?

It seems probable that the planning of school programs could be improved greatly on the basis of certain established principles of procedure. Suppose an attempt be made to establish a few such fundamental principles.

Any school, or any school system, is an instrument of the society which it serves. Therefore, a school first serves to promote the welfare of the social organization which controls the school. In a democratic society it is believed that a public school should contribute to the welfare of all the people.

Principle of social integration (to develop likeness + conformity)

The primary principle to guide the selection of parts of a school program is that it should first include those learnings and experiences that are needed by every individual who comes to school, in order to fit him best into the society in which he must live. This is the principle of social integration. That part of the school program determined by reference to this principle is commonly called *general education.* Note that all of the recent discussions of *life adjustment education* are concerned with the same fundamental issue and receive their final justification in this same principle.

REQUIREMENTS IN THE SCHOOL PROGRAM. In determining what part of a school program is to be *required* of the pupils, it is necessary to find out what every pupil of a given maturity should learn in order to adapt to the present society. The application of the principle of group necessity determines school requirements.

In order to live together all people must learn to be alike in some ways. Modern education has so often stressed the importance of individual differences that we sometimes forget that it is quite necessary to develop some likenesses in people. We are inclined to resent conformity; yet some degree of conformity is necessary for a society to function. There is a needed body of *common education* which every person must acquire. Common education in this sense means that each person must have some of it; the standard or level of attainment need not be low.

APPLICATIONS OF THE PRINCIPLE OF SOCIAL INTEGRATION. Suppose that a few of the common elements of school programs are reviewed in terms of the need for certain likenesses in people.

1. Common means of communication. Any given society operates more easily and economically if its members use the same language. Perhaps the most generally accepted need of young people in the schools of the United States is to learn to speak, write, and read in English. In considering requirements, all young people should be required to have experience in speaking, reading, and writing English. The case is made easily. On the other hand, fixing a standard of performance, determining the quality of speech acceptable, or defining the level of attainment for reading are extremely difficult.

2. Social integration and citizenship. As with the social necessity for a common medium of communication in language, it is also generally agreed that young people need to accept certain common beliefs about the nature of government and the relationships of the citizen to his government. If the elements of American democracy, or "the American way of life," can be defined each member of each successive generation must understand and interpret these elements. In many ways the understandings and interpretations of stated beliefs must be alike in order to make a democratic society work. If youths are drafted into the armed services to support democratic faiths, it is justifiable to require them to study these faiths in the classrooms of public schools—in other words, to require experiences in a particular interpretation of the "social studies" of all young people who attend our public high schools. How many units of credit in the social studies shall be required? Over how many years of schooling shall the required experiences extend? These questions are not answered so easily.

As further illustration of the necessity for requirement within the social studies, it might be well for each reader to review the "Bill of Rights" in the Constitution of the United States. Do you believe that every person attending a public high school in this country should read these statements in the Constitution? Should experiences in interpreting their application to the daily affairs of citizens be required?

3. Need for common science. Scientists, too, have demonstrated facts that contribute to human health and well-being. The incidence of smallpox can be almost completely eliminated by appropriate vaccination. Inoculation of children for diphtheria can protect most of them. Epidemics spread by polluted drinking water or by contaminated milk supply can be reduced. Such knowledge should become the common property of all people. So also should the habits necessary to implement the preventive measures which make the knowledge function. Thus it is justifiable to require general biology or hygiene of high school pupils.

At least two new issues are now raised. There are some members of society who do not believe in the germ theory of the causation of certain common diseases. In some cases this disbelief is supported by an interpretation of a religious faith. Must these people be required to consider the scientific findings along with all the other pupils?

If biological training is required of all, is it for the protection of each as an individual? No one will deny a concern for the health and welfare of an individual. However, the proposal to *require* is based upon the protection of the group rather than of the individual. One cannot have smallpox alone. In some schools a pupil is refused admittance unless he has been inoculated for diphtheria. This is done in spite of any beliefs of his parents to the contrary. In whose interest is the enforcement made?

4. *Limitations on requirements.* The principle of group integration and needs of the society seem to preclude the requirement of certain subjects. An illustration of the point at which the application of the principle will no longer hold is found in religious freedom. If we attempt to guarantee freedom of individual conscience in matters of religious faith and belief, we cannot support in a public school the requirement of experiences that lead toward the acceptance of a common religious interpretation.

In the same way, we would not attempt to set up a social studies program to indoctrinate young people in the political platform of any single political party.

5. *Common cultural needs.* Another important issue arises in the application of the principle of requirement to the whole area of the fine arts. Are there certain elements in the culture of a people that serve as binders in the society? Are there some elements of a common culture which serve well the purposes of social integration? If so, certain selected experiences in music, literature, drama, and the graphic arts might well be required of all the pupils in secondary schools. Again, the basic principle is easy enough to state but difficult to apply in its details. Using this principle, it is extremely difficult to make a case for having every pupil in the ninth grade read *Silas Marner* or *The Merchant of Venice.* But should every

pupil have a chance to thrill to "The Battle Hymn of the Republic" or have the opportunity to be moved by "White Christmas"? The answer lies in the extent to which the common emotional experiences in the arts serve to pull groups together. Hymns of hate or pieces of literature which tend to arouse racial and religious differences would not fulfill the proposed function of group integration and therefore should never be required in public school programs.

Teachers of physical education may well review the bases for requiring common physical education experiences of all high school pupils. If the situation is viewed without bias, it will be found difficult to justify the common physical education program in terms of its contribution to common health gains or maintenance for all pupils. If the health issue is raised, the case is better made for mental health through wholesome recreation and group participation than for mere physical well-being through directed exercises. The case is still better made upon the grounds of the integrating forces of a common culture.

Assume that baseball is an important part of our total American culture. Without doubt the sport serves as a center of common interest for millions of our citizens. Is the game of sufficient importance as a social integrator to require some experiences with it for all people who come to our schools? This same question may well be raised concerning certain other sports. Consider basketball or bowling.

The physical education proponent might consider also the contribution of *group* games as means of developing within individuals the qualities of leadership, followership, and mutual give-and-take needed for the operation of groups in general. Do the group games make enough of a contribution to these factors of social integration to justify the requirement of some experiences with them?

New subject matter in the school program. The illustrations given so far are applicable to parts of the secondary school program that have been generally accepted. To be completely useful, the principle must operate also with changing social conditions and be applicable to situations in the present and future society.

Americans have become accustomed to many devices which aid in communication, such as the typewriter. Courses in typewriting in the secondary school program for training secretaries and office workers are taken for granted. If the idea is extended to include the use of the typewriter for the improvement of all written communication, a case can be made for requiring typewriting for all high school pupils. The use of the typewriter for common communication has now become so nearly universal that the need for skill

in typewriting is now as great as the need for good penmanship in
the world of the nineteenth century.

Another illustration of the impact of the machine upon problems
of the school program is found in the school shop. Since every person in our world is confronted constantly with various tool and machine manipulations, some facility in the handling of tools and the
control and manipulation of machines becomes a necessity for everyone. A cursory examination of a modern kitchen, office, or the
equipment of the armed forces will support this proposition. A general shop with proper equipment and a well selected array of tool
and machine experiences might provide the best school solution for
the need described.

General shop and the need for it on the part of boys—as well as
girls—has a counterpart in the need for some education in homemaking for all young people. People have become accustomed to
the idea of courses in home economics for girls in our high schools.
These have gone far beyond the cooking and sewing of the early
home economics. Many are now designated as vocational home
economics courses and are intended for young women who expect
to make a primary vocation of homemaking. The world changes
here too. An increasing number of young women have careers outside the home and are at the same time homemakers. Even the
bachelor girl wants an apartment. This at once presents problems
of housekeeping.

Since it is still true that the primary directing force in most house-
holds is the wife and mother, quite a good case can be made for
requiring education in homemaking of all girls. But men and boys
live in homes too. Why not require homemaking education of all
the boys too?

There are many more illustrations that could be drawn from the
needs of modern life. A case might be made for certain requirements in mathematics implemented by an increasing use of statistics, mathematical symbolism, and more frequent recourse to exact
measurements of all kinds. There are those, too, who see a need
for requirements in consumer education, driver education, and conservation education. Whenever we consider the merits of the requirement of learning in one of these areas we should attempt to
judge in terms of its fitting our proposal of common need in order
to better fit individuals into the group of which they are a part.
Each is to be judged in terms of its importance for needed group
integration.

One further danger must be pointed out here. If the need for
all the proposed requirements is supported, a completely required

program that may be just as untenable as a program with no requirements may result. Too much may be required.

Principle of individualization *(differentiating education)*

The second important principle for selecting content in the school program is the principle of individualization. The preceding section stressed the need in a society for some degree of likeness in its members. But there is also a great need for freedom for growth of the individual. Each school must provide both a certain amount of social indoctrination and freedom for the growth of each pupil. One of the great contributions of the movement toward a scientific psychology has been the discovery, or perhaps the rediscovery, of the facts of individual differences in human beings.

That part of a school program intended to provide for differences can be designated as *differentiating education* as distinguished from general education. If the primary function of general education is to produce likenesses in people, the primary function of differentiating education is to promote and extend desirable differences in people. The secondary school must provide for both.

Note that the qualifying term *desirable differences* used above places a limit upon the nature of the school provisions for growth. The school does not provide merely a cultural medium for undirected growth of human biological organisms. Certain individual tendencies to growth should be restrained, pruned, directed, or in some cases repressed. The development of many of the interests and bents of individuals is an asset to the society of which each is a part. We need leadership, scientific insight, political acumen, creative literature, great music, high dramatic talent, etc.

Electives in the School Program. The principle of individualization or of differentiation forms the basis for the introduction of optional or elective experiences in the school program. In the formulation of a program, elective courses and choices of extra-curricular activities are to be defended in terms of the differentiating principle.

In planning the program for a whole school, there are practical administrative limits on the range of provisions that can be made for individuals. It is not administratively feasible to provide a vocational curriculum for two people out of a student body of five hundred. The costs of operation become prohibitive if the school attempts to set up provisions for creative expression in dramatics for six people. Is it wise to provide facilities for competitive basketball for seventeen boys and at the same time deny an opportunity for recreational sports for a hundred and fifty?

In some cases the best provision for opportunity for growth in the direction of an unusual talent may be in guidance to the person concerned. It may be difficult to set up adequate facilities for growth for one musically gifted student in a thousand. The gifted pupil and his parents may need to consider where the pupil should go for the training suited to his unusual talent. In this, the high school guidance facilities and the advice of the music teachers should be available.

APPLICATIONS OF THE PRINCIPLE OF INDIVIDUALIZATION. The differentiating principle, then, forms the platform upon which the elective program of the school is to be built. There are some rule-of-thumb generalizations which may help in the application of the principle in actual program construction.

College preparation. All college preparatory subjects, *as such,* should fall into the group of electives. In the great majority of high schools the college-bound group is a distinct minority. In general, approximately a third of high school graduates enter college. In turn these graduates represent only about 45 per cent of the group in school at the fifth-grade level. Of those entering college only half graduate. These graduates from a four-year college amount to about 60 or 70 out of the thousand in the fifth grade. Assume the suitability of a sequence of college preparatory subjects for the group attending college. There may be no reason for imposing these subjects upon the majority with differing educational needs.

Vocational education. All vocational courses or vocational curricula should be elective. There is a necessary diversification of occupations in our society. There is no basis for proposing that different people should follow the same occupation. Our society would not function if too many people were forced into one vocation with none in others.

Because of customary usages in current terminology there are some cautions on the application of the rule just proposed. A case may well be made for experiences in homemaking as a requirement. Many such experiences are now included in the *vocational* home economics program. If all girls, or all young people, need home economics, it becomes a part of general education and may be required. If some girls specialize in some phase of home economics in order to develop a means to a livelihood, such home economics becomes vocational and elective in the school program.

Typewriting is customarily a part of the secretarial training curriculum. As such it is a vocational skill and to be elected by those expecting to become secretaries. On the other hand, if we assume that typewriting is a needed means of communication for every person regardless of his particular occupation, the typewriting is no longer a vocational subject as such. It becomes a part of general education and may well be required.

Specialization.   Courses intended to afford pupils an opportunity to specialize in some one subject-matter field should always be elective. In most cases this implies that upper-year courses of the senior high school in the common fields of subject matter should be electives. Illustrations are to be found in physics, chemistry, advanced algebra, solid geometry, trigonometry, advanced art, harmony, English history, advanced American history, civil government, physical geography, botany, and zoology.

Courses set up especially to serve certain special interest groups should be elective. Illustrations are art for artists, music for musicians, creative writing, debating, dramatics, senior speech, membership on competitive athletic teams, photography, journalism, school band, boys' glee club, and woodworking.

Foreign languages.   In public secondary schools of the United States, courses in foreign languages should be elective. The common language for general purposes of communication is English. Justification for requirements in English can be made easily. (See p. 33.) The case for the *requirement* of a language on any other basis except that of need for communication seems doubtful. Even in terms of needs for worldwide communication, it is probable that the most satisfactory language is English. Two world wars and the modern mechanical means of communication and travel have spread English around the globe. The most nearly common international language is now English.

A possible exception to the making of all foreign languages elective may be found in a few schools in bilingual communities. An obvious illustration is found in the schools along the Mexican border where Mexican children speak Mexican Spanish and need to speak English also. In these schools there may be a case for requirement of experiences with two languages.

What was just said concerning the making of instruction in foreign languages elective does not preclude the offering of languages in many schools. Where pupils feel a need for, or have an interest in, another language, opportunity may be provided.

Selection of content for courses and units

The principles which we have set up as guides to the selection of parts of the school program can be applied also to the selection of the units which are to constitute a course or a core program, or to the selection of the subject matter and pupil experiences to be used in implementing the objectives which are chosen for a particular unit.

In setting up a pattern of units for a given course, the teacher needs first to consider the objectives agreed upon for the course and to use these as a frame of reference within which to develop the course pattern. In considering the possible units for inclusion within the course, the teacher will first give consideration to those units most needed by all the pupils that are to be included within the class group. In effect, these units will become requirements within the limits of the selected course. If there is time for more than the required units, optional units will be proposed in terms of the peculiar needs or interests of the pupils.

As illustration consider the selection of the units to be included in a junior high school course in English, or in communications. Think of the writing needs of most people and of adolescents in particular. Probably the most frequent writing need is that of letter writing. Therefore, in the communications course a unit on letter writing is to be included, in which everyone is expected to participate. The ordinary small-group or living-room conversation is a commonly met speech need. So, the course includes a unit on improving conversation. Suppose that eight or ten common units of the type indicated are chosen. It might be good fun to let some people try to write simple radio skits and present them before a "mike" at a school assembly. Certainly such a unit would not be forced into the communications course pattern. But if the people are reasonably clever, there is some initiative in the group, and interest develops, a place might be made for the radio broadcasting unit. Its value should be compared with other possible options, and the characteristics of the people in the group should be considered. Perhaps the members of the class group can make a final decision when several options are presented to them.

When the details of a particular unit are planned, the same issues arise. Are there certain experiences which every member of the group should have? These would be included first in the unit planning. At the same time the needs of the people in the class will vary. What provisions are to be made for differing experiences?

What has been said applies equally to required and to elective courses. If a required course is being planned, the units selected first will be those which will be thought of as socially necessary for all young people coming to high school. But, within the limits of a required course there should be some room for expression of individual needs. Therefore, the teacher of a required course needs to study the characteristics of the pupils in any class and provide either for possibly optional units or for variation in standards of attainment for particular pupils. In the planning of exercises and experiences within the limits of a given unit, there should be considerable freedom of choice under the direction and guidance of the teacher.

In reverse, if the course in question is elective, there are some things that all people who purport to have the training represented by the course should experience. In effect, these experiences become requirements within the limits of the elective course. The element of choice entered into the situation in the selection of the course itself and its assumed fitting to the needs of the pupil. At the same time provisions must be made for a considerable variation in the differences in the people who make up the class.

An illustration of this latter case may be found in a proposed high school course in artcraft. First, it seems perfectly clear that this course is elective. No one is to be forced into it. If the pupils are to have good art experiences, certain principles of design and color must be incorporated in the chosen units. These principles are to be learned by all the pupils. They may be set up as units of design and color or the principles may be built into units centering about projects in selected crafts. It is possible, too, that certain craft experiences are so common with all amateur craftsmen that these should be included as units for all pupils. Block printing or poster making may represent such units. On the other hand, the inclusion of a unit on leather tooling for all the pupils might seem doubtful.

If a tentative pattern is set up for the course, the same issues arise in the choice of actual projects to be carried out within a craft. It may seem desirable for every pupil to attempt a poster. The choice of theme and the expression of the theme in design and color may vary with every pupil in the class. The teacher may say, "Let's all try hand blocked Christmas cards." But certainly all the cards produced by a class of twenty-five should not be alike. Keep in mind, however, that there are principles of balance in design to be expected of all pupils throughout all the illustrative proposals used.

Course layouts

This unit has been concerned with an elaboration and illustration of basic principles of selection as applied to the school program, the secondary school course, or to the units within the course. However intriguing and necessary these ideas may be, the teacher has certain courses to plan and teach. The theories must be made to operate in practice.

Return briefly to Unit I. (See pp. 8 ff.) The teacher has developed a course introduction. The introduction contains a statement of course objectives as interpreted for teacher and pupils. The teacher has checked his course introduction against the institutional policies of his school to see that what is proposed for the class is consistent with the direction of the whole school within its particular community setting. The next step then is to set up a *layout* for the course within the framework of its objectives.

The layout for a course represents the pattern for the course set up in such fashion that the teacher can visualize the whole course at one time before he undertakes its implementation. Assume the desirability of this complete visualization of a course before undertaking its details. Assume also the desirability of being able to present this whole pattern to the pupils. Certainly it seems reasonable that the pupil is entitled to know what he is getting into. It is his time and energy that is to be invested in the venture.

The teacher's need to see his course as a whole can be demonstrated in terms of two quite common occurrences. The young teacher just out of college and full of *his subject* tends to overlook the difficulties of slower learning and less mature high school pupils. He begins at the front of the subject matter of his course and covers the material in a hurry. It seems simple stuff to him. If by April the course is covered, he knows nothing else to do except to *review* for the remainder of the school year. A better viewing of the course as a whole at first would avoid this trap.

Conversely, the older teacher tends to talk too much. He can think of too many illustrations or must always repeat the stock ones. If he begins at the front of his course and proceeds to cover the subject matter in order, he never gets through. By April he is only half way along. The latter material, and sometimes the more important, gets scant attention in the hurry to "finish on time." An exaggerated case is that of the teacher who says, "Oh well, we are getting short of time. Read the remainder of the text and I'll hold you responsible for it on the final examination." This, too, can be avoided by better planning, a viewing of the course as a whole. Such cases as these involve in detail the applications of our proposed basic principles of selection.

ELEMENTS OF A SATISFACTORY COURSE LAYOUT. In developing a layout for a course a teacher needs to consider:

1. The selection of the units that are to constitute the course. This implies consideration of the relationship of units to the course ob-objectives and the maturity of the pupils in the group.
2. The sequence, order, and arrangement of the units.

3. The timing of the units and the relationship of the timing of each unit to the total time which is available for the course as a whole.

4. An attempt at headlining unit titles so that something of the organization, interpretation, and direction of the unit can be determined by inspection of the title.

If the teacher carries out the stages outlined above, he may expend considerable time and thought on the process. However, in the end he should be able to get the product in the form of a layout on one letter-size page, certainly at the most on two pages. He then has a blueprint for his proposed course which he can easily examine or re-examine at a sitting.

The large unit in layouts. Throughout the discussion in this chapter the *large unit* as the center of educational planning has been assumed. The assumption just made perhaps gives the simplest definition of the unit. It is a large whole which becomes the center of both teacher and pupil planning. The unit as defined should have certain important characteristics to serve its purpose well.

1. The unit should have meaning and significance for the pupils who are to work with it.

2. The unit should have some obvious center, theme, or problem about which it can be organized.

3. The unit should have definite social worth. It should not contribute to just some currently superficial whim of the pupils. It should have content that is worth learning.

The work of the typical unit will take from two to six weeks to complete. This means that in a school year of thirty-six weeks there will be approximately six to twelve or fourteen units in a given course. Hence, the teacher can lay out a course which can be seen in its entirety.

A caution on the number of units for one course needs to be observed. If the teacher has selected sixteen, eighteen, twenty, or more units for a course, either it has been cut into segments which have relatively little significance in themselves, or too much has been planned for accomplishment within the limits of the school year. There is a tendency for teachers to try to crowd too much into a single course.

If a course has too few units, the units themselves are often so large as to be unwieldy. Such units tend to sag in the middle and break in two of their own weight. It is difficult to sustain the drive, interest, and willingness of pupils to work on a unit that takes nine, twelve, or fourteen weeks to complete. The obvious remedy, assuming the worthwhileness of a selected unit, is to subdivide the unit at normal breaks in the organization. Recall the criterion that a unit should have within it some center about which it can be organized.

Variation in the nature of units. The nature of the unit and the center about which it can be organized will vary with the nature of the course and with the unit objectives. There will be considerable variation in the nature of units as determined by the fields in which the work is done. Then, too, the nature of the learning experiences will have much to do with the characteristics of particular units.

If a physical education course is to consist entirely of experiences with common group sports, the sports themselves will form the pattern of units. If an art course or a general shop course is to consist largely of a series of constructive projects, the projects themselves will determine the units.

Certain courses lend themselves to laying out units in terms of large blocks of subject matter. This can be done with general science, biology, physics, chemistry, American history, world history, and elementary economics.

At the same time these courses can be organized by attempting to select significant problems, trends, growths, or evolutions. The point of view for the course will determine whether a topical or a problem approach to selection is to be used.

Shop courses, many vocational courses, and at least part of home economics can be built about the important jobs to be undertaken in the field. This procedure is commonly used in vocational agriculture. The whole of a given type of farm undertaking is called an enterprise. The enterprise is broken into the more important operations and jobs necessary to its successful completion. These are usually set into a seasonal sequence. The operations, or jobs, become the basis for selecting the experiences which constitute the whole enterprise.

Distributed units. In certain courses a part of the objectives imply a long-sustained series of drills carried on over a relatively long period of time. Illustrations are found in spelling, speech, foreign language, music, typewriting, stenography, and perhaps others. In such cases many teachers say that it is impossible to apply the notion of large-unit planning. They will tend to revert to a series of daily lessons based upon the drill exercises needed. However, such learnings *can* be planned as units.

It will be to the advantage of a teacher in planning to think of some units as long-range units with some estimate of the total time needed for learning but with time *distributed* over a considerable number of weeks. The time for one of these units on a given day need not take up a whole class period. Perhaps the unit will require twenty minutes of practice every day for nine weeks, or thirty minutes three times per week for ten weeks. In the total layout for the course, the teacher will show these as units, estimate the total time involved, and mark the unit as a distributed unit. It may be necessary to develop a simple time chart to show the utilization of time in the whole course and the time interrelationships of the various units, but a clever teacher can easily construct such a chart.

Illustrative units which may be treated as distributed units are tenth-grade spelling, mastery of the typewriter keyboard, Spanish pronunciation, improved enunciation in speech, ear training and sight reading in music. Many teachers will at once think of others.

Sample layouts. Following are a few samples of layouts for courses as set up by students in the author's classes. These are presented as suggestive samples and not as models to be followed by teachers.

General Mathematics
9th Grade

Unit		Weeks
1	Measurement—its history and its use today	6
2	Geometric construction as used in the modern shop	4
3	Drawing to scale	4
4	Ratio and percentage	5
5	Pictorial mathematics and the graph as shorthand methods of representing ideas and showing facts	5
6	The use of money; the mathematics of home and personal business affairs	7
7	Short cuts in computation through the use of formulas and equations	5
	Total	36

American History
11th Grade

Unit		Weeks
1	The American Ideal	1
2	Europe looks west	3
3	Nationalism and democracy vs. English imperialism	4
4	Expansion, sectional conflict, and preservation of the Union	5
5	Economic freedom and the growth of power	3
6	In the meantime, the neighbors	4
7	Transitional America and world war	4

8	Government in business and business in government	3
9	America in an interdependent world	5
	Total	32

World History
10th Grade

Unit		Weeks
1	Early civilization—how and where it began	3
2	Greece and changes in early civilization	3
3	Birth and decay of the Roman Empire	4
4	The rise of Christian civilization	3
5	Life in Medieval Europe	2
6	Europe expands	4
7	Church revolts	3
8	World-wide revolutions and their significance to present civilizations	5
9	Beginnings of democracy and nationalism	4
10	Modern civilization—its trials and hopes for the future	5
	Total	36

Secondary School Chemistry
11th or 12th Grade

Unit		Weeks
1	Matter and energy—a challenge to present-day scientists	3
2	The smallest particles known to man—the structure of atoms and molecules	3
3	The chemist's shorthand—symbols, formulas, balancing equations	6
4	The periodic classification of the elements, atomic numbers	4
5	Acids, bases, and salts	3
6	The family tree of chemistry—the halogens	3
7	The general properties of gases	3
8	Metals and nonmetals	3
9	The chemistry of food and shelter	3
10	A glimpse into the organic chemist's world	3
11	Chemistry as a cornerstone of the world today—drugs, poisons, cosmetics, plastics, atomic power	2
	Total	36

Critic's comment: Time allowed for later units too short.

General Biology
10th Grade

Unit		Weeks
1	Basic structure of all living things	6
2	Variability and numbers of plants and animals	4
3	Classification of plants and animals	6
4	Foods, their nutritional content and their effects	4

5	Reproduction of the species	5
6	Improvement of the species	3
7	The unseen hand of death and disease	4
8	Conservation of life	3
	Time adjustment	1
		—
	Total	36

Critic's comment: Query, time allotment given to classification.

Industrial Arts
General Shop
9th or 10th Grade

Unit		Weeks
1	Lines, the draftsman's language	1
2	Freehand sketching, the draftsman's notes	2
3	Scaled drawing, the worker's guide to construction	3
4	Woodworking skills and techniques as necessities and hobbies	5
5	Machine working decreases time and labor	6
6	Sheet metal working	3
7	Artistic metal work	3
8	Bench metals, forging and metal forming	6
9	Plastics, the field of opportunity	5
	Time adjustment	2
		—
	Total	36

General English
9th Grade

Unit		Weeks
1	Social letters and letters of friendship	2
2	Adventures in the appreciation of good poetry	2
3	Everyday uses of grammar	5
4	Using the library and the dictionary	1
5	Building vocabulary Improving spelling	2 (distributed)
6	The appreciation of books	4
7	Improving skills in conversations	3
8	Improving abilities in reading aloud	2
9	Keeping well informed	2
10	An attempt at creative writing for the fun of it	3
11	Drills in mechanics	1 (distributed)
12	Forming opinions through discussion and argument	2
13	Dramatics and public speaking	3
14	An excursion into the modern short story	4
		—
	Total	36

AIDS IN DEVELOPING COURSE LAYOUTS. With the discussions and illustrations of layouts for secondary school courses it has not been the intention to leave the impression that the teacher is to spin his materials for layouts out of the blue sky. The experienced teacher can rely much upon his background of experience and his breadth and depth of training. The new teacher needs considerable help in laying out a course. All of us can profit by observation and examination of the products of other professional workers.

Textbooks as aids. The most obvious help in laying out a course is the textbook. Perhaps next in importance is a collection of textbooks other than the adopted text. Before beginning a layout, the teacher may well examine the content and sequence of material in the texts available. He should gather any pertinent information that he can get concerning the characteristics of the people who are to form the class. The teacher may then make a rough list of seemingly desirable units in the form of ideas, topics, or problems. This original list need not be in the order to be followed in the completed layout. Perhaps the next stage is that of arranging these rough notes in a tentative order.

Then comes the estimate of time for each unit. The time estimate can be used as a crude measure of relative importance of units. Important units will tend to receive more time, less important ones, less time. This is conditioned, of course, by consideration of work rates of the pupils. The attempt to allot time may lead to the omission of some units, the combining of some, or perhaps the addition of a unit.

Finally the teacher will try to polish the units by expressing his ideas of emphasis in appropriate headlining for each unit.

The mature teacher having developed layouts for the courses assigned to him may in turn use these in an attempt to find a textbook to implement best the course as planned. The course layout thus used is perhaps the most valuable guide to the selection of a textbook that a teacher can devise.

No particular textbook is in and of itself infallible. Any textbook is a means, not an end in itself. The text is an instrument to promote desired learning. Therefore, the text is to be chosen as a means of achieving the objectives of the course.

Teachers often say, "What is to be done with material in a given text that does not fit the course at hand?" First it would be well to select a text that will most nearly fit the learning situation. If some of the text material does not fit, let it alone. There is no longer any compulsion in most schools merely to cover subject matter.

On the other hand, the pupils may have need for material not found in the text, or perhaps not available in any textbook. Hence other sources will be needed. In fact, if the material of a course is actually adapted to the needs of the pupils, practically every textbook will need supplementing from other sources.

Courses of study as aids. Another source of help in laying out a course is to be found in published or mimeographed city and state courses of study. Every teacher should begin a collection of such materials for his own use. Again, courses of study are prepared by professional workers or by committees who volunteer or are assigned to the project. They are useful and suggestive but do not constitute the final word concerning what a particular teacher is to do with a course to fit his own pupils. At present it is believed that courses of study should present useful ideas and stimulation for teachers but not be considered as prescriptive.

Aid from teachers and pupils. Cooperative work among teachers interested in planning similar courses will often be found especially helpful. Teachers may themselves form into groups of similar interests. Sometimes the school administration may aid in setting up planning workshops among the teachers. In some schools, committees are assigned the responsibility for planning a part of the program. This procedure has been especially successful in a few schools attempting layouts for a core curriculum.

Some city and some state school systems have a corps of special supervisors who are capable of rendering considerable assistance to teachers in selecting units for courses. This arrangement is especially frequent in such fields as speech, art, music, home economics, vocational agriculture, physical education, and trades and industries. It will pay the teacher to become acquainted with the specialists in his field in his own city or state system.

The teacher who will take the pains to become really acquainted with his own pupils will pick up many ideas concerning pupils' needs from the pupils themselves. Many such ideas may find expression in the revision of a course layout intended to serve the pupils' needs.

A good course should contribute much to the use of the materials, ideas, or skills contained in it. Almost every course can be improved if the teacher will continually observe the uses made of his teaching materials by people outside the school situation. In this sense what the teacher is able to see people doing with potential content for his course forms one of the most significant aids in selecting units for the course layout.

Unit implementation

UNIT ORGANIZATION

1. Schools must teach that subject matter which may be demanded of every individual, regardless of special capacities or interests, in order that the individual may serve the best interests of the group of which he is a part. This is the principle of social need or group necessity.

2. Schools should provide training beyond that demanded of every individual to fit the work of the school to the individual abilities, interests, and needs of the persons being trained. This is the principle of. adaptation to individual needs and differences.

3. Each high school course, whether required or elective, should first contain that material best adapted to the needs of all the pupils enrolled in the course.

4. Each high school course, whether required or elective, should contain some material which may be adapted to the particular or immediate needs of those individuals in the course in the present year.

5. The principle of group necessity determines the nature and kind of required courses included in a high school program.

6. The principle of individual adaptation determines the nature and kind of elective courses offered in a high school program.

7. The principles of group necessity and of individual adaptation apply as well to the selection of content for particular units as to the course as a whole.

8. Subject matter is any solution worked out as a part of the culture as a means of meeting a human need.

9. *General education* includes that part of the school program which is concerned primarily with the development in pupils of those types of likenesses that are necessary for proper social integration.

10. *Differentiating education* includes that part of the school program which is designed to meet the specialized needs and interests of individual pupils.

11. The pattern of units selected for a particular high school course should be consistent with the objectives previously set up for the course.

12. The details of content and the assignments selected for any given unit should be consistent with the unit objectives.

13. Adequate planning of a high school course implies organization of the content and work of the course into relatively large instructional *units*.

14. An instructional unit implies selection of work and of needed subject matter for the accomplishment of a small group of closely related learning objectives.

15. An instructional unit should have within itself some definite basis for organization. *theme, center, problem* .

16. Units should be of considerable concern to the pupils.

17. Units should have definite social worth.

18. The *layout* for a high school course should include the pattern of units to be included within the course and estimates of the approximate time pupils will need in accomplishing the work of each unit.

19. Units appearing in the layout for a course should be titled in such fashion as to indicate the direction of each unit and at the same time appeal to the sense of values of the pupils in the course.

20. Units in a course layout should be arranged to show the sequence of development to be followed in the course.

21. The approximate time needed by pupils in gaining the objectives of each unit should be shown in the margin of the course layout.

22. The sum of the time estimates suggested for each unit must fit within the total time available for the whole course.

THINGS TO DO

1. Imagine yourself free to prescribe courses for pupils in a given high school. List the courses (not subject groups) which you would require of all high school pupils.

For each of these required courses indicate the chief social needs which seem to justify the requirement.

2. Would you place courses in your major field of interest in a required or an elective group of courses? Outline in a page or less the argument justifying your position.

3. Examine the list of requirements for graduation from high schools in your state.

Show how each of these requirements may be justified in terms of the principle of social integration, if possible.

Write out your objections to such a pattern of requirements.

4. Secure a copy of a recent textbook, or course of study outline, for a high school course in your field. Select a single chapter of the text or a section of the course outline for treatment. List the items that you would require all pupils to learn.

5. Make a layout for one high school course which you expect to teach. List the units which are to make up this course. Give each unit a title which will indicate its content and at the same time appeal to high school pupils as being worthwhile.

Arrange your pattern of units in the order which seems to make the best learning sequence. Number the units to indicate the sequence.

Estimate in weeks the time needed in carrying out the work of each of the units. Indicate this time estimate by appropriate figures in the margin after each unit title.

Check your list of units with your original statement of objectives for the course, or with the course introduction.

If necessary, modify your selection of units until the pattern of units is consistent with the stated objectives.

6. Select a high school textbook which seems best to fit the course planned above.

Compare the content of the selected text with your pattern of units. What is to be omitted from the text? What supplementary material will be needed? Where can the needed supplementary material be found by your pupils? What provisions are to be made for rapid learners? Slow learners? Special interests of pupils?

7. Make course layouts as indicated in exercise 5 for other high school courses which you expect to teach.

Helpful Readings

ALEXANDER, WILLIAM M. and SAYLOR, J. GALEN. *Secondary Education.* New York: Rinehart & Co., Inc., 1950. Chaps. 13, 14, and 15.

Chap. 13 deals with subjects for general education; chap. 14 with subjects for specialized education; and chap. 15 with the core curriculum.

AMERICAN YOUTH COMMISSION OF THE AMERICAN COUNCIL ON EDUCATION. *What the High Schools Ought to Teach.* Washington, D.C.: American Council on Education, 1940.

A general statement of policy.

ASSOCIATION FOR SUPERVISION AND CURRICULUM DEVELOPMENT. *What Shall the High Schools Teach?* Washington, D.C.: National Education Association, 1956. Chaps. 3, 4, 5, and 6.

Chap. 3 includes a survey of what high schools are teaching and the common requirements for graduation. Chap. 4 deals with the selection of content for the school program. Chap. 5 considers the foundations of general education. Chap. 6 distinguishes between general, special, and vocational education.

BILLETT, ROY O. *Fundamentals of Secondary School Teaching.* Rev. ed. Boston: Houghton Mifflin Co., 1940. Chap. 7.

Contains a good, brief treatment of the teacher's problems in the selection of subject matter.

BRIGGS, THOMAS H., LEONARD, J. PAUL, and JUSTMAN, JOSEPH. *Secondary Education.* Rev. ed. New York: The Macmillan Co., 1950. Chaps. 4 and 6.

Helpful in formulating principles for the selection of content.

DEWEY, JOHN. *The Child and the Curriculum.* Chicago: University of Chicago Press, 1902.

Read as an original source of much that has been written since emphasizing the importance of pupil growth in selecting educative materials.

DOUGLASS, HARL R. (ed.) *Education for Life Adjustment.* New York: The Ronald Press Co., 1950. Chap. 20.

Chap. 20 suggests a basis for selecting problems and subject areas from community sources.

——. *The High School Curriculum.* 2d ed. New York: The Ronald Press Co., 1956. Chaps. 5, 6, 10, 11, 13, 15, 16, and 17.

Chaps. 5 and 6 give the social and economic setting in which the school program must fit. Chap. 15 is on large units as a basis for course construction; chap. 16 on course construction; and chap. 17 on the teacher's function in course construction.

FEATHERSTONE, WILLIAM A. *A Functional Curriculum for Youth.* New York: American Book Co., 1950. Chaps. 1 and 2.

Valuable largely for the expression of a functional point of view on selection.

FRENCH, WILLIAM MARSHALL. *American Secondary Education.* New York: The Odyssey Press, 1957.

Read chap. 9, "The Curriculum Crisis," for an interpretation of controversies in the selection of content for the modern secondary school program.

INGLIS, ALEXANDER. *Principles of Secondary Education.* Boston: Houghton Mifflin Co., 1918. Chaps. 9 and 10.

Contains the "classic" statement of functions of secondary education which all secondary school teachers should know.

JONES, ARTHUR, GRIZZELL, E. D., and GRINSTEAD, W. J. *Principles of Unit Construction.* New York: McGraw-Hill Book Co., Inc., 1939.

The one best source on definition and interpretation of the large unit as a center of planning and of course construction.

Romine, Stephen A. *Building the High School Curriculum.* New York: The Ronald Press Co., 1954. Chaps. 8, 9, 10, and 11.

Contains effective helps and suggestions on the selection of content, definition of the unit, and course construction.

Smith, B. Othanel, Stanley, William O., and Shores, J. Harlan. *Fundamentals of Curriculum Development.* Rev. ed. Yonkers, N.Y.: World Book Co., 1957. Chaps. 6, 7, 10 and 12.

Deals with principles for the implementation of general and differentiating education in the school program.

Unit III

How Can the Teacher
Organize for Learning?

Suppose that for a class you have selected a unit as most important for accomplishing the objectives for a course. In terms of good learning, does it make any difference where the pupils begin the work of the new unit? In what order is the work to proceed from the determined beginning point? How do you find out where to begin? How do you determine a good learning order?

Many teachers have simply followed the adopted textbook. Obviously, for them the place to begin is the first chapter of the text, or, for a particular unit, the chapter in the text which applies, used in the order in which it is written. Is this always good procedure? Does it make any difference that pupils have never heard of what is in the chapter?

Often pupils have no concern with what is presented in a text assignment or for what the accepted course of study calls for. What is the teacher to do about this lack of a feeling of need on the part of the pupils?

Does a teacher dare change the order of material in a text prepared by a specialist in his field? If the teacher changes an organization to fit the needs and experiences of pupils, what is to be done to avoid leaving pupils with an unorganized and unrelated mass of detail? Is organization, as such, important? How important? Are some forms of organization better than others?

What to look for in this unit

1. Of what value is an organization of subject matter?

2. In what sense is a logical organization *artificial* rather than *natural* organization?

3. What is the elemental basis for all types of classification?

4. What fundamental differences are there between *learning* and *economical and convenient use?*

5. What determines relative ease of learning?

6. How is ease of learning related to psychological *readiness?*

7. Why is progressing from the structurally simple to the structurally complex not always the best learning order?

8. Why is a readiness order most often superior to a strictly logical organization in the early stages of learning?

9. What factors determine the selection of a good beginning point in learning?

10. At what point in the development of any given learning is logical organization to be introduced?

11. What types of logical organization are commonly used to classify materials in your subject matter field?

12. How may high school pupils be trained to use the logical organizations common to your teaching field?

13. What kind of an outline of subject matter should the teacher include in his own unit plan?

14. Why should a unit plan contain an outline of subject matter?

4

Readiness Organizations
in Learning

The teacher has the problem of arranging the items of subject matter and the sequence of learning experiences in an order which will promote learning. In the unit introduction the importance of the beginning point in the organization of learning is stressed. However, the problems are larger than this seems to indicate. There *is* the problem of determining for a given group of pupils the best first point of attack Also, there is at once the problem of arranging the succeeding ideas and experiences. Finally, there is the problem of an ultimate organization that is to be left with the pupils.

To many teachers there seems to be no problem of organization. The attention of the teacher is centered upon the subject matter to be covered in his courses. Such subject matter seems, because of long accustomed use, to fall naturally into its own arrangement. All the teacher needs to do is to begin with the logically first item of the subject matter and follow along with the logical development of the subject matter itself. This is easily illustrated by the teacher of American history who begins with the discovery of America, either by Columbus in 1492 or by Leif Ericson in 1000, and follows the chronology of happenings to the present worldwide international crises.

On the other hand, there are some teachers who ignore the

problems of organization because they do not see the significant contribution of the processes of organization to learning. Such teachers tend to follow the immediate interests of pupils and often leave a period of three or four weeks of work with no organization that will enable pupils to interpret or use the ideas.

A good illustration of the need for consideration of the problems of organization in learning is to be found in the story of the teaching of reading in the elementary school. In early American elementary schools, and well down into the twentieth century, reading was taught by beginning with the simplest structural elements of language and proceeding to the next more complex structural elements. For example, the beginning reader must learn first to recognize the letters of the alphabet. Next, the young reader learned to spell and recognize one-syllable words of two, three, and four letters. These structurally simple words were then combined into short sentences of two, three, or four words. Then followed the introduction of words of five, six, or more letters, and words of two syllables. These were combined into sentences, and as reading progressed the sentences were lengthened. Words were grouped into related structual groups such as cat, rat, hat, mat, bat, etc. But always words had to be spelled. Most beginning reading was oral reading. The process was slow, stumbling, and halting.

Children did learn to read by the process just described. But lip reading was almost universal, and there were comparatively few rapid silent readers. Words often had to be spelled for recognition.

It took American school teachers nearly 150 years to discover that there were other important factors than the degree of complexity of structure of the language elements which condition readiness, or ease of learning, in reading. Some of these factors are: (1) the need or desire of the young reader for the ideas which make up the content being read; (2) the relationship of the ideas represented by the reading symbols to the individual reader's own experiences; (3) the satisfactions attained by each reader in carrying out the reading process.

When some teachers finally became aware that these factors might condition reading readiness, attempts were made to change the selection and order of reading materials. In the first place, children began the school approach to reading by not reading. The clever teacher gathered the children into small groups to get them to talk about the things which concerned them as children. By this process the teacher could find out what might be appropriate content for possible future reading materials. He could find, also, some things about the nature of the existing experiences of different pupils in the group.

The first words for reading recognition probably went on the blackboard. Pupils were not taught letters of the alphabet, nor were they taught to spell. The word as a whole stood as a symbol for an idea of importance to the children. The length of the word was not important. Short sentences were introduced from the beginning and read as wholes. It was always important that the ideas intrigue the pupils and that they be pleased with the results of their attempts at reading.

The present-day youngster may read more readily such words as automobile, airplane, bus, tractor, television, radio, and touch football, than such words as horse, cow, dog, cat, rat, sheep, goat, and crow presented to children beginning to read a generation ago. Note that the spelling and the structure of the words proposed are not the primary issue.

Readiness factors

Suppose that the factors conditioning readiness for reading may apply also to the conditioning of readiness in all learning situations. Then all teachers working under this assumption must consider the possibility of organizing learning to take advantage of these conditioning factors.

In planning the work of any unit the teacher will need to give consideration to the problem of the immediate need of the pupils concerned for the content. Other things being equal, it might be well to begin the unit with an issue or problem which is of great present concern to the pupils. There is also the possibility that there is better leverage for early learning if the unit begins with something within the range of the experiences of the pupils. Certainly, there is considerable evidence to indicate that there will be much better understanding and interpretation if the early learning materials of the unit make contact with pupil experiences. Finally, the continuance of effort on the part of the pupils will be conditioned by the degree of satisfaction experienced by the pupils as a result of the earlier efforts at learning.

The arrangement of elements within a unit applies to the selection of a first unit for a course and to the arrangement of the sequence of units.

There is space for only a few secondary school illustrations of the principles of readiness. Should a course in world history begin with a unit on pre-history merely because the subject matter occurs first in an arrangement based upon chronology? Is it possible for a group of tenth graders who are daily confronted with the doubts of a war-torn world, who read in the newspapers and hear the television commentators on the conflicts between the western world and the eastern world, to begin a course in world history by trying to discover some differences in the cultures of the peoples of the western world and the eastern? What might make a good first unit in world history considering the need for sound information and the present experiences of tenth graders?

Assuming that we are to work out the details of a unit in world history of the kind just suggested, how could the unit be started? What historical content would follow? It is possible that a beginning could be made with the western nations as contrasted with those nations included in the Russian orbit of communism. The clue to this as a beginning point would come out of newspaper reading, current-event magazine reading, and listening to news commentators, coupled with possible fears and dreads of the pupils growing out of such reading and listening. The following historical materials would be selected from those which would interpret the growth of nationalism in western Europe, the democratic revolutions among these peoples, the place of the United States in relationship to these nations, the association of Canada and Australia with this group, questions of the status of the other remnants of the British Empire such as that of India and the African colonies to the western nations, the common elements of culture that tend to unite the western nations. In contrast with this, the late emergence of Russia as a nation, the Russian revolution, the possible differences of Slavic peoples from the peoples of western Europe, the various Balkan disturbances, the culture of the Slavic and Balkan peoples, the appeal of communism to newly freed masses, and the issues of World Wars I and II might be considered.

Many topics are suggested, and no complete historical coverage of all these topics could be made in any short period. With careful selection, enough might be done to develop a sufficient understanding to meet the rather critical needs of a group of adolescents for interpretation of some of the present world crises. If violence seems to be done to the traditional time relationships of history, pupils might well attempt to develop a summary or time chart that will set the facts in proper chronological perspective.

A further illustration of readiness principles may be taken from high school physics. Nearly every high school physics course begins with the nature and properties of matter and energy and proceeds to measurement, to mechanics, and to force and motion. The treatments of heat, light, and electricity come later in the course.

Imagine a group of juniors and seniors in a rural high school. These pupils live in homes that have just been reached by recent extensions of R.E.A. power lines. They and their parents are much stimulated by the possible application of the new source of energy to home and farm appliances. Is it possible to begin a course in physics for this group with the unit on electricity? Could certain basic concepts of the nature of matter and energy be introduced in relationship to electrical phenomena rather than to gravitational phenomena? There is here a need in the pupils that would be almost sure to provide motivation and drive for the work to come. Most of the pupils have, or are getting, some experiences with electrical appliances and electric circuits. There is a possible experiential basis for building better understandings.

If it is agreed to use the electricity unit as a starting point for the course, what now is to be done with the unit? In the traditional physics course the usual first topics are those of static electricity and magnetism as illustrated with fixed magnets. The needs of the pupils are for an understanding and better means of control of electric circuits with established power lines. They have similar needs in relationship to electric appliances. Then try beginning the unit on electricity with electric circuits, sources of power, safety measures in control of circuits, conductors and nonconductors, and the principles upon which the different basic electrical appliances operate. No one will object to a summarization of what is learned into primary laws or principles. A re-application in the form of an interpretation of the R.E.A. wiring regulations may be in place too.

Organization and understanding

From the two brief illustrations it seems obvious that the application of principles of readiness to the arrangement of learning materials will produce better motivation for the majority of pupils. It is the next thesis that the application of these principles provides also the approach to understanding of new ideas or generalizations, or to the development of new skills. At any one moment the working psychological capital of any individual consists of his existing experiences. He can understand new experience only in relationship to that which he has.

The statement that a jet-propelled plane operates on the principle of a Fourth-of-July skyrocket is meaningful only to those who have observed the flight of skyrockets. The statement probably means more to those who have set up and fired skyrockets. It may mean more yet to those who have dissected skyrockets or torn up the "duds" to find how they were constructed. It is probable that, for a mixed group, the statement means more to the boys than to the girls. Do you see why?

Such relationships to existing experiences may lead to misconceptions too. In the case of the skyrocket—rocket plane analogy, some folk may jump to the conclusion that the fuel of the rocket plane is gunpowder. As a matter of fact, the term rocket applied to a plane tends to imply powder as a fuel to a great many people. In the same way, if the term "motor" is applied to the driving mechanism of the rocket plane, many will think of the conventional gasoline motor with its pistons, cylinders, connecting rods, and drive shaft.

We need to emphasize the difficulties of understanding arising in much of our formal secondary education that deals so largely with generalizations and abstractions expressed in language or in symbols. Illustrations can be found in the daily quarrels over the meanings of the terms "democracy" and "communism." Pupils are almost invariably confused in the interpretation of the physicist's use of the term "work" because of the casual interpretations in ordinary conversation of work as human labor.

Clearly the placing of new ideas and abstractions in true relationship to the existing experiences of the pupils is a primary problem of organization for the teacher. The teacher must know the experiences of the people with whom he works and be able to find clever and imaginative possibilities of relationship with the teaching at hand.

Organization and motor learning (developing skills)

What has been said concerning the interpretation and understanding of ideas applies at least in part to motor learning too. It is highly important that teachers of physical education, shop, typewriting, music, home economics, and vocational agriculture see this. Each learner has experiences in the organization of skills. Having mastered some skills, these in turn become possible working parts in the organization of new skills. As with the interpretation of ideas, existing skills may interfere with the formation of the new ones. For example it might be possible to say to a would-be golfer, "Swing the club as you would a grass whip." If the learner is city bred, this becomes a very doubtful approach. The reverse might work also. One could say to the golfer, "In cutting weeds, swing the grass whip as you do a golf club." The response will not be a perfect one at the first attempt, but it may be a useful beginning. Teachers of sports techniques need to study the common household, yard, and sand-lot skills for beginning suggestions for sports skills. Have in mind that study of these processes may turn up reasons for much awkward play in terms of interferences transferring from the learner's earlier experiences. In reverse, the teachers of work-type skills may be able to find many suggestions for beginning skills from the sports experiences of their pupils.

Applications of readiness organization

What has been said in these last two sections can be summarized in two rather arbitrary rules of procedure, set up as case situations.

Case I: The teacher assumes that pupils have a considerable amount of experience that can be related to the proposed new learning. If this assumption can be verified by checking the experiences of the pupils, the new material is to be presented in its appropriate relationship to pupil experiences. The tools of the teacher here are those of the parable, analogy, comparison, role-playing, and case situations.

Case II: The teacher assumes that the pupils have few or no experiences that can be related to the new learning. Again a check on pupil experiences needs to be made. Sometimes the assumption is false. In the absence of pertinent experiences with which to make appropriate connections, the teaching tools of Case I fail. The teacher must now use the classroom and its equipment to build within the pupils the experiences that are lacking. Here is the appropriate function of the workroom, the shop, the laboratory, visual aids, models, dramatization, and the extension of the classroom into excursion, field trip, directed observation, and work experience.

Before listing the commoner attempts at readiness organization, it may be well to summarize and to set up a working definition of the concept of readiness organization. A readiness organization is an attempt to arrange experiences of learners and items of subject matter into a sequence to promote learning for a particular group of learners. In a readiness organization, there is always the attempt to relate the new learning to the immediate needs and to the existing experiences of the particular learners. There is at the same time an attempt to see that the efforts of the learners lead to some degree of satisfaction in the achievements produced. In some other textbooks within the fields of educational psychology and methods of teaching, the term "psychological organization" will be found often.

Common types of readiness organization

Those types of experiential organization that have been tried frequently and can be identified readily and described are: functional organization, applications-to-principles organization, problem organization, project organization, and job organization.

FUNCTIONAL ORGANIZATION. Functional organization is an arrangement in terms of common or frequent use. It may be distinguished from a structural organization in that usually the first point in a structural organization is the simplest element of the structure, whereas in a functional organization the point of familiar use may be with some element which possesses a relatively complex structure.

For example, in a unit on current electricity, simpler structure would be involved by beginning with direct current of low voltage from dry cells. Such an approach will deal with circuits and appliances seldom used by the pupils. With the exception of the common flashlight, the pupil of today seldom works with such circuits. Even the electric toys of today operate with transformers off the household alternating current. From the point of view of a functional organization, it might be possible to begin the unit with the household circuit and the many and various appliances which operate from it. The structure seems much more complex, but the teacher can begin at the point of frequent and often needed use with the learners.

The apparent advantages in possible learning effects in functional organization are in motivation and in the existence of experiences in making some degree of interpretation at the point of beginning learning. The teacher taking advantage of such organization assumes that pupils will want to learn more about those things which they use, and that they can understand more readily those things with which they have had some experience.

APPLICATION-TO-PRINCIPLES ORGANIZATION. In application-to-principles organization, teaching begins with *applications* of principles to be taught that are within the range of experiences of the learners. The interpretation of the principle is derived by an exploration and extension of the pupil's experiences with the applications. After the principle is established, new applications are introduced to be sure that the learner can see the relationship of the principle to further new cases.

The teacher assumes that the pupils are probably more concerned with what can be done with a principle in its application than they may be in an abstract statement of the principle. He assumes, also, that applications are far more frequent in the experiences of the pupils than mere verbal statement of a principle. The experiences with the application may furnish ideas with which the pupil may attain some degree of understanding of the principle. In general, the proof of this latter assumption is found in the success of the learner in making reapplications in new situations.

PROBLEM ORGANIZATION. Problem organization [1] begins with a problem which has reality and significance for the pupils concerned. The relationship of the facts gathered is that of pertinency to the problem at hand. If ideas seem useful in working out a solution to the problem, they are kept and used in an appropriate relationship in the attempts at solution. If suggested ideas seem not to relate to the solution of the problem of the moment, they are discarded as irrelevant.

In the use of problem organization, the teacher assumes the motivation growing out of the *need* of the pupil for a solution to his problem. There may be relatively little experiential background from which the pupil may work. There is the accompanying assumption that better understanding can be attained by the pupil in the process of developing his own solution to a problem. He understands the solution because he knows how it has been put together.

Many of the subproblems of textbooks turn out to be relatively simple quiz questions rather than problems. For example, a problem expressed as, "What were the underlying causes of the Russian Revolution of 1918?" causes no problem-solving reaction in the typical high school youth. He merely turns to his text in world history and lists or memorizes the causes given by the author of the text. The stated "problem" is a very thinly disguised quiz question. The teacher can almost always recognize the quiz question by judging the possible reaction of the pupil to the "problem." If the pupil can turn to a readily available reference and quote a ready-made solution, then there is no problem.

In terms of the assumptions concerning the possible learning values of problem organization, the common element in many attempts to express problems is found in the fact that they tend to miss the element of concern for the *individual* pupil. They are, in general, teachers' or textbook authors' problems, not pupil problems. Nearly always they are very large-scale adult problems. They fail to furnish the impetus to the individual inquiry that might truly motivate the youthful investigator.

Above all, a problem of major value in learning has personal concern to the individual learner. It is *his* problem, or at least he accepts it as such. He must want to find a solution very much, not merely carry out a classroom exercise. This means that there must be a variety of problems. Few problems will fit whole class groups. For the teacher it is most important to see that problems are to be *found*, or discovered, in working with pupils and not invented.

[1] A further elaboration of the teacher's relationship of problem organization to problem-solving learning will be found in Unit IV, chap. 8.

In spite of all the educational literature on the values of problem-solving organization as an approach to good learning, perhaps the most significant attempt at classroom evaluation casts some doubt on the learning values as compared to simple topical organization. Before arriving at a final conclusion concerning problem organization much further investigation needs to be made under actual classroom conditions and further refinement in the distinguishing of true problems from the usual classroom tricks of the pedagogue's trade.

One final caution needs to be observed concerning problem organization in teaching. Not all learning can be approached through problems. There are many skills that are to be mastered through arduous practice.[2] The patterns for many of these are known. Some of the patterns can be established through imitation. Many appreciations,[3] if not all, come as a result of emotional responses. The attempt to rationalize appreciations by setting problems in the arts may produce negative rather than positive reactions. Only that learning which lends itself to the problem-solving processes can be enhanced by attempts at problem organization.

PROJECT ORGANIZATION. The *project* has certain of the characteristics just described under problem organization. A project has been defined as a wholehearted purposeful activity carried to completion in a natural setting. Under this definition, the essential feature of a project is the purpose of the learner. The organization of subject matter necessary for carrying the project to completion is that of pertinency to the given purpose. That subject matter needed in furthering the purpose of the worker is kept and used. That which is nonpertinent is discarded.

The learning value of the project is found in the motivation accruing from the intensity of the purpose of the learner. There is the assumption that if the subject matter and processes needed are determined by the needs arising from the learner's purpose he will work strenuously and retain what he has learned in the process. The relationship of the new subject matter to the learner's existing experiences may be close or remote. Understanding is built up in the process of completing the purpose. Insofar as the learner understands what he is doing, he can interpret the completed project because he himself will have carried it out.

Teachers often say, "What is the difference between a project and a problem?" If a problem is relatively complex and a true prob-

---

[2] For further treatment of this issue see Unit IV, chap. 8.

[3] For further development of the learning factors involved in the development of appreciations see Unit IV, chap. 7.

lem, so that the will to find a solution is the purpose of the problem-solver, then there seems to be no difference. In general, projects seem to be larger than problems, so that the carrying out of a given project may involve the need for solution for a whole series of problems.

As with problems, projects are to be discovered rather than invented. If a proposed project becomes merely a vehicle to motivate learning of subject matter of concern to the teacher, in most cases it ceases to be a project because it at once loses the learner's purpose. It is much easier to find individual projects than it is to find those that have the element of true enthusiasm for a group. On the other hand, group projects are possible, and when found, have the added values of the utilization of group integrating forces. A class picnic is often such a group project.

The literature dealing with the use of projects in teaching seems to emphasize largely activities which deal with things or those in which the activity itself is predominant. Construction projects are common in the shop, in the crafts of the art class, in clothing, and in farm shop. The planning and carrying out of dramatics and music programs illustrate group projects where activity seems to predominate. This does not mean that investigative and appreciational projects are impossible, but the more concrete types of activities seem to occur more readily to both pupils and teachers.

Uses. In the fields of home economics and vocational agriculture, there have long been efforts to tie the learning of the school to normal home and farm living through projects. The girl in home economics attempts to carry out the marketing and meal planning for her own family for six weeks. She plans, overhauls, repairs, and makes necessary new purchases, within her clothing budget, for her spring wardrobe. The boy in vocational agriculture buys or is given a dairy heifer. The calf becomes his. He rears her under normal farm procedures. If he sells her, the proceeds are his by agreement with the farmer parent. If she reaches maturity and has a calf, the calf belongs to the boy and the proceeds from the milk sold are his. He must provide the necessary feed and keep records on the business transactions involved. The 4-H Club movement among farm youths depends almost entirely upon the project approach.

Evaluation. The experimental evidence about the learning values of project organization shows good learning of factual subject matter. In one such pioneer experiment in general science, pupils carrying on relatively unrelated projects learned incidentally more subject matter than did comparable pupils devoting time to attempting to learn the subject matter of the textbooks and following the textbook organizations. Practically all experimenters with project teaching point out the possible added values of concomitant learnings such as the factors of persistence and perseverance in work, learning of problem-solving processes, and so on. In general, these claims seem sound but are not specifically proved.

Drawbacks often presented by teachers who question the desirability of project organization are: (1) the discontinuity and seeming lack of logical organization in the total subject matter covered by the class; (2) the possibility that not all of the subject matter for which the teacher feels responsible in his field will be covered during the school year; (3) the strains upon the teacher's range of information and training and upon his skill in pupil management.

There seems to be no doubt that the number of projects and the number of pupils for which a teacher can be responsible will be limited if any large scale attempt at utilization of projects is made. The typical present enrollments of pupils in classes in vocational agriculture, home economics, and shop, as contrasted with enrollments in classes that depend largely upon books and reading assignments, may be sound evidence on this latter point.

PUPIL PARTICIPATION IN PLANNING. A popular extension of the idea of the project is that of pupil participation in planning. In such planning, the teacher presents to the pupils suggestions for work. In turn the pupils are encouraged to make suggestions either for work to be done or for ways to develop one of the teacher's proposals. In many cases, the blackboard is used for suggestions which are made by pupils and teacher. In good usage, these notes are put into some system, and the final plan replaces the notes on the board. Pupils take the parts of leaders in the planning. There may be a temporary pupil chairman, a recorder for making the notes on the blackboard, a secretary, and some resource assistants to find needed materials in references. The actual organization of the subject matter used may be varied depending upon the nature of the unit planned and the maturities and experiences of the pupils.

The assumptions of learning value are that the pupils will see the need for the work to be done if they participate in the planning, and that better understandings will be developed through pupil participation in organization.

Critics of pupil planning have pointed out that in most cases a clever teacher has previously done the planning and that the machinery of pupil participation has become a thinly veiled motivation device. There is a tendency for bright and loquacious pupils to dominate the group with relatively low participation on the part of a majority of the class members. Final organizations of subject matter tend to be relatively crude. Selection of units, if actually left to pupils, may be determined by temporary values and immature judgments. Basic skills, such as composition, arithmetic calculation, and spelling may be poorly formed. The primary subject matter for which the school seems responsible may not be covered well.

It must be remembered that pupil planning as currently carried on is a *group* process. As such, it takes clever and imaginative teacher direction and management. It does not lend itself too well to individualized learning. Its proponents are often more concerned with the effects of the group processes as concomitants than with the subject matter that can be learned or the individual skills developed.

Experimental evaluations of pupil participation in planning have depended largely upon such evaluation devices as teacher impressions, pupil testimonals, and partial case records. There has been little objective testing of results. Within the limitations of the means of evaluation, there are a considerable number of favorable reports on the results of pupil planning.

JOB ORGANIZATION. A different approach to experiential organization has been developed by teachers in industrial education. This is known as job organization. It was first attempted by teachers of trades. The process of organization is that of an analysis of an actual job to be performed in the order of its normal sequence of operations. The analysis is made on the basis of observations of the work of expert workmen to determine how they perform the operations and the order of the operations. The apprentice is shown the analysis and in his training taught to follow the order of operations of the expert workman. He is taught also to perform the operations in the way that these are carried out by the expert.

The assumptions concerning learning in job organizations are: (1) that the young learner can see the value and importance of the job as something he wants to learn how to do; (2) that the normal sequence of operations of the skilled workman will make sense to the learner; (3) that the transfer of learning from the training situation to normal work activities will be great in amount.

Shop teachers have borrowed the job approach from the trade teacher, so that a great many school shops use job sheets showing the analysis of operations to be used.

Attempts at extension of job analysis and planning have been made by teachers in such fields as home economics, sports coaching, mathematics, science, and English composition. A primary difficulty in the application of job organization to these fields is the identification of the jobs.. The invention of a job and an armchair analysis of the operations may become as artificial as any of our traditional school organizations. There are almost no controlled and objectively measured experimental evaluations of the results of job organization.

The types of readiness organizations that we have described are not the only ones possible. They are those that have been widely discussed and often tried in schools of the last thirty years. The teacher who is observant and imaginative will no doubt find and try others.

Note: For Unit III (chapters 4 and 5), the Unit Implementation (summary, exercises, and recommended readings) will be found at the end of Chapter 5.

5

Logical Organization
in Learning

Most learning does not take place merely for the sake of learning. People expect to do something with what is learned. At least this is true of what may be characterized as purposeful learning, a deliberate attempt to learn in order to carry out some selected objective.

If, then, something is to be done with what is learned, it is necessary to be concerned with efficiency and economy in use. This is apparent in situations in which the accumulation of details becomes large. It is necessary to arrange a large number of learned items into some system in order to be efficient in using them.

An analogy can be found in the housewife's kitchen equipment. The beginning housekeeper with only a few pieces of equipment may be able to leave them on the stove or in the sink and manage reasonably well. But when she acquires enough equipment that it has to be moved or stacked to find a needed piece, she needs formal organization or arrangement. It becomes necessary to find places of storage—equipment for greatest convenience. The desirability of the arrangement depends upon the nature of the work, the size and shape of the kitchen, the housewife's height, and many other immediate and personal factors. Although there is no one "best" method of arrangement, it is possible to make one that will promote efficiency and economy of time and effort.

Ideas also need systematic arrangement. Ideas are to be used. For most efficient use, ideas need to be arranged into systems. As with the kitchen equipment, the formation of a system of ideas will save time and energy for the user. The attempts to arrange ideas into systems, classifications, rules, and laws to promote efficiency and economy in use are called logical organization.

Need for organization

Systematization also aids the process of learning, but generally at its culmination rather than in the earliest stages. Use aids learning too. The combination of building a logical organization with the uses which are made of the learned and systematized ideas serve to fix the learning. Organization and continued use seem to be primary factors in retention of what is learned. Moreover, the learner who has built up his own logical organization of learned ideas understands the relationships better than if he had accepted a readymade organization.

The objections that have been raised to the older approaches to learning are not objections to logical organization in and of itself. The objections are to the introduction to learning through a readymade system which the pupil does not understand and for which at the moment he feels no need. Almost all learning is incomplete without logical organization, but this stage comes later in the learning process than the worshipers of logic have been willing to believe in the past.

In summary, logical organization is a necessary part of the total learning process; it should come toward the completion of the learning; organization aids in both fixation and understanding; use becomes both more efficient and more economical with effective organization. If possible, the learner should be aided in making his own organizations.

Common types of logical organization

Certain types of logical organization in most frequent use are quite familiar. The more familiar ones are those of structure, chronology, function, and cause and effect. It must be recognized, also, that not only these schemes for systematizing ideas but also the formulation of rules, principles, generalizations, laws, and patterns and form for skills are kinds of logical organization.

It is useful to see that the commoner systems for logical organization of things and ideas have a common basis. These organizations classify items that are in some degree alike into related groupings. In general, they depend upon the placing of like things into certain described categories.

STRUCTURAL ORGANIZATION. Perhaps the commonest form of logical organization is based upon likeness of structure of the materials used. The structural likeness may consist of the nature or the composition of the items, size, shape, color, or a similarity of constituent parts.

Some familiar cases of structural organization are found in the arrangement of words in the dictionary, the arrangement of parts in a repair shop parts department, the arrangement of glass and chinaware in a department store, the classification of plants in the botany manual, or the grouping of birds in a bird key. Note that all of these involve an assumption of convenience to the user, worker, or customer. The convenience of structural organization is so obvious that it need not be argued.

Simplicity of structure and learning. Structural organizations present certain difficulties to teachers because of a very common confusion. Teachers tend to confuse the idea of ease of learning with simplicity of structure. Unfortunately in conversation the terms "simple" and "easy" are often interchanged. It would be well for the school teacher always to reserve the term "simple" in application to the notion of structure and the term "easy" in its application to readiness in learning.

The fact that a thing has simple structure does not necessarily imply ease of learning. Another item has complex structure, but it is possible that it can be learned easily. Complexity of structure in and of itself does not necessarily indicate difficulty in learning.

Other factors tend to govern ease of learning. As noted previously, factors include the *individual learner's* need for the learning, the relationships of the new learning with his existing experiences, and the degree of satisfaction derived from the learning. It is possible that a structure can be so complicated that the structure itself enhances the difficulties of learning, but this is not invariably true.

Complexity of structure and learning. The customary practice of trying to break learning materials down into simpler structures and beginning with the smaller pieces is not always a good one. Pupils are more often concerned with wholes rather than parts. This fact suggests presenting the whole to the beginning learner rather than trying to break it into simpler parts. This is equally as true for many motor skills in the shop and on the athletic field as it is for memorizing verses or appreciating paintings and musical selections.

A familiar case in which simple structure presents considerable difficulty whereas some complex structures seem relatively easier is found in the stumbling blocks of spelling. The greatest number of spelling demons are relatively short words, often words of one syllable and few letters. True, they often have structural peculiarities but the words are still far from complex. Note: *to, too, two; receive, believe; piece, peace; there, their.*

Finally, it is well for the teacher to reserve structural organization for its use as a device for arrangement of items already learned in order to make their continued use more efficient.

CHRONOLOGICAL ORGANIZATION. Chronological organization is an arrangement of items in relationship to time. Those elements that are alike in that they happened, or came into existence, within a selected time span are grouped together. The items may be very different in nearly every other respect except in time relationship. The reader will be familiar with many cases of such organization: Events in the Elizabethan period, Theodore Roosevelt's administration, the period from World War I to World War II, the poetry of the romantic period, nineteenth century music, Victorian house furnishings or manners.

Most chronological organizations involve the additional factor of time sequence; that is, the items happened within the selected time and are also arranged in the *order* of happening.

The arrangement of events in the order of time sequence is often a great convenience. In many cases it contributes to better understanding because the time of happening makes it possible to see relationships between the events. The teacher needs to see, however, that mere chronology without emphasis on other significant relationships is of little value.

There are often other relationships that are more important than that of time. Or at least the teacher needs to see that in nearly every case something else needs to be done other than the development of a time sequence. This is peculiarly true of the events of history. The Declaration of Independence was signed July 4, 1776. So what? What did it mean to the signers? Where did Franklin and Jefferson get their ideas? What does the Declaration mean to us today? Are we to take all of its statements literally? Are all men created equal? In what sense? How does our thinking on this issue differ from that of the American revolutionists? These issues must be organized on some other basis than time. Merely to memorize the date without raising the issues is useless.

There are conveniences in having histories of literature, art, music, science, and even of physical education. However, the needs of the young learner are seldom satisfied by the "period" approach. He is much more likely to be concerned with the art, music, literature, or sports of *his period.*

It is extremely doubtful if anyone was ever encouraged to begin to read by an introduction to a literary period. The same thing can be said concerning listening to worth-while music or making desired responses to works of art. The learner must know a considerable range of literature or have contact with much music or with many paintings before having any great need for arranging them into chronological periods.

Even with history, the immediate concern of youth may be with an interpretation of the present, and with prediction of the imminent future than with the events of the past. Historical interpretations are most useful in trying to determine "how we got this way." Much can be said for beginning certain history units with present contacts with issues and using historical resources as a means of interpretation. Period arrangements, time lines, charts, or genealogies come later as a means of convenient classification and as a contribution to retention of the factual materials. Chronology has its uses, but it also has its abuses.

FUNCTIONAL ORGANIZATION. Functional organization is a classification of items into categories based upon like or similar uses. Most often the items are arranged in order of frequency of use.

There are great possibilities in convenience and economy of effort in a use organization. Nearly all users of tools and equipment finally come to at least a partial functional organization. The garage mechanic may have a neat structural array of tools in a rack over his bench, but he carries in the pockets of his coveralls the pliers, wrenches, and screwdrivers that he has found by experience are used on nearly all his jobs.

Functional and structural. In many situations there is a tendency to break up structural organizations to form functional organizations for greater convenience and economy of effort. School spelling lists were once arranged in terms of the structure of words. First lists were words of two, three, and four letters of one syllable. The complex words came at the back of the speller. There was no relationship between the words of a spelling lesson and the words used by the pupil in his normal writing of the day. It took teachers a long time to find that spelling is *used* in writing, rarely otherwise. Then teachers began to explore the writings of pupils to find first the words most often used and secondly the words which frequently give spelling trouble. Today spelling lists include words most often used in writing, graded in terms of the maturity of the pupils. Special functional lists are tailored to fit the uses and needs of individual pupils.

Functional and chronological. For some purposes a functional organization may be preferred to a chronological arrangement. The reading lists of the National Council of Teachers of English are arranged about the reading interests of young people rather than into chronological periods. It is assumed that young people read largely for recreation and information, and that leisure reading should be arranged in terms of the uses which pupils have for such reading.

Functional organization is less open to criticism as an approach to learning than either structural or chronological organization. For this reason it is included with both the readiness and the logical organizations.

CAUSE-AND-EFFECT ORGANIZATION. In another commonly found logical arrangement of ideas the controlling factor is the cause and effect relationship. Such an organization groups those ideas that are alike in that they contribute to the same effect. If possible, the cause which seems to be most significant in producing the effect is placed first.

Cause-and-effect classification is reversible. It is possible to group all the effects that grow out of a given cause together. Those effects related to a single cause can also be arranged in a sequence of assumed importance.

The cause-effect relationship has been much used in the natural sciences and in the social sciences. In the field of history, attempts at historical interpretation almost always take this form. For example, the historian who says that certain factors were the causes of World War II is using a cause-effect organization of ideas. The reverse organization is implied by the historian who says that these are the effects of the Russian Revolution of 1918. Sometimes such organizations are based upon certain stated assumptions, and the cause-effect relationship is not always completely proved.

In the field of natural science the daily weather map and its predictions in the morning newspaper or television program give a good illustration of arrangement of data into a cause-and-effect relationship.

The great advantage of the cause-effect organization is in the analysis of the relationships of the ideas that are classified. When a user builds up the organization for himself, he is likely to have a better understanding of the material organized.

Cause-effect organization is often abused in the classroom by having pupils memorize the skeleton of an outline given by the

author of a textbook without seeing the significance of the relationships upon which the outline is based. How often teachers have
said, "Learn the causes of the Revolutionary War as given in your
textbook." Or, "Be able to tell the diets which produce rickets in
children." The pupils may be totally unaware that the author of
another history text might give another set of causes for the war.
The girls in the home economics class might recite the diets assumed
to produce rickets, without seeing *why* these diets may produce de-
formed bones in children.

Forming and using logical organizations

Logical organizations are manmade; people do not use them naturally. Pupils must be taught to organize. Most learning is incomplete without a final step of organization. Therefore, it becomes a
part of the teacher's obligation to direct pupils in the formation of
needed organizations. The organization chosen should fit the situation and the nature of the subject matter and at the same time
contribute to efficiency and economy in use.

The teacher can help pupils learn to organize by including exercises leading to organization in the assignment directions for each
unit planned. All teachers are familiar with organizational devices
that can be included in unit assignments. As a reminder, some of
these are: outlines, summaries, abstracts, chronologies, genealogies,
time lines, classified listings, tabulations of data, maps, graphs, pic-
tographs, statements of principles or rules, charts, conjugations,
paradigms, plans of strategy, programs, patterns, meal planning,
diets, and work plans. Every teacher will think of some others. In
the use of such devices it is important that the pupil not only form
an organization but that he be able to interpret its significance and
make reapplications in further use.

Standardized organizations

So far the treatment of the relationship of organization to learning has emphasized the desirability of beginning with some form of
readiness organization and working toward a culminating logical
organization, with emphasis upon the need for understanding and
interpretation as a part of the total process.

As with a great many desirable practices, there are certain exceptions to the general rule. There are organizations that are in
such common everyday use that people need to learn to use them
as they stand, without necessarily understanding why they were put
together in a particular form. There are many illustrations of these
organizations that are to be taught "as is" without taking time to

develop reasons for them. Some occur in almost every field of subject matter. The order of the letters of the alphabet makes a good
example. Others are the typewriter keyboard, the system of musical notation, the piano keyboard, the arrangement of the strings on
a violin, or the holes in a flute, the standard-gearshift pattern for
passenger automobiles, the basic rules for any sport or game, and
the Dewey decimal system, which is used for classifying books in
libraries.

Although such organizations are to be taught as they are, without attempts at explanation of their arrangement, the point at which
they are to be introduced is that of need on the part of the pupils.
As illustration, pupils do not need to memorize the letters of the
alphabet in sequence to be able to read. Probably beginning reading will be better if the process is not encumbered by distinctions
of letters and spelling. When, then, should pupils learn the alphabet? Perhaps one good answer is at the point where they begin to
use the dictionary. The abuse in the teaching of all standardized
organizations is found in the teacher who requires their memorization with no immediate use on the part of the pupil. One does not
learn the gearshift pattern until he is ready to drive.

The teacher's organization

In this unit, up to this point, emphasis has been on the relationship of organization to the learning of pupils. It is important for
the teacher to realize the need for teacher organization of subject
matter in the planning of instructional units. In spite of all that
has been said in the emphasis upon pupil growth and activity, and
the accompanying de-emphasis of subject matter, there is no learning without the learning of subject matter. The person who learns,
learns something. What he learns—ideas, relationships of ideas,
generalizations, principles, modes of behavior, customs, skills, ideals,
and biases—makes up the subject matter. If there are directive objectives in the school situation, it becomes necessary for the teacher
to be able to identify and interpret the subject matter to be used in
reaching the objectives. There is much to be said in favor of the
old academic slogan for teachers, "the good teacher must know his
subject matter."

From this point of view it is proposed that each unit planned by
a teacher should include a brief working outline of the subject matter to be included in the unit. Even with pupil-planned units it is
necessary for the teacher to give direction in the planning and to be
able to anticipate the subject matter to be needed. Otherwise the
teacher will be ill prepared to work with the pupils and can render

only insignificant aid as their needs develop in the expansion of the unit.

In the teacher's planning cycle as outlined so far, the teacher examines the relationship of his teaching to the institutional objectives accepted by his school. He then sets up suitable course objectives for each course to be taught. The course objectives are often best expressed in the form of an introduction to the course. Within the framework of the course introduction, the units for the course are blocked out in the form of a course layout.

FUNCTION OF TEACHER'S ORGANIZATION. In the planning of a unit of the course layout, the teacher first formulates a unit introduction which includes his thinking concerning the unit objectives. As the next step, he should outline the subject matter to be used in the development of the unit. The subject matter outline should serve these purposes for the teacher:

1. It should enable him to identify and clarify the exact items to be included. This implies a consideration of the suitability of the subject matter to the maturities of the pupils and its pertinency in accomplishing the unit objectives.
2. It should provide the teacher with any review that he may need in connection with the subject matter.
3. It should provide an opportunity to bring in new subject matter or check the accuracy of older items.
4. The development of the outline will provide the teacher an opportunity to re-examine sources and to reconsider the references recommended to pupils.

The teacher's outline is his working outline, not the pupil's. Copies need not be made for pupils. The outline should be complete enough to serve the teacher's needs as indicated above, but brief enough that it does not become a burden in preparation. In general, it will take the form of a logical organization, although the sequence may show the order to be followed with pupils. Experienced teachers working with familiar subject matter will make quite brief outlines. New teachers, or teachers working in new fields or with core curriculum materials, will tend to make more elaborate outlines.

FORM OF TEACHER'S ORGANIZATION. Many teachers make topical outlines. Any teaching outline is better than none, but a simple topical outline often fails to do well what the teacher's outline should do. In almost all cases a sentence statement outline serves better the function of the teacher's unit outline.

The primary advantage of the sentence outline is in its clearer identification and interpretation of each significant item of subject matter. It helps the teacher to nail down exactly what is to be taught.

The need for sentence outlining can be illustrated by the following story. A good many years ago a teacher wrote the following as an objective for a half-unit course in sociology for high school seniors. "To teach the commonly accepted principles of sociology." Does anyone have any clear idea at all of just what this teacher proposed to do? Having in mind the newness of sociology as a science, it might be appropriate to say to the teacher, "Name six or seven accepted principles of sociology. Can these be *stated as principles?*" It seems extremely doubtful if a teacher can get pupils to learn principles which he himself cannot identify and state.

Consider the following teacher's outline.

The World's Water Supply

1. Water supply and the location of cities
2. Sources of water supply
3. Characteristics of a good water supply
4. The water supply and community health
5. How water is distributed to consumers
6. Water supply and sewage disposal
7. Industrial water supply
8. Pollution of water supplies
9. Conservation of water

Perhaps the teacher knows what he expects the pupils to learn about the relationship of water supply to community health or of the *characteristics of a good water supply,* but his outline fails to show it. It would be just as easy to write into the outline in the first place, "The water used by cities and towns comes from natural or artificial lakes, rivers, or deep wells. The most important characteristic of a water supply is that the source should be great enough to supply the water needs of the community during all the seasons of the year." When so written the reader knows exactly what the teacher believes should be learned, and presumably the teacher knows. A critic might differ with a teacher about his proposed interpretation, but he can at least identify what the teacher intends to do.

Following are a few sample sentence statement outlines of subject matter for selected units:

The Musical Structure of Christmas Carols

1. Harmony consists of sounding notes together in a pleasing way.
2. There are certain rules that are usually followed in writing music.
   a. The strongest chord in the scale is the tonic or I chord.

  b. The sub-dominant or the IV and V chords are also very brilliant chords.

  c. These three chords are the major chords in the scale.

  d. The minor chords in the scale are the II, III, VI, and VII. These chords are not brilliant, but very dull. To most of us they seem sad.

  e. Many Christmas carols are very happy songs. A few are sad.

  f. The happy Christmas carols are composed of many of the bright major chords.

  g. Some sad Christmas songs are based upon the minor, or dull, chords.

  h. These chords may be inverted and any of the notes in the chord may be the lowest note.

  i. In chord inversion there are possible three inversions of every chord.

3. Christmas carols follow either the solid block of harmony (chordal) or an antiphonal style.

4. Antiphony is the singing of two choirs—one in answer to the other.

5. A number of Christmas carols are written in antiphonal style.

6. In trying to sing carols observe the following suggestions:

  a. Listen first to your neighbor.

  b. Never sing so loudly that you cannot hear the people on either side of you.

  c. If the neighbors make mistakes, you can correct them.

  d. We can learn the feel and sound of harmonies by singing them.

  e. Make notes accurately, but put meaning into your singing.

Consumer Economics [4]

I. Consumers

1. All members of society are consumers. The producer of one commodity is a consumer of many others.

2. Under our present economic system, production has often progressed more rapidly than have the means of distribution of commodities.

3. At present, distribution—including transportation, selling, advertising, packaging, etc.—is often the bottleneck in getting goods to the consumer at a price which he can afford to pay.

4. For many commodities the cost of distribution exceeds the cost of production.

II. Prices

1. The final price of food, clothing, and other consumers' goods is determined by a complex of such factors as relative scarcity, quality standards, fashion, monopoly, quantity purchases, and cost of advertising.

2. Modern techniques of production tend to reduce the total scarcity of the articles produced. Such mass production tends to reduce prices.

3. The inability of workers to earn wages with which to purchase commodities is a large factor in the oversupply of some kinds of consumers' goods.

[4] Excerpt from a unit on Consumers' Economics from the course in American Problems. From Bul. 4A, 1941, *Social Studies*, Missouri State Department of Education, Jefferson City, Missouri, 1941, pp. 442–43.

4. Many potential consumers cannot buy what they need because of inability to earn enough to make the purchases.

III. Standards of Living

1. The standard of living is a term used to describe what people feel they must have in order to satisfy their wants from day to day. If people have learned to want more things, or better things, and are able to have them, we say that the standard of living has changed.

2. Most folk would say that, when people begin to eat white bread instead of black, they have raised their standard of living.

3. Ordinarily we think that when people want and demand more of the things of a highly civilized life (as compared with simpler living) the standard of living has been raised.

4. An improved standard of living is usually thought of as meaning less severe physical labor and fewer hours given to labor.

5. Usually, higher wages make for improved standards of living.

6. Increased production makes for higher standards of living, if people can earn wages which enable them to purchase what is produced.

DIFFICULTIES IN SENTENCE STATEMENT OUTLINING. Sentence statement outlines are relatively easy for teachers to make in the natural sciences, in the social sciences, in history, in home economics, and in vocational agriculture. Teachers often run into difficulties in modern languages, in literature, in art, in music, in physical education, and in shop courses.

Identification of subject matter. The difficulties involved are in the identification of the subject matter itself. The teachers in the latter fields are often so engrossed with the detailed activities of the learning situation that they are unable to determine just what it is that the pupil is learning and just what is to be left with him when the activity of the class period ceases.

Substitution of procedure for subject matter. Beginners at sentence outlining often substitute either a description of a classroom procedure or a list of exercises for the subject matter to be learned. Both of these substitutes are often useful to the teacher, but presenting them in place of subject matter in unit planning indicates confusion on the part of the teacher. In making the working outline for a unit, the teacher needs continually to raise the questions, "Just what are the pupils to learn?" or "What is to be left with the pupils when the learning processes are complete?" Sometimes, "What must I know in order to teach this unit?"

Pupil memorization of teacher's outline. A final caution concerning the teacher's unit outline should be made. Pupils are not to be expected to learn or memorize the statements of the teacher's outline. This outline is a significant part of the teacher's planning in preparing his work for the unit. Pupils should be encouraged to formulate their own organizations of what they have learned. There is no special value in having a teacher make his own sentence outline of a unit for pupils to memorize in place of materials in the textbooks. The value of the subject matter outline in unit planning is in its effects upon the teacher's thinking and in its protection of pupils against malpractice. An abuse of the outline is in itself also a form of malpractice.

Unit implementation

UNIT ORGANIZATION

1. Items of subject matter are classified (organized) to serve functions of convenience and economy in the use of the subject matter.

2. *Logical organization* is the classification or grouping of similar items into a related sequence to further convenience or economy in use.

3. *Readiness organization* is the arrangement of items or processes to be learned in an order that fits into the existing experiences or needs of the learners concerned. The function of readiness organization is to encourage learning.

4. In customary usage, some textbooks in educational psychology and methods of teaching use the term psychological organization as a synonym for readiness organization.

5. Common examples of *logical organization* are structural organization, chronological organization, functional organization, and cause and effect organization.

6. Examples of readiness organizations commonly tried in secondary schools are functional organization, applications-to-principles organization, problem organization, the project, job organization, and pupil-planned units.

7. With the individual learner, need for formal organization occurs when he has sufficient experience with an area of subject matter to need to organize for more efficient use.

8. All types of formal organization are artificial, that is, man-made. No organization of subject matter is natural in the sense that it merely grew in an accustomed organized form or in the sense that human beings just naturally think that way.

9. The essential element in all types of logical classification of subject matter is some kind or degree of likeness or similarity.

10. Ease of learning (readiness) is determined by such factors as the relationship of the thing to be learned to the learner's experiences, by the relationship of the thing to be learned to a need or problem of the learner, and by the satisfaction of the learner in increased control of the new learning.

11. Ease of learning (readiness) may be determined in part by the structural relationship of the parts of the subject matter involved. It is probable that other factors are more important in most cases of learning.

12. For much school subject matter there is no established positive relationship between relative simplicity or complexity of structure and relative ease or difficulty of learning.

13. A good beginning point in teaching may be found at the point where the subject matter of the new unit crosses the experiences, needs, or interests of the learners. Preferably, the beginning point should provide a striking introduction to challenge attention.

14. The logical first item in a section of subject matter is not always the best beginning point for teaching.

15. Formal or logical organization is to be introduced toward the completion of a unit.

16. Subject matter should be left with pupils in a logically organized form.

17. High school pupils should be guided in making their own logical organizations of subject matter insofar as practicable.

18. Pupils should be trained to *use* those organizations of subject matter peculiar to a particular field that are in common current use in the world outside the school.

19. The teacher's unit planning should include an outline of the subject matter to be included in the unit.

20. In order to identify clearly the items of subject matter for a given unit, the teacher's outline should be in sentence statement form.

THINGS TO DO

1. Secure a copy of a recent textbook or course of study outline for a high school course in your teaching field. Select a single chapter of the text or a section of the course outline for treatment. List the items that you would require all pupils in the course to learn.

As a criterion of value use the following question: "What items would I expect these young people to be able to remember after ten years?"

2. Examine a group of recent textbooks or course outlines for high school courses in your field.

What types of organization are found in these?

How is the subject matter adapted to the needs of high school age people?

In what respects do these books differ from college textbooks with which you are familiar in the same field?

3. Select one teaching unit from one high school course for work. Indicate the course from which the unit is taken. Describe the pupils for whom the course is intended: age, sex, previous training, social background, economic status, general experience.

Make a logical outline of the subject matter for your selected unit.

Set up what seems to you to be a workable experiential sequence for this unit in terms of the description of the pupils given above.

4. Make suitable arrangements with your teacher and the administrative head of a selected school for visiting a high school class which interests you.

Upon visiting the class, characterize the pupils in the class: grade classification, chronological age, sex, seemingly retarded or accelerated pupils, first exposure to the subject matter treated or previous training, possible out-of-school experiences related to the subject matter, apparent general type of previous experiences of pupils, family background.

Use no names of pupils in characterizing the class. Identify pupils as A, B, C, M, Q, Y, etc.

Give a name or title to the unit being treated in class.

List the topics or subdivisions of subject matter that are used during the class period in the order in which they appear during the class period.

Is the order of development used in class a part of a predetermined *logical* organization? If so, what type of organization is used? Present any available evidence supporting your answer.

What means are used to tie in the subject matter with pupil experiences? Give cases.

What devices are used to insure leaving subject matter with the pupils in the form of some type of organization that will help pupils *use* what is learned? Give illustrations.

Does the teacher organize for the pupils or use exercises for training pupils to make their own organizations? What evidence can you give to support your answer?

5. Select one unit from a course which you are planning to teach. Make a logical topical outline for this unit.

Convert this topical outline into a declarative sentence statement outline for this unit.

6. For the unit outlined in exercise 5, list the pupil experiences which you would assume high school pupils to have had with each item of the outline. What must you know about the pupils to be able to do this?

In the margin of the original outline mark the point at which you believe your selected class should make a beginning.

What is your suggestion for a beginning class activity in this situation?

7. Set up an outline of the Industrial Revolution beginning with the impact of the Industrial Revolution upon the present living of a group of 11th-grade pupils in an urban high school.

Show the sequence of historical information to be used.

Set the finished outline in sentence statement form.

8. Assume that a group of 10th-grade pupils are working in a core curriculum organization. Assume that one of the units deals with labor unions.

Outline the subject matter that seems desirable for this unit. If this seems impossible without more definite goals, set up the objectives for the unit and write its unit introduction first.

Put your finished outline into sentence statement form. To what extent does this finished outline seem more workable than your original efforts? To what extent does the formulation of the sentence statements seem a waste of time?

HELPFUL READINGS

ANDERSON, VERNON E. *Principles and Procedures of Curriculum Improvement.* New York: The Ronald Press Co., 1956. Chap. 6.

Presents learning in terms of the developmental tasks of youth. This chapter pertinent to the teacher's problems of the organization of learning.

The Boners Omnibus. Toronto: Blue Ribbon Books, Inc., 1931.

A humorous presentation of purported pupil answers to examination questions. Interesting for the teacher to attempt to discover the experiential background of the pupil which leads him to respond as he does.

DEWEY, JOHN. *Experience and Education.* New York: The Macmillan, Co., 1938.

A short monograph. Read all. Fundamental for an interpretation of the possibilities of experiential organizations. Contains no comfort for either the progressive or the traditionalist.

MORT, PAUL R. and VINCENT, WILLIAM S. *Modern Educational Practice.* New York: McGraw-Hill Book Co., Inc., 1950.

Examine supplement A "Thirty Psychological Guides to Good Teaching." See especially principles 3, 7, 13, 14, 15, 20, 23, 25, and 28.

MURSELL, JAMES L. *Successful Teaching.* 2d ed. New York: McGraw-Hill Book Co., Inc., 1954. Chaps. 5, 6, 7, 13, and 14.

Perhaps contains the greatest number of useful suggestions to the teacher on the problems of organization of learning and learning materials.

NATIONAL COUNCIL OF TEACHERS OF ENGLISH, THE COMMISSION ON THE ENGLISH CURRICULUM. *The English Language Arts in the Secondary School.* New York: Appleton-Century-Crofts, Inc., 1956. Chaps. 4 and 5.

Contains many suggestions for the organization of reading programs in terms of pupil experiences and around centers of reading interests of pupils.

ROBINSON, JAMES HARVEY. *The Humanizing of Knowledge.* New York: George H. Doran Co., 1924.

A brief monograph. Read all. A plea for the organization and interpretation of the findings of science so that all human beings can learn and profit from these findings. Should be on the reading list of all teachers.

SEENEY, JAMES A. *A Synthesis of the Experimental Evidence on Subject Matter Readiness Organizations Included as an Integral Part of the Instructional Process.* Unpublished doctoral dissertation, Graduate School, University of Missouri, Columbia, Missouri, 1955. Available on microfilm from University Microfilm Service, Ann Arbor, Michigan.

For a summary of cumulative evidence from recent sources on various types of readiness organizations described. Presents recent evidence on the values of problem organization, project organization, pupil participation in planning, and organizations in the sequence in which pupils seem to learn best.

SPEARS, HAROLD. *Principles of Teaching.* Englewood Cliffs, N.J.: Prentice-Hall, Inc., 1951. Chap. 5.

Principles of learning applied in the classroom situation. Part of the principles in this chapter apply to readiness organization.

STILES, LINDLEY J. and DORSEY, MATTIE F. *Democratic Teaching in Secondary Schools.* Philadelphia: J. B. Lippincott Co., 1950. Chap. 8.

Note especially the section of this chapter on the "determiners of learning."

TROW, WILLIAM CLARK. *Educational Psychology.* 2d ed. Boston: Houghton Mifflin Co., 1950. Chaps. 13, 14, and 15.

Read especially the part of chap. 13 on the availability of past experience, chap. 14 on the development of understanding, and the parts of chap. 15 on learner's cues and transfer and retention.

WOODRUFF, ASAHEL D. *The Psychology of Teaching.* 3d ed. New York: Longmans, Green & Co., Inc., 1951. Chaps. 7, 8, 9, 19, and 20.

A psychologist's suggestions concerning the application of the principles of learning in classroom situations. The chapters listed are applicable to the teacher's problems of organization. By all means read.

Unit IV

What Must Pupils
Do To Learn?

As a teacher, you must become increasingly aware that learning is primarily an active process. Young people learn through their own activities. In this sense what the pupils do is relatively more important than what you may do as a teacher. Your success in getting boys and girls to learn will depend primarily upon what you are able to encourage them to do. This is not to say that activity is its own end, but rather that the activities of youths must be directed toward the attainment of certain desired goals. The *effect* of the behavior upon the learners is of ultimate importance. Activities are selected and encouraged to attain the desired effects upon pupil growth and development.

You will need to begin to analyze the teaching situations that arise in your own field to determine what learning activities are involved. You should be able to see the shortcomings in the learning values of certain typical school activities.

For example, a group of girls play speedball in a physical education class daily for several weeks. These girls are never observed playing speedball outside the physical education class or away from the school gymnasium. Apparently, the activity has no game value for these girls. Why does the teacher select this sport? Does the activity lead to any goals of worth to the girls?

You will be expected to develop some skills in formulating pupil exercises intended to aid in the attainment of clearly defined objectives in your own area of instruction.

The four chapters into which this unit is divided may be regarded as subunits. These subunits represent types of behavior frequently found in schools. The division is not entirely artificial as you can recognize the same types of learning behavior in many situations outside of school. The types of learning activity about which the subunits are built are drill, information or idea getting, problem solving, and appreciation building.

The division of the unit into these chapters, or subunits, is not intended to indicate that learning can always be broken into the distinctly different types indicated by the titles of the chapters. It is recognized that many learning situations involve several or all of these types of behavior at approximately the same time. It will be convenient, however, for you as a teacher to be able to recognize the practical possibilities of emphasizing certain distinct types of activities as clearly related to the desired learning objectives. It is probable you can better fit proposed pupil experiences to particular learning situations if you are aware of the simple analyses suggested by this division.

6

Drill Experiences in Learning

What to look for in this subunit

1. What types of frequently occurring learning situations which require practice are to be found in high school courses in your teaching field?

2. What do the terms "practice" and "drill" mean in your own thinking?

3. How are motor skills built up in learning situations outside of schools?

4. Can habits be formed by practice? Without practice?

5. How do ideas become fixed in ordinary out-of-school situations?

6. How are patterns of conduct formed in normal situations?

7. What factors must be considered in setting up a practice program for a complex skill?

8. What may be done in a school situation to insure the practice of desirable patterns of conduct?

9. How may sufficient repetition of ideas to be remembered be insured in a series of school situations?

10. What is the significance of "practice in setting" in the control of drill activities?

11. What are some of the common weaknesses to be found in school drill programs?

12. How may variations in drill "carriers" be secured without change in the essential drill pattern?

13. What is meant by distributed practice?

As indicated in the unit introduction, this entire unit is concerned with the learning processes of pupils and with the teacher's part in the direction of pupil learning experiences. For purposes of clarity in treatment and for greater convenience in working with materials, the unit has been divided into four chapters, or subunits, each dealing with one of the primary types of learning behavior that occur most frequently in the school situation. This chapter will deal with those learning experiences in which a predominant element is that of repeating a process or pattern of ideas until there is some degree of fixation. In customary conversation such learning is called practice, or sometimes drill. In this chapter no distinctions will be made between the terms "practice" and "drill."

Planning drill experiences

In any given situation, the teacher will attempt to define clearly what he is attempting to accomplish with pupils. He will also attempt to get the pupils to see what they are going to try to do. Then must be determined what is to be done in order to reach the agreed-upon goals. In other words, activities are selected, or assignments made, to accomplish what has been set up to learn. It is to the teacher's advantage if he can analyze the proposed learning activities for a given unit into the predominant learning factors involved.

For example, a teacher of ninth-grade English has said that his pupils need to learn to write approximately one letter-size page of straightforward English prose without gross errors in spelling and usage. This teacher needs to see that what is involved for the pupils is extended *practice in writing*—not memorization of rules of usage, discussion, problem solving, appreciation of examples from great writers—but simply *enough repetition* of the writing processes to fix the skills needed in day-to-day composition.

In the analysis of learning experiences there are commonly three kinds of learnings which we attempt to establish by drill. These are motor skills, patterns of associated ideas, and patterns of conduct or behavior.

In addition, it is more than probable that attitudes are fixed by repetitions of the responses associated with the attitudes. The teacher who wishes to establish in pupils a given attitude will find opportunities in which the pupils can practice the responses ordinarily associated with the attitude. Preachments, or lip service expressed in terms of the desirability of a certain attitude, seem to have little to do with its actual attainment.

There has been a tendency in much recent educational thought and in educational literature to minimize the importance of drill. There has grown up the idea that day-to-day routine drills were typical of the "old school" and that the "new school," with its emphasis on interest, motivation, pupil planning, individual growth, and personality development can get along without drills or practices—"Drill represents formal education. The new education should be informal."

In the past there has been much routine drill work on learnings for which the pupils had no immediate need—drill that pupils considered so much drudgery to be done under the compulsion of a teacher-taskmaster. On the other hand, in school or out, there is much to be learned that requires repetition, arduous effort, and sustained application. Almost no efficient skills are acquired without continued conscious practice of an accepted form. There are associations of ideas that should be memorized. There are accepted patterns of conduct that are attained by positive repeated imitation of desirable behavior. Such things are seldom learned well by chance or as mere concomitants to developing maturity. Cases in point involve skillful use of the typewriter, written composition, skills in any sport, tool uses in the shop, competence with a musical instrument, singing, assembly behavior, good manners, courteous behavior, correct usage in a foreign language, chemical relationships, number combinations, time associations in history, and automobile driving. There will always be a place for well-directed practice or drill as an approach to sound learning both in and out of school.

Pupils in general do not object to drill as such, nor do boys and girls have any rooted objection to repetition. Things which they truly want to do, they do over and over again. Observe the informal practice on the basketball floor when team practice is not in session, the efforts of a youth to master a saxophone, or the monotonous repeating of a recent popular ditty on the record player. The assumption that young people never want to practice or object to the monotony of repetition is undoubtedly fallacious. The question is largely whether or not the youth can get satisfaction out of the product of his repetition.

PLANNING IN TERMS OF DEFINED OUTCOMES. In planning a sequence of practice exercises, the teacher must have clearly in mind what effect the practice is to have upon the pupils. Teachers often rely on sets of readymade exercises to be found at the ends of chapters in textbooks, in workbooks, drill manuals, and teacher handbooks. Often these sources do contain desirable experiences for pupils. But teachers must *select* from such sources always with a goal in mind. In general, the teacher should not say, "Work the next ten problems"; "Write out the next fifteen sentences"; "Translate the next half page"; "Line up in a circle and pass the ball around until I blow the whistle"; "Practice exercise 14 in your typewriter manual"; "Do these bowing exercises for thirty minutes every day this next week." Rather the teacher should examine the available readymade practice exercises to choose those which can serve as experiences through which the pupils might expect to reach the goal set up. He needs to examine printed exercises to determine whether or not the *pattern* to be practiced occurs in the exercises and the extent to which the desired pattern is repeated through the sequence of the exercises.

It is not enough for the teacher to know what he is doing in assigning practice exercises. It is necessary also that the pupils know what is expected of them. They must be aware of the desirability of the goals established and undertake the drills willingly and with enthusiasm. Nothing is to be gained by trying to tell the pupils they are playing a game when the teacher has definite work-type goals in mind. Teacher and pupils should pull in the same direction. Agreement on ends is necessary to achieve this. Working at cross purposes with pupils will almost never arrive at useful and satisfactory learning. The teacher must explain to pupils what is to be accomplished before assigning a series of practice exercises. The pupils must be able to see the desirability of the task ahead.

PLANNING THE ATTACK. There is a difference between knowing *what* is to be accomplished and *how* to go about it. One may stand at a distance and see clearly a shining mountain peak. He may desire ever so much to reach its top. There is still the question of how. Where are the trails? What are the easiest grades? From which side should the peak be approached? What equipment needs to be taken along?

There is analogy here with the drill assignment. Each such assignment needs to include some charting of how to attack the exercises proposed. The typical breakdown of many drill assignments is evidenced in the traditional study hall situation. The teacher who made the original assignment has gone on to work with another class group. The teacher in charge of the study hall did not make the assignment. Perhaps he is trained in another field and does not know how to do assignments in the field of the first teacher. A pupil is idle. The study hall keeper says, "Haven't you anything to do?" Pupil: "No." Teacher: "Didn't Mr. Z give you any assignment in algebra last period?" "Oh, yes." "Why aren't you working on your algebra?" "I don't know how to do the problems." Clearly the responsibility in the situation lies with Mr. Z and his assignment of algebra drill exercises in that he did not make the *how* of the assignment clear. As a working principle for teachers, pupils should not be sent away from a classroom to work on practice or drill exercises without guidance until there is evidence that they know how to go about the drills and can repeat the pattern involved without gross errors in the pattern itself.

PLANNING THE DRILL SEQUENCE. Earlier, the necessity for the teacher knowing the pattern to be repeated in a series of practices was emphasized. This becomes doubly essential as the teacher tries to choose appropriate readymade exercises from texts or workbooks for assignment. The pattern to be fixed must occur in the chosen exercises. Pupils should practice on the thing to be learned rather than on something else. This is not as simple or obvious as it may seem. For example, how often has the language teacher said to his pupils, "We are going to learn to read French." Then in assigning work to be done has said, "Write out the translation of the French passage in Lesson 22." If pupils are to learn to read French, they must *practice reading*—not translating. Certainly no writing process is involved. The practice of translation will produce translation habits and almost never good sight reading facility.

Again, the pupils in an algebra class say, "If you will state the equation for this prose exercise, we will solve the problem." The teacher has said, "We are learning to do mathematical thinking and interpretation." What the pupils have been practicing is mathematical manipulation and calculation. What they need to practice, obviously, is the thinking involved in translating situations described in language into mathematical expressions. The pupils need much added experience in what they have asked the teacher to do, the statement of equations from the prose problems.

Principles of drill

ADEQUATE TOTAL PRACTICE. Almost all teachers try to get pupils to learn too many different things within a short time period. As a result very little is done with any one of the learnings. Too little repetition is done to fix any of the learning patterns. As a consequence the forgettings are tremendous.

In a great many drill situations the achievements of the pupils are at a relatively low level because there has been insufficient repetition of the same pattern. In other words, there has not been enough practice.

To see the effects of too little practice, examine the accompanying learning curve, which is typical of the learning curves developed by educational psychologists. Inspection of the curve reveals (1) a rapid initial rise in the curve in the early stages of learning; (2) a slowing down in the rate of rise of the curve as learning progresses; (3) some spots of very slow progress, no progress, or retrogression, indicated by plateaus or dips in the curves; (4) a period beyond the plateaus and slumps of continued quite slow improvement.

In much modern school practice, teachers permit pupils to cease practice on any one given pattern at the point on the learning curve that occurs just at the end of the initial rapid rise in the curve. At

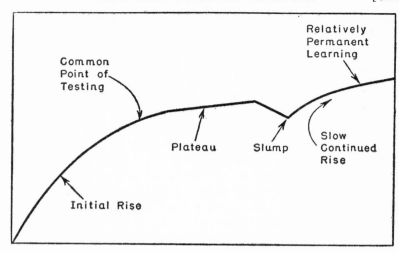

Characteristics of a Learning Curve for New Learning

this point the teacher applies a measure. The results look good due to the initial rapid learning. Practice on this pattern ceases, and teacher and pupils proceed to practice on something else. The teacher fails to see that, if practice ceases at this point on the learning curve, forgetting is likely to be just as rapid as the initial learning. To secure permanent learning, the practice must continue through the plateaus and slumps over into that part of the learning curve which shows relatively slow continued learning. To take advantage of this prospect of permanency, the teacher must begin fewer new learnings and encourage pupils to persist in practices on the few for longer periods of time and for a greater number of practices. Often the psychologist says that a thing to be permanently learned must be overlearned.

Examine the accompanying forgetting curve, which is the reverse of the learning curve. If a thing is practiced to the point where the learner can repeat or go through the motions of the pattern and then the rate of forgetting charted, the curve is almost the reverse of a curve showing the initial rise in learning.

College students will be interested in the fact that these two illustrative curves show quite well what happens in the traditional all-night cramming for examinations. The material crammed goes out by the downhill forgetting curve at just about the rate of intake in the cramming process.

A school illustration of trying to include too many different learnings, and as a consequence getting inadequate practice on any one of them, is found in home economics. Very often in a unit on care

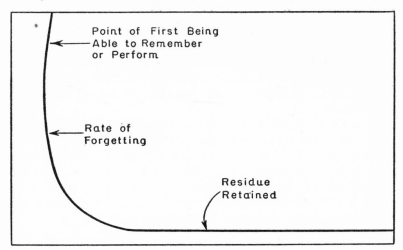

Point of First Being
Able to Remember
or Perform

Rate of
Forgetting

Residue
Retained

A Forgetting Curve

and maintenance of clothing, mending and darning are introduced. The teacher demonstrates the different kinds of darns, and these are shown in worked samples on the classroom bulletin board. Each girl does one worked sample for one kind of darn, and the class then moves on to something else. No girl in the class can make a skillful darn in anything. Why?

Again in home economics, the teacher demonstrates the different types of yeast breads and quick breads. The girls bake one kind of bread once. When the work with breads is finished, no girl in the class can turn out a skillfully made product unless she happened to have learned at home through much practice.

The home economics teacher can say that under modern living conditions it is not worth while to take the time to help girls develop good homemaking skills. One doesn't darn nylons; one just discards them and buys another pair. Bread comes wrapped in cellophane and ready sliced. However, if there are certain skills that are important in modern living, these cannot be learned by demonstration, observation, or by one or two practices. The teacher may try to do too many things superficially in English, mathematics, or history as well as in home economics.

It may be noted, too, that education by television does not in and of itself provide practice for the learner. Merely watching someone demonstrate a performance on a television screen does not insure a skillful performance on the part of the watcher. The viewer may get a suggestion of a pattern from the television performance, but he must still practice to develop any skill at all.

DISTRIBUTION OF PRACTICE.   Along with the common attempt to crowd the learning of too many different patterns into a limited time span and the consequent inadequate practice on any one of the patterns is found a poor distribution of the time devoted to practice.   For maximum efficiency in repetitive learning, practice should be carried on for relatively short periods distributed over a fairly long time span.

This means that, for most of the patterns practiced in the classroom, the time for practice on one pattern should not run for the full class period of 45 to 60 minutes.   For most relatively simple learning, a practice period of 15, 20, or 30 minutes is often better than a longer one.   At the same time, the total practice should be distributed over several weeks rather than crowded into a single week.   The tabulation below will illustrate the point.

	Mon.	Tues.	Wed.	Th.	Fri.	Mon.	Tues.	Wed.	Th.	Fri.	
I.	45	45	45	45	45	. . . .					minutes
II.	20	20	20	20	20	20	20	20	20	20	minutes

The first time distribution shows practices of 45 minutes per day for one week, a total of 225 minutes.   The second distribution shows practices of 20 minutes daily for two weeks, a total of 200 minutes. In general, the second distribution should give greater efficiency in learning than the first, although the total time involved is less.

A number of experiments with practice distributions have been carried on in psychological laboratories.   The results point toward short practices distributed over a relatively long time span.

Some of the early experiments on distributed practice were concerned with typewriting.   At the time, typewriting classes in the high schools customarily were scheduled for double periods of from 90 to 120 minutes.   Later, typing teachers discovered the experimentation with distributed practices.   They proposed to find out the effect on the achievement of typing skills of shortening the daily typing period.   The net result of a number of classroom experiments with typing was the discovery that pupils having single typing periods per day achieved as high or higher levels of skill by the end of the school year than comparable pupils having double periods daily.   As a consequence, better schools have reduced the time for high school typing to a single period a day.

Teachers in home economics, shop, music, art, physical education, languages, mathematics, speech, and dramatics need to be especially attentive to problems of distribution of practice.   Situations in these fields which involve a considerable amount of individual practice for the development of skills should be of special concern to teachers. Music teachers often recommend that pupils practice for one or two hours at a stretch under self-direction. There is great doubt regarding the value of such extended practice without intervening rest periods. Practice at a high degree of intensity and attention for a short interval, with a rest before continued practice, would seem preferable to the mere prolongation of practice with accompanying lowering of attention and intensity.

Without doubt, fatigue factors enter into the effects upon the learner of prolonged practice periods. It is quite safe to recommend that the profitable length of a practice period has been reached when fatigue begins to develop and tends to contribute to an increased number of errors in following the pattern being practiced.

Practice under pressure.   Often a teacher and a group of pupils feel that considerable pressure exists to develop skills within a very limited total time limit. This is frequently true in the basic training of the armed forces, in the preparation of an athletic team for games to be played within the limits of one short season, and in the perfection of performances for public programs in music and dramatics.

At least a partial solution to the distribution of practices in such pressure situations can be found in developing practice schedules that provide cycles of intensive practice alternated with rest periods, or change of pace. If a school schedule can permit, it might be better to hold a practice for a dramatics performance for 45 minutes in the morning, return students for routine schedules of school work until the middle of the afternoon and then hold a second 45-minute rehearsal. This arrangement would seem preferable, at least until the final rehearsal stage.

Too-short practice periods.   A final caution about the profitable length of a practice period: it can be too short. There is a factor of "warming up." In situations that involve associations of ideas, this process seems to involve getting a flow of ideas moving toward the particular ideational pattern to be learned. For motor learning there is the problem of physiological "warming" plus the readiness factor. The practice period needs to be long enough for the pupil to get in motion with his learning, to become attentive to the pattern to be practiced, and to accomplish some actual practice, correction, and redoing. If the period is too short, practice ceases almost at the point of actual readiness to perform. In terms of practical school timing, ten- or fifteen-minute practice periods are probably too short for most situations. There have been school situations in which supervisory officials have urged the use of a part of every class period for "study." Teachers tended to use much of the period for recitation or discussion and wound up with a remaining fifteen-minute "study" period. In nearly every case these residual study periods are almost totally worthless because they are too short.

PRACTICE IN SETTING.   In considering the administrative features involved in planning a practice sequence such as that suggested by the problems of distributed practice, the teacher must not forget that whatever is learned in the drill situations of the classroom must transfer to situations of normal use outside the school. The best assurance of probable transfer is found in another basic principle of drill, that of practice in setting.

The principle of practice in setting is that at least some of the practices on any given drill pattern should take place in a setting which is identical with, or resembles quite closely, the setting in which the performance outside the school is expected to take place.

For example, a pupil in a speech class is to make a formal presentation at a public assembly of students and patrons of the school. He may formulate what he proposes to say. He may rehearse his presentation in his room at home. He may try his speech for the speech teacher. But after all, the setting for the final performance is that of an audience situation. Therefore our would-be speaker needs to have some rehearsal experience with an audience. The speech class might make up the first audience. If the presentation seems of great importance, it might be tried at a high school assembly before the final appearance at the patrons' night. At any rate, the situation of out-of-class use is definitely that of an audience. Practice should provide an audience in order to be sure of successful transfer with some degree of freedom from stage fright and evidences of nervousness.

Most high school coaches are acutely aware of the fact that performance under the pressure and excitement of a crucial game is a different situation from that provided on the home practice field or the local gym floor between games. For this reason the coach attempts to get a green player into as many games as possible as a substitute before he must assume full responsibility as being the only available man for a given spot in a critical game. The early substitutions provide practices in setting to insure ultimate transfers of game skills when such transfers are needed most.

In the early history of home economics teaching in the high schools, laboratories for home economics tended to be patterned after the chemistry laboratories of the period. Girls cooked on single-plate gas burners in small quantities and with relatively small utensils. One thing was made at a time. If the current cookery involved white sauce cookery, tomato soup was made on a given day. All the girls made small quantities of soup. The product was rated and perhaps tasted, but no meal was served. Girls and mothers often complained that the home economics experiences did not seem very "practical" in the home situation.

After some time the home economics teachers discovered that cookery to be "practical" at home had to be practiced in settings approximating the home situation. Few homemakers prepare one dish in isolation. The tomato soup is part of a luncheon. It must be prepared along with the other dishes which comprise a single luncheon. All must be ready to serve and be hot when served. The quantities should be those appropriate for the family setting. What is cooked should be served and the table and kitchen cleared afterwards.

Now almost all foods laboratories for high school home economics are arranged as unit kitchens with full-scale equipment of the kind found in homes—range, refrigerator, sinks, storage cabinets, and work tables. Girls work in small teams and prepare and serve meals. The transfers of learning to the normal home situation should be better through the practice in setting provided.

The principle of practice in setting should lead teachers of all areas to search for normal uses and settings for that which may be learned in school situations. The experiences provided in school should have many elements of normal use and living. Purely artificial and academic learning exercises should be abandoned in large measure. If a pupil is never caught doing one of these peculiar performances of the school outside the classroom or off the school grounds, its desirability may be seriously questioned.

Some normal out-of-school situations cannot be transferred to the school, but if the mountain will not come to Mohammed, Mohammed will go to the mountain. Pupils can be taken into the field, to homes, into business houses, and assigned in normal work situations in the community to acquire suitable practices in setting.

VARIATION IN THE "CARRIER" SITUATION. Throughout the treatment of learning through repetition the term pattern has been used to refer to the thing that is to be learned, or perhaps more appropriately, in a drill situation the thing which repeats is the pattern. Now it is proposed to introduce a companion term which grows out of the discussion of practice in setting. The setting or situation in which a pattern is set up for practice can be thought of as the "drill carrier." This assumes that the important thing in a given set of practices is the pattern. The application or problem in which the pattern is set merely serves as an immediate stimulator which gives temporary significance to the practice of the moment.

The understanding of distinction between pattern and carrier becomes clearer with a few illustrative cases. Suppose a junior high school pupil has arrived at a condition of readiness for writing with a typewriter. He can do little with his proposed learning until he has mastered the proper fingering of the typewriter keyboard, so that he can finger the keys without looking at them or at his hands. The pattern, or patterns, involves the correct fingering of the keyboard in response to the stimulus of a given copy or a given set of ideas to be written. The carrier is the material to be written during any given practice period. Other things being equal, it is desirable that early carrier material be something which the learner truly wants to write. In early stages of learning this type of carrier may be limited by the pupil's control of basic fingering patterns. In general, so far as the mastery of the pattern is concerned, it matters little what the carrier contains—"Now is the time for all good men to come to the aid of their country" or "Dear Aunt Susie, I am writing to thank you for the beautiful muffler which I received for my birthday." It does matter that the written material of the carrier provide opportunity for *correct fingering* of the typewriter keyboard.

A frequently needed association of ideas is found in the statement, "The union of states within the United States was completed with the adoption of the Federal Constitution in 1789." Perhaps the pattern can be shortened to "Constitution of the United States—1789." Carriers of this association of ideas may be any situation which calls for a recall of the date of the founding of the United States, as for example: "In what year was the United States 100 years old? When will it be 200 years old?"; "It is often said that the United States has the oldest government existing in its original form of any country in the world. Is this true? How old *is* the existing government of the United States?"; and so on.

With these illustrations the principle of variation of the carrier in drill situations becomes evident. In a series of practices, the pattern to be repeated should remain the same, but the carriers in which the pattern occurs may vary from one practice to the next.

Note that, although drill carriers may vary, the pattern to be practiced must always remain the same or there will be utter confusion in the learning. Suppose the different carriers for the beginnings of the government of this country involve differing dates for the establishment of the constitution. It is doubtful if a correct

date would ever be learned. The standard gear shift for passenger
automobiles is another case in point. Automobile driving, in general, is made very much easier by the acceptance of the common
pattern represented by the standard shift. The only alternative is
to do away with gear shifting by modern engineering.

There are two basic reasons for a considerable variation of carriers in any given drill sequence. One reason is to avoid monotony
in practice. Without variation in carriers, practices often become
mere rote drudgery. Moreover, learning appears to be facilitated
by sustained interest. Often it is possible to sustain the interest of
learners through a series of drills if the carriers are sufficiently
varied. This is true to the point that the learners may propose
their own variations and participate in planning the practice exercises.

The second argument for variation of carriers is centered in the
issue of transfer. Unless learning developed in school can transfer
to normal living situations, there is little value in the original learning. It becomes obvious that the chances of such transfers to out-
of-school situations are much enhanced if the learner has a variety
of experiences with the pattern. If the pupil has experienced a
given pattern in only one type of situation, he is inclined to react
to the practice situation as a school situation and not think of using
the pattern elsewhere when a need arises. On the other hand, if
he has experienced a given pattern in fourteen different sorts of
carriers, some of which are normal to out-of-school situations, the
chances are great that the pattern will arise in his thinking when
the fifteenth carrier arises as a situation of normal use.

There are greater probabilities of normal transfer of learning
patterns, if varied experiences with drill carriers are provided in
the series of practices.

SATISFACTION IN THE LEARNER. The continuance of effort in
many drill sequences depends on sustaining the interest, willingness, and drive of the learner through several practice periods
extending over a number of days or weeks. Perhaps the most significant clue to sustained high-level effort is found in the satisfaction which the learner obtains from actual achievement and improvement in perfecting the pattern practiced.

This element of satisfaction becomes especially evident in the
early stages of learning. Its role is crucially important at the plateaus and slumps in the learning curve.

At the outset with any new learning, it is essential that the pupil
urgently desire some of what is to be learned. In learning to operate a typewriter, the beginner must want to type and be able to

see what he could do if he could type. On the playing field the prospective player must have an urge to play softball. He must want to hit the ball. He must have a great zeal for catching the ball. Given the urge for what is to be learned, the general outlines of the pattern as a whole need to be set up so that the learner can see what it is that he is trying to practice. Then, as soon as he can go through the form of the pattern, he needs to see that he has accomplished something and, if possible, to be told that he is now on the pattern and making progress. If the pupil practices for some time without making progress, there will be no satisfaction accruing from his efforts and he will cease practice or his enthusiasm will drop to such a low level that further practice is of little value.

Teacher aids to increased satisfaction. At the point of a plateau or slump in the learning curve, satisfaction tends to be lacking. There is little or no satisfaction in standing still or in doing worse than at a previous attempt. Here the teacher may help to restore satisfaction by pointing out the actual achievement attained in reaching the point where the learning leveled off and in holding out the possibility of greater satisfaction to be gained by persistence to the point of higher achievement.

Many teachers are at fault in failing to comment upon or praise limited achievement in the early stages of learning. Too often the teacher points out all the errors at variance from the pattern and criticizes the efforts of the learner. There is a point at which such teacher criticism leads to dissatisfaction rather than satisfaction. All readers can recall situations involving sports form, efforts at English composition, or attempts to play a musical instrument, construct a piece in the shop, or pronounce a foreign language, where the teacher failed to say, "Now you are beginning to get the hang of it; let's try again." Instead, he pointed out all the errors and perhaps ridiculed the performance. The paper in English came back with so many blue marks that it seemed to shout, "You poor hopeless dub, you have made twenty-two errors on this one page. How do you ever expect to learn to write?" As the teacher deals with the early practice efforts of others, he should have an acute realization of the chagrin, defeat, and almost complete dissatisfaction which he felt in such situations as a pupil.

Comparisons with higher achievements of others seldom lead to increased satisfactions for most learners. A lazy performer may be stimulated by the dissatisfaction growing out of the shame generated by comparison. In most normal learning, the satisfaction comes from one's own mastery of what he is trying to accomplish and from the sense of improvement as he progresses in the learning. Evidences of improvement should lead to satisfaction. Most often the comparison should be made with the previous achievement or performance of the individual learner.

Satisfaction in individual achievement. The teacher needs to keep in mind, too, that the thing which carries out the practice is the nervous mechanism of the individual learner and that each pupil should receive satisfaction from the results of his own efforts. Group comparisons and group achievement may be of little value in producing satisfaction with one's own particular degree of learning. The median or average performance is not the basis of satisfaction in typical drill situations but the degree of progress of each individual for himself.

The satisfaction of a learner with his progress in learning is often associated with the standard of accomplishment set in the early stages of learning. If the standard is such that reaching it seems very remote and almost hopeless, the learner will have little satisfaction in seeing his efforts fall far short, or in seeing a few others surpass him. On the other hand, if the goal seems too easy of accomplishment, pupils of good abilities will take little pride in reaching it and so have little satisfaction from the final achievement.

To the teacher this means that such blanket assignments as "Do the next twenty exercises" are almost entirely pointless. The teacher must be willing to tailor practice exercises to the individual work rates of Tom and Bill and Susan. There must be a willingness on the teacher's part to begin with pupils where they are rather than where the teacher wishes them to be. For some, standards of achievement must be within easy reach and praise for early attainment liberal. For others in the same class group, standards should be high, and slipshod or partial accomplishment unacceptable. Satisfaction for these pupils should come from the ability to meet a high challenge and not from "getting by" with as little effort as possible. Almost no readymade blanket set of exercises lifted without modification from a workbook will produce equal satisfactions in achievement for all members of a class group.

BACKGROUND PRACTICE AND FUNCTIONAL PRACTICE. It was stressed in the beginning that the learner should be aware of what he is trying to do and should also have need for doing it. Almost invariably this means that a series of practices is motivated by some proposed immediate use of what is to be learned such as "I want to be able to type my own papers"; "I want to play tuneful melodies for my own amusement"; "I want to be able to drive myself to work"; "I want to be able to converse with the Mexican children in the neighborhood"; "I want to be able to turn ornamental legs for the furniture that I plan to make"; "I want to improve my batting so that the boys in the neighborhood gang will want me on the team."

In spite of this obvious urge in normal drill situations, teachers are prone to break drill performances down into the logical component parts of the completed performance and insist upon preliminary or basic practice exercises on these parts, isolated from any normal usage whatever. We are to practice verb forms, grips on clubs, finger placement, fingering the keyboard, scales, bowing, phonetic sounds, and memorize paradigms, basic dates, spelling of words, place locations, and so on *ad infinitum.*

Whole or part learning. There is much evidence that for most learnings involving drills, practices should be upon wholes rather than upon parts; the learner needs always to keep in mind his use for the learned whole. Let the tyro try to drive the ball. Encourage the budding musician to try to produce tuneful sounds. Encourage the young reader to encompass words, phrases, sentences. Urge the would-be speaker of Spanish to speak, to try words and phrases, greetings, inquiries. Let the singer try his tune. Get the boy into the field to see what he can do with a fly ball. Let the typist try his own name and address.

The teacher needs to know the analysis and be able to suggest suitable exercises for particular parts. But isolated practices broken out of setting are to be suggested as improvements, corrections, or remedies after the whole has been attempted and at the point where the learner begins to realize his need for correction. At this point, the isolated exercises may be continued until improvement is noted and further attempts be continued with the whole in an attempt to reach the stage of effective use as quickly and as efficiently as possible.

The teacher who objects and clings to the notion of long periods spent upon *basic elements* should remember that most people have spent hours drilling on the spelling of *important* and *high-frequency* words which have never troubled them in normal writing, or which they have never had the occasion to use in ordinary correspondence. This teacher must also recall that a few of the greatest baseball players and a considerable number of winning golfers have reached the top of performance with a quite unorthodox sports form. How long can the attention of a group of immature learners be kept through days of memorization of parts of irregular verbs without speaking the language, of making passes in the air with a tennis racquet and never playing a game, or squaring stock without constructing anything, of making whorls and daubs of color but not drawing, of doing finger exercises but playing no tunes?

Background information. Another of the traditional reliances upon basic or background learning is that of expecting pupils to master certain items of information needed for the control of performance before attempting practices upon the performance patterns themselves. Illustrations are found in the attempt to teach phonetic principles or rules before attempting pronunciation in a language, rules of procedure before attempting the procedure, parliamentary rules before trying to carry out a meeting, and many others.

A positive principle may be stated here. Items of information needed for the control of a skill should be developed *along with* the development of the skill itself and inserted as the need for the information arises. There is no point in attempting to memorize control information before the practice begins. If practice is interrupted to find the needed information, practice can be resumed and the information used to control performance at once. For any given drill situation, there should be a minimum of "background" information. Let's get to work on what we are concerned with learning as expeditiously as possible.

A notable illustration of this point has occurred in foreign language instruction when teachers have insisted upon a phonetic approach to the learning of a new language with a mastery of a phonetic system *before* attempting to use the language. For pupils who have limited language experience, the situation which develops is this: they are confronted with learning *two* new languages, the phonetic system and the language itself, say Spanish. Of the two, the language itself is probably the easier. Why spend more time on the preliminary than it would take to do the original learning? The same type of situation has sometimes occurred in classes in speech in English.

Subunit implementation

SUBUNIT ORGANIZATION

1. There must be sufficient analysis of the learning situation for the teacher to be able to determine those kinds of activities which, if carried out by pupils, may be expected reasonably to aid in attaining the desired objectives.

2. Pupils should know the objectives expected to result from a series of learning exercises.

3. Directions for learning exercises must be such that pupils may know *how* to go about assigned work.

4. There must be a clear statement of the thing to be accomplished by means of a sequence of drill exercises.

5. The proposed drill program must include clear statements of the things which pupils are to do in carrying out the series of assigned practices.

6. Practice must be done upon the thing to be learned rather than upon something else.

7. The complete drill program must provide *enough* practice to insure learning.

8. Drills should be distributed rather than concentrated.

9. Provision must be made for some "drill in setting."

10. Provision should be made for variation in drill *carriers*.

11. Practice should result in some satisfaction to the learner.

12. The most effective drill programs begin with the utility of the thing to be practiced.

13. Isolated practice on special factors of a complex learning unit is to be introduced as the need occurs but in relationship to the original function.

14. The information needed for the control of the skill or training should be developed along with the training program. There should be a minimum of preliminary or "background" information.

15. Training programs must always begin where the pupil is rather than where the teacher wishes him to be.

16. There must be individual adaptation of practices. The unit practicing is the nervous mechanism of an individual, not that of a class group.

THINGS TO DO

1. Select some definite body of subject matter suitable for the use of pupils in a high school course in your field.

List the items which you believe that pupils should learn under the following headings:

Ideas to be remembered
Habits to be formed
Ideals to be developed
Concepts or generalizations to be understood.
Skills to be developed.

2. Set up a group of exercises for high school pupils which you believe would insure the learning of the items included in one of your lists in exercise 1.

Be sure that the series of exercises provides enough practice.

Accompany the exercises with a time schedule to show the distribution of practices.

3. Select some one definite thing to be learned. For this one learning item, devise a set of exercises providing variation in the practice situations, but keeping the pattern of learning constant.

4. For the pattern used in exercise 3 list a half-dozen out-of-school situations in which the pattern is commonly used. Devise some exercises to give practice in the normal use of the proposed pattern.

5. Describe briefly how pupils may attain satisfaction with the results of the practices set up for exercises 3 and 4.

6. Repeat exercise 2 for another of the patterns suggested by your listings in exercise 1.

7. Select a set of drill exercises from a published textbook, workbook, or course of study in your field. Review this set of exercises critically in terms of whether or not the pattern is evident and in terms of the presence or absence of the pattern in *each* of the exercises of the set.

8. Revise the selected set of exercises in terms of the meaningful and satisfying repetition of a given pattern. State your interpretation of the pattern for the revised set.

HELPFUL READINGS

BURTON, WILLIAM H. *The Guidance of Learning Activities.* New York: Appleton-Century-Crofts, Inc., 1952. Chap. 18.

Read for practical suggestions on the improvement of drill in classroom situations.

GATES, A. I., JERSILD, A. T., McCONNELL, T. R., and CHALLMAN, ROBERT C. *Educational Psychology.* 3d ed. New York: The Macmillan Co., 1949. Chaps. 9–12.

Read for an elaboration of the laws of learning as applied to practice situations in both motor and informational learning.

GOETTING, M. L. *Teaching in the Secondary School.* Englewood Cliffs, N.J.: Prentice-Hall Inc., 1942. Chap. 17, pp. 361–63.

An effective short summary of drill principles.

HORN, ERNEST. *What Research Says to the Teacher: Teaching Spelling.* Department of Classroom Teachers and The American Educational Research Association. Washington, D.C.: National Education Association, 1954.

Intended primarily for elementary school teachers but illustrations on exercises, time allotments, context and meaning, and steps in learning to spell will be found suggestive for many school teachers in many fields.

MILLS, HUBERT H. and DOUGLASS, HARL R. *Teaching in High School.* 2d ed. New York: The Ronald Press Co., 1957. Chap. 13.

Chap. 13 contains a useful concise summary of drill principles.

MORTON, R. L. *What Research Says to the Teacher: Teaching Arithmetic.* Department of Classroom Teachers and The American Educational Research Association. Washington, D.C.: National Education Association, 1953.

Addressed to elementary school teachers but principles included in the section on pp. 19–21 will be found useful to most high school teachers.

NATIONAL COUNCIL OF TEACHERS OF ENGLISH, THE COMMISSION ON THE ENGLISH CURRICULUM. *The English Language Arts in the Secondary School.* New York: Appleton-Century-Crofts, Inc., 1956. Chaps. 10 and 11.

What to do in planning experiences for learning grammar, usage, composition, and reading.

NATIONAL SOCIETY FOR THE STUDY OF EDUCATION. *41st Yearbook. Part II. The Psychology of Learning.* Bloomington, Ill.: Public School Publishing Co., 1942. Chaps. 1, 4, 5, 7, and 10.

The selected chapters indicated interpret principles of learning applicable to drill situations as seen by different psychologists contributing to the Yearbook.

———. *49th Yearbook. Part I. Learning and Instruction.* Chicago: University of Chicago Press, 1950. Chaps. 1 and 3.

Principles of learning in drill situations more practically applied to classroom conditions.

SCHORLING, RALEIGH. *Student Teaching.* 2d ed. New York: McGraw-Hill Book Co., Inc., 1949. Chap. 9, pp. 232–41.

Suggestions on drill as applied in classroom situations written for student teachers.

TROW, WILLIAM CLARK. *Educational Psychology.* 2d ed. Boston: Houghton Mifflin Co., 1950. Chap. 15.

Chap. 15 deals with motor learning. To be read by teachers of physical education, shop, home economics, typewriting, and others.

———. *What Research Says to the Teacher: The Learning Process.* Department of Classroom Teachers and The American Educational Research Association. Washington, D.C.: National Education Association, 1954. Pp. 17–23.

Includes a short section which presents such topics as perceiving things in patterns, cues for meanings, cues for motor learning, why practice is necessary, repetition for retention, and repetition for improvement.

WOODRUFF, ASAHEL D. *The Psychology of Teaching.* 3d ed. New York: Longmans, Green & Co., Inc., 1951. Chap. 15, pp. 270–85.

A short 15-page guide to important principles of drill.

7

Acquisition and Understanding of Ideas

What to look for in this subunit

1. What are some of the most frequently used sources of information for people outside of school?

2. What processes are commonly used by people outside of schools in acquiring information?

3. How can we check the reliability of sources of information?

4. Under what circumstances do we customarily seek information?

5. What uses do we make of ideas?

6. How are understandings developed?

7. What types of information are pupils most frequently expected to acquire in high school courses in your major field?

8. How do school processes and sources of information often differ from out-of-school sources and processes?

9. How may pupils come to realize a need for the types of information available in your field?

10. How may pupils secure training in getting reliable information within your subject matter field?

11. How can pupils learn to check the reliability of out-of-school sources of information?

12. What are the reliable sources of information, other than school textooks, that are available in your subject matter field?

In the last chapter, or subunit, those learning situations in which great dependence is placed upon the repetition of a pattern of learning in order to insure fixation of the pattern were discussed. Some of the patterns to be fixed by drill processes are associations of ideas. This chapter is concerned with the kinds of learning situations that set off the search for new ideas. It is assumed that, once the desired ideational pattern is recognized, its further fixation can be perfected by repetition in use.

Traditional schools have been criticized by the progressives in education as being subject-matter-centered or as paying more attention to the transmission of inherited knowledge than to the growth and maturing of the individual pupil. In other words, schools of the past have been charged with being too much concerned with the storage of ideas and too little concerned with the learner's ability to find and use significant ideas in cases of immediate need. Neither the traditionalist nor the progressive will deny the value of ideas, even those inherited from previous generations.

Too often schools have emphasized the storage of sets of ideas merely because humanity at one time found them valuable. Such storage has been imposed upon young learners long before they were aware of any need to use the stored ideas. In most cases such storage of learning results in forgetting to such a point that, in case of need, nothing remains of the stored ideas. The schools are then condemned for poor teaching.

Acquisition at point of use

The first teaching principle concerned with the acquisition of knowledge is that ideas are best acquired and better remembered if they are made available to each learner at his own point of immediate need. Obviously, the need for specific bits of information will occur with different people at different times. Presenting the same information on the same day to thirty-five different young learners may often violate the aforementioned principle of best acquisition and best retention of information.

One way to resolve this conflict between a sound principle of learning and practical school management is to place much greater emphasis upon where to find significant information, how to search for facts, and how to interpret the facts in terms of the present situation. At the same time relatively less emphasis may be placed upon attempts to remember ready-made sets of ideas not needed at the moment.

This latter point of view does not preclude keeping a class group within the general limits of a given subject area or within the bounds of the particular unit of a core chosen for work. Neither does it imply the abandonment of the canons of logical organization of the ideas finally selected as significant for the problem at hand. It does suggest that how to find facts, and knowing what to do with them when found, may be more important than mere storage. It implies also that what may be discovered and organized at a point of need for information may be well remembered and understood.

The reader will be aware that he has on occasion struggled to retain sets of ideas for which, up to date, he has never had any use. He may have been embarrassed by a situation in which he did not know *how* to find out what he needed to know. This becomes a very practical matter for the school teacher. If he has a reasonable control of the factual material in his field, he need not be embarrassed to say to an inquiring pupil, "I do not know." But at the same time he should be able to say to the pupil, "But I do know where to find out and I can show you how to get at the answer to your question."

NEED FOR IDEAS. The situation which sets off a search for information can be characterized as a problem.[1] A problem arises at the point where one's present experiences, existing knowledge, and habitual ways of acting break down. This breakdown tends to set the individual whose behavior is blocked off on a search for new ideas or new ways of acting that will carry him beyond the breakdown or block. Almost everyone has embarked upon a search for more information about automobile motors when his car has stalled on the highway. At other times he seemed content with the limits of his present knowledge of motors.

MATURITY AND NEED. Many assignments intended to get pupils to search for and acquire information need to be centered about problems that are significant in the living of the pupils. Certain bodies of information about which the pupils have no present problems may be delayed until the pupils reach a stage of maturity where they do have problems which point to the information in question.[2]

All teachers of home economics know that it is relatively easy to get fifteen-year-old girls to search for ideas and to consider grooming principles that have to do with hair arrangement. The adolescent girl is acutely aware of her own personal problems of hair arrangement. On the other hand, many fifteen-year-old girls are not vitally concerned about problems of child care. In spite of the importance of information about child care to most young women, it may be that the point of maturity at which such information is best acquired is that of the expectant young mother, or at least the young woman about to be married. Perhaps the subject matter is better adapted to teaching in hospitals for young mothers

---

[1] For a more extensive treatment of methods of problem solving see Chapter 8.

[2] For the relationship of problem organization to readiness factors as such, review pp. 65–68 of Chapter 4.

rather than to the high school for quite young girls. At least the information is to be acquired at the point where the problem actually exists. If such information is stored with the fifteen-year-olds, the chances are that most of it will be forgotten in the next several years or that the stored information may have become obsolete with better scientific knowledge in the intervening years.

Problem organization of assignments has become commonplace in many secondary school textbooks in the last thirty-five years. Many of the problems presented in the text materials of the secondary schools present the difficulty that they have problem form but do not in any way represent normal problems of high school youths. Much of the material of the textbooks consists of the *topics* of a previous generation converted into question form. There is still the artificiality of imposed subject matter.

Illustrations of such lack of normality are to be found in the following.

What is the importance of water to plant and animal life?

How can electricity do work for us?

How does man obtain different kinds of fuels?

How do plants and animals secure food?

Mary likes to sleep late. Her mother plans for her to help with the breakfast dishes and to put her room in order before she goes to school. Mary says that her mother expects too much of her. What responsibilities are in keeping with the privileges Mary enjoys in her home?

Sue is doing a home project on canning and preserving food. She is now ready to judge her products. What points should be included in Sue's score card?

How has religion been a force in the lives of all peoples?

How does the state protect the worker?

How does the federal government aid banking and insurance?

Why does the state maintain a system of primary and secondary roads?

On examination of these samples, it should become obvious that for high school pupils there may be no real or normal problems. All of the samples are either question-form restatements of topics or finally resolve themselves into relatively simple quiz questions.

In the search for normal problems the teacher needs to keep in mind that most problems for the immature learner and the adult layman are problems of application. They do not involve the solution to world-shaking questions or the discovery of great new principles. They are concerned with unknown answers to questions about how a known principle can be applied in a given unique situation. The solution probably cannot be quoted from the text-book, and the teacher may not know the immediate answer any more than the pupils. These are the unlooked-for queries of youth and often the kinds of things that the four-year-old presents to the embarrassed parent.

For the ninth-grade pupil in general science there is no problem in the assignment to prove Archimedes' principle of buoyancy. If he can read his textbook and has any curiosity at all, he knows that Archimedes proved the principle three hundred years before the birth of Christ and that it is stated as a law in his science book. Nor is he inclined to question the validity of the stated law in its general application.

On the other hand a group of boys planning to build a raft for a local lake and expecting to use empty oil drums as floats might be intrigued by the problem of how much weight a raft with a given number of such floats can support. Simply, "If we make a raft with four oil drums of fifty-gallon capacity and six two-by-twelve-inch pine planks ten feet long, how many boys can ride on it safely?" This is a problem of application. It might prove useful with a group of boys interested in raft building who might actually construct a raft and have a place to float it. It is not necessarily a problem for other boys and probably of no concern to most girls.

Sources of ideas

Many of the customary sources of information used in schools are seldom found in use outside the school walls. In many schools the primary sources of information are the textbook and the teacher. A cursory examination of the ordinary behavior of youths and adults out of school shows that people in general seldom consult a school textbook for needed information and that the apron strings which may bind the pupil to the teacher during school hours are quite definitely cut before ideas are crucially needed. If this assumption is accepted, the question may well be raised, "Does typical school experience adequately equip young people to use and evaluate out-of-school sources of information?" What are some of the most frequently used out-of-school sources of ideas?

Suppose that a young housewife wants information about a cake recipe. What will be her normal reaction? It is improbable that she will turn to a high school text on foods. She might hunt for her recipe in a commercial cookbook. She might step across the back yard to the door of her neighbor, known to be an expert cook. She might pick up her telephone and call her mother. At any rate her normal behavior will be to ask someone who knows or to refer to a common commercial reference. In this latter category she might readily read a satisfactory recipe on a package of cake flour or use a cake mix.

The amateur gardener will most often seek information from other gardeners, garden magazines, directions on seed packets, garden catalogs, advertising, by visitation to the gardens of others, and possibly from pamphlets such as the *Farmers' Bulletin* series or those of his local state experiment station.

The boy seeking sports information will consult the sports magazines, the sports page of the newspaper, official manuals of sports, observation of amateur and professional games, television, and radio programs.

Uses of sources in assignments

With these illustrative cases as a beginning we may make an extended general list of common out-of-school sources of information. Such a list would include: friends, relatives, neighbors; specialists such as the physician, dentist, surgeon, public health nurse, banker, architect, county agricultural agent, or lawyer; advertising, radio and television programs, newspapers, popular magazines, specialized magazines, ordinary observation, travel, visits to museums, home reference books, libraries, bulletins, pamphlets, and motion pictures. The list is incomplete but suggestive. Each teacher should form his own working list of common sources of information and check it by observation of the ordinary learning of the people that he sees about him.

Without doubt the uses of such common sources can be improved for most people. If these are the sources that are to be used in everyday living, the school experiences should be such that the pupil who comes out of school should have become adept in using the sources that are available to him.

The teacher who cares to explore a bit will find that many pupils of senior high school age do not know how to use the index of a book. Many do not know what words to look for in an index in order to search a book for a given bit of information. Often pupils have had no experience with an historical atlas, the *World Almanac,* or *Statesman's Yearbook.* The dictionary is a crude and inept tool in the hands of many persons. Often people fail to use a library because they have no idea of how to use its resources. Many senior high school pupils have never arranged for an interview with any local specialist.

Each teacher has the obligation to survey the common and valid sources of information in his own field and then, through a continuing series of assignments, see that each of his pupils has experiences in using such sources. The pupil should know where to look for information in the given field and how to go about finding the specific ideas which he may need. Such goals must be set up and carried to achievement in every field represented in the school. Training in the knowledge of sources and their uses is not the sole responsibility of the English teacher or the school librarian.

In order to achieve such training, pupils should have experiences with as wide a range of possible sources of information as it is possible for the school to provide and arrange. Some things may be studied intensively and a few memorized verbatim. But to reach a working knowledge of out-of-school sources, the range of sources should be as wide as possible. The experiences with sources should be extensive rather than intensive.

In the field of reading there is now good experimental evidence [3] to indicate that extensive reading from a variety of sources produces better learning than the intensive reading of a limited number of sources. The experimental evidence on this point has accumulated in such fields as general science, American history, and literature.

Reliability of sources

Frequently, popular sources provide information that is false, partial, biased, or ill fitted to the specific needs of the investigator. Fully as important as knowing where to look and how to use is some power of discrimination between the reliable and the unreliable. The teacher's obligation in his own field, then, extends to include helping pupils set up suitable criteria for distinguishing between the true and the untrue.

SELF-INTEREST OF SOURCE. There is always the question of whether or not the purveyor of information has a vested interest in that which he purveys. Advertising of citrus growers for vitamin content and health-giving qualities of citrus fruits and juices might be questioned on the grounds that the growers who pay for the advertising are interested in promoting the sales of their products. If such claims can be verified from the findings of a professional nutritionist who is employed by an independent health laboratory and who owns no orange groves or any interest in a grapefruit juice processing plant, there is an assumption of greater reliability in the claims.

---

[3] See the treatment of extensive reading programs, Chapter 12, pp. 272–76, on teaching procedures.

The physician has a vested interest in the health of his patient. However, this interest of the physician's coincides generally with the interest of the patient in his own health.

Life insurance statistics on death rates from various causes involve also the vested interest of the insurance company in the longevity of its clients. Again, the interest of the insured coincides with that of the company so that the insurance statistics may be considered reliable unless they seem to conflict with similar data derived from other apparently reliable sources.

USE OF MULTIPLE SOURCES. Two or more sources are almost invariably better than one. In case of disagreement among sources, further information needs to be sought. Sometimes in such disagreement the inquirer will decide that the problem is unsolved. In case of agreement among the several sources, the inquirer will tend to accept the common finding. This situation is illustrated by the diagnosis of severe illness requiring extensive surgery. The patient is thoroughly justified in having the diagnosis checked by a second surgeon before the operation is performed. In case of disagreement, he will ask for still further check and diagnosis. If the experts agree, he will probably submit to the surgery. The modern clinic attempts to furnish the crosscheck in terms of opinions of the several specialists suggested in the process of verification above.

REPUTATION OF SOURCE. Newspapers, magazines, and book publishers establish reputations as do individual people. Some are known for good reporting and careful editing. Others are known for their sensationalism and biased reporting. As with people, publishing firms build up their own classes of associates. Magazines and newspapers of doubtful reliability are often filled with advertising of spurious and doubtful merchandise. Books of questionable firms are often sold by somewhat dubious merchants often in association with other goods of low quality. These reputations and associations can be determined. Pupils in school should find them out and be led to formulate their own judgments in terms of such criteria.

SPECIALIZED TRAINING OF SOURCE. The scientists and professional workers of our day are required to have considerable training in known institutions of higher learning. Pupils need to be able to recognize a reputable college, university, or graduate school. They need to know about how long it takes to educate a modern physician. What kind of school does he attend? For how long? What hospital and internship experiences are required? What are the requirements for licensing physicians? What earned degrees does the physician have? Are the associations of a particular doctor those to be expected of a reputable practitioner? Similar questions can be raised concerning other professional workers. There are no secrets about professional education. No honest practitioner should object to such inquiry. All laymen should learn to ask such questions and to use the implications of the information acquired. The school teacher who reads professional books in education might well raise questions such as these concerning the professional status of authors of the books which he reads.

Informational assignments

In many cases, school assignments have been directed toward the acquisition of blocks or segments of information. Traditionally the teacher has said, "Read chapter 11" or "For your next lesson read in your text pages 222 to 234." A good informational assignment should begin with some reason for acquiring the information. The assignment as made should in and of itself answer the pupil's possible query of, "Why should I read that stuff anyway?"

Modern teachers in stressing the importance of the ideas sought have sometimes neglected the specific lists set with the older types of assignments. The teacher may say, "Let's find out why the southern states have nearly always represented a solid block of Democratic votes" and at the same time forget to add that, "Some good information on this point is contained in chapter 17 of your text and in an article on the recent election in the issue of *Time* for December 15th of this year."

DEFINING THE ASSIGNMENT. Two things about good informational assignments have been emphasized. Such assignments should set up with the pupils definite indications of what to look for and some criteria for judging relative importance of the facts presented. At the same time the assignment should have definite limitations in its range of sources, in order that the pupil not be led to waste time in trying to find information where it does not exist.

If the teacher wishes a pupil to be able to learn to find sources of information for himself, the assignment should indicate this. Such assignments almost always need a direction for preparing a simple bibliography dealing with the problem or topic at hand. Suggestions of possibly pertinent general sources useful to the pupil in preparing his own bibliography should be included in most cases. A list of pertinent sources or a proper bibliography cannot be made by the pupil until his problem or topic is clearly defined and specifically limited.

SUGGESTING THE ATTACK.   Another weak point in the "read the chapter" type of assignment is that it makes no provision for doing anything with the information contained in the chapter. Good learning implies the building up of reactions to ideas, not mere memoriter acquisition. Therefore, the assignment should include exercises built about directions or suggestions for the use or further application of the information involved. It is extremely doubtful if the young learner is in any way aware of the significance of a set of items of information until he has gone through certain active processes in their use.

For example, a teacher of general science is concerned with having pupils learn facts concerning the relationship of heat to the circulation of air. He could say to his pupils, "Henry said yesterday, 'When I stood in front of the refrigerator to get the peanut butter for a sandwich I could feel cold air about my ankles. The cold air seemed to fall out of the refrigerator. Why?' We should be able to answer Henry's question if we read what our general science book says in chapter 8. In your reading try to find out which is heavier, hot air or cold air. Why does cold air seem to fall? Why does air circulate in a heated room? What causes air currents?"

It would be well, however, for the teacher to add to this assignment further suggestions of definite things to do with the ideas concerning the relationship of the circulation of air to heat. For example:

1. Make a diagram of a stove or furnace firebox which shows all drafts and dampers. Show how these should be regulated for slow, medium, and rapid burning. Trace the flow of air through the stove or firebox. Where does the cold air come in? Where do the hot gases escape?

2. Adjust the collar on one of the laboratory Bunsen burners to admit different amounts of air and notice the changes in the flame. Where does the air enter the burner? Where do the hot gases escape?

3. Make a cross-sectional diagram of a home hot-air heating system. If you do not have this type of heating in your home, diagram the hot air system of a neighbor's home. Place arrows in the diagrams of the piping to show the direction of the air currents. What makes the air move? What is the difference between a "forced air" heating system and a "gravity" system?

4. Make a diagram of your room at home which shows the location of all windows, doors, and heat sources, registers, radiators, or stoves. Show how to ventilate this room on a cold winter day;

also on a warm summer day. Place arrows in the diagram to indicate the directions in which the air moves.

5. Try exercise 4 for the classroom at school.
6. Make a brief "floor talk" on what makes the air move in an air conditioning system.

ADAPTATION AND VARIATION OF ASSIGNMENTS. As indicated in the sections of chapter 6 concerning the adaptation of practice exercises to maturity, experiences, and needs of different individuals, there needs to be opportunity for a considerable variety in the experiences proposed as assignments. This principle of variation of proposed exercises while at the same time holding relatively constant the pattern of learning involved is equally as valid in the learning of factual information. In the aforementioned illustration, the general notion that heated air rises and colder air falls or sinks may be shown for different people with differing illustrations. It is not necessary or always desirable that different individuals have identical experiences. Henry may be challenged by the chilled air about his ankles in front of the refrigerator while at the same time Susan is intrigued by rising "heat waves" above the toaster at the family breakfast table. The principle of "variation of the carrier" holds as well for the learning of associated ideas as it does for the practice of drill patterns.[4]

In the preceding discussion, it is assumed that different individuals learn in different ways and through somewhat differing media. If this assumption is accepted, then it follows that people of differing maturities will need to use source materials adapted to their own particular stages of maturity. There are at least two practical ways in which the teacher can provide for these differing maturities. One is in assigning different exercises to different people and at the same time suggesting sources of information suited to the levels of the people concerned.

The second way is to provide the classroom library, or the reserve shelf in the school library, with different source materials dealing with the same ideas and principles. In the ninth grade, one pupil might make a report concerning atomic structures from a recent edition of the *Encyclopaedia Britannica* in the school library, while at the same time a second pupil might use a spread with colored pictures from an issue of *Life*. A third pupil in the same class might use with profit the explanation of an author of a sixth-grade science text.

In trying to adapt source materials to the needs of pupils of vary-

[4] See pp. 99–101 of Chapter 6 for the discussion of the principle of the variation of carriers for learning patterns.

ing maturity, the teacher may well have in mind that in every class there will be differences in reading ability, in vocabulary range, in basic experiences, and in present interests.

A teacher of a junior high school reading and literature class found that in the same group of about twenty pupils, there were individuals who still read typical juvenile books, those who read books commonly included in junior high school reading lists, and those who read the same books read by their parents, who were sophisticated college graduates. Obviously an assignment to the same chapter in the same book might not work with all members of this class.

Understanding

What has been said concerning the fitting of informational sources to the relative maturities of young learners implies the desirability of the pupil's being able to make interpretations of the ideas. The teacher's clue to the improvement of understanding is in the nature of the assignment or direction of the work of the pupils.

RELATIONSHIP OF UNDERSTANDING TO EXPERIENCE. Any human being understands a new idea in terms of his accumulated experiences. Each new experience is colored by its relationship to the previous experiences of the same individual. For years teachers have laughed at the odd responses of pupils to examination questions and have frequently characterized many such replies as stupid. Typically the unexpected have been described as "boners." What teachers often fail to see is that if enough were known about the pupils' experience the nature of the "boner" would become obvious. In many cases the pupil's response is the only one that he could have made within the limitations of his own experience. Everyone is familiar with the tale of the lad who on listening to a sermon on the text, "Fear not the Comforter will come" reported at home that the minister had said, "Don't be afraid, you'll get your quilt."

Many of us do not understand why the masses of the people in India do not understand our interpretation of democracy. We fail to consider that we have lived "American democracy" and that few Hindus have.

The assignment, then, which deals with information should help pupils to see relationships between the new material and their existing experiences. To make such an assignment well, the teacher must study the experiential backgrounds of his pupils, especially as these may relate to learning in his particular teaching field. This study of pupil experience can never be abandoned because interpretative experience is an individual matter and the experiences of people in one class group in any given school year are not those of the members of the next group.

Useful in establishing relationships with pupil experiences are such devices as the teacher's introduction which uses anecdote, analogy, and contrast, preliminary *discussion* of the assignment, brief reports of pupils of present reactions and proposals related to the next work of the class, and conferences with individual pupils.

CONTINUED USE OF IDEAS. The precept that pupils should *do something* with the ideas in the assignment needs to be repeated in this connection. The active reaction of the pupil should tie in with his present experiences and at the same time tend to extend his experiences with the new ideas.

The spread of many common micro-organisms can be checked by common measures of cleanliness, application of heat, and exposure to sunlight. The pupil should be able to react to simple questions concerning the use of soap and water on eating utensils and the scalding of drinking glasses. He should then be able to make recommendations concerning what should be done with utensils, clothing, and so on in a household in which there has been an epidemic of common colds. Or, what should be done with football uniforms, shoes, pads, etc. worn by last year's team? It should be relatively easy for any teacher who knows his pupils to extend the potential reactions of pupils to the original idea almost indefinitely. It is possible, too, that experiences in examining micro-organisms under a microscope before and after drying and exposure to heat and sunlight will be of value in *seeing* what the hygienic measures accomplish.

Further understanding as well as fixation of ideas is accomplished by varied and continued use of the ideas. This continuation of use and variation in application can be manipulated, at least in part, by assignments, suggestion, and direction from the teacher. Ideas are never well learned unless they can be used and applied in a variety of situations. In this connection it is highly desirable that the teacher should not abandon entirely sets of important ideas after the first early experiences with them, but from time to time through additional assignments he should revert to their use as they may become pertinent in the solution of new problems.

It must be remembered that appropriate understanding should be developed as information is acquired. The interpretation should not come as an afterthought. The *why* should always accompany the *what*. For example, in the earlier illustration (the spread of many common micro-organisms can be checked by means of common measures of cleanliness, application of heat, and exposure to sunlight) the reasons for the rule-of-thumb statement should be developed at the same time as the application. Micro-organisms are living things. In order to live and grow they must have a food supply, moisture, an optimum temperature, and—for many of the common ones—an oxygen supply. The food supply is often found in wastes and remnants of organic matter. The checking of growth or killing depends upon a control of these life and growth factors. Perhaps with this interpretation many pupils can at once begin to *explain why* cleanliness is necessary, or why boiling water and steam can be used as germ killers.

The teacher who reads this will be inclined to say, "But we always teach the explanation with the new idea or principle." It is hoped that this is true. But can you recall finding out *why* a minus sign before a parenthesis changes the sign of all the quantities within the parenthesis when the parenthesis is removed? Or being aware of *why* most southern congressmen have stood for free trade or tariff for revenue only? Assignments are to be built so that reasons accompany the awareness of the existence of facts. From the point of view of most useful learning, further interpretations of ideas in new situations depend upon this knowing of the why from the beginning. Transfer in the further application of ideas or principles depends upon sound understanding.

ORGANIZATION OF IDEAS. The basic clue to understanding is found in the relationships of the ideas; relationships are at the same time the clue to better retention of ideas. This suggests a final step in the learning of associated ideas: systematizing or organizing them.

It is evident from modern psychology of learning that understanding, retention, and the possibilities of reapplication are better if each learner works out for himself his own organization for any given set of ideas.[5] At least, each learner should participate in the organization of any given set of ideas if he is to attain a maximum of understanding and effective retention.

For the teacher who is attempting to direct learning processes, this means that each series of assignments for informational types of learning should contain some exercises that are definitely designed to get pupils to organize the ideas recently gathered. Every teacher is familiar with the commoner forms of organizational devices. These include the formation of generalizations, conclusions, and rules, summaries, reports, charts, maps, graphs, formulae, programs, pieces of construction, outlines, diagrams, and finished performance.

It is not enough to say to pupils in the history class: "Let's find

[5] See also Chapter 5, p. 72, on the place of logical organization in learning.

out whether or not it is possible for a president of the United States to be elected without having a majority of all the votes cast for president in a general election." In addition to this setting of the proposed problem, the teacher should make suggestions of possibilities in finding and organizing the data to be used in the solution of the problem. For example:

1. Examine the *World Almanac* to find data on presidential elections from the time of George Washington to that of Dwight Eisenhower. Make a table to show the number of electoral votes attained by each winning candidate, the number of electoral votes received by each major losing candidate, and the number of electoral votes received by minor candidates, if any.

   Construct a similar table to show the number of popular votes received by each major candidate.

   Are there any cases of the election of a candidate to the presidency who failed to receive a majority of the votes cast for president in the election?

2. Construct a table showing the electoral votes and the popular votes of the leading candidates for president in the last election by states. Select ten or twelve states which seemed to carry the "balance of power" in this election. How many votes in each of these states would have been needed to swing the election in the other direction?

3. Make a bibliography of books on American history and government that can be found in the school library that make useful interpretations of recent presidential elections.

4. Do you believe that a constitutional amendment which would provide for popular election of the president by a majority of votes cast and the abolishing of the electoral college is desirable? Why do you take such a position? What are the arguments on the other side?

It would seem evident from these sample exercises that pupils will gain both in understanding and in retention of factual material concerning the machinery of presidential elections better than if they merely read what the history text said about elections or better than by trying to memorize by rote the numbers of votes held in the electoral college by "crucial states."

Each reader who is not concerned with learning in the field of history might well attempt to develop some comparable illustrations dealing with the relationship of the factors of organization to learning in the field which most concerns him. What can be done in working with pupils who need to organize isolated skills into significant whole patterns. Teachers of typewriting, stenography, music, sports, shop, and home economics may well attempt sample approaches in the organization of skills. Opportunities to try such sample exercises in learning situations need to be sought, too. It should be easy for teachers of science, mathematics, and social sciences to develop desirable organizing exercises. What can the teacher of speech, Spanish, or English composition do with the concept proposed here?

Subunit implementation

Subunit Organization

1. New ideas should be introduced into a learning situation as the need for them occurs.

2. Information is most often needed in problem solving.

3. The range of sources of information used in high school should be as wide as is possible within the school and community resources.

4. Pupils should be trained in the use of out-of-school sources of information.

5. Each teacher should accept the responsibility for training pupils to use the sources of information commonly available in his field.

6. Pupils working in each field of subject matter should be trained to discriminate between reliable and unreliable sources of information.

7. There is good evidence to support the notion that information is acquired more readily through the use of extensive sources than through intensive study of limited sources.

8. Informational assignments should begin with a definite indication of the specific body of information to be acquired and the values of such acquisition.

9. Informational assignments should indicate definite things *for pupils to do.*

10. There should be variation in the activities for information getting.

11. Most assignments should indicate a definite list of sources.

12. Sources should fit the maturities of the pupils.

13. Understanding should be developed as the information is acquired.

14. Understandings are developed through establishing relationships with existing experiences and through varied use of the ideas in different settings.

15. Ideas should be organized.

16. Opportunities for summarization and generalization should be provided.

17. Pupil participation in organization aids both understanding and retention.

Things to Do

1. List briefly a half-dozen recent situations in which you have experienced a need or demand for a definite body of information. Indicate how and from what sources you obtained the information in each case.

To what extent could you depend upon your previously stored ideas?

2. List as many common out-of-school sources of information as you can readily think of. Can you classify these sources by any suitable scheme? Try your classification.

3. Classify the kinds or types of information most frequently used by workers in your field, *e.g.*, scientific facts, rules, generalizations, directions for carrying out procedures, etc.

Illustrate each type which you list for your field and suggest a few specific cases for each classification.

4. List the commonest sources of information used by people out of school to get at information within your field. Which of these are reliable sources? How do you know?

5. Outline the *information* to be used with pupils for some one definite teaching unit from one high school course in your field. Make this outline in sentence statement form.

6. Describe briefly ten situations which show the needs of high school pupils for information contained within some one high school course in your field.

7. Describe briefly how you as a teacher can check the reliability of new information in your own field.

8. List the sources of information which you believe pupils in courses in your field should be trained to use.

9. List items of information you learned in school courses which are no longer true. How do you know these items are now untrue? What protection can you render your own pupils in such situations?

HELPFUL READINGS

BOSSING, N. L. *Teaching in Secondary Schools.* 3d ed. Boston: Houghton Mifflin Co., 1952. Chaps. 5, 11, 12, 14.

Chapters deal with lecturing for presenting information, assignments, questioning, and verbal illustrations.

The Boners Omnibus. Toronto: Blue Ribbon Books, Inc., 1931.

Reread sections on history and the natural sciences as illustrations of lack of understanding when instruction relies heavily upon verbalism.

BURTON, WILLIAM H. *The Guidance of Learning Activities.* New York: Appleton-Century-Crofts, Inc., 1952. Chaps. 16 and 17.

Deals with informational instruction and with verbalism as contrasted with understanding.

BUTLER, FRANK A. *The Improvement of Teaching in Secondary Schools.* Rev. ed. Chicago: University of Chicago Press, 1946. Pp. 78–106.

Presents the basic issue that words are not substitutes for perceptions in learning.

FAY, LEO C. *What Research Says to the Teacher: Reading in the High School.* Department of Classroom Teachers and The American Educational Research Association. Washington, D.C.: National Education Association, 1956.

Pamphlet. See especially the section, pp. 23–27, on reading in content areas.

NATIONAL COUNCIL OF TEACHERS OF ENGLISH, THE COMMISSION ON THE ENGLISH CURRICULUM. *The English Language Arts in the Secondary School.* New York: Appleton-Century-Crofts, Inc., 1956. Chap. 6, pp. 161–90.

Presents work-type reading and listening as means to the acquisition of information.

NATIONAL SOCIETY FOR THE STUDY OF EDUCATION. *41st Yearbook. Part II. The Psychology of Learning.* Bloomington, Ill.: Public School Publishing Co., 1942. Chaps. 5 and 7.

These chapters deal with the psychological background of informational learning.

————. *47th Yearbook. Part II. Reading in High School and College.* Chicago: University of Chicago Press, 1948. Chaps. 6 and 7.

On work-type reading and the improvement of reading in high school. Gives general support to the value of extensive reading programs.

————. *53rd Yearbook. Part II. Mass Media and Education.* Chicago: University of Chicago Press, 1954. Chaps. 7, 8, 10, 11, 12.

Selected chapters deal with the acquisition of information through modern mass media of communication—newspapers, periodicals, motion pictures, radio, and television. Some attention given to reliability of information distributed through these sources.

————. *55th Yearbook. Part II. Adult Reading.* Chicago: University of Chicago Press, 1956. Chaps. 1–3.

Chapters contain surveys of the nature and quality of adult reading and implications for the high school teacher for improvement of weaknesses shown in the surveys.

TROW, WILLIAM CLARK. *Educational Psychology.* 2d ed. Boston: Houghton Mifflin Co., 1950. Chaps. 11, 13, and 14.

Read chap. 11 for a statement of the laws of association; chap. 13 on increasing retention; and chap. 14 on knowledge and understanding.

————. *What Research Says to the Teacher: The Learning Process.* Department of Classroom Teachers and The American Educational Research Association. Washington, D.C.: National Education Association, 1954.

Pamphlet. See pp. 27–29 on retention of information.

WOODRUFF, ASAHEL D. *The Psychology of Teaching.* 3d ed. New York: Longmans, Green & Co., Inc., 1951. Chap. 16, pp. 280–295.

Contains applications of psychological principles underlying informational learning, retention, and understanding.

8

Problem-Solving Processes

What to look for in this subunit

1. In what types of out-of-school situations do problems occur?

2. Are there cases in which thinking takes place without an awareness of a difficulty?

3. What is the distinction to be found between a puzzle and a normal problem?

4. How may normal or "real" problems for high school boys and girls be found?

5. What is a typical weakness of many school problems?

6. What are the steps usually given in the analysis of the problem-solving process?

7. What is the relationship of information getting to problem solving?

8. What place has human imagination in problem solving?

9. What variations in the techniques of application of the general problem-solving process are used most often in your field?

10. What systems of proof are possible within the limits of the field of your major interest?

11. How can pupils be trained to solve problems within your field?

12. What kinds of learning situations do not lend themselves to a problem-solving approach?

The previous chapter, or subunit, was concerned with ways and means of acquiring new ideas. Clearly, a great issue confronting schools is that of *storage* as contrasted with the acquisition of immediately significant information. In the previous chapter it was emphasized that the primary reason for seeking information is being able to use the information in the solution of problems. In this chapter, an attempt will be made to show how the individual or the group may use ideas in the solution of problems and how teachers in the varying situations of the school can help young people to learn to solve problems.

Origin of the problem

Under what circumstances do people attempt to solve problems; colloquially, when do people try to think? The blanket answer to this query is that human beings attempt to solve problems only as they are confronted with some difficulty. Or, people think only when they get into trouble.

If you, as a reader, are inclined to doubt this offhand characterization of problem solving or thought situations, try to recall cases in which you have actively attempted to find a solution to a problem in which there was no difficulty to set you off on the quest for a solution.

The converse of the proposed thesis is that in the great majority of everyday situations human beings react in terms of habitual behavior. The reactions are in terms of previously learned behavior, including habits, biases, and attitudes. It is only at the point where the habitual behavior breaks down and will not function, or the point at which the individual questions his attitude or doubts his bias, that thought or problem solving begins.

For most people, the routines of daily living present few problems. Habits and biases carry them through. If they are in school, they go to classes on schedule without questioning the desirability of attendance. Most have limited wardrobes. If it is cool, they wear the topcoats in the closet. If it rains, they wear raincoats. When the sun comes out, the raincoats come off. Most persons eat within the narrow range of the food provided. Students read the books and chapters recommended by the teacher. They accept the point of view of the author "because he is an authority." When they reject, they reject in terms of previously acquired biases. In almost none of this is there any thinking. So far there are practically no real problems.

In his *How We Think*, John Dewey has used the analogy of the crossroads situation. In other words, the problem arises at the point of necessary decision. If there is no crossroads, there will be no thought. But when a decision of which way to turn must be made, there is a problem.

It may be helpful to analyze still further the kinds of difficulties that produce problem-solving reactions. Perhaps first is the actual physical difficulty which serves as a block to action. The car door has been locked with the key inside. The car refuses to start on a zero morning. A break in the plumbing begins to flood the bathroom. An opposing halfback intercepts the pass that was intended to carry the home team to a touchdown. A wreck and personal injury occur on the highway. The baby has a violent red rash and a fever. The train connection is missed. The new ribbon for the typewriter seems not to fit. The material purchased for the blouse is inadequate for the pattern chosen. The ice storm has broken the power lines, and the household heating system is out of commission. Each reader can at once add many more.

Secondly, there is the type of difficulty which grows out of a conflict of ideas. "God is the same yesterday, today, and forever" as contrasted with "Man's interpretation of the nature of God changes from time to time." "God created the universe in six days" vs. "The universe has evolved from a gaseous nebula in the course of several million years." "Watermelons and squashes planted in the same field will cross. The product will look like melons and taste squashy." But a noted horticulturist attempted to cross watermelons and squashes over a period of twenty years and was unable to produce fruit from the cross. "When Mary's mother was pregnant she was frightened by a large black snake over which she stumbled in the garden path. When Mary was born she had a snakelike red mark on the skin of her left leg." But there is no direct connection between the nervous system of a pregnant mother and the embryo. There is no physical connection by means of which the effect of a fright upon a mother's nervous system could be impressed upon an embryo. According to the embryologists the thing is impossible. "But it happened. Mary's mother told me so, and I have seen the mark on Mary's leg."

Thirdly, there are difficulties which grow out of conflicts between ideals, attitudes, or biases. "I have always been a Democrat. I believe strongly in the tenets of the party. At the same time I believe in honesty in government. Recent reports of corruption among Democratic officials concern me greatly. Can I bring myself to vote for a particularly upright Republican who is a candidate for Congress in my district?" "I believe in equal opportunities for people of all races. No, I will not sit next to the principal of the Negro school at the next schoolmasters' club dinner." "I believe in tolerance for members of various religious groups. A man's religious faith is between himself and his God. I will not vote for Mr. Levy to be a member of our school board because he is a Jew."

A fourth type of problem-producing difficulty is the possibility of interconflict between ideals, attitudes, or biases and facts. "The members of the 'white race' are superior to the people of other 'races'." However, many reputable anthropologists now believe that mankind is all one species and that therefore, the old concept of separate races of mankind can no longer hold. "The Nordic strain of the white race found in central and northern Europe is superior in every way to all other types of man found on the earth." But the facts of history indicate that central and northern Europe have been overrun for hundreds of years by different peoples. The folk at home and the various conquering hordes have continually intermixed until there is no pure strain of any kind of mankind left in most of Europe. The Nordic strain is a myth. "It takes a big, rugged, and rangy man to play halfback on a modern football team." The leading ground gainer among teams of the XYZ league in 1957 was five feet eight and weighed 165 pounds. "People who have had good training in high school plane geometry can reason better in various kinds of situations because they have had geometry training." However, Fawcett, working in the Laboratory School on the Ohio State campus, found that his geometry pupils could pass reasoning tests involving nongeometric situations only when they were taught to make the transfer from geometric to nongeometric situations.

Finally, there is the type of difficulty commonly characterized as curiosity. The research scientist has no conflicts. He is simply trying to discover the truth. And yet he works on problems. Within the limits of the proposed general thesis, it is possible that the problem arising in curiosity comes about through a lack of satisfaction with the current solution. The difficulty lies in dissatisfaction with the accepted explanation or theory, or with the possibility that there may be other interpretations.

A generation ago chemists taught that there were possible only ninety-two chemical elements. Not all of them had been discovered, but there were places in the system of atomic weights where the unknowns could be fitted. When those which would fit were discovered, there could be no additional chemical elements. Since then, there have been doubters in the field of chemical theory, and now the list of chemical elements has been extended beyond the limits of the ninety-two. In other words, there were a few chemists who were dissatisfied with the explanation of chemical structure commonly accepted by workers in the field. If these men had not allowed themselves to be disturbed by the possibility of other interpretations, the world would indeed have lacked the most recently discovered elements and probably atomic bombs.

From my study window I see a moving object in a bush. What is it? A bird. But what kind of a bird? A warbler. But which of the warblers? And I am off for the *Handbook of Birds* and the field glasses. Note that I could have been satisfied at any of the stages with a simple explanation. I might have gone happily back to the typewriter with, "There's a bird in the haw bush." The problem arose with the refusal to accept so simple an interpretation.

Problem-solving processes

To solve a problem a pupil must define his problem, determine what is known about the situation, come to a possible tentative solution, determine whether this solution will resolve the difficulty, and then use the solution in future situations in which it will fit.

AWARENESS OF THE PROBLEM. It is highly important for the teacher to see that the individual who is to attack a problem must be acutely aware of the difficulty so that he feels that he must struggle to arrive at a solution. Another way of saying this is to suggest that many difficulties exist about which most individuals do nothing. The difficulty is there. The situation exists. But the persons who seem most intimately concerned do nothing. The spark which sets off the problem-solving process is this element of awareness or concern.

A recent news item illustrates the point. In a new housing development a pit, or abandoned quarry, was left which filled with water. In the development of the landscaping for the area this pit went unfilled. A child from one of the families of the neighborhood fell into the pit and was drowned. A child from a second family fell into the pit and was rescued just in time to save his life. At this point the citizens took matters into their own hands. They assembled with picks, shovels, and wheelbarrows to fill the pit. Two men borrowed the contractor's bulldozers. This open pit had existed as a hazard to children for some time. It detracted from the beauty of the landscape. No one was concerned to see that anything was done about it until a child was lost and a second in extreme danger. The necessary awareness for action was created by the tragedy.

In matters of health and hygiene, pain or fright often serve to produce the awareness necessary for action. In a previous generation people did not visit the dentist until a toothache occurred. Whenever there is a toothache the conditions which give rise to the pain have existed for some months, perhaps years, but the ache produces the awareness of need for treatment. In terms of the analysis of problem solving the difficulty existed for some time. No action was taken until pain produced an acute awareness of the existing difficulty.

In modern dental hygiene, people try to use other means of building up awareness of need for dental care, because the pain tends to come at a point too late for many preventive measures. So, the teacher in working with pupils in school will attempt to introduce into school planning and into problem-solving assignments some measures which will aid in getting individual pupils to become greatly concerned with attempting action as a means of meeting the existing conditions which constitute the problem at hand. A negative illustration of a lack of drive arising out of individual concern for the problem is found in many of the "prose problems" of the typical algebra textbook.

DEFINITION OF THE PROBLEM. To be efficient in his problem solving, the solver must be able to locate his problem specifically and set limits to its scope. This important process is familiar in the work of the physician or surgeon. It is called diagnosis. In simple composition many difficulties arise through failure to limit the topic, or title, about which the composition is to be built. Everyone is familiar with the small boy's struggles to write about "Cats." How much simpler would the boy's writing become if he would define his topic as, "What Cats Eat," or "Cat Friends that I Have Had," or "A Night Out with Old Tom," or "Why I Hate Cats."

As further illustration, in the case of a stalled automobile motor such questions as the following serve to define the problem: Is there gas in the tank? Is gas getting to the carburetor? Can I get a spark between the top of a spark plug and the motor head or block? In other words, does the trouble consist of lack of fuel, of stoppage in the fuel line, or in a fault in the ignition system? There is no reason to begin to take apart the ignition system if the tank is empty. There is no reason to disconnect the fuel line if there is no spark at the plugs.

In a given high school there are 150 girls. Of these, 40 ninth-grade girls are enrolled in vocational home economics. But in the tenth-grade class in home economics there are only 18 and in the eleventh grade only 10. The same teacher has the four sections of home economics. What is the reason for the apparently diminishing interest of the girls in home economics? Does the content of the courses fail to meet significant homemaking needs of girls? Are there personality conflicts between this particular teacher and the girls? Is the teaching uniformly poor? Do the more mature girls find other vocational interests in the total scope of the school program which in competition tend to cut down the number of girls remaining in home economics? Are there external social factors which make the girls who begin the home economics program feel socially inferior or which may seem to subject them to ridicule? It may be that in attempting to make an appropriate analysis of the situation all of these possibilities need to be explored. On the other hand, it seems quite evident that it would be more efficient to limit a current investigation to one of them and leave the others until a solution is found for the defined or limited problem. If, for example, it is determined that the teacher has a long record of difficulties in getting along with girls in previous schools and there is evidence of an unwholesome atmosphere in the present classes, perhaps the other problems will not need investigation, at least for the present.

COLLECTION OF INFORMATION.   Problems cannot be solved without facts or information. Having defined his problem, the problem solver will proceed to determine what is known about the situation. Technically, this stage is often called that of collecting data. Sometimes a distinction is made between "background information," or what is now known about the situation, and the collection of new information, "the data," needed for the ultimate solution.

Practically, a person commonly approaches the gathering of needed information by beginning with, "What do I know about this?" "What did I do the last time this kind of thing happened?" "Did I ever see a case like this?" "What have I seen other people do in such situations?" Obviously, this is a stage of recall, remembering, recollection.

Next, there is the stage of, "Who else might know?" "Who has attacked a similar problem?" "What did he find out?" "Are there any specialists who are known to work on related problems?" "What could these specialists suggest?" "Are there any books or published studies that might help?" "What can I find in the library?" Recourse to books and printed materials becomes in this sense an extension of the notion of appealing to the experiences of others who may have worked upon a similar problem.

Sometimes a relatively simple problem can be solved by reference to recalled information, advice from others, or reading. However, there are many problems that call for further observation, experimentation, and investigation. Ideas from such sources can be characterized as *new information.*

Whatever the source or however information is obtained, it is always extremely important that it be pertinent to the problem at hand. Whatever information is available must have something to do with the problem. Its present worth is to be determined by its usefulness in dealing with the problem to be solved. This issue is an extremely crucial one in schools. Schools are often accused of mere storage of information. It has been said that often schools have trained pupils to read with sponges or attempt to remember everything. From the point of view of problem solving, pupils should read with sieves rather than with sponges. They should recall selectively. The basis for selection, or the nature of the mesh in the sieve, is the query, "Does this have any bearing on the defined problem?"

FORMATION OF THE HYPOTHESIS.   When a problem is defined and the solver begins to collect information, somewhere in the information-gathering stage an hypothesis concerning a solution is formed. The hypothesis is a suggestion of a possible solution. It is a tentative or temporary solution.   Midwesterners have a common colloquial expression which fits: "I guess this will work."   Have in mind that the guess must be probable, or fit the present known facts.   The guess should be intelligent.

Suppose a motorist deep in the countryside has run out of gas. Having verified the fact that he is out of gas, he might propose that he could get gas at the farmhouse just passed.   Note that he forms this hypothesis because he observed a tractor in the farmyard.   His guess is probable.   He does not just walk back to the farmhouse with no means of checking the probability of his guess.

TRIAL OF THE HYPOTHESIS.   The hypothesis formed by the problem solver must be possible for the particular problem at hand.   But it must also be probable.   Its probability can be assured by certain processes developed for checking guesses at solution.

Many people tend to jump at conclusions.   They accept a possible guess too readily.   Or they plunge immediately into trial-and-error experiment, perhaps act too soon upon what is at best only a beginner's guess at a solution.

Hypotheses can be tried by two general processes.   These are (1) trial in imagination and (2) trial and error, or experimentation. In most cases it is more efficient to use experimentation as a last resort and to utilize imaginative trial first.

Imagination trial.   Trial in imagination refers to the facility which human beings have of inventing situations that have not yet occurred and attempting to predict consequences based upon these invented situations.   The elements out of which an imagined situation is built consist of factors that can be recalled from previous experiences, things observed, things heard, and things read.   Technically, the imagined situation is built out of an organization of the data gathered by the problem solver from the various sources available to him.

As an illustration of imaginative trial consider the daily weather prediction.   The forecaster gathers the reports which come into his office from all the other weather stations.   These reports include data on air pressure areas, temperatures, precipitation, relative humidity, wind direction, wind velocity, and so on.   The forecaster plots such data on a map.   He then forms an hypothesis concerning the kind of weather that will occur in his particular locality within the next twenty-four hours. To support his hypothesis he may make a weather map showing tomorrow's weather. Note that the conditions of this second map do not yet exist. It represents the imagined consequences drawn from the data shown by the first map and data on the rate of travel of potential storm areas. In all likelihood, the forecaster will try to verify his imagined weather by comparing his forecast map with the map of actual conditions today and possibly by reference to previous records showing similar weather conditions. In this case there is no way to try experimentally the hypothesis; it must be done by imaginatively projecting a condition that has not yet occurred. There is no proof or disproof until the weather conditions either occur or fail to occur.

Trial and error. On the other hand, there is the story of the college professor who was spending Saturday afternoon enamelling the electric stove in the family kitchen. When he was ready to do the top, he placed the palm of his hand on one of the hot plates to find out whether or not it was hot. The reader can present at once a whole host of other things that he could have done. Certainly, he immediately checked as false his hypothesis that the current was off and the plate cold and with the same stroke proved the solution to his problem. In spite of this, the reaction is that only a fool would resort to immediate experimentation under such circumstances.

The attempt of a girl to fit the pattern for a garment to a given yardage of cloth represents a nice balance of imaginative and experimental trial of an hypothesis. Suppose that the hypothesis is stated something like this: "I believe that with careful planning I can get *this* garment out of the recently purchased remnant of nylon." There follows the spreading out of the goods, the examination of the pattern, the reading of the pattern directions, and certain experimental laying on and turning of pattern pieces, with imagined consequences and rejections. Finally, by way of experimental verification, all of the pattern pieces are pinned to the material. No cutting has yet taken place. Even after the experimental pinning, there will need to be certain checking with directions and with the pattern picture on the package. "Do I have all the pieces? Have I provided for both sleeves? Are the pieces all turned properly?" How foolish it would be to say, "The piece looks big enough," and then begin to cut. How foolish to cut two sleeves for the same armhole without first having done the complete check for all the parts!

The teacher needs to become aware of the essential importance of the stage of imaginative trial in the processes of problem solving. So far as we know, this is an essentially human procedure. Animals do solve problems, but apparently the animal process is that of crude relatively unimaginative trial and error. Human beings can take elements of previous experiences, parts of the experiences of others, excerpts from readings, and recalled observations, and combine these into an imaginative projection that may never have existed. It is possible also to modify this imagined picture to portray the consequences of action which has not yet taken place. This seems to be the peculiar reaction which distinguishes human thought from that of the animal.

The use of imagination in problem solving also constitutes the basic economy in human thought processes. This economy includes economy of time, saving in prevention of waste of materials, conservation of human energy, and finally the prevention of certain types of disaster. This economy is readily illustrated by the processes of scientific invention. Consider, for example, the work of the Wright brothers with airplanes. How many planes did the Wright brothers *not* build? How many did they *not* attempt to fly? How many reached the stage of drawings, only to be rejected in terms of imagined flaws? Suppose they had built and tried to fly the first plane which they may have sketched on paper. What could have been the consequences?

Human beings are confronted with many problems that do not lend themselves to immediate experimentation. Often such problems require a considerable span of time to prove. Many social, political, and economic problems involve so many uncontrollable factors that no one individual can arrive at an experimental verification of any hypothesis concerning their solution. But many of these long-range and complex problems are those of greatest significance to human beings.

Some illustrations of the kinds of problems just described which may crop up readily in school situations are the following. In a class in general biology there is invariably a unit on heredity and genetics. The most crucially important problems of genetics are those of human heredity. Generations of human beings are relatively long. To prove a problem of human heredity experimentally would take years. The first experimenter would be long since dead before any conclusions could be reached. Further, the mores of society do not permit experimentation with human production. If it were permissible, the variable factors in normal human life are so many that they would probably not be controllable by the experimenters.

Should teachers therefore refuse to consider problems of human heredity and bar them from presentation in the biology classes of the schools? Certainly not. It is highly necessary to be able to predict the solutions to some of the problems of human heredity.

So, students consider the known "laws of heredity," gather what information they can from experiments with fruit flies, peas, mice, dogs, and fowl, and try to predict what might under certain circumstances happen to human beings. It is well for the teacher and the pupil problem solver to be aware of the fact that the proposed solution is not yet proved and may not so far be possible of proof. The proposed hypothesis fits all the known facts better than any other hypothesis proposed. This falls within the scope of what was called imaginative trial. Some analyses of the problem-solving process call this *comparison*.

Another illustration of the value and the limits of imaginative trial is found in the large-scale social problem. After World War II, it was proposed by American political leaders and certain other leaders in Western Europe that it should be possible to combat the spread of communism and communist revolution by a policy of military containment of Russia and communist satellite nations and by fighting small wars on the periphery of the containment line.

Supposedly this hypothesis of containment was subjected to certain imaginative trials. The hypothesis was checked experimentally by the continuance of troops in Korea, the maintenance of various armies in Europe, and by the French war in Indochina. It is possible that a further consideration of historical records of the results of previous attempts at military containment and an examination of historical records of attempts to stem the flow of revolutionary ideas by military might could have led to a rejection of the hypothesis and avoided the experimentation by a consideration of other hypotheses.

At any rate there is no present proof of the proposed thesis or of any of the optional ones. Only the sweep of history with time, grief, bloodshed, and tears will offer the proof. And yet the problem cannot be avoided. It is necessary to consider the various hypotheses and subject them to whatever evidence can be gathered in the way of imaginative trials. In high schools, teachers and pupils in American Problems classes and world history classes must come to grip with such problems.

At the same time they must not become cocksure that their readings, discussions, and reports have proved the solutions. Most of the pupils attempting to arrive at sound imaginative trials of the proposed solutions will not live to see the conclusions proved. They may, however, be able to formulate more intelligent modes of behavior as citizens whose voices may be heard and whose votes will be counted in the choice of new leaders.

PROOF OF THE SOLUTION.   In effect what has been said about the processes of imaginative trial is that the hypothesis proposed seems to fit the available and known facts better than any other selected hypothesis.   In long-range problems and those of great social complexity, often this is as far as it is possible to carry attempts at problem solving.   Ultimate proof consists of fitting the tested hypothesis into the conditions out of which the problem originated and determining whether the solution will operate under such conditions.   If a person has attempted to find his way out of a difficulty and the proposed solution will resolve the difficulty so that he can condition his behavior in future similar situations upon it, the solution is considered proved and the problem solved.

It must be noted, however, that in some cases the solution to a problem may work once and only once where undefined chance factors are involved.   Ordinarily a solution is considered proved if it can be shown to work repeatedly under the same conditions.   If the solution works upon first, second, third, and later trials, it is considered that it will always work under the same conditions.   It must be noted further that such proof involves enough control of the conditions to hold them constant during the trials. In many complex problems, it is extremely difficult to control all factors affecting the solution, or in many cases some of the conditioning factors are unknown or undefined.   Proof becomes extremely difficult in such cases or may for the time being be only apparent.

It is said often that history repeats itself.   The obvious flaw in this saying is that possible causative factors underlying the conditions in this era are not those of the previous era.   Therefore, the solutions to problems which may have served in the earlier era may not continue to work in the present one.

In the laboratory, the scientific worker attempts to define and control those factors which may have some affect upon the operation of the proposed solution to his problem.   When he has arrived at an hypothesis which stands up under imaginative trial, he tries it experimentally under his controlled laboratory conditions.   If the hypothesis works out experimentally, he repeats the experimentation until he and others are convinced that the solution will continue to work under the same conditions.   The caution to be observed here is that such a solution to a problem may not always operate because outside the laboratory, the controls are lacking.

An illustration of this latter caution can be found in the rather typical experimentation of the psychological laboratory.   The psychologist works with a problem of behavior.   For obvious convenience, he uses animals as his experimental subjects.   In the laboratory he sets up conditions which isolate his animal subjects from factors which might affect their behavior, other than those with which he chooses to experiment. When he finds that under the controlled conditions his animals always behave in a certain way, he announces a solution to the particular behavior problem under investigation. And yet the animals released from the laboratory may under apparently similar conditions behave differently. Again, what has been determined for animal behavior may not be true for human behavior. The conditions which could be controlled for experiments with animals may not be controllable with human beings. Extreme caution needs to be exercised concerning a tendency to jump at conclusions concerning human behavior, e.g., that of children in school, where the implications derive from apparently proved solutions to animal behavior under laboratory conditions.

USE OF THE SOLUTION. The final stage in problem solving is the continued use of the solution in the future situations in which it will fit. This brings us back to the stage at which the problem-solving process begins. At the point where the accepted solution fails to work, we arrive at a new difficulty and so start the problem-solving process all over again to find a way out of the new difficulty. It is interesting to observe that solutions once proven finally fail to work further because certain factors inherent in the conditioning of the earlier problem change in time, or new factors are introduced. Sometimes added information or new facts point to a *better solution* to an old problem.

Illustrative of this latter point are the changes in health practices and in medical treatments. There was a time when people in the Midwest wore full length and heavier underwear in the winter. Such garments could not be left off before Spring. Colds and pneumonia would have been predicted as a result of premature change of clothing. Such practices have changed for the great majority of people. Were the predictions ever true? Or, what does modern household and office heating and riding in heated automobiles have to do with the changed practice?

Variability of problem-solving process

One of the dangers involved in attempting to outline in general the steps in problem solving is that teachers and pupils may be led to believe that there is only one problem-solving process and that all problems are attacked in the same way. This conclusion often leads teachers of particular subjects to lay claim to their own subjects as having particular virtue in training for problem solving. Other teachers may be inclined to leave the teaching of problem solving to a few teachers and, therefore, neglect the obligation to help young people in learning to solve a variety of problems which fall outside the province of the "preferred fields."

To be quite specific, teachers of mathematics and science often believe in the peculiar virtues of courses in their own fields for education in problem solving. When this becomes evident, teachers of social studies, physical education, art, home economics, and shop may be inclined to leave problem-solving to the scientists and mathematicians.

This tendency has been exaggerated by the scientists and science teachers in their presentation of the scientific method of problem solving, which seems to imply that there is only one scientific method that in and of itself has some particular magic for unraveling any and all problems. Without doubt it would be far more desirable to recognize that there are many *scientific methods,* not merely *one scientific method.* Although the steps which we have just outlined may seem to be the same for any problem, the technicalities of application to problems in different situations and of the use of different resources in solution tend to vary tremendously. For example, the solution to a problem of color effects in a painting is not solvable by the same techniques as those used in the biology laboratory to solve a problem of heredity involving the genes of fruit flies.

Responsibility of the teacher

If it is agreed that scientific methods of problem solving are plural and that the detailed techniques applicable vary with the nature of the materials involved, at once the necessity for a variety of experiences with problem solving in practically all the classes of a high school becomes evident. The teacher in each field, then, must assume the obligation for identifying problems common within his field and for determining the special techniques that may be brought to bear upon them. Each such teacher has also the obligation of furnishing pupils with experiences which will enable them to master such techniques in some degree. The diagrams and logical processes involved in the proof of a theorem in plane geometry are not necessarily applicable to a problem of determining the best treatment for finishing a piece of walnut furniture in the shop. Pupils need school experiences with techniques suitable for solving both kinds of problems.

There is a tendency for teachers to stereotype problem-solving processes in their particular fields, to reduce the process to formula and then teach the formula. Having done this, the teacher assumes that the pupil will transfer the formalized process to any and all out-of-school problems that may be related to the field or subject. There is abundant evidence to indicate that pupils make transfers of problem-solving processes from the formal in-school learning situation to the informal out-of-school problem only when they are taught how to make the transfers. For example, the logical proof based upon the precedent of previous assumption or of previous proof that is used in plane geometry is applicable to situations outside geometry. Most pupils use the thought processes of the geometry proof in nongeometric situations, however, only when shown how these processes can be brought to bear upon the nonmathematical cases.

This means that the application of laws of simple machines from science to the shop must be shown and taught, not assumed. What was said about imaginative trial of the hypothesis in connection with long-range social problems must be demonstrated in its application to problems presented in today's newspaper. The need for a control in a scientific experiment must be carried from the confines of the laboratory to its application in the interpretation of common advertising claims presented in magazines, by radio, and by television.

Pupils in school must be trained to attack a variety of out-of-school problems involving different types of subject matter and differing systems of proof.

Artificial problems

Many of the assignments of high school teachers which purport to be problem-solving assignments are highly artificial. They may be classified better as puzzles rather than as normal problems. They tend to lack the element of awareness or concern on the part of the individual worker with which all true problem solving begins. The distinction which we should make here is that which we commonly make everywhere with puzzles. A friend brings in two crooked nails hooked together and says, "I'll bet that you can't get these unhooked in ten minutes." The convalescent patient in a hospital bed has brought to him a set of numbered blocks in channels in a frame. The trick is to rearrange the blocks in numbered sequence. Many newspapers and some magazines publish crossword puzzles. There are riddles and match trick arrangements. Most of these can be thought of as time-killers for bored people. They become problems only as the bored individual permits himself to become involved with some degree of mild concern. It is just as easy to say, "Go peddle your wares elsewhere. I can't be bothered with unhooking bent nails," or "Who wants to spend time with crossword puzzles if he can engage in challenging conversation with friends, read a worthwhile book, or listen to fine music?"

There is a further characteristic of the puzzle. This is expressed by the impudent adolescent's, "So what!" In other words, the solution to a puzzle has no intrinsic value when it is attained.

In terms of the concern or awareness of the pupils and in terms of value upon reaching a solution, many of the problem assignments of the classroom are mere puzzles. True, some pupils allow themselves to become intrigued with these puzzles temporarily. There are always a few people taken in for a while by most puzzles. On the other hand, probably there are many pupils who may be too polite or too school-conditioned to say, "Why be bothered with this stuff?"

The proofs of theorems in the traditional geometry class tend to be puzzles for most of the pupils. Only the mathematically or logically minded pupils allow themselves to become intrigued with proofs that have been long since proved and which most people are willing to assume. For most people the problems of geometry are in the constructional, household, agricultural, and engineering applications of known theorems, not in the theoretical proofs long since developed by geometricians.

What was said of geometry is true also of much of algebra. Factoring "problems" are primarily drill exercises in the manipulation of algebraic expressions. Some of them represent puzzles. For many pupils there are few true problems. The typical "prose problems" of the algebra texts concerned with rates of travel of boats, trains, and planes are puzzles but are not within the range of immediate concern for most adolescents. The perennial challenge for the high school mathematics teacher is that of finding significant problems for young people that do not resolve themselves into mere mathematical puzzles. The whole of the *17th Yearbook* of the National Council of Teachers of Mathematics (1942) is devoted to source materials for real problems for the mathematics teacher.

School puzzles are not confined to the field of mathematics. The science pupil who is sent into the laboratory "to prove Archimedes' principle of buoyancy" knows full well that the text states the principle and that Archimedes made the discovery before the birth of Christ. He may have a science puzzle but certainly no problem in a true sense.

The pupil in the American history class, whose teacher makes an assignment to prove what might have happened in the reconstruction of the South if Lincoln had not been assassinated, knows quite well that the conditions of the proposed problem violate all the facts of history and that no proof is possible. Should this be classified as a puzzle or condemned because of its impossibility?

It may be admitted that some people enjoy puzzles, at least occasionally. But the teacher should not confuse the puzzle with important and true problems. If puzzles are to be used, they should be introduced frankly as puzzles with no other claims to importance other than that pupils may enjoy struggling with typical puzzles that have entertained many people for a great many years. The teacher will find that pupils appreciate such frankness and perhaps respond more readily to the presentation of the next real problem.

In the past many teachers have been inclined to justify the use of puzzles and various kinds of artificial problems on the ground that such problems furnish training in how to think, although the problems in and of themselves are of no importance. It should be obvious that such claims are based primarily upon a psychology of general discipline. What a pupil may learn as a result of experiences with mathematical puzzles is facility in developing solutions to such puzzles. What else he may learn is at least in doubt. Certainly his motivation in learning particular problem-solving processes is likely to be better if his experiences are directed toward the solution of problems that have significance to him. If there are disciplinary values, these will be diminished in no way because the solutions of the problem seem worth while to the learner.

Sources of significant problems

It should have become apparent that problems of concern to normal people and especially those that seem important to youths are to be found in working with the persons concerned. Most problems are concerned with the application of known principles in unique situations, not with the discovery of new principles. The high school youth is not likely to discover a method of heating homes based upon some principle of heat transference not now known to the physicists and engineers. But he may become concerned with a way to improve the heating of his own home within the limits of the facilities available in his community and the economic limits of his family. The youthful radio "ham" is unlikely to add anything to the known principles of electronics. He may be able to work out a way to improve the reception for his own station within the limits of the equipment he has or is able to purchase. Each teacher should discover what needs for problems of application exist with his own student group rather than attempting to invent or borrow from published sources pseudo-problems pitched at the rediscovery of known principles.

A device for collecting problems suggested by pupils or observed by the teacher in the community may be useful. If problems are to be observed, discovered, or found, each teacher concerned with problem solving should keep a cumulative card file of problems appropriate to his teaching and suited to the maturities of his pupils. Index cards with tabs corresponding to the units customarily used in a course may be used as a means of classifying the cards upon which the discovered problems are recorded.

Whenever a pupil brings in a problem, whenever in conversation with a pupil a teacher finds a need for problem solving, whenever a significant problem situation is observed in the community, whenever the local newspaper raises an important issue, the teacher should record the problem and its possible limitations on a card. Later, pupils and teacher may add suggestions concerning sources of information or bibliography. Often the back of the card may show a record of a solution worked out by a high school pupil or a group of pupils in a given school term. The wider a teacher's experiences with pupils and the more acute his observations of the local community, the more rapidly such a file will grow. The teacher's file of problem situations then becomes a tremendous resource for suggestive problem assignments.

There is a need for an urgent caution in connection with the teacher's problem file. It should not be allowed to drift into a bag of tricks to be used in the same way with each successive class group. Old problems that are no longer pertinent need to be discarded. Variations with new pupils need to be noted. If not added to, renewed, revised, and consistently weeded, the cumulative file of problems drifts back into the puzzles and artificialities which its inception attempted to avoid.

The raising of a problem or its formulation through cooperative planning with a pupil group is a part of the teacher's assignment technique. It may be well to summarize a few simple statements of principles which apply to the raising of problems in the formulation of assignments.[1]

1. Assignment problems should be of a kind which are of concern to high school pupils.
2. Problems used for school work should include problems which normally occur to people out of school.
3. Sources of data to be used in problem solving should be readily available to high school pupils.
4. Problems must be defined and limited for profitable and efficient work.

[1] Additional suggestions of teaching techniques for the teacher in handling problem-solving situations will be found in Chapter 4, pp. 65–66, and in Chapter 12, pp. 255–57, on problem methods.

5. In problem solving, information is to be accepted or rejected in terms of its pertinency to the problem at hand. Pupils need to learn to reject nonpertinent information.

6. Problems used for school assignments should be worth solving.

7. The problems selected for school use should be possible of solution.

8. Problems may be solved by a variety of methods. Young people need to be encouraged in developing ingenious and imaginative approaches to problem solving.

9. Look for problems of application. The pupil may need to identify the principle involved but almost invariably his difficulty is concerned with an application in a situation which is new to him.

10. Problems in assignments should be stated in such a way as to stimulate thinking rather than acceptance of an authoritative ready-made solution.

Nonproblem learning

Although this chapter emphasizes the necessity for learning to solve a great variety of kinds of problems, the teacher will need to see that much learning is not concerned with problems. Modern school literature emphasizes the problem-solving approach and the so-called problem method. Yet there are many learning situations that are not inherently problem solving in nature.

The skills of the shop, the art room, the clothing workroom, the typing class, the gymnasium, and the athletic field are attained by practice and drill techniques. As was said, the lists of "problems" in the handling of algebraic expressions are primarily drill exercises and not problems. Much of English composition, speech, and group singing is learned through practice rather than by reasoning.

The teacher of one of the fine arts must realize that appreciations are largely concerned with emotional responses and that emotional responses are not attained by problem-solving approaches. If the teacher is concerned with emotional reactions to a poem, pupils are unlikely to develop such responses with a problem of proving why the author wrote the poem by citing episodes from his biography.

Teachers of literature, drama, art, and music need to beware of struggling to throw assignments into problem form and of attempting to prove the reactions that should be made if the goals are appreciations.

Human thinking is important. Human beings must be able to solve many problems and to prove the solutions. On the other hand, imitation, practice, drill, and emotional responses are also human and necessary in normal growth and maturing. In the beginning of this chapter it was suggested that problems arise at the point where customary reactions no longer seem to work. This should be kept in mind clearly in attempting to attain a balance among learning experiences of the school.

Subunit implementation

SUBUNIT ORGANIZATION

1. Problems occur in situations in which there is some difficulty for the person concerned.

2. Human being tends to react to situations in terms of learned behavior unless some factor interferes with the learned reaction.

3. Difficulties which often produce problem solving are:
    a. physical difficulties, actual physical blocks to action
    b. conflicts of ideas
    c. conflicts of ideals, attitudes, biases
    d. conflicts of ideals, attitudes, and biases with ideas
    e. lack of satisfaction with a current solution

4. Problem solving is synonymous with the term "reflective thinking" as often used in educational literature.

5. The person who attempts to solve a problem must be aware of the existing difficulty and accept it as his difficulty.

6. The techniques of problem solving differ in different types of situations and in different subject fields.

7. Pupils in school need to be trained to attack out-of-school problems involving differing types of subject matter and differing systems of proof.

8. Puzzle-type problems have limited values. Puzzles should be labelled as such when presented to pupils.

9. Problems must be defined for profitable and efficient work.

10. Trial of hypotheses in imagination is the essence of economical thinking.

11. The teacher should build up a cumulative collection of normal out-of-school problems in his own field.

12. In problem solving, information is to be accepted or rejected in terms of its pertinency to the problem at hand. Pupils need to be trained in the rejection of nonpertinent information.

13. Artificial problems have little training effect upon most pupils.

14. Problems are to be discovered by the teacher rather than invented or borrowed from ready-made sources.

15. Assignment problems should be of a kind which are of concern to high school pupils.

16. School assignment problems should include problems which normally occur to people out of school.

17. Sources of data for problem assignments should be available readily to high school pupils.

18. Problems used in assignments should be worth solving.

19. Problems selected for school use should be possible of solution.

20. Problems in assignments should be stated in such a way as to stimulate thinking rather than the acceptance of an authoritative ready-made solution.

21. Not all learning lends itself to a problem-solving approach.

22. Appreciations in the arts are primarily developed through emotional reactions rather than through problem solving.

23. The teacher should not strain to throw assignments into problem form when other forms of learning are more appropriate to the situation at hand.

THINGS TO DO

1. Examine a list of suggested problems for high school pupils taken from a textbook or workbook in your field. Review these problems critically in terms of their fitting the characteristics for problems indicated in this chapter. Which would you select for use with your pupils? Why? Which are you inclined to reject? Why?

2. Illustrate with five questions and five problems from your own field the difference between quiz questions and problems.

3. List the types, or kinds, of out-of-school situations in your field which present problems to individuals under normal conditions. Are these likely to present problems to tenth-grade pupils whom you know? What evidence do you have to support your judgment?

4. State a typical problem from a course in your field as you would state it for high school pupils. Outline the specific steps to be taken in the solution of *this* problem (not just any problem) as you would attempt to solve the problem. State the conclusion. Is the conclusion what appears to be the best of several hypotheses, or a proved solution?

5. For one high school course in your field make a list of problems that appear to be suitable for ninth-grade pupils. What evidence do you have that ninth-grade pupils may be concerned with some of these problems?

6. Repeat exercise 4 for other problems.

7. What is the difference between a practice exercise and a problem? Illustrate with specific cases taken from your field.

8. List the techniques of problem solving more commonly used in your field. Outline in detail the processes followed in each of these techniques in so far as you can. How can you incorporate these as suggestions to pupils in problem assignments?

9. Enumerate the limitations of proof most often met in your field. Write out a problem assignment in your field which incorporates these limitations as cautions to pupils in their work on the assignment.

HELPFUL READINGS

BILLETT, ROY O. *Fundamentals of Secondary School Teaching.* Boston: Houghton Mifflin Co., 1940. Pp. 87–106.

Treats problem-solving processes under the heading of "learned behavior." See especially pp. 99 ff. Worthwhile, but not easy reading.

DEWEY, JOHN. *How We Think.* Boston: D. C. Heath & Co., 1910.

Contains the analysis of the problem-solving process from which nearly all subsequent analyses are derived. The reading of Part II with its clarifying illustrations is recommended before reading Part I.

FAWCETT, HAROLD P. "A Description and Evaluation of Certain Procedures Used in Senior High School to Develop an Understanding of the Nature of Proof." 13th Yearbook of the National Council of Teachers of Mathematics. *The Nature of Proof.* New York: Bureau of Publications, Teachers College, Columbia University, 1938.

A significant piece of experimentation which shows that the general proof of theorems in plane geometry is transferred to nongeometric situations only when pupils are taught how to make the applications.

GATES, I. A., JERSILD, A. T., McCONNELL, T. R., and CHALLMAN, ROBERT C. *Educational Psychology.* 3d ed. New York: The Macmillan Co., 1948. Chaps. 13 and 14.

The educational psychologists' interpretation of problem-solving processes.

MILLS, HUBERT H. and DOUGLASS, HARL R. *Teaching in High School.* 2d ed. New York: The Ronald Press Co., 1957. Chap. 14.

Chap. 14 is on teaching problem solving in the high school.

NATIONAL COUNCIL OF TEACHERS OF MATHEMATICS. *13th Yearbook, The Nature of Proof.* New York: Bureau of Publications, Teachers College, Columbia University, 1938.

Contains the Fawcett study above with others indicated by the title of the yearbook.

———. *17th Yearbook, A Source Book of Mathematical Applications.* New York: Bureau of Publications, Teachers College, Columbia University, 1942.

Title indicates content.

NATIONAL SOCIETY FOR THE STUDY OF EDUCATION. *41st Yearbook. Part II. The Psychology of Learning.* Bloomington, Ill.: Public School Publishing Co., 1942. Chapter 12 on problem solving.

———. *49th Yearbook. Part I. Learning and Instruction.* Chicago: University of Chicago Press, 1950. Chap. 8.

Application of problem-solving processes in instruction.

———. *53rd Yearbook. Part II. Mass Media and Education.* Chicago: University of Chicago Press, 1954. Chap. 8, pp. 185–87, and chap. 12.

How mass media may be used in problem solving. Points out dangers in propagandist uses of mass media.

SCHORLING, RALEIGH. *Student Teaching.* 2d ed. New York: McGraw-Hill Book Co., Inc., 1949. Chap 7, pp. 171–78.

Suggestions to the student teacher on problem solving in instruction.

TROW, WILLIAM CLARK. *Educational Psychology.* Rev. ed. Boston: Houghton Mifflin Co., 1950. Chap. 12.

See especially sections on guides to correct thinking and scientific method.

———. *What Research Says to the Teacher: The Learning Process.* Department of Classroom Teachers and The American Educational Research Association. Washington, D.C.: National Education Association, 1954.

Section, pp. 24–27, on how children learn to think.

WOODRUFF, ASAHEL D. *The Psychology of Teaching.* 3d ed. New York: Longmans, Green & Co., Inc., 1951. Chap. 16, pp. 301–07.

Further analysis of problem solving processes with suggestions for classroom application.

9

Appreciation Building

What to look for in this subunit

1. What is meant by the term "appreciation"?

2. What special significance is given the term "aesthetic appreciation"?

3. What subjects, or parts of subjects, are concerned largely with aesthetic appreciations?

4. What problems of developing appreciation concern all secondary school teachers?

5. What special problems of developing appreciation often occur with pupils in your own teaching field?

6. How are realizations of new values developed in out-of-school situations?

7. What factors influence the development of normal appreciations outside of school?

8. What is the relationship of skill in performance, or production, to appreciation for individuals of little ability in performance, or production, in a particular field?

9. How is the analysis of "wholes to be appreciated" related to the growth of appreciation in individuals?

10. How is the difficulty of interpretation related to final appreciation? Can you explain this in terms of the psychological expression of the satisfyingness of a response?

11. In normal out-of-school situations, how does the biography of a producer or performer enter into the appreciation of a work of art?

12. What can be done to develop improved appreciations through school experiences in the fine arts?

13. What is meant by a consumer of the fine arts?

14. What difference is there in the appreciations of the consumer and those of the specialist in a given art?

15. What is the responsibility of the teacher in one of the fine arts to the potential consumers in that field?

This unit as a whole has been concerned with the learning activities, or experiences, of high school pupils. For purposes of convenience these learning experiences of young people have been grouped into drill or practice experiences, information getting experiences,

149

problem solving, and appreciation building. The first three subunits (chapters 6, 7, and 8) have been concerned with the first three of these. This chapter, or subunit, deals with the learning situations that are primarily concerned with appreciations.

It must be remembered that much learning cannot be cut distinctly into these categories. The learner's appreciations are not set aside from ideas and information. Seldom does he begin to practice before attaining some degree of appreciation of the thing that is to be practiced. Very probably, as his skills develop with attendant satisfactions, his appreciations are enhanced. However, it seems possible to give needed emphasis to the processes involved in building up appreciations by treating them separately.

At the end of the previous subunit (chapter 8) it was indicated that there are many learning situations that do not lend themselves to a problem-solving approach. It was suggested that appreciations are developed as a result of emotional responses rather than through reasoning. The present chapter, or subunit, explores further the processes that are closely related to the development of appreciations.

Appreciation as awareness of value

In common usage, to appreciate means to value, often to increase in value. The owner of real estate often says that his property has appreciated in value. The investor in stocks and bonds speaks in the same terms. Any awareness or consciousness of value constitutes an appreciation. This seems clear enough. But what is a *value?* A value is something which has worth to the person concerned. Thus appreciation is a consciousness of worth in something on the part of the person concerned.

The things of value may be tangibles, such as our ordinary possessions. A value may consist of relatively intangible relationships between people. "James is my friend." "I love Sarah." Values may also be associated with relatively intangible qualities, traits, or virtues: the love of truth, honesty, being a good sport, democracy, "blessed are the meek," and so on. Values may also grow out of satisfying responses to the senses. Obviously, likes for different foods belong in this category. Most response to music probably belongs here. We respond, also, to color, form, and shape. "This is a beautiful landscape." "What a gorgeous sunset!"

These are by no means all the kinds of appreciations which human beings can have, but these few will serve for the moment to explore the notion of value.

It may be well to point out that all of these values tend to have their negatives. "This watch is no good." "The stone set in this ring is worthless." "James is an enemy." "I dislike Susan." There are such traits as untruthfulness, dishonesty, and bad sportsmanship. There is undemocratic behavior as well as democratic. There are the haughty as well as the meek. There are discordant sounds and clashing color combinations.

SOURCES OF VALUES. What happens to people to establish the values which they may have at any given time? There is no complete answer to such a question. However, some of the kinds of experiences which seem to establish values can be suggested. Customary and long-established satisfying use is beyond doubt one of the kinds of experiences which establishes value. Father values his old hat. Mother and daughters look upon it as a public disgrace, but it has value to Father. Most of us have favorite pairs of shoes or slippers, best-liked chairs, favorite spots in the library, hymns we prefer, flowers we always plant, people we like to be with.

Other values may derive from rarity, difficulty of attainment, envy of people who have, and the urge to be like one's peers. Jeans rolled to the knees have value because the other girls wear them. Diamonds have value because they are scarce and difficult to obtain. If they were as common as pebbles, they might lose their value. The velocipede has value to Billy because for the moment Harry wants it.

Some values seem to be acquired through strong and relatively sudden emotional upheavals. Note that such emotional disturbances are often associated with physical responses too. Such values are illustrated most easily with the negatives. "I no longer eat chocolate." "I'm afraid to be in a house alone at night." "I do not like bearded men." "Grating noises annoy me."

A great many values are attained through association with some previously acquired value. "This *was* my mother's Bible." "This is my wedding ring." "This is Willie's first shoe." "This is the place where we had our first date."

Often an associated value has worth because it can be used as a means of gaining control of some previously existing value of great concern. "I shall save money so that I can have a car." "I shall go without lunch so that I can have a sylphlike figure." "I shall study hard for this course so that I can make an impression on the teacher and he will give me a good recommendation for a teaching position."

Values rest largely upon emotional reactions even more than upon rational processes. Values are *felt* rather than reasoned out. The perennial query, "Why do you like me?" has no rational answer. None of the possible answers make any real sense—"Because you have curly hair," "because you have such beautiful brown eyes," "because you're slim, plump, tall, short, talk so entertainingly or know when to keep still, and so on." But finally simply *because*. All of which means "That's the way I feel."

The doubter here might carry out a little bit of superficial investigation among his friends on why they prefer the cars they drive. What is the advantage of my Ford over the neighbor's Plymouth? Is there any significant reason to prefer a Buick to a Chrysler? Probably a Chevrolet will do anything in the way of useful transportation that a Cadillac will do. A Ford may serve its purpose in congested city traffic and in limited parking areas better than a Lincoln, but try to convey such ideas to the man who drives a Lincoln.

DIFFERENCES IN VALUES. Values vary extremely with individual human beings. Most of our keepsakes are of worth only to ourselves. Often there seems no way to explain the preferences of others for taste in hairdos, choice of friends, wives, or husbands, preferences for strange foods, likes for music, and selection of home furnishings. At least there are often qualities in connection with each of these that are peculiar to the individual who makes the choice or has the taste.

This latter issue is of tremendous importance to all teachers. It means that in attempting to build up appreciations of new values the teacher must know many things about the existing values of the individuals concerned. It should also make the teacher extremely cautious in attempting to impose some uniform standard of taste upon all members of a group. Why should *all pupils* be expected to have tremendous emotional reactions to *Silas Marner?* It is possible that there are other great pieces of literature that many would prefer to read. Do *I* have to like modern art?

Appreciation as a general problem

Wherever a teacher attempts to get pupils to see *values* in what may be learned, the problem is one of appreciation. If a pupil is to work willingly at a given assignment, he must feel, or see, that it is worth doing. This is true for the theme to be written in the English class, the theorem to prove in plane geometry, skill in blocking on the football team, or the bookends to be constructed in the shop. Fundamentally all motivation is a matter of appreciation. The utilization of various factors of appreciation as an approach to motivation in learning will be considered in the following chapter. The remainder of this chapter is concerned particularly with appreciations as they are developed in the fine arts.

Aesthetic appreciation

In secondary schools the teachers who are most often concerned with appreciations in the arts are the teachers of art, drawing, music, literature, poetry, drama, and dancing. Many teachers of other subjects will find large areas of artistic elements within their fields. Aesthetic elements are involved in all of the following: posture in physical education; design and color in clothing and home furnishing; symmetry and geometric form in geometry; balance, fitting, squareness, trueness, finish, in the shop; uniforms and cleanliness in physical education; alignment, freedom from strike-overs and erasures, margins, and centering in typewriting; headings, margins, spacing, alignment, page appearance in English and mathematics papers; enunciation, local accent, pronunciation, and tone quality in speech; people "who appear to be" honest and trustworthy, in sociology.

Teachers of the fine arts or teachers of parts of other fields which involve questions of taste, form, or beauty are concerned with problems of aesthetic appreciation as distinguished from the total of appreciation which involves the awareness of any and all kinds of values. A dictionary definition of aesthetic appreciation suggests that it is a form of appreciation which is concerned with the development of a sense of, or a feeling for, beauty. If the original definition of appreciation as an awareness of value is accepted, then aesthetic appreciation is an awareness of beauty in some form as a value. This definition seems to hold until the teacher runs into various accepted forms in the arts which many people do not feel to have beauty. For example, there are discordances in music; the grotesque in drawing and painting; violent contrasts in most forms of art; literature which deals with the morbid, with squalor, and with the psychopathic; verse which is not rhythmic and has no rhyme; forms of both art and music and some verse which are abstract and symbolic and have no meaning for the uninitiated. A common reaction of those uneducated in the arts to these latter art forms is that they are either ugly or meaningless. This difficulty of definition can be avoided by broadening the meaning of the term "beauty" to include contrasts and negatives or opposites. It might be simpler to say that aesthetic appreciation is concerned with the development of values in the fine arts. Then it is necessary only to list the fine arts or those parts of subjects that have artistic elements, and expect the artists, the artistic interpreters, and the teachers to list and define those values with which they are concerned.

Common problems of appreciation in the fine arts

Perhaps the first and greatest problem for teachers of the arts is that of bringing about the pupils' acceptance of the materials within a given art as having any value at all. The teacher feels that everyone should love the world's great music. Everyone should like to read the classics of literature. All should react with enthusiasm to Shakespeare. Anyone with an opportunity to visit New York City should go forthwith to the Metropolitan Museum of Art and sit enthralled before the great paintings displayed upon the walls.

Problems arise when some teachers discover that there are pupils who seem not to read at all. But, there are those that do read comic books, "whodunits," and westerns. "I hate poetry" is a common expression. The level of art is represented by pinups of movie stars. Music listened to consists of boogie woogie, be-bop, rock-and-roll, or juke box ballads. Shakespeare is dead; let's go watch the latest TV thriller. What can the teacher do to introduce such people to the fine in the arts?

A second familiar problem of teachers of the arts is that which involves the quality of the art, the level of taste, the standard to be set. Common terms used are, "the great," "classic," "fine," "the world's finest," "everyone should know," "masterpieces," and "cultural." Negatives are "cheap," "tawdry," "crude," "lowbrow," "trash," "worthless." Every teacher is familiar with similar terms used to describe those tastes which he considers undesirable in his pupils. The teacher describes his problem as that of developing improved tastes or of raising standards.

Aesthetic appreciations out of school

At least partial solutions to the problems of the teacher may be found by an examination of the ways in which appreciations are formed in normal out-of-school situations. Experienced teachers of English know that in every class there are some pupils who read a wide variety of literature willingly and who at the same time do read and respond to selections of approved quality. As a matter of fact it would be extremely difficult to prevent these pupils from reading. In the same way music teachers find a considerable number of willing listeners to worthwhile music *before* formal experiences in music listening are introduced in the class.

EASE OF PARTICIPATION. If case records of pupils who read before they reach the high school English classes are made, some common characteristics of the pupils are found that are useful to the teacher. First, such pupils *can read* without difficulties. They read with easy comprehension, and they are generally rapid readers. The reading process itself does not interfere with the satisfactions attained in reading. Stated in reverse, the pupil who cannot read well can get little satisfaction out of his reading and therefore tends to shun all reading. This may be one reason why comic books are popular with pupils of low-level literary appreciations. The pictorial representation aids in comprehension, so that the story can be easily followed with understanding and with satisfaction. Text without the graphic aids cannot be read with ease and rapidity by many of these people. In the same way the continuity of a television program or of a motion picture can be followed with relative ease and with considerable satisfaction by the viewer. If the same tale is presented in language only, in oral language or in printed words, many in the audience will follow with greater difficulty and with lessened satisfactions.

The teacher must not misinterpret at this point. Many excellent readers and those with quite good tastes for other literature also read comic books and detective stories, sometimes in wholesale quantities. They also like to watch television.

EARLY EXPERIENCES WITH THE ARTS. A second factor common to the case records of those who read much is that they began early. Some of these people began to read before entering school, in spite of the admonitions of the school reading experts. These are the children who in the first year of school begin to boast by the opening of spring, "I have read thirty books this winter." Of course, the thirty books are primers and first readers. Note that there is implied an exposure to a quantity of reading materials. The case record will show further that many of these children have had libraries of their own books, have had a children's magazine at home, and were accustomed at least to thumb through and examine the pictures in adult magazines before they could read. Many of these children were read to by adults before they themselves could read. These people know Mother Goose, fairy tales, *Alice in Wonderland*, A. A. Milne, legends, and often the Bible stories.

ACCESS TO GOOD MATERIALS. This suggests at once a third factor generally common in the case records of readers. They have had access to a quantity of suitable reading materials. In the homes of these pupils there have been newspapers, magazines, and books. In the elementary schools which they have attended, the classrooms were equipped with extensive and well-selected grade libraries. Often they have had access to other libraries in the local community. In general, reading of literature of acceptable quality is closely associated with the availability of a quantity of suitable materials for the prospective readers.

A study done by a graduate student at the University of Missouri supports this point. The investigator studied the quality of reading of pupils in three small Missouri high schools. She found that the quality of reading of groups of pupils in these schools was in direct proportion to the availability of books and magazines. In the first school the pupils had access to a limited school library and to the magazines available on the newsstand of a local drug store. In the second school the pupils had access to a better-equipped school library and to the library of a small college in the community. In the third school the pupils had access to an adequate high school library, to a well-stocked local library, and to a college library. The reading of pupils in the first school was approximately at the level of the poorer periodicals from the newsstand of the drugstore. Reading quality in the second school was better, that in the third school higher still.

Another investigator in the same institution, working under the supervision of the author, examined the home reading materials available to pupils in a small rural high school in which the reading levels of pupils were distressingly low. This investigator found that there was practically nothing available for reading in the homes of the pupils. Most of the homes had no daily newspaper. A few had the weekly farm edition of a nearby city newspaper. A few had a fifty-cent-a-year monthly farm journal. In several of these homes, the only book was a subscription book on the diseases of farm animals. One wonders what became of the family Bible. Since the library in the high school had only a few hundred volumes and no newspapers or magazines and there was no public library within fifty miles of the school, the pupils read little and the quality of reading tended to be low.

ASSOCIATION WITH THOSE WHO APPRECIATE. A fourth common factor in the case records of good readers is that many of them were continually associated with other readers. In the situations in which they grew up people read. It was the thing to do. No one ever questioned the fact that people spent time reading. Parents read. Friends and neighbors read too. Very often what was read became a center of conversation. Reading was an accepted way of spending time. It is possible to predict that in families and neighborhoods where watching the television programs becomes the way to spend the evening and the accepted way of recreation, pupils of the next generation will have become versed in television themes and will have less conditioning to reading.

Teachers concerned with developing listening in music may well review similar cases of pupils whose listening habits were formed before the time when they entered the music class. It will be found that these pupils have had enough musical experience to listen with satisfaction. These pupils will have listened to wholesale music from childhood. They will have had access to music of quality. They will have had music facilities at home and at school, record collections, attendance at concerts, opportunities for listening to selected music programs by radio and television.

A recent investigation [1] of the abilities of intermediate grade pupils to identify the moods expressed by instrumental music found that many pupils of the described maturity could distinguish the moods expressed by music. In trying to find factors which contributed to this ability, the investigator found that those pupils who preferred to listen to music programs by radio had significantly higher scores on the testing device than did pupils who listened to other types of radio programs. Apparently home listening to music is related to certain forms of musical appreciation.

Teachers of the other arts should review those factors which are identified as affecting the formation of appreciations in the area of reading and literature. It is probable that similar factors affect the appreciations of pupils in all of the arts.

Application of out-of-school experiences to appreciation

CONTINUED CONTACT WITH WHOLESOME MATERIALS. If the factors enumerated hold in the development of appreciations in literature, music, and art in out-of-school situations, how can the teacher manipulate such factors to build appreciations in the classroom? First, pupils must have continued contact with that which is to be appreciated. Each pupil must read much. Each pupil should listen to some music every day. There must be pictures, designs, and colorings always around the pupils. Pupils will have to *live with* those things that are to be appreciated. The "musts" and the "have to's" here are not to be interpreted as compulsions, but rather as continually recurring opportunities and a manipulation of the pupils' school environment. The availability of materials is extremely important.

In the literature class, time needs to be given to satisfying silent reading and to occasional oral reading when something is found by one reader which he feels will appeal to other members of the

[1] Moon, A. C., "The Ability of Intermediate Grade Children to Identify Moods Expressed by Instrumental Music" (Doctoral dissertation, University of Missouri, 1953). Available on microfilm from University Microfilm Service, Ann Arbor, Michigan.

group. The equipment and the arrangement of the classroom should be conducive to reading. Books, magazines, and newspapers should be readily available to pupils on open shelves and on tables in the classroom. Collections should be changed frequently and materials of current concern displayed often. The whole environment of the pupils should be conducive to reading. Some browsing should be encouraged. Obviously the school library experiences can be made an extension of the classroom situation.

In the field of music pupils must have opportunity to listen to well-selected music. Because of the timing of the radio and television programs in relationship to school hours and schedules, record collections are often more effective than radio for listening. The present LP records make a whole host of music selections easily available at reasonable costs. Considerable time should be given to listening. Practically all assembly programs should present some music. Here the school music organizations and those of the community can be utilized. The lunch hour and the intervals before and after school present opportunities for listening. Most modern high schools are wired for sound. With a suitable reproducer and a good school record collection, music can be put into the cafeteria, assembly hall, gymnasium, or corridors. Some schools have a listening room where pupils may listen quietly to music from records. This arrangement can serve the same function for music that the library serves for readers. As a matter of fact, this kind of listening program can be administered through the school library. Some schools have clubrooms sponsored by the student council. Most such clubrooms have juke boxes and record collections. Here is another opportunity for hearing music. The pupils can be encouraged to work on the problem of "What music?".

In the field of art, the school itself should be used to produce an environment which might develop tastes in pictures, design, and coloring. The art room should be decorated with suitable illustrative examples. Too often the art room is a workroom only and possibly the messiest room in the whole school. If the nature of the work to be done in art and in the crafts is such that a workroom is necessary, another room is needed suited to effective showings of samples of student work in art and in crafts. The shop may join the art classes in the displays. These must be changed frequently. In some schools art displays may be borrowed from the outside for temporary exhibition.

The pictures used in classrooms should contribute to the program of appreciation. Often the pictures in the English room, the history room, the science room, and the principal's office have not been changed in school generations. Some of these are school landmarks, like the spot on the ceiling above the stage where the roof leaked in the great storm. Most of these old pictures should be stored. More pictures should be owned by the school than can be appropriately hung at one time. Changes should be frequent. The art classes can be responsible for selection, rearrangement, and hanging. This need not be elaborately expensive. Frames with open backs can be used. Many high-quality prints are available. Colored prints are often effective with modern processes of color reproduction. Corridors and the school cafeteria can be used as display centers. The whole idea is that of using school facilities to surround pupils with the kind of art to be appreciated.

Control of quality. In all of these illustrations, the *quality* of the appreciations developed can be controlled largely by the selection of the materials used. The tastes in reading will be governed to a large extent by the books and magazines selected for the school library and for the classroom collections. The records selected in the development of the music program will tend to determine the levels of listening produced. The pictures displayed throughout the school should reflect the standards of art desired.

Limitations. Two cautions need to be observed in this attempt to determine quality through the processes of selection. If the materials for appreciation are too far beyond the present tastes of the pupils concerned, the program will fail or tend to produce negative results by turning pupils away from the art. For pupils of limited appreciations, the teacher will need to make a very broad interpretation of quality. Often in these cases the standard may be set by such a term as *wholesome* rather than in terms of *high art.* For example, there may be boys in the English class who, the teacher says, do not read at all. If it is proposed that these boys read *Atlantic Monthly, Harper's,* or *The Yale Review,* the game is lost. On the other hand, some of these boys will read, or at least look at pictures in, *Popular Mechanics, Field and Stream, Popular Science Monthly.* The teacher will say that such magazines contain no literature. However, the point is that it is desirable that these boys begin to read and that they form habits of satisfying use of magazines. Moreover, the question of quality is to be determined by the standard of wholesomeness of the content. Perhaps later, the boys can mature into some appreciation of reading that can be classed as literature. Teachers of music and art may consider this same issue in determining the selection of beginning materials for appreciation.

The second caution is the reverse of the first. There are some pupils in every class who come into the class with high level appreciations which may approach the standards of cultivated adults. In selecting materials for these pupils, care needs to be exercised that the quality be kept high. Particularly, avoid materials that will seem to such pupils to be childish or juvenile. Boys at this level will read *Science News Letter,* or *Scientific Monthly,* or Vallery-Rodot's *Life of Pasteur* as well as *Popular Mechanics.* Some of them will read the *Merchant of Venice* with pleasure and satisfaction.

In this discussion of the use of in-school appreciation-developing processes that operate out of school, there is no implication that everyone should appreciate or experience the same thing at the same time. There seems to be no valid argument to support the thesis that all ninth-grade pupils should read *Silas Marner* and discuss it in class. It is difficult to support the notion that all pupils in a given music class should listen to Schubert's "Ave Maria" and have a relatively uniform and satisfying emotional response.

SATISFACTION IN APPRECIATIVE EXPERIENCES. A second teaching principle to be gleaned from the formation of out-of-school appreciations is that the appreciative experiences be satisfying. In practice the application of this principle has three phases. First, in order to attain satisfaction, the pupil must be able to do whatever the experience demands. In reading a given selection the pupil must be able to read it with ease. Few ninth-grade pupils can read Kipling's *Kim* with ease. To listen to a music selection pupils must be attentive to the end. Probably they must identify and follow the theme or melody. Relatively few ninth-grade pupils can listen to a whole symphony with great satisfaction.

Secondly, the content of the selection must arouse a satisfying emotional response. Pupils who tap with their feet, nod their heads, or clap hands for a dance tune or a rhythmic march are achieving such an emotional response. The girls who weep during an intense scene in a dramatic presentation are *enjoying* the drama. The content of the materials selected for appreciation must be consistent with the emotional maturities of the pupils concerned.

Thirdly, the appreciations of adolescents are largely conditioned by limitations set by the approval of their peers. This is readily illustrated by styles. If all the girls in a given set are to appear at the opening of school in sweaters and skirts, this is the accepted style for the set. The temperature may be ninety degrees and all may be acutely uncomfortable, but the girl who appears in a summer print will be unhappy and all attempts of adults to get her to be rational about the choice of clothing in terms of the temperature will not lessen her unhappiness. Boys are just as bound by peer approval as girls, even in matters of clothing.

In selecting materials for appreciation for the arts classes, the teachers must be aware of the limitations of peer acceptance for the particular group and time. What are adolescents now reading? What is the popular music? What dance music is accepted? What motion pictures must be seen? Where do people never go? Although the teacher's selection may not be determined by such limitations, he must know at least that, in order to get results, the attitude of the whole group must be affected. The individual's appreciations will be attained more readily if the gang is with him, not against.

It may be well to summarize those suggestions which derive from observation of the development of appreciations in the arts in normal out-of-school situations. An attempt should be made to surround the pupils with the kinds of things for which appreciations should be built. The contacts of the pupils with the arts should begin as early as possible and the opportunities for contacts should be frequent and continuous. The school should provide a quantity of materials for appreciation—books, magazines, pictures, records, opportunities for listening.

Pupils must be able to attain satisfactions from those experiences which condition appreciations. The content of materials for appreciation must produce satisfying emotional responses. The materials selected must fall within the framework of peer approval of adolescents. All pupils need not react to the same work of art. Quality or standards of appreciation can be controlled largely through the process of selection of materials. The level of appreciation possible with pupils varies with the maturity of each individual. The teacher needs to adapt the standard set in terms of such varying maturity.

Classroom practices for appreciation

What has been said lays a groundwork for attempting to build appreciations in the arts. However, there are certain problems which occur perennially in classes in the arts and frequently lead to confusion in the determination of suitable teaching procedures.

Skill in Performance. One such confusion arises out of the assumption that skill in performance in an art is necessary to attain appreciation of the products or performances of others in the field. For example, "It is necessary to attempt to write verse in order to appreciate the poetry of the great poets." "One must be able to sing to appreciate the singing of others." "We must try to draw or paint in order to appreciate the paintings of the masters."

There is no attempt to deny that poets, playwrights, musicians, painters, and architects may attain levels of appreciation not reached by the rest of us. The problem in the typical school situation is that of the possible level of attainment to be reached by the amateur reactor in these fields. The thesis here will be that some degree of satisfying appreciation is possible for the tyro in the arts.

It may help to make a suggestive classification of potential users of the arts. In this classification there are: first, the creators and producers—poets, authors, playwrights, composers, painters, sculptors, and architects; second, the high-level interpreters of the arts —actors, concert performers, motion picture producers; third, the critics; fourth, the amateur participators—amateur musicians, members of school and community bands, orchestras, choruses, amateur actors, local contributors to magazines and newspapers; and finally, the great audience masses—the readers, listeners, viewers, ultimate consumers.

An hypothetical enumeration of these may help to see the issue. Of a thousand young people in a high school there will probably be about the following numbers of each class described above.

Creators of lasting fine arts	1
Great interpreters, e.g., concert musicians	2
Art critics	3
Amateur participators	494
Audience, listeners, readers	500
Total	1000

Whatever minor variations there may be in allotments to each class, it should have become clear that the great obligation of the secondary school is to the 994. Note that the amateur musician is at the same time a reader of literature and a member of the audience in the theater.

No doubt the member of the school orchestra is aided in his appreciation of music through his participation and performance. Here again the law of satisfaction will tend to govern. If he can play his instrument and carry his part readily enough to give satisfaction, appreciation may be enhanced. This principle will govern in other types of participative experiences in the arts.

The common difficulty is that great numbers of pupils feel that they cannot perform. Perhaps they could learn with great expenditure of energy and time. But there is the feeling, "I can't sing," "I can't draw," "I can't do creative writing." For these, an attempt to force creative efforts or performance as an approach to appreciation is futile. The effect may be to drive the pupil away from the art rather than pull him into it.

This does not imply any criticism of attempts to get pupils to participate in activities involving the fine arts. Without doubt there is need to increase the opportunities for participation of youths in bands, choruses, orchestras, crafts, applied arts, amateur theatricals, public speaking, and creative writing. But it is possible to attain some degree of appreciation as a reader, a listener, or a member of the audience. For those people who feel inadequate in developing skills within the arts, something must be done other than a forced participation.

After all, the readers, listeners, viewers, and audiences are the ultimate mass consumers of the arts. They need help in forming tastes, making selections, and in attempts to interpret what they read, hear, and see. Here is the great opportunity of the teacher of fine arts in the secondary school. Some degree of appreciation may be attained without the development of skills in performance.

ANALYSIS OF SELECTIONS. The teacher of a fine arts class feels something must be done with the selections proposed for appreciation. One alternative is to take apart the poem, play, music, or painting. The process can be called dissection.

The proposal to use the class period for analysis stems from two assumptions on the part of the teacher. One is that appreciation must begin at the top. The beginning pupil must begin with examples of the greatest literature, the finest music, classic art. The specimens chosen for treatment are not comprehended by the beginner. To enable the beginner to understand what the artist was attempting to convey, the work must be taken apart. The teacher fails to see that such dissected works seldom are put back together. The bewildered pupil is left with the fragments. The situation is very like that of the small boy who has taken apart a clock to find out how it ticks and is left with an expanded spring and an assortment of cogged wheels which he cannot reassemble. The clock no longer ticks.

The second assumption which leads the teacher to classroom dissections is that a detailed knowledge of the relationship of the parts and of the artist's techniques of production is necessary to an appreciation of the finished whole.

Suppose a positive counterassumption is set up. A great work of art is to be appreciated as a whole, not piecemeal. The listener reacts generally to a whole piece of music, at least to a whole movement. The reader reacts to the whole poem, not to a phrase, a line, a figure. The viewer sees the whole painting, not the individual daubs of paint. Everyone knows that a painting loses its perspective if examined at close range.

Certain analogies may help to see the value of the whole approach. The design and color of the latest model automobile on the showroom floor appeals to the prospective owner and driver. In driving the new car, the rhythm, the flow of motion, and the feeling of easy control of great power make their impressions. However, for most owners and drivers the car tends to lose its beauty as it is dissected in the shop. The hood is removed. The head comes off the motor. Pistons, gears, pins, and bolts lie in black greasy heaps in pans on the garage floor. The mechanic who takes the motor apart may admire the closeness of fit of the parts and the fine tooling. The owner turns away in distress. The car has lost its appeal as a beautiful whole. Mostly, he wants to know, "When can you have it put back together again?"

What significance has the analogy for the teacher of the arts? The initial presentation of a work of art should be of the whole. The picture should be viewed as a picture. At first, people should hear all of a piece of music. The whole poem should be read. All of a play should be seen.

The first impression should be pleasant or satisfying. The poem should be read aloud by someone who can read, and read well. The narrative should be well told or well read. The rendition of the music should be expert and expressive. This should mean an end to stumbling reading in turn in the class with an expectation that both the halting reader and his auditors are gaining in appreciation. It means that the teacher himself often needs to be a skilled performer and interpreter in his field.

At this point someone always objects, but many works of art need to be analyzed to be understood. A presentation of the whole fails to convey what the artist was trying to say.

The answer to this objection lies in the selection of the work of art to fit the maturity levels of the people in the class. If a work of art as a whole cannot convey its message to the pupils in a given class, that in itself may be evidence that the selection is beyond the maturity of these pupils. The solution is not in prolonged classroom analysis, but in the selection of a piece that can be interpreted. Perhaps later the pupils will grow enough in maturity to be able to interpret the more difficult selection. Pupils who may get nothing from Milton's *L'Allegro* or *Il Penseroso*, may respond readily to the poet's sonnet on his blindness. Some of them may reach an adult stage in which they can respond to the first two poems mentioned. Analysis now will tend to kill the work of the poet forever for the majority.

Length of a selection from literature and perhaps complexity of structure in the graphic arts should be considered. An epic poem is difficult to present as a whole. Some plays put even educated adults to sleep. Some operas and a few symphonies take all afternoon to present. This suggests that in the beginning stages of appreciation building, shorter selections that can be presented as wholes are preferable. It might be well to consider a presentation of Shakespeare's songs before attempting a full-scale play. One-act plays may better serve as an introduction to drama than any of the longer spectacles. Sometimes a movement from a symphony that has entity in itself is preferable as a beginning point to a longer experience with further complications upon the theme. Usually a short story is a better approach to experiences with a narrative than a lengthy novel. In spite of the popularity of the tale, nearly all youthful readers get completely lost with the full original text of Defoe's *Robinson Crusoe*. Some episodes from *Ivanhoe* are exciting and romantic, but it takes forever to read the whole in class.

Very often if a teacher knew his field well enough, he could find acceptable shorter selections from the same "masters" who have produced the lengthy. Scott wrote *The Talisman* as well as *Ivanhoe* and *Lady of the Lake*. It is possible to listen to the "Waltz of the Flowers" or the "Dance of the Sugar Plum Fairy" without hearing all of the *Nutcracker Suite*. Kipling wrote the short stories in *Soldiers Three* and the poems of *Barrack-Room Ballads* as well as *Kim*. It should be possible to find a dance, a march, or a symphonic poem from a great composer. Quite respectable dramatists have done one-act plays. Menotti's *The Medium* or *The Telephone* might serve as an introduction to opera.

With literature, painting, and sculpture it is probable that the best attitude for the teacher to adopt is that the reader or viewer is entitled to make his own interpretation. With music, enough analysis to be able to identify and follow the theme or melody is desirable. Again what the theme *means* to the listener is *his* interpretation.

Perhaps a general rule for the teacher of the arts is that, when inclined to have pupils spend much time in analysis of a work of art, it is time to go lightly and probably an occasion to reconsider the wisdom of selecting the piece proposed.

USE OF BIOGRAPHICAL DETAIL. Another common practice in art classes which seems to grow out of some confusion on the part of the teachers is the presentation of biographical details concerning the artist as an approach to appreciation and understanding of his work. Schumann's life is studied before listening to his music. Poe's biography is read before reading one of his short stories. The life of Michelangelo is assigned before pupils have seen one of his pictures. Is it possible that many pupils are almost totally unconcerned with biographical details of the lives of artists and that many such pupils are lost before reaching the work to be appreciated?

The thesis proposed here is that the thing which lives is the *work* of the artist. If the work is sufficiently good and if it has sufficient appeal, pupils may become concerned about the man who produced the work. Simply, the thesis is that appreciation of the *work* of an artist comes *before* any concern about the artist as a person is possible. If this thesis is sound, in most cases the teacher will reverse the customary order of use of the biography of the artist.

What is proposed amounts to this: The selection to be appreciated should stand on its own merit and appeal. After some degree of appreciation of the selection is attained, the question may be raised, what kind of man produced this piece? It is preferable that the question concerning the producer come from the pupils. "I like O. Henry's short stories. What kind of man was he to have such a keen insight into human nature?" "I like animal pictures. It is remarkable that the best of the pictures we have been seeing could have been painted by a woman. I would like to know something about Rosa Bonheur." "The most tuneful waltzes that we have been hearing seem to be the work of one man. Who was Strauss?"

Perhaps the present thesis will seem less controversial if we take it out of the field of the arts for the moment. What lives about Louis Pasteur? Certain knowledge about micro-organisms, the causes of anthrax in cattle and sheep, the possibility that one of us can hope to survive if bitten by a rabid dog. These important items of knowledge persist. Pasteur died in 1895. If pupils become concerned about the scientific knowledge involved, they may want to know about Pasteur and so read a life of Pasteur. There they can find something of the man, and something about his methods of work. They can find that the process which is known as pasteurization was first applied to the wines in France and not to milk. If it were not for the science which remains, people would not bother to read about Pasteur the man.

There is a further caution to the teacher concerning the use of biography as an aid in the appreciation of an artist's work. Knowledge of the artist may not aid. Indeed, such knowledge may detract from appreciation. Ravel was insane through much of his adult life. Schumann died in a mental asylum. Tschaikovsky is said to have been mentally ill at times. Does this knowledge add to the responses which the listener may make to the music of these composers? Does a knowledge of the details of Byron's life add to an appreciation of his poetry? Sometimes we seem to leave with youths the impression that in order to be a great artist, a person must be a "screwball," a dope fiend, a drunkard, a rakehell, or a polygamist. The contribution of this kind of impression to a deep appreciation of great artistic works is at least open to question.

There is the additional factor that in some cases involving the greatest works of art so little is known about the creator of the work that nothing can be gained from biographical study. Some great pieces of sculpture are marked simply, "artist unknown." Who carved the Venus de Milo? The world's greatest drama is usually credited to Shakespeare. Almost nothing is known about Shakespeare, the man, which can throw any light upon his work. As a matter of fact so little is known about Shakespeare that there has long been a dispute concerning the authorship of some of the plays attributed to him.

However, much great art has a time, place, and social setting. Often a knowledge of the setting can contribute much to an understanding and appreciation of a work of art. *The Scarlet Letter* has a setting in colonial New England. Shakespeare's plays were written and performed in Elizabethan England and staged in a theatre peculiar to the times. Michelangelo's paintings adorn a great and ancient cathedral of the Catholic church. The language of the King James version of the Bible is that of seventeenth-century England and of course the setting is that of the Church of England.

To summarize, biographies of artists are to be used after some degree of appreciation of their work is attained and to the extent that such biographies can lend to the valuing of the work. It may be wise to add that biographies add most as the demand for knowledge of the artist arises from the pupils who have been stimulated through experiences with his work.

SELECTION IN TERMS OF MATURITY. The primary problem of the teacher of appreciation in the fields of literture, art, or music is that of selecting particular works of art to be used with a given group. Often the teacher tends to be pulled between two forces, the standard of the "world's finest" as judged by the critics in the field, and the stage of readiness or maturity of the young learners in the class. An earlier section dealt with the problem of overanalysis of appreciative materials. The common difficulty here can be defined as that of overselection.

Perhaps the problem can be seen more clearly by an analogous situation and diagram. The world's finest literature can be designated as being the "seventh heaven" of appreciation. The literature of this seventh heaven is that which is enjoyed and presumably understood by the literary critics and by a relatively few adults highly educated in the field of literature. The teacher proposes that young people in the ninth or tenth grade strive to reach this seventh heaven within the next three weeks. These young folk are not highly educated adults. Their experiences are limited. They live on the earth, not in the seventh heaven. There are no celestial elevators or rocket ships that will within a few hours transport them from their present earthbound immaturity to the seventh heaven of the literary critics. Any progress in the general direction of the heaven will seem tremendously slow and have to develop from their earthly experiences.

As with all other learning, appreciation is dependent upon such factors as the feeling of need on the part of the learner, the nature of the learner's existing experience, and the degree of satisfaction attained in the learning. (Here the reader may well review the treatment of readiness in chapter 4 on the organization of materials for learning.) For the teacher of the arts this means that selection must be made in terms of the present needs and the nature of the experiences of the particular group of pupils now in the class.

In dealing with the arts it must be remembered that the largest element of experience tends to be emotional. This is peculiarly true of the satisfactions attained from experiences with selections within one of the arts. The reaction is not fundamentally a rational one. One does not appreciate merely because there are good reasons for so doing. He does not enjoy because he is told that it is the proper thing to do. He does not like because the selection meets the proper standards. He reacts in terms of his own emotional responses to the selection at hand. These responses are determined in large measure by his previous experiences with other selections within the same field of art.

Understanding is always related to experience. Some degree of understanding is necessary for appreciation. In literature, limited vocabulary is often a stumbling block. A pupil cannot appreciate a poem or a short story if he cannot read it. Neither can he appreciate well when the teacher reads if the ideas are beyond his range or if he does not recognize the significance of vocabulary items. To appreciate a painting, it is necessary to be able to identify what the artist is attempting to portray. In listening to music, identification of the melody or theme is necessary. Where this becomes lost the listener may be lost too. Enough experience with the tones of different musical instruments and different voices to be able to identify the instrument or the voice carrying the theme may help tremendously.

It is extremely difficult for people to catch the imagery and the figurative expressions of the artist if they themselves lack the experiences upon which the imagery is built. The rippling of the brook probably means nothing to a junior high school pupil who has grown up among the tenements and on the pavements of Brooklyn. The sweep of autumn color of a Missouri landscape in October led Mark Twain to liken heaven to October in Missouri. This may mean very little to the lad from Los Angeles who is unfamiliar with the yellows, scarlets, and greens of hard maples or the darker hues of the oaks in the background. The smooth athletic flow of muscular strength in an Apollo means almost nothing to the high school girl from mid-Iowa who has read no classical mythology. She has seen no Apollos among the corn-fed youths on the local basketball court. What does "Junoesque" mean to her masculine compatriot with even less experience with classical allusions? Even Biblical references are often lost upon modern youths with very limited reading experiences, irregular Sunday School attendance, and perhaps no church affiliation.

In order to begin to build appreciations, the teacher must know something of the nature of the experiences of the pupils, and especially something of the kinds of art selections now appreciated by them. Perhaps a suggestion of a general pattern of approach to selection in terms of an acceptance of the thesis of beginning with the pupils where they now are will be in place.

BUILDING NEW APPRECIATIONS. In the beginning, assume that probably there is no such thing as zero appreciation in any one of the fine arts. Every person of secondary school age, having learned to read, reads something and has preferences for that which he reads. Almost all boys and girls listen to some kind of music, sing, hum, or attempt to whistle. Most people look at pictures, or even collect certain kinds. People do have choices of clothing in both color and form. All these responses represent possible present levels of appreciations in the arts.

Some of these preferences and likes are not those which the teacher or educated adult would like to have young people exhibit. Perhaps some of the existing undesirable preferences of young people can be defined as negative appreciations, below zero. At least, these are tangible and furnish the teacher with a beginning point for building others.

The teacher is to be reminded that not all youths have low-level appreciations. The tastes of some boys and girls in school are quite high, often as high as the teacher's. Some junior high school pupils read very much the same literature as that read by the adults in their families. The music listening of some high school pupils is at a very high level. Some pupils have collections of unusually fine music records. The teacher must know these pupils, too, and build with them from their present levels, not assume that all pupils in a given group have low appreciations.

Next the teacher must admit that the basic elements which make the human appeal in any given form of art, either cheap or fine, are very much the same. The highly colored adventure tale of the pulp magazine is built around the same elements of appeal as *Treasure Island, Two Years Before the Mast,* or *Kon Tiki.* There is the nude over the bar in the tap room of the swank hotel, and there are the nudes of the paintings of Rubens and Titian. There are the headlines in this morning's tabloid and there are also the stories of Cain and Abel and of David and Bathsheba in the Old Testament. The dance tunes of the juke box overemphasize the rhythm, some of them are noisy and brassy, many contain off-beat elements. But there is also the music of Ravel which is sometimes overly insistently rhythmic. What is noisier than Wagner? Who is more often offbeat than Brahms?

So true is this latter assumption that every teacher of the arts must be ready to defend with the pupils the difference between the acceptable and the trashy in his particular art. Why not read a Van Dine mystery when we are told that Poe's *Murders in the Rue Morgue* is a great piece of literature? Why is *Robinson Crusoe* literature and *Swiss Family Robinson* not? Why listen to Strauss and not to Cab Calloway's arrangements?

In order to begin building appreciations at the points where the pupils are two assumptions are proposed:

1. All the pupils respond to something; there are no zeros.
2. The selections preferred by the pupils contain the same elements of appeal that are found in some of the approved selections.

Having established these assumptions a systematic approach is suggested.

1. For any particular group of pupils, first find the things within the the art which these pupils now value.

2. Analyze those things in the art which are now appreciated by the pupils to find the elements which seem to make the appeal.

3. From the range of available selections within the art that can be considered wholesome and relatively desirable find those which contain the *same elements of appeal* as the things now enjoyed by the pupils.

4. Use these latter as the first selections for the class.

In almost every case use several selections rather than one or a few. Be careful not to overshoot the pupils at the lowest level.

Be careful not to insult pupils who can begin at a higher level.

Choose selections that will tend to carry themselves by making their own appeals.

Keep analysis at a minimum. Avoid obvious comments. Never mind details about the artist, composer, or author. Do not try to do too much to the selection.

5. Find other reputable and wholesome selections that can be associated in some way with the original selections chosen.

Possible associations that can be used are: other materials on the same theme; material of the same kind, type, or style; work of the same artist, composer, or author; performance by the same artist or interpreter.

6. Continue excursions into other wholesome and reputable selections based upon any possible associations with the earlier ones. Attempt to raise the standard of later selections proposed as choices. Build relatively slowly.

Be sure that each pupil is able to make the responses needed in working with a particular selection, e.g., that a pupil *can read* his short story or verse.

Do anything that can be done in the class situation to produce satisfaction with the responses to the selections.

Attempt to carry group approval (peer approval) along with the selections proposed for the class.

AN ILLUSTRATION OF APPRECIATION BUILDING. To illustrate the steps proposed, a situation in a junior high school reading and literature class in which there purported to be a high percentage of nonreading boys is described.

Investigation with the boys revealed that it was not exactly true to say that they did not read. Rather, what they read did not have the wholehearted approval of educated parents or of the English teacher. What they read consisted mostly of highly colored adventure tales from the pulp magazines. Others seemed not to read much in books or magazines, but they did read comic strips, better characterized as adventure strips.

Knowing the kind of reading matter appreciated by these boys, the elements of appeal in the highly colored adventure tale are as follows. The stories deal with strange and unusual places, perhaps with unusual modes of travel. At present this may involve expeditions into interplanetary space in flying saucers or space ships. The characters are almost all males. Boys in this group are not particularly concerned with women and girls in their stories. The male characters are rough and rugged. There is the element of hero worship for the leading character. There is usually an obvious villain. The action is swift. There are frequent fights or battles. Frequently there is mystery and suspense. In the more appealing of these adventure stories there is a young character of approximately the age of the boy reader. This latter characteristic makes it possible for the boy to fit himself into the character of the lad in the fiction and more actively participate in all of the episodes of the adventure.

The next step for the teacher is an attempt to answer the question, "What selections from reputable literature contain most of the same elements of appeal?" The first response will likely be Stevenson's *Treasure Island*. An analysis of *Treasure Island* indicates that it contains all the elements of appeal of the adventure tale except space travel. The only difficulty with *Treasure Island* as a selection is that many of the boys will have read it along with the "trash." Other selections that come to mind are Dana's *Two Years Before the Mast* and Kipling's *Captains Courageous*. The fact that all of these have appeared in motion picture form may be an asset. Other possibilities can be found in Jules Verne's *Twenty Thousand Leagues Under the Sea* and *From Earth to Moon*, although they are not considered to have the literary merit of those first proposed. Melville's *Typee* and Defoe's *Robinson Crusoe* will occur to many readers.

There should be little difficulty in getting the boys to read any of the selections proposed providing their reading skills are such as to permit them to get satisfaction out of the reading. A clever teacher with adequate acquaintance with literature should be able to list at least fifty more such selections. There is this possible difficulty. These are full-length books. Much of the adventure reading of the boys has been with short selections often from magazines or strips. It may be well to include in the early proposals adventure literature in short story form, perhaps some from current magazines.

How is the transition to be made to other literature? Suppose that a beginning was made with *Captains Courageous*. The boys should respond to other sea stories. Perhaps some of the boys will say, "We liked this last book. Did Kipling write anything else that we could read?" Suggest that Kipling did write some very adventurous and amusing tales of soldier life in India. The transition to *Soldiers Three* should be easy. Again, the boys may respond, "We liked Sergeant Mulvaney and his companions. What else did Kipling write about soldier life in India?" Suggest that some of the *Barrack-Room Ballads* deal with soldier life in India. Please note that probably the boys will want to know about the books that Kipling wrote that they will want to read. They probably will not want to know much about Kipling himself or how he lived.

If this chain of association can be made to work, it should be possible to get a group of boys to begin reading with picaresque sea tales and move through the short story to the reading of selected verse. If in the beginning it had been proposed to these boys that they should read poetry, the response would have been decidedly negative.

It should be remembered that the preceding paragraphs illustrate a process. The actual selection for a given class group will have to be developed for that particular group. There is no guarantee that the illustrative case will work with any other group of junior high school boys.

The process illustrated is workable for selections in art and music. Teachers familiar with materials in these fields should be able to illustrate the process as an additional contribution to thinking about how to approach the *building* of appreciations in the arts.

This chapter has been concerned largely with the question of how aesthetic appreciations are developed. There may have been a tendency for teachers of social studies, mathematics, science, and vocational subjects to be complacent about the treatment of the chapter with the attitude that after all these problems concern only the teachers of fine arts.

It may be well to close the chapter, as it began, with the suggestion that the basic approach to appreciation within the arts is merely one phase of a larger process which operates for all kinds of appreciations. The following chapter deals with the over-all approach to motivation. Since motivation is dependent essentially upon an awareness of values, it seems desirable that all teachers follow the suggestions concerning the processes contributing to the development of appreciations as an introduction to and a means of better understanding of the larger problems of motivation.

Subunit implementation

SUBUNIT ORGANIZATION

1. Appreciation is an awareness of value.

2. All teachers should be continually concerned with problems of appreciation.

3. Aesthetic appreciation is an awareness of the values that are peculiar to the fine arts.

4. A useful partial definition of aesthetic appreciation is found in the statement that aesthetic appreciation is awareness of some form of beauty as a value.

5. Teachers of fine arts are primarily concerned with aesthetic appreciations.

6. The fine arts include such fields as literature, poetry, drama, painting, sculpture, crafts, architecture, music, opera, and dancing.

7. Realizations of value, out-of-school, are built by forming associations between existing values of individuals and those other values needed for better control of the existing values.

8. In the fine arts, skill in performance or production is not uniformly necessary for some degree of consumer's appreciation.

9. Appreciation in the fine arts is concerned usually with wholes. Overanalysis may kill appreciation for the nonspecialist.

10. New appreciations must be related to existing ones and not too far removed in level of maturity. Appreciations grow and are seldom reached by broad leaps.

11. The thing to be appreciated must produce some satisfaction in the learner. The process of learning to appreciate should not set up dissatisfactions.

12. Appreciation in the fine arts must begin with the individual at his present level of appreciation rather than where the teacher wishes him to be at the end of his training.

13. Appreciations may be negative but are rarely zero.

14. Biographies of producers or performers in the arts contribute to appreciation only after the learner has developed some appreciation of the work of the artist. The work is the thing to be appreciated, not the individuality of the producer.

15. Most fine arts appreciation for high school pupils should contribute to the needs of consumers of the arts.

16. Exercises for appreciation should appeal to the existing values of high school age people but move in the direction of socially approved standards.

17. Experiences in the arts should *begin* with cleverly chosen selections which tend to make their own appeal, not with personalities of the artists or producers.

18. As far as possible, art experiences should surround the learner with the things and values which he is to appreciate.

19. In many cases, the in-class experience with a selection from the arts should stand on its own merits and be left alone with a minimum of formal analysis or comment.

20. Selections from the arts for school experiences should be chosen for their fitting into the emotional and artistic needs of young people rather than being chosen to illustrate periods in the evolution of the arts as such.

THINGS TO DO

1. Select some value of your own, about which you feel that you have a real concern. Analyze and describe as well as you can how you have happened to develop an appreciation for this value.

2. List values that exist in a course in your subject, which you believe should be possessed by high school age pupils.

3. Find a typical high school age boy or girl whom you know well. In one column list twelve key values appreciated by this person. In an opposite column present evidence for the existence of each of these values for this individual.

4. Select some one of the fine arts—drawing, art, music, crafts, literature, drama—in which you had grade school or high school experience. Enumerate the processes carried on in school by the teachers in this subject, presumably to develop better appreciations. Which of these processes aided you in developing improved tastes? Which seemed to you to develop a dislike for the subject? Can you give specific instances on either side?

5. Outline a program for developing improved appreciation for the "consumer" in one of the following situations?
   a. A liking for worthwhile poetry for the enjoyment of leisure.
   b. Improved taste in the selection of literature from current magazines.
   c. A liking for folk music.
   d. A liking for music above the jazz, boogie-woogie, or rock-and-roll level.
   e. Better taste in the selection of color combinations in clothing.
   f. Improved taste in the selection of designs for house furnishings.
   g. The selection of worthwhile motion pictures for temporary entertainment.
   h. The selection of novels for vacation reading.
   i. The selection of worthwhile television programs.

6. Criticize briefly current teaching methods for building appreciations in a fine arts field that interests you.

7. Lay out a proposed technique for developing appreciations in some one of the divisions of the fine arts.

8. Analyze the out-of-school processes by which pictures, dramas, songs, or books become popular. Outline your analysis. Can you suggest how this process might be applied in teaching a course in the fine arts in high school?

HELPFUL READINGS

BILLETT, ROY O. *Fundamentals of Secondary School Teaching*. Boston: Houghton Mifflin Co., 1940. Chap. 14.

A pertinent and useful chapter on music and art in the secondary school.

BURTON, WILLIAM H. *The Guidance of Learning Activities*. New York: Appleton-Century-Crofts, Inc., 1952.

See p. 129 for definition of appreciation only.

CROSS, E. A. and CARNEY, ELIZABETH. *Teaching English in High Schools*. Rev. ed. New York: The Macmillan Co., 1951. Chaps. 2, 3, 18, 19, 20, and 22.

Chaps. 2 and 3 are on trends in English in secondary schools; chap. 18 on the treatment of the short story; chap. 19 on novels and adventure and mystery stories; chap. 20 on poetry; and chap. 22 on the use of newspapers and magazines.

DARRELL, R. D. *Good Listening, A Guide to the World's Best Music.* New York: Mentor Books, 1955.

Paper back. Title indicates content. Includes a preferred listing of long playing recordings as of the date indicated. An illustration of the kind of information which the music teacher needs. Listings of recordings will need to be brought up to date with later comparable publications.

DEWEY, JOHN. *Art as Experience.* New York: Milton Balch, 1954.

The title indicates the point of view.

DEWEY, JOHN, et al. *Art and Education.* Merion, Penn.: Barnes Foundation Press, 1947.

A suggestion for "enrichment reading" for the superior student expecting to teach art.

DYKEMA, PETER W. and GEHRKENS, KARL W. *The Teaching and Administration of High School Music.* Chicago: C. C. Birchard & Co., 1941. Chaps. 2, 27, 32.

Contains many useful suggestions on practices in music education.

FAY, LEO C. *What Research Says to the Teacher: Reading in the High School.* Department of Classroom Teachers and The American Educational Research Association. Washington, D.C.: National Education Association, 1956.

Read and reread the paragraph at the top of p. 27 on reading in literature.

GATES, ARTHUR I. *What Research Says to the Teacher: Teaching Reading.* Department of Classroom Teachers and The American Educational Research Association. Washington, D.C.: National Education Association, 1953. Pp. 6–7.

Supports the general theses of the need for exposure to a quantity and variety of reading materials and of the spread of reading through contacts with others who read.

KLAUSMEIER, HERBERT J. *Principles and Practices of Secondary School Teaching.* New York: Harper & Bros., 1953.

Chap. 12 presents "principles and practices" as applied to the teaching of appreciation.

MURSELL, JAMES L. *Music and the Classroom Teacher.* New York: Silver Burdett, 1951.

Music teachers should read. Others will be interested in the point of view on appreciation.

NATIONAL COUNCIL OF TEACHERS OF ENGLISH, THE COMMISSION ON THE ENGLISH CURRICULUM. *The English Language Arts in the Secondary School.* New York: Appleton-Century-Crofts, Inc., 1956. Chap. 5.

Ways to achieve appreciation in literature. Selection of content and the management of reading programs are emphasized.

NATIONAL SOCIETY FOR THE STUDY OF EDUCATION. *40th Yearbook. Art in American Life and Education.* Bloomington, Ill.: Public School Publishing Co., 1941. Chaps. 21, 23, 27, and 29.

Stresses the point of view that applied art can be good art and worthy of appreciation. Emphasizes art for the consumer.

——. *35th Yearbook. Music Education.* Bloomington, Ill.: Public School Publishing Co., 1936. Chaps. 1, 2, 3, and 10.

Chapters from various specialists in music education. Stresses importance of appreciation for all.

——. *47th Yearbook. Part II. Reading in High School and College.* Chicago: University of Chicago Press, 1948. Chaps. 6, 7, and 8.

Approaches to reading for appreciation. Stresses the importance of facility in the reading process as fundamental to appreciation. Supports contact with a wide range and variety of reading materials and of association with others who read.

———. *49th Yearbook. Part I. Learning and Instruction.* Chicago: University of Chicago Press, 1950. Chap. 7.

On the psychological background of appreciation as a process.

———. *53rd Yearbook. Part II. Mass Media and Education.* Chicago: University of Chicago Press, 1954. Chaps. 7 and 11.

Possibilities and pitfalls in the application of mass media to the arts.

SEASHORE, CARL E. *In Search of Beauty in Music.* New York: The Ronald Press Co., 1947.

An introduction to the science of music. Each chapter opens a new avenue of approach to the psychology of music and esthetics.

TROW, WILLIAM CLARK. *Educational Psychology.* 2d ed. Boston: Houghton Mifflin Co., 1950. Chap. 16.

The psychological aspects of aesthetic learning.

WOODRUFF, ASAHEL D. *The Psychology of Teaching.* 3d ed. New York: Longmans, Green & Co., Inc., 1951. Chap. 16, pp. 295–99.

Stresses the importance of emotional responses in appreciation.

Unit V

How Can the Teacher Direct Learning?

If learning is conditioned primarily by the activities of the learners, the chief function of the teacher becomes that of the direction of the work of the people in the group assigned to him. Some of the problems of the teacher included in the direction of learning experiences of pupils are: the stimulation of interests; planning work to be done, the setting up of appropriate teaching procedures; the direction of work and study; and the management of pupils.

As a teacher you will be expected to become familiar with acceptable teaching practices and to develop some skill in carrying out those processes. It is to be hoped that what is presented here will find immediate and direct application in the classroom situations in which you will find yourself. You will be expected to learn to analyze teaching situations in terms of the principles of learning involved and to plan desirable pupil experiences in terms of such analyses and in terms of the goals established. The experiences proposed for this unit include a beginning attempt at unit planning on the part of the prospective teacher.

In the previous unit, school situations were presented in terms of the pupils' learning. Every effort was made to make the pupils the center of the stage. Their reactions were of major concern. In the present unit it will be expected that you fit yourself into the

179

teacher's role and, in the various school situations described, raise the question, "If I were the teacher, what would my job be?" Unit four was concerned primarily with the activities of pupils dominant in learning. This unit will be concerned with the activities of the teacher in his attempts to direct learning and to provide suitable situations in which effective learning can take place. This unit deals frankly with the methodology of the teacher plus his planning and the management of pupils in the classroom.

The unit begins with the attempts of the teacher to find and maintain interests in the learning at hand. It proceeds to the problems presented in modern unit planning. Next the selection of those methods appropriate to any given learning situation is considered. Finally, attempts to direct learning outside the classroom and those management factors which can develop desirable conditions for learning are treated.

10

Motivation

What to look for in this subunit

1. What are the relationships between the teacher's processes of motivation and those of appreciation?

2. To what extent are interests to be found, or discovered, rather than created?

3. What is the distinction between the appeal to "generic values" and the appeal to "immediate values" of pupils?

4. What weaknesses occur in motivation by appeals to generic values?

5. What two types of analyses must the teacher learn to make in order to build better motivation in his own classes?

6. How can the teacher learn to find the values of pupils?

7. How does the teacher determine the values which should exist within his own courses?

8. What is to be done with unmotivated subject matter?

9. What are the flaws in "gingerbread motivation"?

10. Which pupils within a group can be reached by appeals to competition?

11. How can individual improvement be used as motivation?

12. Explain: "Selection of appropriate subject matter is the key to the best motivation."

13. What should a unit introduction contain?

The final chapter, or subunit, of the preceding unit was concerned with the ways in which appreciations are developed. Special emphasis was given to aesthetic appreciations. Appreciation was defined as an awareness of values. It was further emphasized that new values are developed in relationship to those which exist with the learners at any given time and that readiness in the development of new appreciations is largely conditioned by the appreciations now in existence with the learners.

This chapter, or subunit, will be concerned with what the teachers of various subjects can do to motivate learning. The perennial and colloquial expression of the teacher's problem here is expressed by the plaint, "What can I do to get my pupils interested in the work they are supposed to do?" Or, "How can I get pupils interested in my subject?" Perhaps in the modern school the teacher says, "How can I find the interests of my pupils?" Or, "How can I persuade my pupils to express their interests?"

Interest and appreciation

In the shift from the pupil's development of appreciations to the teacher's problems in building interests, much of what is done is to insert new terms for very similar processes. If a return is made to the basic definition—appreciation is an awareness of value in something—it is possible to say that if a person appreciates a thing he also must have interest in it. Or, to reverse the statement, if a person is interested in something, he is at the same time aware of some value in it, at least for him.

As an illustration, a music teacher discovers that one of his pupils collects jazz records. It would seem obvious that these records have some *value* for the pupil and further that the teacher is justified in assuming that the pupil has some appreciation of jazz music. At the same time it is possible to say that the pupil is interested in jazz. Further, the teacher should find it relatively easy to transfer some of this interest to other highly rhythmic and off-beat music selections. Do you suppose that a physics teacher who is working with this same pupil could get him interested in the physics of tone production of the piano, the trumpet, the clarinet, the saxophone, or the bass viol?

A popular and relatively superficial approach to problems of interest is to ask people to tell what interests them, what they like, or what they would like to do. Indeed some serious studies of school practice have used just this procedure. However, this kind of approach to interest is often misleading. A person interviewed may say that he is interested in improving the parking facilities in his community. If at the same time this individual does nothing that may lead to parking improvement, his interest may be questioned. A good church member expresses great interest in getting a new organ for the church. When the canvass for funds is made, the member contributes two dollars toward a fifty-thousand-dollar organ. How great and how sincere is the interest? In general, actual behavior is a better index of values, or of interest, than a mere statement of likes or dislikes. For this reason, the illustration on jazz music begins with the boy who collected records rather than with the boy who just said, "I like jazz music."

The teacher who has become superficially enthusiastic about pupil participation in planning school experiences may be tremendously fooled about the true interests of the pupils by merely attempting to follow the expressed wishes of the majority. Sometimes there are pupil groups whose values at the moment lie in mere activity, noise, confusion, and the avoidance of work. The biology class that urges the teacher to use the afternoon for an excursion to collect aquatic insects may be interested in aquatic insects, but they may be interested in not having to spend an afternoon in reading relatively difficult text material in biology, or just in getting out of doors and poking around in water and mud.

The development of interests is dependent upon the values which pupils have. Interests can be developed if the learner can find out that the thing of potential interest is related to a value which he now has. Or better still, interests can be developed if the learner can be convinced that the thing of potential interest can be used for *better control of some value* which he now has. Remember, however, that behavior reactions are better clues to the present values of learners than statements of likes and dislikes.

In the truest sense the teacher finds or discovers the interests of pupils rather than creating or developing them. At least, in order to develop apparently new interests, the teacher must find out what values the pupils now have.

A teacher of history works with a high school group for several weeks. He becomes discouraged and says that this group has no interest in history whatever. Probably his sweeping statement is not entirely true. Most of the pupils in the group have certain present values that are in some ways associated with the historical. The teacher just doesn't know enough about his pupils or is not at all clever in developing historical associations with the values which he finds the pupils have. Suppose that the group in question is an eleventh-grade group and most of the pupils are sixteen years old. It is probable that some boy in the class collects stamps. How can one collect stamps without having some degree of historical interest? Another of the boys reads historical novels. One of the girls is concerned with costume design. Another of the girls comes from an old family in the community and has great family pride. The mother of another of the girls is a specialist in antique furniture. A boy collects guns. Another is an ambitious would-be politician. The teacher must first find these interests and values, and anything that can be done with interest in history must grow out of them.

The process of developing interests can be described generally as follows. A person is found to have a value which he has only partially attained. The value stands as a goal to be reached. Anything which can be made to seem useful in reaching the goal, or in controlling the value, can gain interest through the association. Diagrammed the process appears as in the figure below.

The person ──────────────────→ Something ──────────────→ Value to
                                that may   be reached
                                help in
                                reaching value

For example, suppose a boy of junior high school age wants to own a bicycle. He may be willing to carry a paper route on foot in order to get money to buy the bicycle. The unattained value is the ownership of the bicycle. The boy is interested in the paper route insofar as it will help him to get his bicycle. His interest in money is also related to the bicycle. He has some degree of interest in *walking* the paper route, at least until he has the bicycle upon which to ride. It is possible that the teacher of his arithmetic class at school could get some interest in certain simple accounting problems and in improved accuracy in addition, if the boy can see that he needs the skills in keeping the records of his paper route straight and, therefore, attain more readily and with less effort the desired bicycle. To make this approach effective the teacher must find out the value now motivating the activities of the boy. The teacher must know about the bicycle and the paper route and make a clever association of the arithmetic processes with them. It should be equally clear that other members of the class probably have other values and will not be motivated with accounting problems associated with a paper route and the acquisition of a bicycle.

Classification of pupil values

At this point it seems useful to set the potential values that motivate human beings into certain categories. Values may be characterized as *generic* or *immediate*. They may be grouped also as *static* or *dynamic*. These two proposed classifications are not mutually exclusive. Certain values can be classified both ways.

GENERIC AND IMMEDIATE VALUES. A generic value is one which has a very wide general appeal to most people in a great variety of situations. Some of the generic values are negatives easily recognized as the common fears of human beings. Illustrations of generic values are: concern for the members of one's immediate family, the adolescent's response to the approval or disapproval of his peers, fear of being smashed in an automobile accident, responses to rhythm, bright color, movement, an urge to surpass the other fellow, wanting to possess things that other people have, and many others.

Values in this category tend to be timeless. Our grandparents responded to most of these same values. Probably our grandchildren will still respond to them too.

An appraisal of the appeal of common generic values can be made by an analysis of the appeals in current advertising. Materials useful in doing this are billboards, magazine advertising, radio and television commercials. Automobile tires are often sold through emphasis upon tread designs that are supposed to give a better grip upon slippery pavements and therefore provide safety from the turnover on a curve which many drivers fear. Life insurance is sold by an appeal to the concern of the purchaser for the welfare of members of his family. Life insurance as such is of no immediate value to the buyer. He will be dead when the benefits are collected. Many commodities to be sold are introduced by feminine models. Who does not respond to a pretty face and a graceful figure? How much of the appeal in automobile selling is rooted in a kind of snobbery, a car that has a longer wheelbase, a motor with a higher horse power, an interior with more luxurious fittings than the neighbors? How much selling is based upon the urge to be like everyone else? A million people buy this soap. A million people can't be wrong. Therefore, you too must use this soap.

Some school motivation is at the same level. "The critics all agree that this is a fine play. Therefore, you must see it and must like it." "Thousands of people have enjoyed this great music. You are musically illiterate and uncultured if you do not like it too." "This is great nonobjective modern art. Everyone *who understands art* should respond to its appeal." "Aren't you ashamed of the behavior of the students in our assembly today? What do you suppose parents would think if they knew about it?" All of these are appeals to generic values. Can you put your finger upon the particular value in each case?

Immediate values are those that make specific appeal to particular invididuals *now.* "This was *father's* watch." "It is old fashioned. You couldn't even pawn it. No one else wants a watch of that kind." "But it keeps good time and *I* prize it because it belonged to father." Why do some men marry the women they do? Why did some women select the husbands they have? Harry wants to be an anthropologist. No one else in his class even knows what the word means. Sarah wants to be a florist. Bill collects bugs. Patricia wants to appear in television shows. All these ambitions and interests are immediate values.

DYNAMIC AND STATIC VALUES. Values can also be classified as *static* and *dynamic*. A static value is one that stands still, that can be attained and passed by. A dynamic value is one that moves ahead, perhaps can never be completely attained nor controlled.

To revert to the diagram of the motivating process on page 184, those things which are motivated by a goal which stands still may be abandoned when the goal is reached. The junior high school boy may abandon his paper route when he has acquired his bicycle. The politician makes abundant promises in his campaign. Sometimes he forgets the campaign promises when he has been elected to office.

If the goal to be attained is not static but moves ahead of the person motivated by it, the intermediary values will tend to be kept so long as they are necessary to the pursuit of the moving goal. High-level professional ideals tend to fall into this category. I desire to be an effective teacher. This motivates my study of research investigations in the psychology of learning and my continued observations of the behavior of young people. I can never cease these studies and observations because the moment I do, I tend to lose my effectiveness as a teacher. If a politician is motivated by high ideals of service in representing his constituents, he must be careful in making campaign promises and at the same time continue to struggle to get something done about those made *after* he is elected to office. A man with an ambition to be a great surgeon must continue to keep up with all those things which contribute to the profession of surgery. New developments in the field of surgery are such that at the moment the surgeon ceases his quest, he begins to lose that which might keep him in the ranks of great surgeons.

Motivation through the stronger values

Many of the school values often used by teachers in attempts to motivate school work which seems to the pupils dull and of little worth are both generic and static. Among these are school marks, certain types of school awards, fear of not being promoted with the group, fear of failure, loss of prestige with parents or other adults.

A difficulty with the school mark as a motivating value is that it tends to be an artificial school device of less consequence outside the school. The mark is not associated closely with values which should be inherent in work of a given course. The same mark is used without distinction as bait in all of the courses pursued by the pupil. Marks are used as appeals from year to year throughout a pupil's whole school experience. There are no relationships to the immediate values of any particular pupil. Marks are held up as desirable to every Tom, Dick, and Susy in every class every year. Marks may serve as motivators for those pupils for whom they are associated with more personal values, as pride in achievement, a means of securing parental approval, or an indication of having won over other near competitors in a competition. For those pupils who have already lost these other more personal values, marks have little motivating force. For the pupil long since accustomed to receiving "F" and "D" marks, the appeal to work harder to receive a "C" or "B" has practically no effect. To the pupil who knows that he commonly receives "C's" in all his work, there is no appeal in striving for an "A".

In the appeal to marks as values there is the further difficulty that a particular mark is static. Having once had the mark set on the school records, the pupil can proceed to forget all that he tried to learn in getting the mark. The exaggeration of this is shown in the occasional book and paper burning in celebration of the completion of a disagreeable course. "The marks are in. Hurrah! We do not have to suffer any more. Let's get rid of all that reminds us of the course." Even superior pupils who make high marks, where the marks have been the chief goal, tend to slough off the temporary learning built up in the attainment of the marks.

What was said about marks applies also to other related artificial school values such as credit in a course, meeting a requirement for graduation, or being eligible for interscholastic athletics.

Better approaches to motivation are to be found in appeals to values that are immediate and dynamic. For a particular course the teacher needs to hold up to pupils things of truly significant value inherent in the course that can be closely related to the things which the pupils now desire. To be able to do this, knowledge of values of individual pupils may operate better as motivating material than knowledge of adolescents in general. It may be well to review here what was said about readiness in chapter 4.

Dynamic values of pupils tend to be those that have relatively long-range effects. They include ideals, ambitions, vocational and professional choices. Possibly a certain amount of hero worship can be placed in this category. Illustrations are found in the boy who wants to be a doctor, the girl who has an urge to be a nurse, the would-be musician, the concern with hot rod cars, the girls' ideals of personal appearance and grooming, the urge to find out all that can be found about radio, planes, photography, or electronics. If the content of a selected course in high school is closely related to one of these long-range urges and the pupil can find satisfaction in the relationship, the teacher should find no difficulty in motivation. The teacher is fortunate to find a pupil who has set up a professional goal and tries to relate his high school experiences to the attainment of that goal. The teacher should have no difficulty in the motivation of a course in physics for a would-be engineer. On the other hand, the teacher of a stereotyped course in period literature may have great difficulty with the same lad. However, the teacher who is willing to work with the boy should be able to find a considerable number of literary selections that will appeal to the young engineer. It is also possible that the embryo engineer has other values that can be reached through literature and not through physics and mathematics.

Motivations are stronger and more effective if appeals are made to immediate and dynamic values. It is also true that appeals to generic and static values are often ineffective or tend to lose in appeal as the static values are attained. It takes a clever teacher to find and work with the immediate and dynamic values of varying and different individual pupils. Almost any relatively stupid teacher can appeal to hard work to make the next higher mark or threaten with fear of failure or lack of promotion.

Teacher exploration of pupil values

In many ways the motivation process is one of tying together or associating two sets of values. One set is to be found in the values of pupils. The other set of values consists of those which are inherent in the body of subject matter or the patterns of behavior to be learned. In order to aid the pupils in tying the two sets of values together, the teacher must have made some explorations into both. It is impossible to tie two things together if one cannot be identified. This means that an effective teacher must be almost continually professionally observant. He must be alert to the behavior of adolescents and continually questioning about why they behave as they do. Also, he must be ever attentive to what human beings all around him are doing with the material that he is charged to teach.

INTEREST SURVEYS. It is useful to most teachers to conduct simple interest surveys in their classes. The findings may be helpful in shocking teachers out of a complacent assumption of values in their courses. These surveys could best take the form of queries concerning things which pupils do, but any relatively formal questionnaire approach by the teacher is susceptible to certain apple-polishing biases on the part of pupils. What the teacher needs most is a continuing observation and perhaps some informal testimony taken in normal situations out of class.

OBSERVATION OF PUPIL BEHAVIOR. At school, the teacher needs to observe pupils in the corridor, as members of the audience at assemblies, at school parties, in the bleachers at basketball games, in the lunchroom, in classrooms before classes begin, as they come to school, and as they leave. Teachers should make every effort to engage in friendly conversations with pupils on topics about which they are willing to converse. Too often teachers sit at the teachers' table in the lunchroom or in a forbidding police squad at assemblies. In conferences with pupils, it is possible to introduce a few general questions which will lead a pupil to talk about himself, his activities, and his values. Such interviews should take the form of friendly conversations and never become attempts at pumping pupils about personal affairs which are often not the concern of the classroom teacher.

Probably the truest pictures of pupil behavior can be found in the observation of normal reactions out of school. Often the teacher is advised to close the school doors upon his professional problems but a real concern with youth and youthful activities would not violate this advice. The teacher can learn much of youthful values by noting the behavior of young people on the streets, on playgrounds, at work, at church, at motion pictures, on the buses, in parks, and in various places through the summer vacation. Sometimes there are opportunities to observe adolescent behavior in homes.

BOOKS ABOUT ADOLESCENTS. Often when confronted with a particular problem the teacher tries to find the solution in books. What can the teacher read that would help him to a clearer vision of adolescent values? Of course, there are the books on adolescent psychology. These are often helpful in establishing general principles and in suggesting the kind of things to be looked for in young people. They are often inadequate in suggesting specific clues to the behavior of boys and girls. Some of the case studies included in the modern literature in the field of guidance may be found more useful.

Some writers of fiction have had a keen insight into the mainsprings of youth behavior. Many times the teacher can read such fiction with profit. Perhaps the teacher should begin to add to his personal library pieces of fiction which are most helpful in the understanding of boys and girls. The teacher who searches can find a considerable volume of fictional materials of importance in assaying values of youth. The woman teacher who has never been a tomboy needs to read literature on boys with an attempt at understanding. The man needs to read books about young girls.

One other suggestion may be significant for beginning teachers. One should remember his own youth. Too many teachers age too rapidly in attitudes toward the young people with whom they work. The boy of fifteen thinks that the teacher of twenty-five is "old." The teacher who says that modern youth "is going to hell on a bandwagon," is truly getting old in his reactions toward young people. The issue is not one of actual chronological age but of attitudes. Some teachers are too old to deal effectively with youngsters at twenty-three. Others have succeeded in remaining relatively young at sixty-five.

Teacher exploration of subject values

The knowledge of youthful values is only half of the teacher's stock in trade for the processes of motivation. He must be keenly aware of the human values inherent in what he teaches. Too many high school teachers merely assume the cultural values of the subjects which they teach. It never seems reasonable to them to question values in their own subjects. Of course, everyone needs English. Algebra is good for people. Science is necessary to understand the world in which we live. Spanish adds to your culture. All people should appreciate good music. Physical education assures a sound mind in a sound body. But none of these assumptions is satisfying to the pupil who comes to the principal's office to drop plane geometry, or English III, or physics, or French I. Neither are the often stereotyped statements of purposes of school subjects and courses found in published state and city syllabi of any great value in dealing with the pupils who must respond to the courses. How then can the teacher come to grips with subject values that can seem to be of significance to the people in his classes?

The clues to values are to be found in what people *do* rather than in what they may say about values. In chapter 3 the term "the intrinsic function of subject matter" was used. In this previous discussion the intrinsic function was interpreted as the uses which people outside the school situation find for any bit of subject matter. This, then, would suggest to the teacher in search for the more tangible values of his own subject to look into the world outside the school to see what people are doing with what he is trying to teach.

Such questions as these immediately arise. Where do people use algebra? How do people use algebra? What kinds of problems do ordinary folk have which lend themselves to solution by algebraic processes? What do people do with history? What understandings of issues in the present world could be improved by some knowledge of history? What kinds of things do people read when they are let alone? What books do people buy? What magazines do people read? What in these magazines do they read? What books do people talk about? What do people say when they discuss the things which they read? Is it true that most people are continually and intimately concerned about their own *personality growth?* If this isn't true, what does concern people? To what extent are many people more concerned about the welfare of others? What about the welfare of others does concern altruistic people? To what music selections do people of good taste listen? What decisions do many people have to make which involve principles of design and color? Such questions are almost endless, but each teacher within his field must be continually attentive to them.

Teachers must try to find out what human beings in the world about them do with subject matter. Emphasis must be placed upon the actual and potential uses of subject matter rather than upon past uses.

The social science teacher must be widely read and continue to read. His reading must include the daily newspapers, the current events magazines, the proposals of the politicians, economic trends, and social changes.

The teacher of English must read with great diversity. He must know magazines as well as books. He needs to keep up with motion pictures, radio, and television programs. He should know neighboring libraries. He should know something of book publishers and be informed about the costs of books in varying editions. Possibly he should know some things about the market for writing in order to be able to advise some ambitious pupils who yearn to do "creative" writing.

The teacher of mathematics should explore business, scientific, industrial, agricultural, and engineering uses of mathematics. He should know statistics and become skillful in the graphic representation of mathematical data. He should be observant of building construction. He should find out something of elementary surveying and its farm applications. He should observe the applications of geometry in the design of fabrics, wallpaper, and floor coverings. He should be or become familiar with the uses of such implements as the carpenter's square, the compass, the calipers, the micrometer screw, and the slide rule.

The science teacher should read not only a serious journal in his major science field but also the popular science magazines. He should make some explorations in aviation, radio, television, and photography. If he teaches chemistry he must find out about the chemistry of foods, soils, fertilizers, water softeners, soaps, soapless soaps, cosmetics, insecticides, fungicides, antiseptics, the rarer metals, heavy water, isotopes, fuels for jet propulsion, and atomic piles. If he teaches biology, he must know the out-of-doors. He should

know trees, wild flowers, weeds, birds, wildlife conservation, do-
mestic animals, human genetics, and many things developing in the
fields of plant and animal breeding.

The art teacher needs to be concerned about interior decoration,
furniture, wall paper, floor coverings, textiles, fashions, architecture,
flower arrangement, and the design of automobiles and planes. He
needs to read or look at the house and garden magazines. He needs
to know what is available in the nearest art museums where fine
prints of good paintings can be purchased. He should know many
craft processes such as block and silk screen printing, weaving, art
metal working, and perhaps wood carving.

The music teacher should know records. He should be a student
of the record catalogs. He should know something of recording and
reproducing equipment. He should be able to offer advice concerning choices between several recordings of the same music. He
should be familiar with hymns and the more often used church
music. He must know the musical side of the radio and television
programs and observe music as it is used in motion picture production. He should keep up with developments in modern music. Perhaps he should be aware of what is on the records of the juke boxes
in the "jelly joints" across the street from the high school. It is
highly desirable that he know musical instruments and something of
comparative values in the choice of instruments. If he can perform
acceptably with an instrument it will be to his advantage. He
should be able to sing in tune. Every music teacher should be able
to illustrate what he needs with the piano.

The suggestions in the preceding paragraphs are only samplings.
Teachers in other fields should be able to lay out similar suggestions
for themselves. The suggested samplings can be expanded. Many
of the suggestions are not learned by teachers in the college courses
that they have had. Practically all of them can be learned by an
alert and aggressive teacher who is truly professionally minded.
The teacher who learns such things will grow both in his general
culture and as a teacher. From the point of view of the possible
motivation of his pupils he will tremendously enlarge his potential
capacity by having so many more subject and human values to
present.

Classroom practices

But suppose that we are faced by the teacher who says, "I have
done all of the things suggested here, and I still have some people
in my classes that seem to have no interest in some of the things that

I am supposed to teach. A number of the pupils can see no values in part of our work. What am I to do?"

INDIVIDUAL ASSIGNMENTS. Perhaps the first answer is that we cannot expect all pupils to respond equally well to all the values that may be inherent in the content and experiences of a given course. The implication is that of a considerable individualization of the work within the course. An illustration is found in the laboratory exercises in the science class. There is no reason to expect that all pupils will work at the same laboratory assignment or, if they do, that they will make the same responses. The problem of the teacher is that of finding challenges to fit the science needs of varying pupils in the class. There is also the possibility of encouraging different pupils to express their varying reactions to the same problem.

RE-EVALUATION OF SUBJECT MATTER. A second answer is that, if a relatively large number of pupils in a class fail to respond to the values of the subject matter presented, there is need to re-examine the content of the course in relationship to the needs of the pupils. The lack of response in the pupils may be a truer index of the values of the course than tradition, the thinking of the school program makers, the author of the textbook, or the opinion of the teacher. At least, lack of motivation on the part of any relatively large number of pupils in a course suggests a reconsideration of the values of the course as a whole, or a scrutiny of the course content in terms of pupil values.

OMISSION OF SUBJECT-MATTER ITEMS. A third answer to the query of what to do with unmotivated subject matter is to omit it or delay introducing it until the pupils concerned are sufficiently mature to become aware of the values. Of course there is always the possibility that some individuals may never reach a condition of maturity in which they will be concerned about some of the things that teachers propose to teach in the schools. As an illustration of readiness in relationship to maturity the introduction of junior high school boys to football will serve. Many teachers of physical education are in agreement that the bone structure of most thirteen- and fourteen-year-old boys is not sufficiently rugged to take the rough play of blocking and tackling in football. It is proposed therefore to introduce tag football for these boys and delay the introduction of regular football until greater physical maturity is reached. In this case there is adequate motivation for football for most boys, but physical maturity is not in proportion to their ambitions. However, teachers have found that the boys respond unusually well to tag football and that there are fewer serious injuries.

SOCIALLY CRUCIAL SUBJECT MATTER.   Apparently there are some cases where omission or delay of unmotivated material seems doubtful either from the point of view of the safety of the pupils or from the point of view of social welfare.   For example, the shop teacher will insist upon the learning of certain regulations for the use of power equipment in the shop whether or not at the moment the boys express any interest in such regulations.   The teacher of a driver education course will insist upon the pupils learning the speeds that are safe for rounding curves, coming over the crest of a hill, or approaching an intersection, whether or not the pupils want to have such information.   This attempt will be made for the sake of other highway users as well as for the safety of the youthful driver.   From the adult point of view, it is probable that we shall always take this position concerning certain seemingly crucial subject matter.   On the other hand, the level of learning will be low in all probability in all situations in which pupils see no reason for the learning.

"GINGERBREAD" MOTIVATION.   Another approach to the teacher's insistence upon the continued use of unmotivated material is that of the application of extraneous and relatively superficial motivation devices.   The name of "gingerbread" motivations is proposed for these devices.   The story is told of an old-time German schoolmaster who had difficulty in getting his beginners to recognize the letters of the alphabet as he tried to teach them to read by the alphabetic and spelling approach.   After some days he appealed to his wife.   She rolled out gingerbread and cut out the letters of the German alphabet.   When these were baked, the schoolmaster took them to his pupils.   When a youngster could recognize one of the letters, he could eat it, hence the term gingerbread motivation.

A gingerbread motivation is one in which the interest of the moment is in the device itself rather than in the thing that is worth learning.   In the case of the German children the interest was in the gingerbread rather than in the alphabet or in reading.

Another common characteristic of gingerbread motivations is that they are often extremely roundabout and remote in reaching the value to be motivated.   How much gingerbread must be baked and eaten so that thirty youngsters may finally fix the identities of the letters of the German alphabet?   Pounds of gingerbread for a few ounces of improvement in reading.

At the elementary and junior high school levels the gingerbread approach is illustrated in the tendency of teachers to make games of school work.   Instead of presenting the worth of what is to be learned and gaining the willingness of pupils to put forth serious effort, the teacher tries to camouflage the situation by saying, "Now we are going to play a new game. I'm sure you will have great fun in playing this game." Often the pupils will respond to the game proposal for the sake of the excitement, the confusion, and the fun of manipulating the motivation machinery. However, little is accomplished in establishing increased value for the learning which is supposedly motivated by the "game." In some situations the teacher is the person who is misled. The pupils actually use the game to avoid the work implied by the learning which the game supposedly motivates.

Common cases of gingerbread motivations often found in secondary schools include soap carving of historical objects, translating and singing silly American juke box tunes in Latin, Spanish, or French, illustrated and decorated notebooks, scrapbooks, lead-up games in the physical education class, a considerable number of the bulletin board devices, showing a movie in place of the normal day's work, at least some field trips and excursions, mnemonic devices for retaining names, dates, and figures. Many school notebooks and scrapbooks are suspect as are most classroom games.

The issue is not that all school work should be drab, colorless, and without enjoyment to the pupils. If a game has a normal function within the limits of goals of a course, it has a place. If a notebook is of any value to a pupil as a record of what he has been doing and the record will be used later, the notebook has a justification.

Some insight may be gained by raising the question of the normal function of some of the activities used as devices for motivating school work. Games have the function of serving as a means of recreation. People engage in them for the fun or enjoyment of participation. If a game presented in school as a game has true game value for the pupils, presumably some of the pupils will be found playing the game out of the class and out of school hours. Softball has game value. The evidence is to be found on playgrounds, in parks, and on vacant lots. The game value of speed ball may be questioned. Did you ever find any normal high school age pupils playing speed ball out of school hours or anywhere except on the floor of the school gymnasium?

A point of view concerning gingerbread motivations can be summarized by suggesting that the teacher carefully scrutinize all proposed *motivating devices*. Wherever it seems that the pupil tends to have his attention fixed upon the machinery of motivation rather than upon the values to be learned, some other approach is indicated. Wherever the machinery of motivation is extensive and time consuming for a relatively small learning of values of greater importance, the teacher needs to consider the issues of triviality and waste of time. Perhaps the game isn't worth the candle.

COMPETITION. Another common means of stimulating pupils is the appeal to do better than other members of the group. The social and psychological desirability of reiterated appeals to competition can be questioned. It may be that in our complex society cooperation is a much more valuable slogan than competition. Assume, however, the strength of the competitive appeal. How useful is it in getting the majority of pupils in a school group to multiply their endeavors for reaching the established learning goals?

Quite probably only those pupils who have a chance to win are stimulated by competition. To see that this thesis may be tenable it must be realized that pupils in a school group very soon become aware of the comparative abilities of the various members of the group. The teacher has access to the school records. He can find marks showing previous scholastic achievement for each pupil. He can find the recorded I.Q. for each one. He may have a case record from the guidance clinic. But the pupils who have attended school together know at the beginning who can win games on the gym floor, who can draw, who can play a musical instrument, who can "cozy up" to the teacher, who will antagonize the teacher, who can write beautifully, who is the class comic, who plans the mischief in the group, who is clever in mathematics, who is sleepy, who is the ladies' man, who is the science wizard, who can do languages.

An analogy can be found with groups of animals. A farmer turns into a pasture fifteen or twenty seven-months-old shorthorn calves. Within twenty-four hours, all but two or three have ceased to try to be first at the water tank or to hold a position at the preferred end of the feed bunk. In another twenty-four hours, the order of precedence of the first three is settled. Pupils in school find out about one another almost as readily.

If the pupils can predict who will have a chance in any competition proposed by the teacher, in a class of thirty-five no more than three or four can be stirred by trying to see who can make the nicest poster or write the finest theme.

Furthermore, the people who can be motivated by competition usually need such motivation least. The pupils in a group who are making the highest marks have pride in achievement. They are constantly alert to keep ahead of anyone who might challenge their leadership. Most parents take pride in high marks, too, so that they encourage the competition and sometimes contribute to the misery of the second best. Sometimes bright pupils are overly aggressive and make themselves obnoxious to the other members of the group. In general, it would be better for the teacher to try to get "winning" pupils to see something of worth in the work to be done other than in surpassing a neighbor. In terms of the earlier classifications of values, winning a competition is a static value. It loses value when it is acquired. It can be passed by. It is possible that things learned in winning are discarded and soon forgotten when the record is once down.

APPEALS TO IMPROVEMENT. A possible option for competition within the group is that of competition or comparison with one's own record. If a high school physical education teacher has a boy who can run a hundred yards in ten seconds, it will be difficult to get him to try harder in order to win from the other boys. However, he may work ever so hard to cut his own record by a fifth of a second. The boy who can do the hundred in twelve seconds will not strive to win from the boy who can do it in ten. But he may be willing to struggle to reduce his own record to eleven and a half.

For pupils to be willing to work to improve their own records, the thing to be done must seem to them worth doing in the first place. A pupil may work quite earnestly to increase his speed in typewriting. But he must first want to typewrite and see the value of good speed in writing. A boy may practice strenuously to improve his tone quality with a bassoon. First he must want to play a bassoon. He must have an ear that will recognize tone differences. He must want to improve the quality of the music performed by his orchestra. A girl often will work to improve the quality of writing of her school papers. But she must be convinced that school papers are worth while and that good writing is desirable.

The improvement of one's own status also affords the possibility that the learner can keep his records and participate in making the comparisons upon which progress is judged. The pupil in typewriting can keep his own records of speed and reduction in the number of errors. The pupil in the speech class can play back a record of an early speech performance and compare it with a recording of his latest attempt. Each pupil in an English class can keep a folder of dated samplings of his attempts at writing. With the teacher he can compare samplings taken at different intervals to appraise his progress. The girls in the clothing class may compare the seams made in a first garment with those made in another garment three to six months later. A pupil in an art class can preserve a folio of art samples as was proposed for English. The boy in the shop can compare joinery and finish of a recent woodworking project with one made earlier. The basketball player can file and compare his record for goals, free throws, and fouls through a series of games. Each teacher should be able to make similar suggestions for work in his own field. Score card devices may become effective as an extension of the idea of comparing samplings of products or performances.

In most school situations and for most pupils, the appeal to improvement will tend to get better responses than an over-all appeal to competition within the group. It must be kept in mind that to make the challenge of improvement work the original attempts must have had worth for the pupils.

Importance of selection

It is extremely difficult to get human beings to respond to motivation that corresponds to the bundle of hay tied to a pole on the shaft of a cart dangling ahead of the donkey. Sooner or later even the donkey will find out that the hay is a subterfuge and cease to trot. Bait, sugar coating, threats, frightening, awards, and bulldozing apparently are not effective ways to encourage learning.

For pupils to learn, it is preferable that they work willingly. If the learners can see that the values inherent in the work to be done are of worth to them, there should be willing response. If the pupils cannot see that the work at hand is worth doing, it may be necessary to delay the work until pupils have reached a stage of maturity in which they can see the values.

For the teacher, the practical manipulation of motivation rests upon the selection of subject-matter values consistent with the values and maturities of the pupils in the school group. Of course, there are always the limiting factors of supposed fundamental worth and of social approval for the selections made for a particular group.

Suppose that it seems desirable for a high school group to sing. The group expresses no particular desire to sing. A clever teacher who knows many songs should be able to find a song the group will be willing to try. Possibly a demonstration from another adolescent group who sing the proposed song with vim and vigor will help. A rousing recording might serve too. Basically the problem is to find a song that has some worth and that will appeal to the group as something to sing.

The proof of geometry theorems may seem extremely dull. An imaginative and observant teacher should be able to find occasions for the use of the geometry that will catch on with most youths.

Almost always hidden away in the background of pupils' thinking are the questions, "What can we do with the stuff?" and, "What does anybody do with such stuff out of school?" Basically the teacher needs to struggle continually with valid answers to these questions rather than with time-consuming extraneous machinery of motivation.

Course and unit introductions

If much of the primary approach to the teacher's problem of motivation is to be found in a frank appraisal of values that are to be gained by the work at hand, then the teacher needs to look for the opportunities for presenting or considering the values to be reached. Some of these opportunities were examined in Unit I which deals with objectives of learning and teaching. In this first unit it was suggested that a good way to express the objectives for a course is found in the informal course introduction addressed to the pupils and not to other school workers. In the same way it was proposed that unit objectives be expressed as informal unit introductions addressed to the pupils. A few brief samples of course and unit introductions were presented on pages 11 and 13. It is obvious that the objectives of a course, or of a unit, are expressions of the values to be attained. Therefore, the teacher's opportunity for stressing the values of school experiences are always at hand whenever a new course or a new unit is to be introduced.

Too much enthusiasm cannot be expected on the part of pupils who are thrown into the midst of a course without any awareness of what they may expect, or any knowledge of what may happen to them in the progress of the course through the school year. Pupils have every reason to expect to be informed about each course which they enter. This information should include some description of the nature of subject matter, some ideas of what pupils may do in the course, an indication of what may be expected of pupils, and concrete illustrations of what people outside the school do with what can be learned in the course. The teacher should not neglect illustrations to show what the young people in the class can do with the learning *now*. Another way to put these suggestions for the course introduction is to say that we expect certain changes to take place in young people as a result of their experiences in a particular class situation. The boys and girls most concerned are entitled to know what these expected changes are.

In the same way, whenever a new unit is to begin, there is opportunity in the unit introduction to interpret the values of the unit. The unit introduction gives better opportunity than the course introduction for very specific and somewhat detailed elaboration of immediate values. This is true since the work to be done is much nearer in time and opportunity than some of the values presented at the begining of the course may seem.

Assignments, too, may be introduced by some consideration of what the worker can expect to accomplish if he carries through with the designated work. "What can I expect to gain by making this chart of accomplishments of the various sessions of Congress?" "What values for me are there in these time-rate problems in algebra?" "Why should I cut out pictures to represent expensive kitchen arrangements and paste these in a notebook for the home economics class?" Pupils should have answers to such questions as the assignments are made.

Teacher-pupil conferences also provide opportunities for exploring values. In this case the values explored may be both the values of the school work and the present set of values which the pupil now has.

In closing this brief treatment of motivation processes the impression is not to be left that in introducing a course or unit the teacher just gets up and "tells 'em." An introduction can take the form of a joint exploration of potential values with pupils making suggestions and often turning to an observation of uses and applications in the world outside the school. Very often an introduction may begin with the cooperative, "What do you suppose that we can learn in first-year English?" "What do you feel that you need in improving your reading, writing, speaking, or listening?" "What do successful business managers, engineers, farmers, housewives, and secretaries need in English expression?" "What do you do in a 4-H Club, or in working with the school newspaper, that we can improve through this class?" At least these suggestions of a down-to-earth cooperative approach seem to express the point of view of the newer school teacher as he attempts to *work with* his pupils, neither driving nor following, but saying, "Here seems to be something worth doing. Let us see what *we* can accomplish with it."

Subunit implementation

Subunit Organization

1. The motivation of school work is dependent upon the appreciations of pupils, that is, upon the extent of the awareness of values on the part of pupils.

2. Interests are to be discovered by teachers, rather than created or invented.

3. Interests and values of pupils are discovered best by observing their behavior in out-of-school situations.

4. New interests are developed by relating the values to be learned to existing values of pupils.

5. Values may be generic or immediate.

6. Generic values are those which appeal to many individuals in a wide variety of situations.

7. Immediate values are those which appeal to particular individuals, perhaps not to others, and often in a limited situation.

8. Much school motivation is based upon appeals to generic values.

9. General appeals are often weak because of the temporary effects and because of the reiteration of the same appeal.

10. Appeals to immediate values of individuals more often provide effective motivation.

11. To attain satisfactory motivation a teacher must be able to analyze the existing values of the high school boys and girls with whom he works.

12. To secure interest in a high school subject, the teacher must know the values which various parts of the subject have for people in the world outside the school. Most often this implies familiarity with many homely uses and applications of the various parts of the subject.

13. The best solutions to problems of motivation lie in the selection of inherently worthwhile subject matter.

14. Competition, as motivation, reaches only those having a chance in the competition.

15. Improvement of an individual record may serve as a useful means of motivation.

16. "Gingerbread" motivation is an appeal to the superficial in an attempt to get temporary concern for something of much greater potential worth.

17. Pupils are not fooled by gingerbread motivations.

18. Interest developed through gingerbread motivation tends to be lost as the transitory concern with the gingerbread device wanes.

THINGS TO DO

1. Select a particular school age boy or girl whom you see frequently. This can be a younger brother or sister. Observe the out-of-school behavior of this young person. As you can, talk with him informally. Make a list of important values which seem to affect his behavior. Which of these seem to have any possible relationship to values in one of the courses which you teach, or hope to teach?

2. For one high school course in your field make a list of those parts of the course which are most often uninteresting to high school pupils.

Indicate which of these things might be either omitted from the course or left until some later course without serious damage to the pupils.

3. Select and list six or eight principles, rules, laws, concepts, big ideas, or complex skills which you are convinced should be learned within the scope of a particular high school course.

For each of these indicate three or four *applications* or *interpretations* which you believe would appeal to high school pupils as having definite value. Where, outside of school, do people use the applications? How often do teen-age people need to use these applications?

4. List the "gingerbread" motivations which you have observed in use in courses in your teaching field. Indicate why each of these is not likely to hold beyond the period of temporary class use.

5. Work out an illustrative case showing the operation of the appeal to

individual growth or improvement as applied to some one learning element found in a course in your field.

6. Grades, fear of punishment, approval of the teacher, promotion, graduation, and approval in the opinion of one's peers are common generic values often used as motivation in school. Show the weakness of one of these in securing permanent appreciation of some desired learning in a course within your field.

7. Write a unit introduction for a selected unit of a high school course in your field.

8. Select a piece of advertising from a recent issue of some one of the popular advertising media such as *Life, Saturday Evening Post, Good House-keeping, Ladies' Home Journal*, etc. Analyze the processes used for catching the interest of the reader. What values, commonly held by consumers, are played upon? How are the associations between the values of the consumer and the values of the advertising made?

9. With the assistance of several other members of your class set up a *role-playing* situation for the class. One person plays the role of a pupil asking to drop a particular course. Another takes the role of the principal, another the role of a parent, another the teacher of the course. Add other characters if you desire.

10. Get a list of test marks for thirty pupils in a high school course. Indicate which pupils probably can be motivated by means of a prize offered to the pupil writing the best essay upon a topic proposed by the local post of the American Legion.

Helpful Readings

Billett, Roy O. *Fundamentals of Secondary School Teaching.* Boston: Houghton Mifflin Co., 1940. Pp. 112–15.

Read the section on the goal and attention, motivation, interest and the direction of learning.

Burton, William H. *The Guidance of Learning Activities.* New York: Appleton-Century-Crofts, Inc., 1952. Chap. 3.

Helpful treatment of pupil purposes as inherent in effective learning.

Klausmeier, Herbert J. *Principles and Practices of Secondary School Teaching.* New York: Harper & Bros., 1953. Pp. 74–86.

Suggestive practices for securing motivation in the classroom.

Kettelkamp, Gilbert C. *Teaching Adolescents.* Boston: D. C. Heath & Co., 1954. Chap. 2.

Chap. 2 contains a very effective presentation of adolescent values.

Mursell, James G. *Successful Teaching.* 2d ed. New York: McGraw-Hill Book Co., Inc., 1954. Pp. 314–16.

A very brief presentation of problems as the basic source of motivation.

National Council of Teachers of Mathematics. *17th Yearbook, A Source Book of Mathematical Applications.* New York: Bureau of Publications, Teachers College. Columbia University, 1942.

An excellent illustration of potential motivation through out-of-school values in the application of a subject.

National Society for the Study of Education. *41st Yearbook. Part II. The Psychology of Learning.* Bloomington, Ill.: Public School Publishing Co., 1942. Chap. 8.

The psychology of motivation.

——. *49th Yearbook. Part I. Learning and Instruction.* Chicago: University of Chicago Press, 1950. Chaps. 2 and 5.

Suggests classroom approaches to motivation.

——. *52nd Yearbook. Part I. Adapting the Secondary School Program to the Needs of Youth.* Chicago: University of Chicago Press, 1953, Chaps. 1 and 2.

Analysis of the needs of youth as potential centers of motivation.

——. *55th Yearbook. Part II. Adult Reading.* Chicago: University of Chicago Press, 1956.

First few chapters present what adults read and the values to be attained by reading. Suggests applications as approaches to motivation of adolescent reading.

STILES, LINDLEY J. and DORSEY, MATTIE F. *Democratic Teaching in Secondary Schools.* Philadelphia: J. B. Lippincott Co., 1950.

Read chap. 9 on creating a desire to learn. Contains a good summarization of the factors of motivation.

TROW, WILLIAM CLARK. *Educational Psychology.* 2d ed. Boston: Houghton Mifflin Co., 1950. Chap. 4.

Read the latter part of chap. 4 on needs and the quest for values.

——. *What Research Says to the Teacher: The Learning Process.* Department of Classroom Teachers and The American Educational Research Association. Washington, D.C.: National Education Association, 1954.

Pamphlet. Pp. 12–17 deal with motivation.

UMSTATTD, JAMES G. *Secondary School Teaching.* 3d ed. Boston: Ginn & Co., 1953. Chap. 5.

Chap. 5 contains a significant treatment of adolescent drives.

WOODRUFF, ASAHEL D. *The Psychology of Teaching.* 3d ed. New York: Longmans, Green & Co., Inc., 1951. Chaps. 7–10.

Extensive psychological treatment of motivation.

11

Unit Planning

What to look for in this subunit

1. What should be the size of the unit in unit planning?

2. What factors must be included in the teacher's planning?

3. What redefinition of the idea of the lesson is necessary for improved planning?

4. How may instructional units be defined in your field of teaching?

5. How many units can be included in a single course in your teaching field?

6. How much writing is necessary for good unit planning?

7. What are economical *forms* for unit plans?

8. To what extent can the teacher expect to depend upon commercial forms of ready-planned teaching devices?

9. What uses are to be made of completed plans?

10. To what extent can the teacher plan work in cooperation with pupils during the class period?

The major question used as the title of this entire unit ("How Can the Teacher Direct Learning?") implies a concept of teaching in which the pupils are considered as the effective workers and the teacher is the leader or director. An analogy can be found in almost any observable working group out of school with a foreman in charge. Suppose that the workmen are engaged in some large scale building enterprise. There are carpenters, form builders, steel workers, brick layers, stone setters, mortar mixers, concrete finishers, hod carriers, and common laborers. Before the work of these people becomes effective, the structure to be built must be planned; the blueprints and working drawings read; and the order of work determined. There must be a general foreman to direct the activities of the workers. The work must be planned, and the plans must be interpreted. Without planning and intelligent direction, the work will bog down in utter confusion.

The analogy is not complete, for the teacher is both architect and general foreman. The teacher formulates plans, interprets them, and directs the day's activities.

There are many teachers who hurriedly cover allotted subject matter and, not knowing anything else to do, spend the remainder of the school year "reviewing" the same content and repeating the same exercises. There are also teachers who spend so much time upon the early units of a course that the course is never completed or the latter units receive inadequate treatment for proper learning. The basic protection of pupils against the malpractices inherent in these situations can be found in improved planning on the part of the teacher. It must be kept in mind that planning without implementation is futile. The plans must be carried through, or modified and the revised planning put into action.

Responsibility for planning

There are people who will object that the responsibility for planning falls upon the author of an adopted textbook or upon the compilers of state and city syllabi. It can be admitted at once that a great many teachers accept not only the contents of their textbooks but also the sequence and order. They simply follow through the text material as it is written. The only planning is that of determining the size of the dosage to be administered on a given day. In some cases even this is predetermined by the "lesson" indications of the text makers.

Suppose that some of the effects of this practice upon the pupils are examined. With all due respect to the authors of many very useful textbooks, the authors are human beings with limitations in their experiences and contacts with young people. It would be helpful for most beginning teachers to become intimately acquainted with some author of books to find out just how many human frailties the person actually has. The contents of books and the order of their use are not "handed down from Sinai."

For illustration, imagine a group of pupils in the ninth grade of a village high school in Utah or Arkansas. They are using as a text in citizenship a text written by a professor of political science in Massachusetts and a professor of education in Michigan. These two authors are now fifty-five and sixty years old. The book was written in 1955. The pupils are struggling with problems of citizenship in their own communities in 1960. The authors never saw the pupils who are using the book now. Probably they have never visited the towns in Arkansas or Utah where the book is being used. Can the book be taught just as it was written? How do parts of the text fit the needs and experiences of these village youths? Is it necessary to suplement the text from local and recent materials, or from human resources near at hand? Should some parts be omitted? Can the order or sequence of learning be rearranged to fit better the nature of the experiences of these particular boys and girls? The responsibility for adapting text materials to the people in a particular class group falls upon the teacher.

Consider also the use of workbook exercises. The author of a workbook should know what the effects of the proposed experiences might be upon pupils. And yet the author never saw the pupils in the classes in which the workbook devices are used. The selection of the exercises from the workbook to fit the development of particular pupils is always the responsibility of the teacher in the local situation.

USES OF TEXTBOOKS, WORKBOOKS AND SYLLABI. Textbooks and workbooks are tools for the encouragement of learning. Most of those available are good tools. However, the *uses* of the tools come within the competence and discretion of the teacher. Therefore, the planning of school work ultimately falls upon the teacher, however good and useful the ready-made teaching materials may be. Merely following an adopted textbook does not constitute adequate instructional planning.

In some fields, teachers tend to follow general outlines or syllabi rather than textbooks, especially in such areas as physical education, music, art, and large parts of home economics. There are no textbooks for most curricular cores. Curriculum directors in city school systems and in the offices of state departments of education frequently issue courses of study, syllabi, or "curriculum guides." Teachers sometimes feel that they must follow such official publications. "This is what the state course of study calls for. I must teach it." "The front office expects me to be teaching tumbling in Februruary." "I must have these songs ready to present at the spring festival." "The supervisor will check to see that I am following the official guide."

It seems necessary to remind teachers that administrators, supervisors, and curriculum directors have also been becoming professionally educated in the last twenty-five years, perhaps even more rapidly than the school teachers themselves. A teacher who plans adequately for the immediate needs of his own classes needs to have little fear of a professionally trained supervisory staff. A review of published course materials from the cities and states will show that they are almost always set up as suggestions and recommendations rather than as prescriptions. The teacher is expected to use the published materials in planning work for *his own classes*. The teacher who doubts this probably has not read carefully the recent materials published by his own state office or his own city administration. Again the responsibility for planning and making immediate use of published aids to teacher and pupils rests on the teacher in the local situation.

TRADITIONAL LESSON PLANNING. The notion that the teacher should plan the work to be carried out in the classroom is in no way new. The literature dealing with teaching includes a great volume of material on planning. From the beginning of campus laboratory schools, student teachers have been expected to plan their work. City school principals and supervisors have often required teachers to prepare and submit for inspection written lesson plans. Some supervisors have insisted that teachers keep plan books in which the series of plans are filed. The complaints of teachers about the added drudgery of writing out lesson plans have been almost as frequent as the practice of requiring them.

If planning is to be built around the writing out of lesson plans for each lesson taught each day, perhaps others should join the clamor of protest raised by the teachers. It is not probable that a teacher in service is going to write out the details of 180 lessons for each course which he teaches. The time and drudgery involved inhibit this approach to planning.

Daily lesson planning presents another and more serious difficulty: it makes for discontinuity in organization and the accompanying effects upon the learning of pupils. With emphasis upon the day's lesson, pupils often fail to see relationships which lead to any awareness or wholeness in the learning. Lessons are day's tasks to be endured, accomplished, and in many cases abandoned. Seldom do teachers, or pupils, attempt to bring a series of lessons into a related sequence which has meaning in terms of a completed skill, a new concept, or the understanding of a basic principle. Very often the suggested organization of the author is abandoned in favor of quantitative segments sheared off to fit the convenience of what can be done in today's class period or as an overnight assignment. One hundred lines are assigned to be read. Half a chapter is to be prepared for tomorrow. Ten problems are to be worked. Twenty sentences are to be written. After a succession of such assignments, both teacher and pupils are apt to have forgotten what was in the first hundred lines or the preceding chapter, or the point made by the problems or sentences.

Sometimes extensive periodic *reviews* are undertaken to recover the pattern of organization which never became evident to the pupils in the passing procession of the daily lessons. Seldom do such reviews achieve for pupils significant organization and meaningful interpretation. Usually they are merely hurried repetitions of the quantities of ideas or skills passed over in the preceding days.

Often pupils and parents express a liking for the quantitative assigned daily task. The responsibility of the pupil is reasonably clear, definite, and limited. He is to read these twenty pages of world history text. When he has read these twenty pages, his responsibility is ended. He can watch the television show and trust that he will not get embarrassing questions in the morning. If a parent says, "Did you get your history lesson?" he can say, "I have read the twenty pages the teacher assigned." There is no question of how the content of the twenty pages can be used to interpret the relationships of laboring groups to those who own land, mines, or manufacturing establishments, or if it fits with the chapter read last week. Often, there is no thought of reading the remainder of the present chapter to find out what the whole chapter can convey. The conscientious student, who is concerned with remembering what was read until it can be delivered in class on the morrow, merely rereads the assigned twenty pages.

There is the same reaction from the pupil who has fifteen algebra problems to solve. Probably he doesn't know, or care, about the mathematical principle which the problems illustrate and apply. He is to get answers to fifteen problems. When this is achieved the lesson is completed. He can go to the neighborhood movie with a clear conscience. Or, if his work is done in study hall, he can now read magazines. The algebra lesson is complete. If a pupil cannot find solutions to five of the fifteen, he can borrow the solutions of a neighbor and when he has copied these solutions along with his ten, the lesson is finished. It is a rare teacher who will say, "If you are convinced that you see the mathematical principle in these fifteen problems and feel sure that you can work others like them, you needn't do the simpler ones. You may need to do only eight or nine." It is a rare pupil who will continue to work the remainder of the set of twenty-five presented in the text if the teacher said, "Work fifteen." It is indeed a rare pupil who will look ahead to see if the next set of problems is like the one assigned today.

Frequently, the laboratory exercises now being done in the chemistry class have little to do with the chemistry dealt with in class yes-terday. Seldom are the illustrative laboratory exercises performed on the day that the principles involved are elaborated. Problems assigned for chemistry often have nothing to do with the current laboratory experiences. Does it seem important that the planning of the chemistry teacher be synchronized so that some notion of wholeness and relatedness is achieved in the pupil's varying experi-ences with chemistry?

Large-unit planning

At least one promising solution to the difficulties inherent in day-to-day lesson planning is found in the current attempts at large-unit planning. Such planning attempts to center the work of the school around meaningful whole patterns and to make the work of succeed-ing days continuous around a central theme until some degree of unified learning is attained.

A comparable statement was presented as a definition of the unit in Chapter 3. This section should be re-read now.

CHARACTERISTICS OF THE UNIT. A restatement of the characteris-tics of the unit in the present setting may not be out of order.

1. A unit should have meaning and importance for the pupils con-cerned, in terms of their present levels of maturity.
2. It should have social worth.
3. It should have some center, theme, or problem about which it can be organized.
4. It should have the possibility of completion, within the maturity levels of the pupils, within reasonable time limits.
5. It should *fit* the course, area, or core pattern within which it is taught.

Units chosen and planned to fit these criteria should tend to solve the problems of lack of relatedness and wholeness in learning which have been so often characteristic of day-to-day lesson planning and lesson hearing.

SIZE OF UNITS. However, the teacher is faced with certain prac-tical and concrete situations in unit planning. What is the quantita-tive size of a unit? What are its time limitations? How many units constitute a course? These questions cannot be answered categori-cally for all secondary school courses. The objectives to be attained, the subject matter, and the nature of pupil experiences implied are all conditioning factors.

Content courses. Certain rules of thumb may be useful, how-ever, in thinking about the sizes of units and their relationships to whole course patterns. A preliminary treatment of this empirical approach to the size of units has been presented in chapter 2. Most teachers have a tendency to lay out too many units for a given course. For courses which involve experiences with large bodies of subject matter, sometimes referred to as content courses, the number of units may be ten, twelve, or fourteen. This suggestion can be applied to courses in the social sciences, the natural sciences, geography, and possibly some courses in mathematics.

As an illustration, a course in American history may operate very well if planned in twelve units. Ten might work also. Fourteen becomes a possibility. Six will present problems of inadequate content or of units of unwieldy size. Eighteen units for such a course imply either superficial coverage or more work than a class group possibly can do within the school year. Thirty units suggests either units with little significance as wholes, or far too much work for the time available.

As an approach to unit planning it may be well for the teacher to learn to think in terms of *weeks* of the school year rather than in terms of day's lessons. The traditional year for most secondary schools consists of thirty-six weeks. A course which contains twelve units provides approximately three weeks' time for the work of each unit. It should be understood that some units might run for four or five weeks and others for two. The time will be distributed in terms of the emphasis and the nature of the work to be done.

A series of illustrative course layouts together with suggested timing of units in terms of weeks needed to accomplish the work of each is to be found in Chapter 3.

Teachers need to be aware that important learning takes time. A unit planned for one week consists of five working days. If the class period is sixty minutes long, the work is limited to five class hours plus whatever the pupils are willing to do outside the class period. The teacher needs to raise with himself such questions as these: What skills can be developed in five hours? What understandings can be built well and interpreted in five hours ? Can the attitudes of the members of the class be changed in one short week? At once it becomes evident that few important learnings can be matured in one school week. Therefore, the teacher will learn to look with doubt on units for which only one week of work is allotted. In the same way the teacher should be sceptical about layouts for courses which contain many units with very short timing for each.

The other side of the picture is presented by the unit which runs for ten or twelve weeks. Can the wholeness of the unit point of view be maintained by the pupils over such a long period? Is there a possibility that some pupils may forget just where they came into the unit after such a lapse of time? Can the interest of the pupils be retained for so long, or will there be considerable sagging as the unit continues? In general, teachers need to reconsider the organization of quite long units.

Skill-forming courses. Some kinds of school learning involve the formation of complex skills that take considerable time to perfect. If pupils are to achieve satisfactory learning, such units must be comparatively long in weeks. Hence, courses that consist largely of such skill-formation will necessarily include fewer units. Illustrations can be found in such fields as: the sports in physical education; the chorus, band, and orchestra in music; clothing in home economics; typewriting; the skills involved in speech and in art. If the first unit of typewriting is centered around mastery of the typewriter keyboard, it may need eight or nine weeks. Typically, clothing construction units in home economics run long. The teacher faces the continual struggle to keep them short enough to retain interest in the garment under construction while at the same time maintaining high standards for the needed skills. An art course may well have six or eight units rather than the twelve or fourteen of the history course. If physical education is organized around a seasonal sequence of sports, the course for the year may include six units, or fewer.

The total number of units in a given course is influenced also by the number of class periods per week. Some high school courses are scheduled for two or three periods per week rather than for five. This may be true for physical education and for music, occasionally for art and shop. If a course has only two class meetings per week, the number of weeks needed to reach a given achievement will be greater, and the number of units that will make up the course pattern will be few. A chorus meeting twice a week has only 72 meetings in the school year. A program of four units will provide only 18 hours of participation for pupils within any one unit.

UNITS IN CORE CURRICULA. Recently schools have been experimenting with core curricula, pulling together large segments of human experience into organizations which, taken together, may represent the most needed areas of general education for all young people. Without exception, these core patterns have been planned in large units. Since the core is intended to care for the general education of a particular group of pupils in a given school year, from one third to one half of the school day is given to it. In terms of traditional class periods the core program may be scheduled for ten or fifteen class periods per week, 360 to 540 per school year.

Therefore, single units of considerable size can be attempted and the number of units sometimes increased.

Stages of planning

The teacher's planning will normally fall into three stages or steps: planning the course as a whole; planning of each unit, which comes within the scope of the course pattern; and consideration of what needs to be done each day.

A Suggested Procedure for Unit Planning

Step One: The Course Layout

1. List the few most important course objectives which are to determine the nature and direction of the course as a whole. Incorporate these in a *course introduction* addressed to the pupils.
2. With the objectives of the course clearly in mind, block out the major units which are to constitute the pattern of the course.
3. Arrange the units in the order in which it is assumed they can be learned best.
4. Headline units with appropriate titles which may give some indication of the nature or direction of each unit.
5. Estimate the time needed for each unit. Write the time estimate in the margin after the title of each unit. Check the sum with the total available time.
6. Reconsider the total pattern and timing in terms of the course objectives and the implied emphasis upon each unit. Consider needs for adding or omitting units from the course pattern. Readjust timing, if necessary, in terms of relative emphasis for particular units.

Step Two: The Unit Plan

1. List the specific objectives to be attained in the unit chosen. Consider the feasibility of accomplishing these objectives within the time estimate given the unit. Incorporate the objectives into a unit introduction addressed to the pupils.
2. In view of experiences gained in working with a particular group of pupils, re-estimate the time needed for the accomplishments of the unit.
3. Outline briefly the *subject matter* to be used or emphasized in the unit. Write the outline in sentence statement form.
4. Select and list the pupil experiences which will insure that pupils will reach the desired objectives. Check the proposed experiences in relationship to the subject matter outlined for the unit.

   Write out the needed directions in exercise form as they are to be given in assignments to pupils.

   Provide for individual differences here.

   If pupil participation in planning is to be utilized, indicate here the approaches to be developed with pupils.

   If ready-made assignment material from texts or workbooks are to be used, indicate them by specific reference to sources. This process may be used to shorten the writing out of details of original exercises if the borrowed assignments *fit the proposed unit objectives* and the outlined subject matter.

Check total group of proposed pupil experiences and assignments in terms of consistency with the unit objectives.

5. List the references and materials needed for carrying out the work of the unit.
6. State the means to be used in evaluating the learning of pupils in carrying out the work of the unit, or accompany the unit plan with the test to be used in measuring results. Check the test against the unit objectives, the outlined subject matter, and the learning exercises.

Step Three: The Day's Work

(Note: Plans for the day's work need not be written out in elaborate detail. The teacher should avoid the daily lesson plan approach. Only such rough notes as are needed as memoranda or reminders need to be written. These may be discarded when their function has been served.)

1. Note the things that need to be done in class on a particular day. Marginal notes on the unit plan may serve.
2. Note, or review, points of subject matter to be emphasized. See subject matter outline in unit plan. The notes needed may be checks or symbols in the margin of the unit outline.
3. Check on materials, or equipment, that need to be provided for the day's work.
4. If necessary, write key or guide questions to direct class discussion. Try a 3-by-5-inch card that may be carried in the pocket or clipped to a roll book as a carrier for these questions.)

Planning the course

Theoretically a competent and experienced teacher should be able to assay the needs of the secondary pupils in the local community as these needs relate to the limits set by the field or subject which he is assigned to teach. He should be able to set up the goals to be attained by pupils in the course and to state these as a part of the course introduction. On the basis of the introduction he should be able to lay out the units for the course. When this is done, he should canvass the available textbooks and select for use the one which most nearly fits the course which he has planned.

Practically, most teachers will work within the limits set by accepted textbooks or published state and city courses of study.[1] Therefore, it is suggested that when the teacher has developed an introduction for the course he examine the textbooks that are available for such a course as well as any courses of study, or "guides," that can be found.

If several teachers in the same field are employed in the school, planning should be cooperative. In larger schools, several teachers may teach sections of the same course. Each teacher should be free to make modifications in terms of the needs of individual pupils in

[1] See the suggestions for teacher aids in developing course layouts in Chapter 3, pp. 48–49.

the various sections, but the general layout of the course should be agreed upon by the group of teachers. If one teacher is assigned an accelerated section, the acceleration should be planned around the course layout agreed upon for all the sections. In the same way, the teacher of a slow section may be expected to begin with the central layout for the course as a whole and modify in terms of possible omissions, simplifications, and adaptations to experiences of slow learners.

Many school systems have a corps of special supervisors in such fields as music, art, physical education, speech, reading, home economics, and industrial arts. One of the primary functions of such supervisors should be to furnish advice, suggestions, and consultation in the planning stages. Therefore, it is assumed that the special supervisor, where there is one, will participate in formulating the course layout.

The administrative officer of a school must assume the responsibility for the planning of the instructional program of the school as well as for its administration. In the large school the immediate administrative officer is the principal, in some small ones the superintendent of schools. The administrative officer should know what is planned for a given course. If he does not participate in the original planning, he should at least approve the course layout. He will not be expected to be concerned with details of planning but with the general character of the course and with the selection and possible omissions of major units. It is good administrative practice to file a copy of each course layout with the administrative officer of the school. In periods of social change and of widespread criticism of schools, the existence of concrete layouts for courses and an official filing of such layouts in the administrative offices may serve as protection to the teachers and to the school. Certainly the members of the board of education and the patrons of the school reasonably may expect the administrator to be able to answer specific questions concerning the nature of the courses which the pupils are pursuing.

FRAMEWORK OF THE COURSE. In actually writing the layout for a course, the teacher first jots down ideas or centers about which the ultimate units can be built, but not necessarily in sequence. It is desirable that this first list include more suggestions than may be used in the final layout.

The first listing may consist of a series of topics or of the more important problems, issues, or trends. The choice in expressing these original items will depend upon the teacher's interpretation of the nature of the organization of units, the kind of center around which the units are to be built. If the physical education teacher proposes to organize a course around sports, his first list will be simply a list of proposed sports to be included in the year's program. If a teacher of shop proposes to organize around a series of construction projects, his beginning list will be a list of things that his boys might build. If a music teacher proposes to organize the work of a chorus around programs to be prepared and presented, the original working list will consist of the programs and a few items of sug, gested music for each.

For example, in setting up the units for a college course in educa‚ tion based upon this text, a teacher might make up a topical list such as the following:

1. Objectives for teaching
2. The selection of subject matter
3. The organization of subject matter
4. Learning activities of high school pupils
5. Methods of teachers in directing learning
6. Evaluation, measurement, and marking

If the reader will turn to the table of contents, he will find what happened to these topically expressed ideas for units in the process of evolution into more meaningful and significant units. It will be noted that the topics finally found expression as questions or problems which it is assumed confront all teachers. Further, some of the units turned out to be too big and unwieldy or could not be expressed well as single problems and were, therefore, broken into subunits with specific names of their own.

UNIT TITLES IN THE COURSE. The next step in building up the course layout is that of titling the proposed units. As the newspaper headline should arouse curiosity and lead the scanner of the paper to want to read the story that follows, so the unit title should challenge the pupil to want to find out what comes next. Also, the title should indicate direction and emphasis so that both the teacher as planner and the pupil as worker can see more clearly what the nature of the unit is to be.

The following are illustrations of the significance of selecting unit titles. Probably, any teacher planning work in American history will include the Civil War as a possible unit. Teacher "A" proposes for this unit the title, "A War to End Slavery." Teacher "B" proposes, "War as an Outcome of Economic Differences, North and South." Teacher "C" proposes, "State's Rights Before and After the Civil War." Here are three different units using similar factual materials. The titles indicate the differences and the proposed directions for each of the units.

Teachers need to use discretion in attempts at unit titling and remain within the scope of the proposed functions of unit titles. The teacher who proposed a unit on industrial development in modern America and used the title, "How Americans Bring Home the Bacon," has missed the basic issues in selecting titles for units.

The attempt to formulate titles for units will raise questions of relative importance, need for breaking some units into several, and the possibility of omission of units that do not fit the course pattern. The whole process at this stage is one of reconsideration, balancing, and polish. The teacher will need to keep in mind the basic characteristics of units and to review what he has learned about the elements of *readiness* as these relate to organization and learning. Perhaps a rereading of what has been presented in Chapter 4 will not be amiss at this point.

UNIT SEQUENCE IN THE COURSE. Next comes the stage of arranging units in the sequence to be followed in the course. Here the teacher is confronted with problems of readiness as well as with certain apparently inherent relationships in the subject matter. Perhaps the hardest nut to crack is that of the choice of the first unit. If the course is World History, does the course begin with prehistoric man or with the problem of the pupils' own cultural inheritances? If the course is citizenship does it begin with the pupils as school citizens, with citizenship in the local community, or with the civic conflicts of our nation as expressed in the newspapers?

Some problems of placement in the course sequence are determined by normal usage in the everyday living of people. A unit on touch football belongs in the football season. Probably softball should come in the spring with the upsurge of national interest in professional baseball. A unit for the chorus in preparation for a Christmas program can be placed in only one spot. A unit on clothing construction for advanced home economics might well deal with the construction of a new spring dress and be placed just before Easter. In an election year, a unit on politics, voting, and democratic processes belongs just before and along with the election. If the art course is to include some work with landscapes, the unit needs to be placed when weather is settled and attractive out of doors. Colors may lend an attractive feature. For most of the country, the landscape unit may well fall in October. If pupils in Art I are not far enough along to attempt landscapes in October, the unit may need to be moved over to the early part of Art II. Units for the course in biology which require field experiences must be placed when the field work can be done. Work with insects is usually better done in the fall, that with birds in the spring.

The teacher must keep in mind that the proposed layout which he has committed to paper is always subject to revision in terms of the growth and development of members of the class, and of the problems which may arise in the class. As the teacher works with the pupils, it may become desirable to move a unit from sixth to third place in the sequences, or vice versa.

TIMING THE COURSE. When the units have been selected, titled, and arranged in sequence, the teacher is confronted with the problem of timing. The various issues involved in timing were treated earlier. In the structure of the course layout, the timing may be expressed best in the form of marginal notes of the number of weeks assigned to each unit and which appear in the right-hand margin of the layout following the unit title.

DISTRIBUTED UNITS. One problem of timing arises in situations calling for distributing practices over a relatively long period. Typically, such practices do not take up the whole class period on a series of consecutive days. The skills are such that they cannot be completed in two or three weeks. Consider the ninth-grade group that needs experiences with remedial and improved spelling. The proposed spelling unit is assigned to the ninth-grade English course. Nothing much is to be gained by allotting three weeks to this unit and doing nothing with spelling for the remainder of the school year. The pupils need continuous experiences with spelling through most of the year, perhaps longer. Possibly results can be reached with twenty minutes of spelling two or three days a week for eighteen weeks. If this distribution is done hit and miss, little will be accomplished. The spelling unit needs to be planned as a whole. It may well appear as a unit in the course layout, but the timing will indicate by means of an appropriate notation that the unit is to be distributed and the total time involved estimated. For example:

Unit 3:　Remedial and Improved Spelling
　　　　　(Distributed unit, 20 min., 3 days
　　　　　per week for first semester)　　　　　　　　　3 weeks

The need for distributed units will likely arise in connection with arithmetical computations in junior high school mathematics, in muscular conditioning in physical education, in pronunciation of foreign expressions in French and Spanish, and with enunciation in speech. Teachers in other fields will find comparable situations.

The following example of a layout for eleventh-grade English includes several distributed units.[2]

English for Eleventh Grade

Unit		Weeks
1	Diagnostic Test on Grammar and Usage (Follow by remedial work on weaknesses shown)	3
2	Introduction of Out-of-Class Reading (Follow with approximately 35 days distributed)	7
3	Writing Book Reviews	2
4	Introduction of Discussion of Today's Headlines (Follow with ten days of distributed time)	2
5	Comparison of Literary Types	3
6	Introduction to Occasional Speeches (Ten days distributed)	2
7	Writing Narratives	2
8	Review of Periodical Literature	3
9	Appreciation of Lyrics	3
10	Writing Ballads and Lyrics	2
11	Humor in Literature	2
12	One-Act Plays	3
13	Interviews and Conferences	2

The finished layout should show the course and its timing in broad sweeps, so that the teacher, principal, pupil, or patron can visualize the whole readily. It is desirable to get the layout on one typewritten page, if possible.

Planning a unit

The planning of any particular unit within the course layout repeats in part the processes described for planning the course as a whole. Differences are found in the narrower scope of the unit and in the more specific and concrete treatment of subject matter and of proposed activities of pupils.

Unit planning should begin with a unit introduction which can serve as a frame of reference in selecting subject matter and pupil experiences. In developing the unit introduction, one should have in mind that the objectives are immediate and to be accomplished within a limited time span. The teacher may find it useful to make first a simple working list of things he believes the pupils should be able to accomplish as a result of the work with the unit at hand. In considering this list, the teacher must be aware continually of the maturity levels of the pupils for whom the unit is planned.

Sometimes it will be an advantage to attempt to break down the proposed learnings into types. For example, the teacher may ask

[2] From a class project in Education D446, *Curriculum Construction for Secondary Schools*, in Ralph K. Watkins, et al., *Curricular Modifications in Secondary School English*. University of Missouri Bulletin, Education Series, No. 41, 1946. See also National Council of Teachers of English, The Commission on the English Curriculum, *The English Language Arts in the Secondary School* (New York: Appleton-Century-Crofts, Inc., 1956), chap. 3.

himself, "When we have finished this unit, what ideas, items of information, or generalizations can I expect the pupils to be able to remember for a long time?"; "What habits or skills are to be formed in this unit in the next six weeks?"; "What ideals or attitudes are to be formed or changed?"; or, "What new interests can the pupils develop as we work with this unit?" If this kind of breakdown is attempted, it is highly desirable to remember that the number of objectives proposed for any one unit should be kept small. Neither is it necessary that every unit be planned to include all types of learning. There may be no important skills for some units. Others may stress skills and have few important generalizations to be remembered.[3]

THE UNIT INTRODUCTION. The next stage is to write out the introduction as the teacher expects to present it to the pupils. The proposed objectives will be presented to the pupils in language which they can understand and to which they will respond favorably. A few excerpts from sample unit introductions will be found on pages 12 and 13 of Chapter 1. This process of expressing objectives as an introduction to pupils will help the teacher in clarifying his thinking about the unit and at the same time should help in setting the work at the maturity levels of the pupils.

In working with any group of pupils, the teacher will gain an increasing knowledge of their needs, experiences, and working pace as the work progresses. After the first unit of a course is completed, he will be able to estimate better the time to be allotted to the second unit and so on. Therefore, as details of new units are planned successively, the teacher should check the time estimate of the original layout with the present knowledge of the particular group of pupils.

SUBJECT-MATTER OUTLINE FOR THE UNIT. The next step in the development of a unit plan is that of determining the subject matter needed in its implementation. Some confusion exists in educational literature about the relationship of a body of subject matter to the unit structure. This confusion is reflected in the attempt to classify units as *subject-centered* units, *experience* units, *activity* units, and so on. Such attempts to classify units are of interest to the educational theorists but of little practical importance to the teacher who is attempting to develop his own planning. The position can be taken that there is no such thing as a unit without subject matter. One cannot learn without learning something. Whatever is learned

[3] An earlier treatment of unit objectives and their analysis is presented in Chapter 3, pp. 40–41. This should be reread now along with the suggestions of criteria for judging objectives contained in Chapter 2.

is subject matter or becomes subject matter. No learning takes place unless the learner has experiences and goes through certain "activities." Therefore, every unit is concerned with experiences and activities of the learners. It will be assumed that certain subject matter is inherent in every unit and that it is a primary obligation of the teacher to identify such subject matter and to determine the relative emphasis to be placed upon its parts.

The subject-matter outline for any given unit, then, is concerned with the specific identification of the subject matter needed in the development of the unit and with the problem of relative emphasis. It is not necessary to write a new textbook in developing subject matter for a series of units. On the other hand, if subject-matter indications are offhand and scanty, the unit becomes obscure and hazy both for teacher and pupils.

It was said in Unit III that teachers' outlining is better done in sentence statement form. The same recommendation can be applied to unit planning technique.

Difficulties in lack of specific identification of subject matter in the simple topical outline are shown by the following outline of a unit of a course entitled *Introduction to Music*.

Unit 2: Large Instrumental Forms

1. Overture
   a. Classical
   b. Dramatic
   c. Concert
2. Sonata
3. Concerto
4. Quartet, Trio, etc.
5. Classic Suite
6. Modern Suite
7. Symphony
8. Symphonic Poem

No one quite knows just what the music teacher expects to teach under each of these terms. Possibly the teacher who made the outline did not know just what emphases were to be made. Probably, if the subject matter were properly identified, there is far more here than should be in a beginning course. Contrast with this the more specific indications of content in the excerpts from a student's unit for a similar music course shown below.

Unit 1: Instrumental Forms

1. *Program music.* Program music is music which by its title, descriptive analysis, words, action, scenery, or accompanying pictures tells a story and hence follows a distinct program.
2. *Absolute music.* Absolute music depends entirely upon its own material to establish a mood or create an emotional or intellectual response. It is music pure and simple with nothing but tones to carry its message.
3. *Rhapsody.* A rhapsody is a disconnected and rambling composition, e.g., Liszt, "Hungarian Rhapsody No. 2."

4. *Impromptu.* An impromptu piece is one made offhand at the moment or without previous study, e.g., Schubert, "Impromptu in A flat, Op. 90."

The music teacher who reads this may not agree with the descriptive definitions included, but at least we are reasonably clear about what the teacher who wrote it intended to teach.

The following illustration taken from the planning for a course entitled *School Publications* also illustrates the need for including subject matter.

Unit 6: Special Types of Writing

Primary Objective: To enable students to write effectively criticisms and reviews, accounts of speeches, interviews, and sports events.

Teaching Approach:
1. Have the students make a survey of the metropolitan papers for criticisms and reviews and for accounts of speeches, interviews, and sports events. Clip examples and discuss the general structure and effective wording.
2. School papers may likewise be surveyed for such types of news and the articles compared with those found in the city papers.
3. Students may work as a group studying each type of news story in turn.

Activities:
1. Have students read a book and write a review of it.
2. Have sudents scan a new book and write a review of it.
3. Have students report a musical program.
4. Students may review a motion picture indicating the story and the relationship of the film to a book or stage play.
5. Have students report an art exhibit.

Evaluation of the Unit:
(Detail omitted here)

But where is the subject matter for this unit? What are the characteristics of the varying kinds of news stories? What constitutes a good book review? How does a sports article differ from a front page news story? What characterizes good sports reporting? From the activities shown, the unit seems to be weighted toward reviewing. Is this desirable? What relative emphasis should be given to the various types of writing? Someone must know the answers to such questions. Presumably the teacher should be the person who knows. The unit plan should give concrete evidence that the teacher knows what he is about. The subject matter for the unit needs specific identification.

An additional illustration of the need for including specific implementation of subject matter in the unit plan is shown by the following excerpts from contrasting outlines for a unit from *Home Economics I.*

Unit 3: Preservation of Food for Family Use

1. Nutritive values of foods canned by modern methods
2. Brined vegetables
3. Frozen foods
4. Dried fruits
5. Dried vegetables

vs.

Unit 3: Preservation of Foods for Family Use

1. Modern canning methods depending upon heat sterilization make it possible for home canned foods to retain their nutritive values. Possible exceptions are found in the loss of vitamins B and C in water bath and pressure sterilizing.
2. Brined vegetables lose in food value as compared with fresh vegetables because the salt needs to be soaked out to make them palatable. Soaking removes vitamin and mineral content as well as salt.
3. Properly cooked frozen foods compare favorably in nutritive values with fresh cooked foods.
4. Dried fruits and vegetables have a lower vitamin content than fresh fruits and vegetables.
5. Dried vegetables have a lower mineral content than fresh vegetables.

Teachers of English, history, social studies, sciences, home economics, and agriculture should have little difficulty with the outlining of subject matter. On the other hand, teachers of physical education, shop, music, art, typewriting, stenography, and speech often run into difficulty. The problem of such teachers is not because the units lack subject matter but because of the inability of the teachers to identify clearly the inherent subject matter.

For example, a teacher of physical education in outlining the subject matter for a unit on softball first included the item, "catching a thrown or batted ball." Upon revision this was changed to "thrown or batted balls above the belt should be caught with fingers pointing up; those below the belt are caught with the fingers pointing down."

By contrast in an attempt at sentence outlining another unit on softball included the item, "students will be shown the best way to get a quick start toward first base after hitting the ball." This sentence talks about a proposed item of subject matter but fails to indicate just what the subject matter is. No technique for a quick getaway toward first base is given. Presumably the teacher knows what the item means, but his unit outline is certainly decidedly fuzzy.

A teacher of French put into a subject-matter outline for a proposed conversational unit the following item.

The first conversation to be used takes place between John Carey, an American living in Paris, and the concierge, or caretaker-superintendent, of the apartment house in which he lives. John is complaining about the mail service in the apartment. The concierge is trying to explain to him the local system.

Here the teacher confuses subject matter and procedure. The item presented above should be in that part of the unit plan which deals with learning experiences, activities, exercises, or assignments. It fails to identify clearly the subject matter of the French implied in the situation described. The exercise needs to be moved to the following section of the unit plan and, instead, a working vocabulary list for the conversation placed in the subject-matter outline. There may be need, too, for a few points of French grammar which will apply specifically to such a conversational situation. In order to implement the proposed learning experience, the teacher must have forecast the vocabulary and the possible usage difficulties that may be inherent in such a conversation. It may be that the proposed exercise is too difficult *in French* for the maturity of the pupils. There is no good way to know this without an exploration of the needed subject matter.

Occasionally it is not necessary to use sentences in indicating subject matter in the outline. For the music teacher working with a chorus group, the subject-matter outline for a unit may consist of a copy of the music to be performed upon which the teacher has marked the emphases which he expects to make in directing the group. For a unit in typewriting on the fingering of the keyboard the subject-matter outline may consist of an appropriate chart of the keyboard showing the correct fingering to be learned.

A clever teacher of physical education in planning a tumbling unit indicated subject matter by stick figures showing how each stunt could be performed. Although these examples are exceptions to the general proposal to make such outlines in sentence statement form, they do, however, follow the principle of clear identification of the subject matter involved and at the same time illustrate the possibilities of a need for flexibility in planning.

LEARNING EXPERIENCES FOR THE UNIT. A third step in unit planning is that of selecting learning experiences that will enable the pupils to achieve the goals presented in the unit introduction. In customary schoolteacher's language, these include assignments, exercises, readings, problems, projects, films to be viewed, excursions, laboratory exercises, papers to write, graphs to make, charts, diagrams, maps, oral reports, and floor talks.

This is the crucial stage of planning. What the pupils do will determine what they learn. At the same time, many of the teacher's management difficulties can be solved with clever planning of things for pupils to do which seem to them worth while. The teacher may work ever so hard and yet get relatively low-level learning because the pupils themselves have been comparatively inactive in the process. Class morale may be low because only a few pupils out of the whole group are busy or are contributing anything to what is going on in class.

Ideally the activities for a unit should be so planned and administered that every pupil is busy doing something which contributes to the learning at hand for the whole class period. There is an old adage which applies here, "An idle brain is the devil's workshop." The idle pupil in a class situation is the primary source of many of the morale and management problems of the teacher.

This statement should not be interpreted to mean that all the pupils should be doing the same exercises at the same time. Experience planning is the point at which the teacher can make the individualization of class instruction effective. Variable assignments may be planned. Pupils may be afforded options in exercises. Some experiences may be tailored to fit the needs of particular people in the class group.

In general, it is a good thing for the unit plan to include more things to do than can be done conveniently within the time limits of the selected unit. The teacher's list of learning experiences may be well thought of as a reservoir of potential activities for pupils. Not all of the exercises included in the plan need be used with a particular class group.

Fitting experiences to objectives. Learning experiences for pupils are to be chosen in terms of their usefulness to the pupils in reaching the goals established for the unit. Each proposed experience should be scrutinized also to determine the extent to which it deals with a specific part of the outlined subject matter. Imaginative teachers often think of interesting and challenging activities which pupils may do willingly. Under scrutiny, however, they prove to have little to do with the current objectives, or their relationship to the subject matter of a unit seems farfetched. In the same way, pupils often propose things to do which in and of themselves are reasonably wholesome activities but are not closely relevant to the present learning situation. When these proposals come up the teacher can say, "That sounds interesting, but do you think that it will help us very much with what we are now trying to do? Can you think of things that we can do which will be of more help with this unit? After all, this is what we are trying to do this week."

Directions addressed to pupils. The teacher can clarify his own thinking about learning and be much clearer in his directions to pupils if he will learn to write the learning experiences or exercises for a unit plan as directions to the pupils concerned. Much confusion results from exercises phrased as "I shall have the pupils do thus and so." Nothing is more vague than the inclusion in a unit plan of such a phrase as "We shall discuss," or a direction to pupils such as "Discuss the effects of Korean War."

Following are a few excerpts which illustrate the notion of phrasing exercises as directions to the pupils.

From a Unit on "School Lunches":

Make a list of ten foods which we can easily include in school lunches which will supplement in nutritive values foods planned for other meals of the day. Make a week's menus for three school children to show how the school lunches fit into the meals planned for these children.

From a Unit on "Changes in American Culture":

Canvass your community for any old school books which may be available, especially such books as the McGuffey readers. Bring these books to class to compare with those now being used. What are significant differences between new and old school books? What can you see in the old books that make them seem in any way superior to the new ones?

From an Eleventh-Grade English Unit on "How Others Live":

Read Slosson's *The Fight Against the Potato.* Collect material about some other form of food which people have considered dangerous, unpalatable or poisonous. Examples are the tomato, snails, mushrooms, wild greens. Write your own story concerning one of these.

Read part of Sinclair Lewis' novel, *Main Street.* Write your own interpretation of life in a small town or city neighborhood which you know.

From a Unit on "Heredity and Variation":

Find in the references recommended for the unit, or in the school encyclopedia, a description of Lamarck's theory of the inheritance of acquired variations. Explain his theory using as an illustration the often quoted example of the giraffe. Find out how August Weismann tried to disprove Lamarck's theory by cutting tails off mice. Can you set up some other way of attacking the solution to this problem by gathering certain types of statistical data or by another experiment with animals comparable to Weismann's? Can you find a farmer who has consistently dehorned the animals of a horned breed of cattle for several generations? What kind of records are needed to use this material as evidence on the inheritance of acquired variations?

From a Physical Education Unit on "Basketball":

For improving skills for *pivot* and *pass,* two squads line up in single file as for a simple relay. Allow space for a pivot and pass between lines. Number 1 player in each line, pivot, bounce diagonally sideward and backward and pass to player number 2. Each player continue in the same way to the end of the line. Each file must move in the same direction across the court to avoid collisions. Re-form lines and repeat until the whistle blows.

From a Unit on "Lettering in Commercial Art":

Make a page layout or a subject heading to be reproduced in zinc to be used in the school paper or the school annual. Adapt the lettering to the theme, style, or motif to be used with it.

Not all experiences needed for carrying out the objectives of the unit being planned have to be written out in detail by the teacher. In many cases satisfactory exercises are available in the textbook, a workbook, or a pupil's manual. In such case the teacher needs to select the ready-made exercises in terms of the unit objectives established for the people in his own classes, omitting those exercises that seem not to be pertinent. Those that are to be used can be supplemented by exercises of the teacher's own invention. In writing out the section of the unit plan dealing with learning experiences, the teacher can preface the listing of the usable ready-made exercises with a simple directive indicating what is to be done with them and then list the chosen exercises by page and number.

Obviously teachers of typewriting will use many of the exercises in the typing manual. Algebra teachers will select the exercises needed for the unit largely from those in the adopted text. If the general science teacher uses a workbook, many of the assignments for the pupils will come from the workbook; otherwise pupils should not be asked to buy it. The point at issue is simply that all exercises selected in the planning of the unit must be pointed toward the objectives to be attained.

Provision for individual differences. Provision can be made for individual differences within the class by differing assignments. One way to do this in planning is to group those exercises that most pupils will be expected to do at the first of the list. A second set of exercises, labelled "optional" or "suggestive," will include some challenging and attractive experiences for superior pupils. The teacher can implement his planning for individuals by simple marginal notations on the exercise list in the unit plan.

Equipment, References, and Materials for the Unit. An important phase of the teacher's planning is trying to foresee what equipment will be needed to carry out the work of the class. Much school work breaks down because the materials or equipment needed are not available when the work needs to be done. The pupils have a perfect alibi if the teacher forgets to have the librarian reserve the books for a given assignment. Many of the management and disciplinary problems that arise in class situations come from the fact that the pupils have nothing with which to work. Imagine the school chorus assembled and ready to sing while the teacher has to go to a storeroom to search for forgotten music. Picture also the home economics girls ready to cook when there has been no grocery order to supply the day's cookery.

In unit planning, the obvious spot in which to consider needed books, supplies, and equipment follows the listing of the learning experiences selected to implement the objective. By an analysis of the exercises the teacher should be able to make a working list of the materials that will be needed. There needs to be, then, in the unit plan a list of needed references and materials for the unit.

UNIT EVALUATION. Unit planning is incomplete unless the teacher can make some forecast of how to find out what will be learned. Pupils will be dissatisfied with their work unless they are able to see some fairly tangible evidence of results. Often a teacher will wish he had not begun a given unit because he can find no way to check outcomes. There is always the basic issue of *validity* of unit tests or unit evaluative devices. Too often evaluative devices are set up as afterthoughts when all the work of the unit has been completed. Hence there are often great gaps between what the pupils were told in the beginning and what the teacher proposes to measure. Simply, the test set up may not have anything to do with what the pupils were told they were to learn. When this occurs the ultimate result will be that pupils will soon learn to cram for the types of tests most often used by the teacher and pay relatively little attention to expressed unit objectives.

Evaluative devices and unit tests should be planned as a part of the unit structure and appear as a part of the unit plan. In the construction of test devices the teacher will keep constantly in mind the relationship of test items to the objectives of the unit and plan subject matter items in consistency with that originally outlined in the unit. If the unit is replanned in midflight, appropriate notations need to be made on the unit plan, and tests adjusted to fit the replanning.

Ideally, then, a unit plan should be accompanied by a valid unit test or a description of a means of evaluation consistent with the objectives and subject matter of the unit.[4]

THE DAY'S WORK. This discussion of unit planning has repeatedly emphasized the unit as a whole. There are some things, however, which the teacher needs to keep in mind concerning the work of each class from one day to the next. Such things need to be borne in mind by the teacher but need not always be written down in great detail.

[4] For further details on the construction of valid evaluation devices see pp. 325–31 in Unit VI.

If the teacher will think of his unit plan as an instrument to be used, many of the things which he needs to remember concerning the day's work can be indicated in the form of marginal notes on the copy of the unit outline in current use. For example, this can be done with the application of learning experiences for a particular class section or for individuals in the class. When a marked copy of a unit plan is so filled with notations that it has to be discarded, it is usually time to replan the unit.

Other things needed for today's work can be jotted down as memoranda, perhaps on a 3-by-5-inch card that can be carried in a pocket or clipped to a roll book.

Such memoranda may be a *few* thought or study questions needed for today's asignment or to be used to stimulate discussion, references for reading, perhaps with pagings, supplies needed for the day, things to remind the pupils to bring to class next time, and so on. Such memoranda often have little significant permanent value and may go into the wastebasket at the end of the day. The structure proposed for planning given on page 213 contains the emphatic notation—*not to be written out in detail.*

Forms for unit plans

Teachers sometimes raise the question of what a finished unit plan should look like, and some directors of student teaching and supervisors of special fields prefer that plans be cast in a particular form. The author has expressed certain preferences for ways of stating parts of the unit planning cycle, for reasons indicated in the text. Among these preferences are: expression of course objectives as course introductions to the pupils and unit objectives as unit introductions addressed again to the pupils; the outlining of subject matter in sentence statements; and writing exercises and assignments in the form of directions to the pupils for work to be carried out.

The mechanical arrangement of parts of the unit plan on the page has been left to the convenience of the teacher. Pages will need to fit the teacher's chosen notebook. If notations are to be made on plans, margins will need to be wide and therefore the page size will need to be relatively large, perhaps the standard 8½ by 11 inches. Flexibility of form seems generally desirable. A notebook cover or binder in which amendments, clippings, and changes can be readily inserted will be found useful.

There is good logic in the columnar arrangement of the parts of a unit plan as illustrated in the following diagram.

Unit Title

Unit Objectives	Subject Matter	Pupil Experiences	References	Evaluation

The advantage of such a form lies in the fact that a teacher can see the interrelationships of the parts of the plan at a glance as they are laid out on one sheet.

However, the mechanics of such a layout may present a continuing nuisance. The whole will not go on any standard-size page or fit into a conventional notebook. Even if pages are turned lengthwise the space is not enough across the page. If the teacher typewrites his material, as he should, an adequate sized sheet will not go into a standard machine. If two pages are used there are the problems of pasting sheets together and folding. If for any reason plans in this form are to be printed, the cost of typesetting is enormously increased. If our recommendations of writing unit introductions and sentence statement outlines are to be followed, the space will be cramped indeed. There are no other professional objections to such a form. The issues are primarily those of mechanics and convenience. Generally, it will be found more convenient to use a size sheet which suits the teacher and let the parts of the plan follow in sequential order as the pages are turned. Modification by insertions, notes, and so on are made more readily if only one side of the sheet is used.

Replanning old units

It has been suggested that the teacher make annotations on the margins of plans indicating use, timing, and adaptation to needs of particular pupils. It will be found valuable to make notations, especially on exercises, of those things which seem to produce good learning and those which seem ineffective. Notes on test items and means of evaluation are useful too.

At the end of the school year the teacher may well review his unit outlines and his notes on them. Notes, new illustrative materials, changed reading, revised test items and other revisions should be used in the formulation of new unit plans. Often, many pieces of previous planning can be carried over into the new. Rarely should the teacher use the same plans from one year to the next, for each group of young people is different and there are always differences among the individuals. If the teacher moves, plans will need to be modified in terms of the institutional purposes of the new school and the whole climate of the new community.

Subject matter is constantly changing, and differing emphases need to be made as conditions change. The clothing teacher may have problems with an old text illustrated by out-of-date styles, as does the physics teacher who uses an aging physics text with a group of boys who know planes and automobiles.

This section can be summarized by saying, do not discard unit plans. Keep them, but use them as a basis for building new ones.

Pupil participation in unit planning

This chapter has emphasized the great need for planning on the part of the teacher for the work that is to be done by each group of pupils in progressing toward agreed-upon objectives for learning. In spite of this emphasis, it should be recognized that there is some movement in the direction of minimizing the value of planned school experiences. By extension, it might be said that it is not necessary to plan work in advance. Even the objectives are to be selected by pupils and teacher together on the spur of the moment. Pupils are to be encouraged to determine the nature of their own learning experiences in terms of their own self-direction. Pupils can learn to participate in the activities of a democratic society only when they have the greatest freedom possible in selecting their own goals and their own school activities.

But neither schools nor classes can operate effectively without adequate planning. Spur-of-the-moment planning will result not in democracy but in anarchy.

Many school teachers have vivid recollections of experiences with complete freedom of choice for pupils. For example, there was the English teacher who said to her class of ninth graders, "Today you can write on any subject that you choose." Many pupils didn't choose to write at all. Without suggestions, more than half the class had no ideas for topics. Mostly the pupils just sat and looked at the teacher. Perhaps it was the same teacher who told a class that they should read anything they chose to read. Again, some chose to read nothing, and others had no ideas to propose. Of course, a few superior readers with well-established reading habits might propose to read just what the teacher hoped for.

There was also the general science teacher who proposed that his students choose their own science projects. Anyone who had a burning zeal for experimentation, exploration, and work in the field could now have an opportunity to work on his own investigation. Of course, three boys wanted to make gun powder, and some girls wanted to press autumn leaves. But most had no ideas and no great zeal for scientific investigation. They sat and waited for direction and leadership and were, for a time at least, willing to kill time while awaiting the divine inspiration the teacher seemed to expect. Perhaps these examples seem exaggerated and perhaps the teachers lacked the inspiration and skill of fine leadership. Nevertheless, such situations do occur under a mistaken philosophy that all young people are self-starters moving invariably toward desirable and socially approved goals.

Suppose it is agreed that the teacher must plan, that for good learning pupils must accept the objectives established and work willingly toward their accomplishment, and that learning experiences must fit the maturities of learning and seem to be real and immediate. What choices are pupils to have? How large a part are pupils to have in cooperative planning of their work?

In order to plan at all, the teacher must know, in general, the outcomes for a given course and for pupils of a given maturity. The place in planning for reaching an agreement with pupils on such outcomes is in the presentation of the course introduction. The introduction may take the form of a discussion rather than a telling. In the same way, the time given to the introduction may include exploration of pupil experiences, needs, and interests and the relating of these to the work to come.

The teacher must know the relationship of needed subject matter to the goals to be attained, in other words, the units to be included within a given course. On the other hand, there are many possible variations in the development of a given unit that may be adapted to particular pupils within a group, even to the point where a choice of topics or problems may be possible for individual pupils.

Again, the introduction of a new unit presents the possibility of agreement upon objectives, discussion, illustration, and exploration. Since the unit represents the immediate work to be done, the adaptation possible through the unit introduction can be more intimate and specific than is possible with the course introduction at the beginning of the term.

Ultimately, the best opportunity for choice and pupil initiative lies in the adaptation of learning activities or experiences to the pupils. The suggestion has ben made that in unit planning the teacher always build up a set of "optional" or "supplementary" exercises. Teachers may well invite suggestions from pupils and often substitute their best proposals for some of those in the original plan. Sometimes the teacher may suggest that a pupil carry out a given exercise or propose a comparable one of his own designing. It is always understood that the pupil's proposal must have the teacher's approval and be pertinent to the learning of the current unit. The alert teacher will keep a file of worthwhile activities suggested by pupils and use the material from this file in replanning the unit. Finally such a cumulative file of proposals of pupils can become a tremendous resource for the teacher.

All this does not mean, however, that a teacher is to come to class with no planned exercises. The teacher must always be forearmed with *suggestions of things to do,* and if necessary with a list of experiences *which pupils are to do.*

Source units

A means of providing the teacher with resources from which to develop further planning in a local situation is found in the *source unit or resource unit.* Such a unit differs from the instructional unit in that it is intended primarily for the teacher's use in further planning and is not intended to go into the hands of pupils. Most resource units emphasize the subject matter and its organization. They do not include adaptation of learning exercises to a particular group of pupils. Such adaptive learning experiences must be set up by the teacher or developed with the pupils through cooperative planning with the group.

Source units have been especially useful in core curriculum developments and in the newer areas of the school program where effective textbooks are lacking. Such units are frequently built in workshops for teachers or made by supervisory agencies as suggestions for local planning. Whatever the source, the teacher must still convert the source unit into instructional material for his own class groups.

Subunit implementation

SUBUNIT ORGANIZATION

1. Merely following through in sequence the material of an adopted textbook does not constitute adequate planning of instruction.

2. Writing out detailed lesson plans for each day's work is extremely burdensome and leads to a lack of coordination and lack of organization of learning into meaningful wholes.

3. Adequate planning implies the organization of courses into relatively large instructional units.

4. An instructional unit implies the organization of work and needed subject matter for the accomplishment of a group of closely related immediate objectives.

5. An instructional unit should have within it some definite basis for organization.

6. An instructional unit should contain problems or ideas or potential skills of immediate concern to the pupils.

7. An instructional unit should contain subject matter of social worth.

8. Subject-matter outlines in unit plans should be brief, merely long enough to show the plan of organization, and serve as a reminder of content for the teacher concerned.

9. Sentence-statement outlines of subject-matter are to be preferred to topical outlines for practical guidance of the teacher using the unit plan.

10. The heart of any plan for teaching is to be found in the planning of of work, exercises, activities, or projects to be carried out by pupils.

11. Tests should be constructed as the unit plans are built. Tests made as afterthoughts, when instruction has been completed, are often invalid.

12. Previously made plans may be used as the basis of replanning to fit current conditions.

13. The year's course should be blocked out into major instructional units with rough time estimates for each *before* individual instructional units are planned.

14. The teacher's planning falls into that of two major parts, the course layout and the planning of particular units within the course.

15. The course layout consists of the course introduction, the list of units to be included within the course arranged in sequence, and the estimation of time needed for each unit.

16. A unit plan consists of the unit introduction, an outline of the subject matter of the unit, preferably in sentence statement form, the directions for learning activities or experiences, a list of materials and references needed, and the unit test or means of evaluation for the unit.

17. The planning of the day's work is not to be written in detail, but may consist of marginal notes on the unit plan, or of brief memoranda which may be discarded later.

18. Annotated plans are useful in replanning for another group of pupils.

19. Pupil participation in planning can be implemented as a part of the course introduction, in the unit introduction, or in developing suitable learning experiences for a given unit.

20. The ultimate responsibility for planning falls upon the teacher. Good pupil participation hinges on the foresight of the teacher in laying out the goals to be attained and in the suggestion of experiences which can implement these goals.

Things to Do

1. Write an introduction to a high school couse which you expect to teach. Address this introduction to the pupils concerned. Include a statement of

what the pupils are expected to accomplish in the course. Include illustrations of accomplishments and of work to be done that will appeal to the pupils as worth while.

2. Set up and plan a course introduction in which pupils are to contribute their views of possible goals for the course and in which the teacher uses the introduction as a means of exploring pupil needs, interests, and experiences.

3. Lay out the major units of instruction to be used in the course which you have introduced above. Give appropriate titles for each unit. Arrange them in the sequence in which you think they should be taught. Write in the margin of the layout an estimate of the time needed for each unit.

4. Write out a complete unit plan for one of the units included in the above course. Follow the planning procedures developed herewith.

5. Construct an objective test for the unit planned. Or devise and describe a means of evaluation for the unit.

6. Write out a unit plan for another of the units in your selected course.

7. Block out the pattern of units for a second course which you expect to teach.

8. Introduce to a class group a core curriculum for a given school year.

9. Lay out the units for this core. Be sure to include timing for each unit.

10. Introduce and plan one of the units for your proposed core.

11. Visit a class in which the pupils participate in the planning during the class time. Observe and report on the procedures used by the teacher.

Helpful Readings

ALBERTY, HAROLD. *Re-organizing the High School Curriculum.* Rev. ed. New York: The Macmillan Co., 1953. Chap. 13.

Emphasizes large-unit planning as an approach to curriculum making. Insists that subject matter is necessary part of good planning. Shows some sample course layouts.

ANDERSON, VERNON E. *Principles and Procedures of Curriculum Improvement.* New York: The Ronald Press Co., 1956.

Chap. 15 on unit definition and the development of units. Stresses pupil participation in unit planning.

BILLETT, R. O. *Fundamentals of Secondary School Teaching.* Boston: Houghton Mifflin Co., 1940.

Chap. 16 on the historical development of the unit idea; chap. 17 shows specimen units in academic courses; and chap. 18 specimen units in nonacademic courses.

BURTON, WILLIAM H. *The Guidance of Learning Activities.* New York: Appleton-Century-Crofts, Inc., 1953. Chaps. 12–13.

Useful interpretation of unit structure. Emphasizes the importance of pupil activities in unit development.

JONES, A. J., GRIZZELL, E. D., and GRINSTEAD, W. J. *Principles of Unit Construction.* New York: McGraw-Hill Book Co., Inc., 1939.

The whole book on unit construction. Read. First two chapters are on planning in general in terms of unit interpretation. There follows a presentation of the essential elements of the unit. See especially chap. 6 on unit planning. Latter part of book on sample units and unit tests.

KETTLEKAMP, GILBERT C. *Teaching Adolescents.* Boston: D. C. Heath & Co., 1954. Chap. 5.

First part of the chapter is on planning in general; the latter part on unit planning, including some sample units.

KLAUSMEIER, HERBERT J. *Principles and Practices of Secondary School Teaching.* New York: Harper & Bros., 1953. Chap. 6.

A useful, pertinent chapter on unit planning.

NATIONAL COUNCIL OF TEACHERS OF ENGLISH, THE COMMISSION ON THE ENGLISH CURRICULUM. *The English Language Arts in the Secondary School.* New York: Appleton-Century-Crofts, Inc., 1956. Chaps. 3 and 4.

Planning course layouts and units in English.

ROMINE, STEPHEN A. *Building the High School Curriculum.* New York: The Ronald Press Co., 1954. Chaps. 10 and 11.

Read. One of the good treatments of unit planning. Sample course layouts and sample units included.

SCHORLING, RALEIGH. *Student Teaching.* New York: McGraw-Hill Book Co., Inc., 1949. Chap. 6.

Unit planning as proposed for student teachers.

UMSTATTD, JAMES G. *Secondary School Teaching.* 3d ed. Boston: Ginn & Co., 1953. Chaps. 10 and 11.

Chap. 10 makes a clear distinction between the older concept of daily lesson planning and the newer concept of the unit. Chap. 11 is on teacher practices in unit planning.

12

Teaching Procedures

What to look for in this subunit

1. What is meant by the term, "methods of teaching"?

2. What conflict may occur between a method of teaching and the learning of individual pupils?

3. What should be the relationship between methods of teaching and the objectives of learning?

4. What is meant by the direct attack in teaching?

5. How can you determine when a method is good? To what extent can a teacher predict that a given method is a good one?

6. How can you identify bad methods? Can a bad method be predicted so that its use can be avoided?

7. What are some of the commoner teaching practices described as methods of teaching?

8. To what extent are such methods becoming outworn in modern school practice?

9. What more recently developed teaching procedures are intended to gain increased pupil activity as a part of the learning process?

10. Which of these more recently developed teaching procedures are most often applicable to learning situations in your field?

11. How may the idea of the direct approach to the learning process be applied in designing particular learning experiences for units of instruction in your field?

Some people maintain that anyone can teach, or at least learn to teach for himself. Such folk have insisted that all that is necessary to teach is to know. Mastery of subject matter is the prime necessity for teaching, indeed almost the sole requisite. From this point of view, professional courses in methods of teaching are scorned as having no content and overemphasizing method. The professional educators are accused of proposing that if the teacher knows methodology he can teach without being well grounded in his subject.

Obviously, the author of this textbook on high school teaching believes that people can be taught to teach and that even the greatest expert in subject matter can improve his own teaching.

But there has been an overemphasis on teaching methodology, with the implication that a given method is applicable to any and all learning situations. Indeed, there have been popular waves of pedagogical propaganda in favor of particular methods as panaceas for various educational ills. These have run the gamut from the Herbartian five formal steps, through development method, socialized recitation, problem method, and project teaching to the current vogue of group dynamics.

The position taken here is that the function of the teacher is to stimulate, direct, and aid the learning process. Learning cannot be applied from the outside. It takes place within the learner. There is no sure-fire method for the application of any given learning to other human beings. Therefore, there can be no methodological panacea that can be applied in any and all learning situations. All readers are familiar with the obvious flaw in most patent medicine advertising. It is not specific. A certain nostrum may be useful in relieving pain in aching muscles but when the advertising claims for it are all-inclusive, the reader knows at once that the claims are false. No one should believe that any one compound is good for sore throat, chilblains, falling hair, infections of minor cuts and wounds, insect bites, and muddy complexions. This is too much. If the claims are so great, the possibilities are that the stuff may be good for nothing. In the same way if it is claimed that an approach to learning through a proposed method will produce democratic citizens, a fine knowledge of American history, basic skills in algebraic manipulations, an understanding of atomic fission, and ability to use scientific methods in solving problems, teacher and pupils may well begin to doubt. Can any of these claims be true? Or is it possible that such claims may approach the realm of pedagogical quackery?

Obviously, whatever methods of directing learning the teacher may use, he must know the subject matter to be used in the learning. For a given secondary school course, the teacher should know more about the subject than the pupils. It is to be hoped that the teacher will know more than the brightest pupils. On the other hand, there are often class situations in which problems arise about which the teacher is not completely informed. This is not a case for stalling. The teacher should say, "I do not know the answer, but I do know how and where to find it. I shall be glad to work with you in finding the solution to our problem." In this case the teacher's knowledge in his field is that of the *how* and *where* rather than absolute coverage of all details. Knowledge of a subject-matter field does not make a teacher automatically competent to direct the learning of adolescents. He needs to know *how* to direct learning as well as *what* is worth learning.

Definition of method

What, then, is meant by "a method of teaching"? In the first place the word "methods" should always be used in the plural. There are methods of teaching, not one method of teaching. The idea of method is used to describe what the teacher does, or can do, to direct the learning of others. In general, a particular method consists of the practices of teachers which are accepted as usually effective in producing at least some learning under certain commonly observed classroom situations. In many cases, the acceptance of the method has simply grown up as a result of continued use in the traditional practice of many teachers. Often there is no really sound evidence that any high level of learning is reached as a result of the application of the method. Cases in point are the traditional recitation approach of the grade school and lecturing at the college level.

The literature of teaching includes a large number of named methods. The use of such methods on the part of the teacher is often limited because they are so inadequately described that the new teacher cannot follow them. In some professional literature there is an attempt to distinguish between a *method* and a teaching *device*. For example, the formal lecture, informal lecture, discussion, panel discussion, and laboratory may be spoken of as methods. The use of parables, anecdotes, dramatization, visual aids, demonstration, written reports, and recitals may be characterized as devices or techniques.

It is doubtful that this distinction has any great significance. A motion picture can be a teaching device, a mechanical medium for carrying and conveying a specific bit of information. On the other hand, there are methods of utilizing motion pictures to produce increased and significant learnings. In the same way, an anecdote may be characterized as a trick of the trade to serve as a temporary attention-getter. But there can be a method of using anecdotes to relate new learning to existing experiences of learners in such a way that understandings are greatly enhanced and retention improved.

Characteristics of method

As previously indicated, one difficulty in identifying named methods of instruction may be ascribed to inadequate and vague descriptions in the literature of teaching. One possible remedy for this situation is to attempt to set up a simple formula for analysis of method and to try to describe methods in terms of such a formula. To do this, suppose that the elements of the formula are stated as questions:

1. What kind of assignment is made? How is the assignment made?
2. What do the pupils do during the class period?
3. What do the pupils do outside the class period as a result of directions developed in the assignment?
4. What does the teacher do during the class period and following the assignment?
5. How do the teacher and pupils find out what has been learned?

The application of the analysis formula can be illustrated with the historic and familiar text-recitation methodology. Note that the name of the method ties the recitation to an accepted textbook, and the analysis is made of recitation tied to a text, not any and every recitation.

Within these limits what does the teacher do with the assignment? The assignment is made to the text, which all the pupils are assumed to have. In almost all cases, the assignment tends to be quantitative—so much of the text to be covered. This may take the form of so many pages to read, so many questions to be answered, so many exercises to do, so many problems to solve, or so many sentences to write out. Reference is made usually to directions or helps in the text. Suggestions of the teacher about what to do with the assignment are often at a minimum. Most assignments set a deadline for completion of the quantitative task, usually tomorrow's class period. That is, the assignment is in the pattern of the day's lesson.

What do the pupils do during the class period? They recite on the material covered in the text by the previous assignment. In most cases, this is yesterday's assignment. In response to the questioning of the teacher, they try to recall what was in the text. Oral responses of pupils tend to be brief and without elaboration or interpretation. Many responses are single words. Yes-no questions and answers are frequent. In some classes the oral responses to questioning are varied with blackboard or pencil-and-paper reproductions of solutions to problems, sentence structures, or paragraphs from the text. Finally the pupils listen to the directions for the next assignment and note the area to be covered in the book. Pupils respond at random or in sequence as determined by the teacher. More interested and aggressive pupils volunteer responses. There is no guarantee of the mental activity of any particular pupil between the responses which he himself makes during the class period.

What do pupils do out of class? They prepare for the next recitation. This takes place at seats, in a study hall, or at home. The preparation consists of reading, possibly rereading, text pages in an attempt to remember what the book says. Variations take the form of trying to solve assigned problems, writing out assigned sentences, or writing other pencil-and-paper exercises "to be handed in." Some pupils, frustrated by inability to read or understand the text or interpret the directions for written exercises, do nothing. They just trust to luck that on the morrow they may not be called on or may be able to pick up a garbled response on the rebound. Some pupils copy the written work of others.

What does the teacher do? The teacher determines the amount of the text to be covered during the next preparation and recitation. In some cases the teacher determines parts of the text to be omitted as not fitting the readiness of the pupils. In other cases the teacher finds suitable supplementary sources from which materials can be added to those found in the text. During the class period the teacher questions pupils on the text material of the previous assignment. Questions tend to be many and generally factual rather than interpretative. There is usually an attempt to distribute questions among the members of the class and also an attempt to catch and expose the unprepared and the stupid. The teacher frequently elaborates and comments somewhat at length upon pupil responses. The oral questioning is varied by the reproduction of assigned written exercises at the blackboard and by pencil and paper at seats. The teacher marks errors in written exercises and hands these back to pupils. Sometimes pupils exchange papers in class and mark errors of fellow pupils.

How does the teacher and how do the pupils find out what is learned? Pupils judge their own successes in terms of accepted responses in the oral recitation and by the relative number of errors in returned written exercises, even though the latter may have been borrowed from other pupils. Sometimes an escape from questioning is credited as successful recitation. The teacher judges learning in terms of impressions gained from the oral responses of the pupils in the series of recitations. Added to these impressions are impressions and records of the relative number of errors made by pupils on pencil-and-paper types of recitation. At intervals there are tests which generally take the form of finding out how much the pupils remember of the text material covered.

It must be kept in mind that this presentation of text-recitation is not concerned, primarily, with the merits of the method. It is used merely as a sample of how the description of a method can be set up. Without doubt the reader will form some reactions concerning the desirability of applying the method as he reads the description. But for our present purposes the question is whether the description is clear enough and definite enough that the teacher who reads it can attempt to follow it in a class situation. It is intended as an illustration of our proposed descriptive process for classroom methods in general.

Method and pupil learning

Even when methods are described so that they can be followed, there remains the conflict between a view of *method as method* and *method as a means of directing learning*. An old view of method—possibly that held by some critics of professional education—is that, having learned a given method, the teacher is able to apply learning like a poultice from the outside. A more modern view of learning is that learning always takes place *within* each individual learner and that, furthermore, the learning results from the experiencing of each individual. The evidence of learning is to be found in changes of behavior of individual learners. I cannot dribble a basketball down the court *for* the player on the basketball court. I cannot react to a symphony concert *for* the listeners in the audience. A body of subject matter, such as the Declaration of Independence or the Bill of Rights, cannot be attached to the existing knowledge of a pupil by some process operated by the teacher. To be effective, a method must succeed in getting *pupils to do something* within the learning situation which will produce some of the desired learning in them. Furthermore, what each pupil learns is dependent upon what he himself does in the situation. The group reaction is important insofar as it influences the behavior of individuals within the group. The method, under ideal conditions, should induce each individual within the group to behave so that he learns.

As an illustration, consider the possibilities of learning with a set of written exercises which pupils are to prepare outside of class and hand in. The class is one in ninth-grade general mathematics. There are thirty pupils. The assignment consists of twelve prose problems having to do with the application of percentage to sales prices and profits. Of the thirty pupils, five have been attentive to the teacher's directions and can follow the model problem set down in the textbook. These five work out all the problems with only minor errors in calculation. Ten of the pupils cannot work out the problems independently but, through a process of copying and consultation with the first five, succeed in getting solutions and in understanding the processes involved. The next twelve copy the work of the first fifteen without finding out how the work was done. The remaining three, after a half-hearted attempt at finding out how to solve the problems, become frustrated because they cannot follow directions or interpret the text model, give up, and do nothing further. Here is a method apparently uniformly applied to thirty people of varying abilities. It turns out to be quite effective with one-sixth of the class and at least produces some learning with another one-third. It is completely ineffective with half the class. In the case of one-tenth of the group, it may build up frustrations that will turn them away from mathematical calculations as such.

Method cannot be judged in terms of a procedure to be applied by a teacher. To judge a method, it is necessary also to know to what extent the learners can be brought into such behavior as will result in some changes in them.

Method and objectives

Whatever activities of pupils are set in motion by the method of the teacher should move in the direction of the goals established for that particular learning situation. Language teachers are sometimes vulnerable on the score that the classroom activities of individual pupils do not lead toward the announced objectives. For example, a Spanish teacher has announced that for the next several weeks pupils are to learn to make conversational uses of colloquial Spanish. If we plant an observer in this classroom with a stop watch, the observer finds that one pupil speaks Spanish during the class for one and a half minutes. A second pupil speaks Spanish for thirty seconds. Six pupils speak no Spanish at all during the class period. And so it goes. At the end of the week the greatest amount of experience in speaking Spanish by any one member of the class group is four and a half minutes. There are still some pupils who have made no attempts at all to speak in Spanish. Whatever else the pupils may have been doing in this Spanish class during the week of class sessions, undoubtedly not enough time was spent in activities related to the announced objective to accomplish it. A change in methodology is indicated or a redefinition in goals that may be consistent with the major activities that can be discerned in the class.

Again, suppose that the pupils in this same class are told that they are to learn to read simple Spanish prose at sight. If the classroom activities consist of labored, more or less, literal *translations*, the sight reading objective will not be reached. The method used is inconsistent with the proposed objectives.

Although the position has been taken that methods should be tailored to fit the particular objectives at hand and that what pupils can be persuaded to do is the essential factor in methodology, there are in the literature of teaching a number of recently developed methods which should be known by most teachers. For the most part, these methods tend to emphasize pupil activity and minimize the importance of teacher activity *as such*. These methods tend to move away from authoritative presentation of subject matter and toward increased emphasis upon those activities of pupils which contribute to learning. Responsibility for willingness to work is placed increasingly upon the pupils. The teacher becomes more of a director and leader in the learning process and less of a dictator and police officer.

The direct attack in teaching

As indicated at the beginning of this chapter, the descriptions of named methods used by teachers do not quite cover the whole concept of teaching method. The complete notion of method, which should include the various described methods, is rather simply stated. First, pupils and teacher must see clearly what is to be accomplished, or learned. Secondly, the teacher must be able to visualize experiences of pupils which are so closely related to what is to be learned that going through them will produce at least some of the learning proposed. Thirdly, pupils must be willing to go through the selected experiences, or the teacher must be able to persuade them to do so.

If the goals are quite clearly defined and are within the maturity or readiness scope of the pupils, there must be some experiences which will develop in the pupils some of the desired learning. If the pupils can be persuaded to go through these experiences, they will scarcely be able to avoid some learning.

The difficulty in applying this notion of method has been the insistence of teachers on applying customary and stereotyped methods which are indirect and do not provide experiences which move directly toward the learning proposed. It took several generations to discover that spelling is rarely used except in writing. In the meantime the roundabout approach to spelling through oral exercises and tests continued in the schools.

As was said, foreign language teachers still talk about having pupils learn to *speak a language* and yet do everything else in language classes except practice speaking the language. Some of the same teachers also talk about reading in a language and then practice labored translations which can never produce effective sight reading. Even the teachers of speech in English often spend more time with experiences having to do with the function of the vocal cords and with rules of rhetoric than they do with practice in the kind of speaking which pupils will normally have to perform out of school. Do not throw further bricks at teachers in these fields but examine carefully the practices of teachers in your field with experiences which seem to have nothing to do with the needed learnings.

Again, pupils who practice filling in correct usages in mutilated sentences in English workbooks learn to fill in some correct forms in mutilated sentences, but they do not learn to use correct forms in either their own speech or in their written compositions. Pupils in plane geometry spend class time in the proof of theorems but cannot determine the pitch of a rafter or stair or lay out the pattern for a circular skirt. Pupils in physics memorize and demonstrate Ohm's Law but continue to overload the household electrical circuits with too many appliances.

On the positive side, in answer to "What would you have the pupils do?" there are the following illustrations. In the language class, if pupils are to learn to speak the language, they must have experiences in speaking. One way to do this is to have pupils dramatize very simple conversational situations. Cases could include two people passing on the street and exchanging greetings, a housewife telling the milkman at the door what to deliver, buying a theatre ticket, buying a railway ticket, checking baggage, and so on. If pupils have enough experience with such situations, they can begin to speak in the language. If incorrect forms are used, corrections must be made on the spot and the correct forms practiced. This applies to pronunciation also. The teacher may need to set some correct patterns. It must be remembered that conversational facility in a language involves hearing the language as it is spoken. Experiences with recordings and perhaps with sound motion pictures may help with this side of a conversational approach. If the teacher is clear about the objective, experiences of pupils are to be selected that *can* contribute as much as possible to the learning.

An actual case will illustrate the possibilities of a direct attack in a speech class. A junior college speech teacher proposed to a class that the members should learn to do public speaking at the level of the speech performances most often called for in the local community. To implement this objective, the teacher and class offered to furnish speakers for all special occasions for all the community organizations, clubs, men's dinner clubs, churches, young people's organizations, and women's groups. This involved the preparation and practicing of all speeches called for. But the speeches were *actually delivered* to a normal audience. Each member of the class had considerable experience with such speaking by the end of the year. It may be added that members of this particular class went on to win a national speech contest.

GOOD TEACHING METHOD. The presentation of the direct attack upon learning suggests a way for the teacher to determine whether or not a given method may be effective. If the teacher can suggest experiences which will produce in pupils a clearly defined desired learning, the method is good. The effectiveness of the method can be predetermined to some degree by attempting to predict the immediate relationship of the proposed pupil experiences to the chosen objective. The teacher may well use ordinary common sense in trying to make such a judgment. He can say to himself, "If the pupils go through these experiences, is it at all probable that they will come out with what we have proposed to learn?"

The effectiveness of a particular method cannot be judged entirely in terms of educational theory or of widely publicized methods. Even a popular method may fall short if, in going through the implied experiences, the pupils fail to reach the learning objective. For example, in spite of the extensive treatment of problem method in educational literature, the results attained with it often have been disappointing. Either the problems have not been well chosen or the experiences of the pupils in working with them have failed to produce the objectives frequently proposed for problem-solving procedures. This is not to say that problem method cannot be made to work in some situations. It merely illustrates the point that in some situations a widely publicized method may not be a good one. The proof of the pudding is in the eating.

POOR TEACHING METHOD. The converse of the proposal for judging methods can be made to operate also. If the experiences proposed for pupils fail to produce the desired learning, the method is poor, regardless of recommendations in educational literature. Some methods which have been generally condemned sometimes produce results. For example, having high school pupils go through the experience of listening to the teacher lecture from day to day is generally frowned upon by educationalists. And yet there are cases when such an experience may produce good learning. Of course, much depends upon the nature of the material presented and the skill of the teacher as a lecturer. It may work for some learning and not for other. The question is, "For what we propose to learn, will it be profitable for the pupils to listen to a teacher presentation?

Are there other experiences which would seem to be more profitable?" The method is good or bad in terms of the results obtained through the pupil experiences inherent in it.

This does not imply that teachers should not be informed about methods described in educational literature. There are a number of useful methods which can be adapted to meet various teaching situations, and there is a considerable body of evidence to indicate that these described methods can be made to operate successfully. What seem to be the more significant of the methods now described and available for teachers are treated in the remaining part of this chapter.

Methods stressing individual learning

One group of widely publicized, comparatively recent procedures has been developed by teachers seeking practical means of providing for individual differences under classroom situations. There is the additional feature of getting pupils to accept responsibility for their own work and for the consequences of the work. These methods bear such labels as block or contract assignments, three-level assignments, committee assignments and reports, and individual progress records.

BLOCK OR CONTRACT ASSIGNMENT PROCEDURES.   The block assignment is first a manipulation of assignment techniques. The procedure assumes large-unit organization. It becomes so unwieldy as to become impossible of operation when attempted as a day-to-day lesson organization. Directions for work are set up for the majority of the class, who may be expected to receive a C mark. The second block contains the work of the first but includes also work set up for those pupils who may be expected to receive a B mark. The third block includes the work of the first and second blocks and in addition work for those pupils who may be expected to receive an A mark. Diagrammatically, the block assignment appears as in the accompanying illustration.

In planning a given unit of instruction, the teacher should plan the exercises, activities, readings, etc., for the three blocks for the whole unit before work can begin. Practically, the directions for work will need to be written out and usually typed. The operation will become exceedingly cumbersome unless the teacher has access in the school to good duplicating equipment. Assignment sheets will need to be duplicated and a copy placed in the hands of each pupil.

A time limit is established and a deadline set when all work for the unit at hand must be completed. All pupils begin with the as-

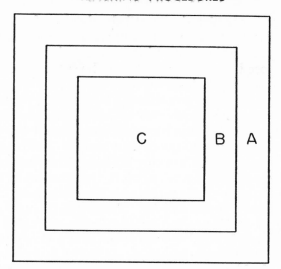

Diagrammatic Representation of Block Assignment

signment for the C mark. Some pupils will spend all their time on this assignment. Some may not be able to complete all the exercises for the C block when the time is up. Those pupils who complete the C block before the time is up are encouraged to work on the directions for exercises for the B block. Pupils who have completed C and B blocks are encouraged to attempt the work outlined for the A block.

To avoid conflicts and misunderstandings with pupils, it is desirable to have directions for the different blocks on separate sheets. In the beginning all pupils are given C assignments and the sheets for the other two withheld. Upon *satisfactory* completion of the C block, pupils are given the sheet with the B assignment. Upon *satisfactory* completion of both C and B blocks, pupils are given sheets with the A assignment.

The contractual feature of the block assignment scheme, which gives it its other name, lies in the layout of the blocks in terms of marks for which the pupils strive. In effect, when pupils are first introduced to the assignment, they are told that if they complete the C block within the time limits set for the unit, they will expect to receive a C mark for the work done. Those who complete both C and B blocks within the time limit will receive a B mark. Those completing C, B, and A assignments will expect to receive an A mark.

It is apparent that the first work done in the classroom will have to do with an elaboration and interpretation of the assignment. Following this, on successive days until the date set for completion is reached, classroom work consists of working upon the exercises contained in the previously prepared assignment sheets, or exercises or problems proposed by pupils which may be substituted for some of those on the assignment sheet.

The whole assignment procedure is intended to permit pupils to work at their own individual work rates. Therefore, after the first day or so of work on the first block different pupils will be working at varying tasks during any given class period. As the work moves on, superior pupils will be working on more advanced blocks while slower learners are still at work upon the assignment of the original block. The classroom tends to become a workshop for doing whatever the assignment sheets call for. There will be little group work for the whole class. The recitation disappears, and there will be few discussions, although pupil reports to the group may become a part of the assignment for some blocks.

Wherever block assignments become the routine procedure, there is a tendency for exercises to become largely paper-and-pencil exercises. The pupils will more and more tend to be doing what the old-fashioned elementary school teacher characterized as seatwork. The seatwork characteristic is not necessarily inherent in block assignment procedure, but the teacher will need to be continually alert to avoid having the exercises of the block assignments degenerate into classroom busy work.

The evaluation of work under a contract system tends to be quantitative—so much work, or so many exercises, for a given mark. This presents the problem of qualitative evaluation of work done and the learning effects of such work. It is possible for a pupil to do all the exercises set up in a block assignment, do them all in a slipshod fashion, and claim the mark indicated for the block. To avoid this, some teachers have set a mark on a unit test as a part of the block contract. For example, pupils are told at the beginning that for a C mark they must complete certain exercises *and* make a mark of 80 on the unit test. Some teachers go so far as to administer a test for any individual at any point of completion of a block assignment. This means that, past the midpoint of the time set, some pupils may be taking a test almost every day until the final deadline for the unit is reached.

Another approach to control of quality with a block assignment is to put into the general regulations of the contract a statement that credit for a C mark will be assigned when the exercises for the C block are completed and *approved by the teacher*. This means that careless work can be disapproved and turned back to the pupil for further correction and improvement before the mark can be attained. Pressure can be applied to such a regulation by withholding assignments for the next block until the work of the preceding block has been completed *with teacher approval.*

Advantages.   Block assignment procedures tend to place responsibility for willingness to work upon the pupil. There is provision for adapting the work of the class to the work rates of pupils. Goals as defined in terms of marks tend to be definite. Some pupils who might otherwise make marks toward the upper limits of D will be willing to put forth extra effort and spend the time to make a C, if they know exactly what to do. Some pupils who otherwise might have marks toward the upper limits of a C will make B. Almost all upper B pupils will try for an A, if they know what is expected.

At once it becomes apparent that there will remain a group of pupils at the lower end of an ability scale, i.e., who will tend to make D and F marks who have no hope of reaching the standards set by a C block assignment. These pupils will not be motivated by such an assignment and may even be discouraged. Their marks will remain unaffected. The lower- and mid-C group who are relatively content with their status will also be unaffected.

It can be said in summary that block or contract assignment schemes tend to be effective in the stimulation of individual differences upward and ineffective in providing for differences downward.

Objections.   Many teachers will object to the emphasis upon marks as motivation which is inherent in the contract notion. The emphasis tends to be upon grade-getting and not upon the learning opportunities which the assignments should provide. Most superior pupils tend to exaggerate the worth of grades, and many parents contribute to this overemphasis. Mark motivation tends to artificiality of school situations. The few B+ pupils in a class do not need especially to be prodded by being shown how to make A's. It might be better for them to be concerned with what they have an opportunity to learn and how this can be turned toward their further growth.

The teacher who uses contract-block assignments needs to be aware of the probability that there will be a disproportionate number of high marks in the distribution of marks for a class as a whole. In technical language, the effect of contract-block assignments is to produce a curve of distribution of marks which is skewed toward the upper end. The teacher will need to advise the principal of the nature of the work being done in his classes so that the principal will understand the reason for the disproportion of high marks.

THREE- OR FOUR-LEVEL ASSIGNMENTS. There have been many objections to block-contract assignments on the grounds that marks are overemphasized and that superior pupils must begin with a mid-assignment. There is the added criticism that there is no provision for the neglected group at the lower end of an ability scale.

An attempt to meet these criticisms is found in the three- or four-level assignment. Like the block assignment procedure, this is primarily a manipulation of the unit assignment to provide for individual differences and varying work rates of pupils. The procedure assumes large-unit planning. Assignments are developed by the teacher prior to the introduction of a new unit. Duplication of assignment sheets is necessary for good administration. Assignments for different groups should be on separate sheets.

Assignments may be designed for either three or four subgroups. The fourth assignment is intended to make provision for the neglected lower-ability group not cared for with the typical block assignment. Theoretically, five or six assignments could be made. In practice, very few teachers attempt more than four. Some do only three.

The three- or four-level assignment differs from the block-contract scheme in two essential ways. First, each pupil *begins* work with an assignment at his assumed level. He does not need to do the exercises designed for pupils at a lower level and does not progress to a block of a higher level. Second, there is no "contract" feature. Assignments carry no mark designations. Under the most favorable conditions teachers avoid any mark connotations for assignments. If tags for assignments are used, these are tags that are almost never used to designate marks. The teacher avoids even such terms as "high (or low) level assignments." Certainly, he does not refer to assignments for bright, average, and stupid learners in discussing assignments with pupils. Sometimes the symbols X, Y, Z, or W, X, Y, Z are used to differentiate assignments.

In the accompanying diagram the varying level assignment appears as a series of strata or layers rather than as blocks.

The grouping of pupils who are to receive the varying assignments is predetermined by the teacher in the light of what he has been able to discover about the abilities and work rates of the members of the class group. The groupings are informal, for this unit only, and are not announced to pupils. Probably the teacher will lay out a list of proposed groups using the class roll as a guide. This is done before the unit is introduced to the pupils. If some pupils do unusually well with a Z assignment on one unit, they can be placed on a list to receive Y assignments for the next. If the abili-

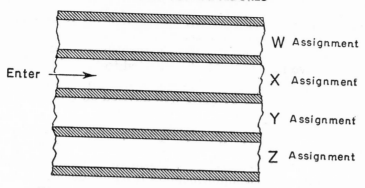

Diagrammatic Representation of Four-level Assignment

ties of some pupils receiving W assignments for one unit have been overestimated, they may be given X assignments for the next unit without any special announcements or fanfare. The groupings are always flexible and subject to change as the teacher discovers more about work rates of pupils, or as pupils show significant growth.

The time of the class period is used by pupils in doing the work indicated by the assignment sheets. As with block assignments, there can be no recitation and there is a minimum of total group discussion. Time limits for work may be somewhat more flexible than with block assignments. Again, there is a likelihood of a drift toward paper-and-pencil exercises, although this is not inherent in the procedure. During the class period as pupils are at work, the teacher may move from group to group or pupil to pupil to see what is being accomplished and offer suggestions. Above all, the teacher needs to avoid sitting at a desk attending to his own routine paper work and leaving pupils to their own devices.

Evaluations applied to the learning and outcomes of varying level assignments may be any of those customarily used by teachers. The usual test and quiz devices are applicable, as are ratings of work and performances of pupils and informal appraisals of progress.

However, it must be remembered that, since pupils have had assignments of assumed varying difficulty, marks of pupils having different assignments are not comparable. The difficulties of administering a procedure based upon varying level assignments lies here. In order to maintain a high level of motivation, it is assumed that pupils receiving Z assignments will be able to receive a full range of marks. This assumption holds also for pupils receiving assignments at other levels. It then becomes possible for a pupil with a Z assignment to receive an A mark along with a pupil who has had a much more difficult W assignment for the same unit. It becomes possible, also, for a pupil having a Z assignment to receive an A, while a superior pupil who receives a W assignment and does it badly receives a D. The variable assignment procedure plays havoc with competitive marking. Marks reported to the school office will need to carry explanatory notes of interpretation. Moreover, pupils and parents will need to be quite well advised on the new marking interpretation.

COMMITTEE ASSIGNMENTS AND REPORTS. Another approach to subgrouping and individually tailored assignments is found in committee assignment and reports. Many teachers are familiar with this procedure in its use as a supplementary teaching device for superior pupils.

Complete Committee Organization.   It has possibilities of adaptation as an overall teaching technique as well. As with the procedures just described, the large-unit organization is assumed. The teacher, in planning the unit, breaks the whole into meaningful parts —problems, subtopics, themes, questions, and so on. Enough are planned so that when the class group is broken up into a number of small committees each has its own problems or subtopics. For example, for a class of thirty pupils, assume seven to ten committees. The teacher may then plan ten or twelve subassignments.

In working with a committee assignment technique, it is desirable to keep working groups small. Rarely should a committte have more than four or five people as members. Many groups will consist of only two or three workers, and a committee of one is sometimes desirable. This notion is supported by the experience of the aging neighbor who often employed the boys of the neighborhood to work in his yard and garden. He found that two boys together almost always accomplished more than two boys working separately. Three boys often made a fine working team. Four or five nearly always wasted time and drifted into arguments, talk, and horseplay. Beyond the four or five, almost no work was accomplished.

In presenting the work of a new unit, the teacher makes the usual unit introduction. Then the proposals for problems, projects, or subtopics are made. These can be listed on the blackboard. Duplication of assignment sheets is usually unnecessary. Suggestions of other or optional subtopics are received from the class and added to the blackboard list. First committee members may be selected on a volunteer basis by asking who would like to work on particular problems. The teacher may suggest that certain pupils can contribute to some of the proposed committees. In some cases the teacher will assign committee members to particular groups. Hesitant, slow, or timid individuals will be suggested as members of some committees. By clever steering of pupils at the class organization stage, differences in both abilities and interests can be cared for. In general, superior pupils should appear on committees working upon more rugged assignments. Slow workers should draw easier jobs. There should be some leadership in each committee.

Classroom work will consist of what the various committees find is necessary to carry out the committee assignment. There will be no class recitations. In the stages of committee work, discussions will be limited to small group discussions within the committee. The teacher may from time to time join any working group as a co-worker or contributor. If reference or book materials are needed, a given committee may adjourn to the school library and spend the class period at work there. In a science class a committee may carry on laboratory or investigative experimentation as part of its classroom work. Finally, each group will need to put together and organize a report of what the members have found out or accomplished.

As the work of committees is completed, their findings are carried back to the class as a whole through committee reports. In almost every case, these will be oral reports supported by summaries, tables, diagrams, illustrations, demonstrations, and so on. There will usually be questions from the group and very often considerable discussion. Committees also may be expected to file a written report which can be kept in the classroom for the benefit of the whole class. There should be an attempt to keep the point of view that each committee accepts the responsibility for contributing something to the group as a whole.

The teacher may gather material from the reports and construct tests of any of the usual forms to be administered to the whole class, both committee workers and listeners. Such tests should serve as incentives to class members as a whole to be attentive to reports.

It has been found experimentally that with a complete committee organization of classes in the social studies the pupils who listened to reports of committee members learned a significant amount of the subject matter involved. On the same tests members of working committees always made higher scores than those who listened to reports. Apparently a relatively poor committee could convey less to the class group than a committee of superior pupils. The experimenter believes that systematic testing is necessary to get good results with the listeners.

Committee reports as enrichment.   Many teachers will hesitate to use a committee-report procedure for all the work done in the class. However, the procedure is used frequently as an approach to "enrichment." The class as a whole may be given uniform assignments, and additional materials may be brought into the class as contributions from committees. Hence it is possible to provide for interests of different groups within the class and at the same time widen the scope of subject matter that can be covered.

A common use of the "enrichment" approach is found in the introduction of current events into classes, especially in social science and natural science classes. Too often the current materials are poorly chosen and the programs in which they are presented almost completely unorganized. Pupils take the current event as another school task and not as a challenge. There is little feeling of responsibility for contribution to the class group. "I have to have a current event today. Where can I find one?" Anything will serve which the teacher is willing to have brought in.

A remedy for the abuse of the current event lies in the committee-report procedure. Instead of designating one day each week as current event day and accepting any random material, the teacher and pupils plan a series of continuing themes for the class. These themes, or centers of interest, are to be pursued by the class through the school year. Committees are formed, taking into account the interests and abilities of pupils. Each committee accepts the responsibility for keeping the class informed and up to date on the theme assigned to it. Several reports will be made by each committee through the year, usually in the nature of progress reports. Oral reports can be supplemented by bulletin board exhibits, demonstrations, projected pictures, graphs, and reading suggestions from newspapers and magazines, possibly with cross-references to current radio and television programs.

INDIVIDUAL PROGRESS RECORDS. Another procedure which may be classified with those which stress individualized instruction and work rates is one which appeals to a pupil's urge for improvement and uses the record of the pupil's progress for judging improvement. Actually such an appeal to improvement is a means of motivation rather than a complete piece of methodology. Assignments, classroom practices, and pupil activities may be various.

The teacher devises some way in which a graphic record of pupil progress can be made. Such graphic devices may include: learning curves; checklists of operations and learnings; lists of problems correctly solved; bar graphs of quantities of work; files of written work or drawings, dated and kept in order. Each pupil should keep his own record up to date on the graphic device used. Charts of individual progress need not be displayed for the class. For some pupils, progress charts should not be placed on public display. Comparisons are always with each pupil's own record. Comparisons between pupils which may result in rivalries and competitions are avoided. For slow-moving pupils, and for very bright pupils who are approaching achievement limits, praise of the teacher for achievement needs to be liberal. Goals for short-range future improvement should be set by agreement with the pupil in terms of what he believes he can accomplish. Very often parents who are informed of pupil progress and shown the charts can help with encouragement and in setting goals.

Marking devices need to be reorganized so that marks become consistent with the progress made. The whole scheme will fall apart when pupils who have made marked individual improvement find that they have been assigned D marks for the term. On the other hand, bright pupils who have been drifting with comparatively little improvement may be severely shocked and complain loudly upon receiving a D mark for achievement which is low for them and yet at a level above that of most other members of the group. The procedure does run into the perennial stumbling block of individualized procedures; the noncomparability of the marks used. Its value, however, lies in the motivation provided by individual improvement, and the marking features should not be overemphasized.

Methods stressing activities, needs, and purposes

Another group of methods centers about the attempts of teachers to find methods which will utilize the motivating forces of awareness of needs and purposes on the part of the pupils themselves. Under this heading will be examined the problem method, the project, and pupil participation in planning.

These three methods were considered in their relationship to readiness organizations of subject matter in Chapter 4. Certain evidence bearing upon their effectiveness was also presented in this earlier chapter. This material should be reread in the light of the present setting of methodology. The treatment of problem solving in Chapter 8 is pertinent also. Here an effort will be made to bring these approaches to learning into the total scope of classroom methodology.

PROBLEM METHOD. As a method of instruction, the problem approach is largely a manipulation of assignment. The teacher attempts to find problems which are consistent with the immediate objectives of the unit, and which will lead to a utilization of the subject matter. Ideally, the problems should be normal problems for the pupils and deal with out-of-school life situations. The assignment is presented to the pupils as a problem or series of problems to be solved within the time limits set for the unit. The obvious place in which to develop the problem setting is in the unit introduction. In many situations a considerable amount of pupil participation in the formulation of suitable problems can be utilized. Under such circumstances there are no appreciable differences between problem method and pupil participation in planning.

There is no exact description of what should go on in the classroom under a problem method. Presumably pupils will do whatever seems necessary to reach a solution to the accepted problem. In the sciences this may involve controlled observation, excursions, and laboratory investigation as well as summarization of data and the formulation of conclusions. In the social sciences class time may be used for selective reading, finding suitable source material, assembling of data, and arriving at interpretations. In mathematics the usual procedures for mathematical solutions of problems are transferred from homework to the classroom setting. Probably greater emphasis will be placed upon applications of mathematics and relatively less upon drills on mathematical manipulation. There will be very little recitation, and discussion will be curtailed at the point where it ceases to add potential data for the solution of the problem at hand.

Out-of-class work will consist of a continuation of the problem-solving procedures initiated in the classroom. The teacher's role in the classroom will be that of making suggestions, helping in finding sources and selecting pertinent processes, and aiding in the organization of data and the drawing of inferences.

As was indicated in Chapter 4, controlled experimentation with the problem method under classroom conditions has not produced the high achievement that educational theory would lead us to expect. Probably this failure to reach expected attainment may be ascribed to the introduction of topics as questions labelled problems, in the artificiality of many school problems, and in the use of adult problems with adolescents.

Wherever the problem method is applicable, learning to use problem-solving procedures becomes fully as important as the recall of the solution to the problem. Tests commonly applied have tried to measure the acquisition of subject matter as a result of a problem-solving method. Generally the tests used have been inadequate in measuring what pupils have learned about how to attack problems. Teachers will continue to be concerned with problem methods wherever they are aware of their obligation to help young people to learn to attack problems for themselves. Adequate measurement of results will depend upon the designing of evaluative techniques for getting at *both* subject-matter achievement and methods of problem solving.

Remember that a problem approach is out of place in situations where the primary goals are either high-grade skills or the development of appreciations. Teachers of mathematics need to make a very clear distinction on this issue. Typewriting is primarily a matter of practice, not of problem solving. Reaction to a piece of literature or to a great piece of music is essentially a matter of emotions and not an exploration of problems involving the psychological makeup of the author or the composer.

PROJECT METHOD. Frequently teachers say, "What is the difference between a problem and a project?" One significant practical difference is that of size. Ordinarily people think of a project as a large-scale or long-range undertaking. On the other hand, a problem demands immediate solution. Projects tend to be complex and may involve the solution of a whole series of problems. For example, a farmer's project might be to establish an adequate farm water supply. The determination of the best available water source for the particular farm will be one of the problems, the best and least expensive means of storage another. If he decides to store the water in a pond, the location of the pond offers a third problem, and so on.

As a method, the first stage is the presentation of potential projects to the pupils as a part of the unit introduction. This can be modified by a composite of suggestions from the teacher and the pupils in the class. Very often there will be no reaction from pupils unless the teacher is ready with suggestions for possible projects. On the other hand, many of the suggestions of pupils may be trivial and nonpertinent to the particular unit, and the teacher must exert some degree of forceful leadership in the early planning stages. It is evident that if projects are merely assigned or planted by the teacher the motivating force of the normal purposes of the pupils will be lost. The purpose around which a project is to be organized must also be the learner's purpose or at least fully accepted by him as worthy.

The best source of suggestive projects for the teacher is in a continuing file of projects successfully carried to completion by his own pupils. Every teacher who works with projects should build such a file for reference.

Since projects are inherently organized around the normal purposing of the learners, pupil participation in the unit introduction stage is a commonplace. As each project develops, the pupils working with it must do the basic planning or many of the learning values are lost.

During the progress of a set of projects undertaken by pupils in the class, the work done is that which is necessary to carry the projects to completion. The carry-over of work done outside the classroom is also determined by what is needed to keep the projects moving. If different people are working on a variety of projects, there will be relatively little class discussion. There will be no place for recitation as such. Reading will be that which is needed for gathering information centered around the projects of the pupils.

In many cases pupils are expected to formulate written reports for each project completed. It is desirable to have each pupil make an oral report to the class group on each project as it is completed. Such reports may be accompanied by demonstrations, displays, charts, and so on. Members of the group should be encouraged to raise questions concerning the work of the pupil reporting.

A whole class may develop a project which seems of value to all members of the group. Such projects have the potential values of group organization and participation. Probably more of the class periods will be utilized for discussion than if individual and committee projects are undertaken. Some illustrations of group projects are "the improvement of assembly programs for our school," "keeping our parents informed about what goes on in our school," "improvement and beautification of the school grounds," "fly eradication in our community."

In undertaking whole-group projects, if several of the pupils are unconcerned about the enterprise, it ceases to be a project for them and so loses the inherent motivation. The unmotivated group can be a considerable drag upon the undertaking. It is much easier for the teacher to find projects for individuals and small groups than to find class projects.

A project approach has become commonplace in many high school fields. Individual farm projects are written into the regulations for vocational agriculture. Most teachers of classes in vocational home economics expect the girls to carry on home projects along with certain other classroom instruction. General shop and art courses are quite commonly built around a series of projects. Projects are quite common in many high school science classes.

An early attempt to evaluate the success of a series of projects in terms of the subject matter learned was carried out by the author in classes in junior high school science. An elaborate objective test covering the common content of general science texts was used. Tests were administered in September and repeated in May. Increases in subject-matter learning were computed in relationship to the pupils' measured intelligence. It was found that pupils in the experimental classes working with a series of projects which had no sequential relationships as a course pattern learned significantly greater amounts of subject matter than did pupils in the control classes who studied the subject matter of the textbooks in the order set up in the texts.

There may be administrative difficulties in handling classes in which most of the work is organized around pupil projects. It is extremely difficult for a teacher having thirty or forty pupils in each section, a total of 120 to 150 pupils a day, to keep up with the details of knowledge concerning the work of each pupil, needed in working with the project method. Freedom to work out projects within the classroom often requires greater floor space and different furniture from that customarily found in classrooms adapted to more formal instruction. A room equipped with armchairs and a teacher's desk is not ideally equipped for project teaching. Classroom libraries with a variety of resource materials are desirable for pupils carrying on projects.

PUPIL PLANNING. A considerable amount of pupil participation in planning work is necessary for the successful operation of projects. An extension of the idea of pupil participation in projects to the planning of all kinds of classroom enterprises has become increasingly popular with progressive teachers. One advantage in a pupil-planning approach lies in the assumed improved motivation. Pupils should be much more willing to work with enthusiasm toward goals which they have helped to establish. In addition there is the learning received in the democratic process as contrasted with an authoritarian approach in which the teacher dictates to the group what is to be done.

The primary emphasis again is at the stage of assignment or the level of the unit introduction. The teacher presents suggestions, proposals, or possibilities concerning the next work to be attempted. Pupils aid in suggesting problems, projects, questions to be answered, or ways of attacking the work. Almost always the language of the teacher is that of the cooperative "we". "If we follow up the work which we have just completed, what should we attack next? How shall we express the problems that we wish to work on? What is the first thing that we should do in attacking our first problem? Whom do we have in class that can do this kind of thing best? Where can we find the information which we need?" The unit introduction takes the form of a quite free discussion rather than that of a lecture or presentation by the teacher.

In many cases it is necessary to get the thinking of members of the class down in writing in the form of an outline, notes, or a series of questions. The teacher may serve as secretary to the group, or class recorders may be used. The blackboard is a most useful device for such recording. Usually the original suggestions need to be reworked into an organized approach. Sometimes this final proposal from the class for an organized attack can be duplicated for future use of each member of the class.

The teacher who encourages pupils in participation in planning is still responsible for preplanning. Indeed, the cleverest attempts at participative planning are carried out by teachers who have previously planned most thoroughly and so have clearly in mind the goals toward which pupils are to be directed as well as imaginative predictions concerning what the pupils are most likely to propose.

Since the introductory stage of the unit provides for a considerable amount of free discussion and contribution from random pupil experiences, the teacher must guard against a prolongation of the planning stage which may finally appear to be time-wasting. The attempt to organize the planning with the blackboard and questions which have to do with the effectiveness or practicality of the work design may serve to conserve time devoted to the initial stages of planning. Sometimes a time limit set for planning presented to the pupils in the beginning will aid.

After the planning stage, the work of the class will follow no set pattern. The classroom and the class time are used for whatever work is necessary to implement the plan.

As the work moves toward completion, some organizing device for the whole should be introduced, such as writing a class report for the project, a dramatization or demonstration to which parents or other guests are invited, or a series of reports from various individuals organized as a program.

Pupil planning has been used most effectively in such areas of the school program as home economics, art, music, English, dramatics, citizenship, and in some measure in science. The activities program of a school presents a considerable opportunity for participative planning of such activities as school parties, assemblies, athletic tournaments, clubs, and the student council.

Experimental evaluations of the learnings resulting from pupil participation in planning have produced somewhat inconclusive and contradictory evidence, owing in part to the inclusion of claims to learning values other than subject-matter achievement that have not been easy to reduce to clear-cut objective measurement. As a consequence, much of the evaluation is based on testimonials of pupils concerning what they believe they have learned. Such testimony tends to be divided. Some pupils prefer the orderliness of logically organized sequences of subject matter and feel that much of the learning under pupil planning lacks good organization and wastes time. Others welcome the freedom to pursue objectives of their own proposing and claim both better knowledge of subject matter and gains in learning how to carry on work processes for themselves.

Methods stressing objectification and direct experience

Another group of methods includes those that have as a primary feature the providing of concrete and direct experiences for the pupils. Common illustrations are to be found in the science laboratory, the industrial arts shop, the art class, clothing construction in home economics, and in typewriting. Often all these school situations are thrown together as laboratory experiences. The teacher's operations seem clearer if a distinction is made between a laboratory and a workshop. In making this distinction, it is desirable to examine the expected outcome or output.

LABORATORY AND WORKSHOP. Generally, in or out of school, the laboratory is a place for investigation. The laboratory is equipped with the furniture, apparatus, tools, chemicals, measuring devices, and so on, that will enable an investigator to arrive at objectively verified information. The worker attempts to get proved answers to questions. The output is in the form of the answers, usually expressed as facts, ideas, rules, laws, formulae. The output is not expected to be an object or thing. The laboratory is a place for inquiry. The output is in the form of the answer to a query.

On the other hand, a workshop is intended to turn out a tangible product. This can be seen by common observation of the out-of-school shops which we see around us. The print shop, the photographer's, the bakery, the garage, the tailor shop, the dressmaker's, the florists's, and the planing mill are cases in point. As with the laboratory, the shop has special arrangement of floor space, furniture, equipment, tools, and materials to further the work to be done.

If the distinction between shops and laboratories is carried back into the school, the following can be identified as shops: the industrial arts shop; the art workroom; the clothing construction room in home economics; the home economics kitchen, or unit kitchens; the typing room; the farm shop in vocational agriculture; and possibly others.

EXTENSION OF THE WORKSHOP APPROACH. It is possible to extend the notion of a shop, in which people work and turn out a definite product, to other areas of school work. For example, it is possible to operate a composition workshop in English. The point of view becomes that of the use of the classroom, class time, and class equipment to turn out pieces of composition, letters, editorials, news stories, narratives, or descriptions which fit the composition needs of the pupils in a particular group. Class time is used to write. Furniture will be adapted to convenient writing, probably tables and chairs rather than tablet-arm chairs or school desks. Possibly the room should be equipped with typewriters. Certainly the reference tools of the writer's trade will be found there: the handbook of usage, the dictionary, the thesaurus, and the style book. There will be little discussion after the introduction and definition of the writing tasks at hand. There will be no recitation. There may be exhibition and criticism of finished products. Most of the class time will be taken up with writing, proofreading, and revision. The teacher will become a source of suggestion, a helper, and a friendly positive critic. It will become unnecessary for the teacher to carry home armloads of formal themes to correct. The reading will be done as each piece of writing develops in the workshop. Each workman will do his own proofreading, correction, and polishing. Indeed, it is probable that few *themes*, in the ordinary usage of the English class, will be written.

Classification of work from this point of view in music, physical education and speech seems more difficult. However, it is possible to accept a fine speech performance as the output of the work of a speech class and so classify such a speech situation as a workshop. The same approach can be taken with groups in applied music, if the public musical performance is considered as the product. In the same way the actual performance of a skilled player in a competitive sport may be considered as the product of work done over a period of days on the field or on the floor of the gymnasium. The performance of forward Williams in the basketball game with Crossroads High School may be considered as the product of his experiences in the basketball workshop preceding the game. The adoption of this point of view places emphasis upon the ultimate performance as a goal and does for speech, music, or physical education what we have tried to picture for instruction in composition above.

LABORATORY INSTRUCTION. When the term laboratory instruction is used, most people think of the science laboratories in school first. In terms of the proposed definition of the laboratory, the school science laboratory should be a place in which pupils search for facts and ideas and *learn how* to verify facts and ideas. Typically, the pupil is supposed to have a problem when he enters the laboratory to work. Typically, his assignment takes the form "to prove that so and so takes place under the given set of conditions." He is issued a set of equipment and spends his time in the laboratory deriving a set of objective data which presumably will support the proof at which he is trying to arrive. He tabulates his data and forms a generalization based upon the tabulation. He then compares his data and generalization with similar experimentation carried out by expert scientists and recorded in the science textbooks.

Science teachers in general have defended the laboratory procedure described above as valuable for training pupils in the use of scientific methods. As a matter of fact, such an approach may be questioned from the point of view of training in the use of scientific methods. In the first place, the pupil is not truly proving anything new and is not dependent upon his own laboratory resourcefulness in arriving at a solution to a problem. Most laboratory assignments propose to have the pupil prove something which has long since been proved, and they deal with ideas or laws that are commonly recorded in science textbooks. There is really no "research." The pupil does not depend upon his own methodology, his own data, or his own conclusions. He works toward what he has previously accepted as true. What he does get is added direct sensory experience and observation dealing with concrete things. He can manipulate apparatus, smell chemicals, see color changes take place, feel the pull of forces. Such laboratory exercises provide for objectification of experience but not for experiences with sound investigative techniques.

LECTURE-DEMONSTRATION. In the literature dealing with science instruction will be found a whole series of experiments which deal with this issue. These experiments contrast the learning of factual material in science from lecture-demonstration with learning comparable facts from laboratory instruction. Where the tests deal with the acquisition of science facts, immediate tests given at the close of instruction favor the lecture-demonstration. Differences, however, are small and perhaps not always statistically significant. Where the tests are given after some lapse of time after the completion of the instruction, there are small differences in favor of laboratory instruction. In other words, retention seems to be better under laboratory instruction, but not very much better, perhaps not enough better to justify the added expense involved in laboratory instruction.

On the other hand an experiment done by Ralph Horton with high school chemistry shows large differences in favor of laboratory instruction where the tests are tests of laboratory skills.

It is possible to interpret these experiments with lecture-demonstration vs. laboratory instruction in terms of the objectification involved in the instructional process. Neither seems to involve true investigation or scientific methodology as such. In one case the instructor with superior manipulative know-how and probably with superior equipment shows pupils what happens under certain controlled conditions. In the other case the pupil with less know-how and possibly poorer equipment handles his own equipment in order to see what happens. The differences are small either way. The issue involves which is the better approach to object teaching and direct experiencing. A third option in modern schools might involve the use of strip film and motion pictures for the same purpose.

In view of the work of Horton cited above there seems to be no doubt but that if manipulative skills are desired the pupil must practice the manipulation for himself. This would seem to apply not only to laboratory skills but also to various shop skills in clothing, typewriting, woodworking and so on.

THE INVESTIGATIVE LABORATORY. There remains the issue centering around laboratory instruction in which the pupils work with problems of considerable significance to themselves, for which the solutions are not commonly known. This implies that the relatively inexperienced learner might attempt to do in the school laboratory on a small scale what the research scientist attempts to do. The pupil would try to find a solution to a problem which seems worth investigating. The solution would be unknown to him and probably to his teacher. A classroom library and the equipment of the school laboratory would be used in trying to arrive at a solution. The youthful investigator would be dependent upon his own collected evidence and laboratory data. He could not doctor his data to come out in consistency with more reliable data published in his textbook.

Obviously the problems investigated by high school pupils will not be of a kind that make modifications in the great generalizations and laws of science. Pupils will not "prove Newton's laws of motion" or "prove Mendel's laws of inheritance." By far the greatest number of problems investigated will be *applications* or *cases* involving well-established facts, principles, laws, or generalizations. In general, pupils will not be creating new science but applying old science. There are literally thousands of unsolved small problems of application. Pupils in science classes bring these to the teacher daily. The teacher is inclined to refer to an authoritative source or to shrug the problem off as not having a known answer. Instead the teacher could say, "Let's use our science library to get what information we can. What principles that we know seem to apply. Let's go into the laboratory and set up a series of experiments that might give us an answer to our question." Or, "Let's see if we can plan a series of controlled field observations that may give us an answer."

The reader is referred to the best of the exhibits and demonstrations of science pupils in high schools shown at the annual science fairs in many cities and reported in the newspapers during the progress of the fairs as illustrations of what can be done with science laboratories in schools.

In the evaluation of the kind of science laboratory experiences just described there are four possibilities:

1. The solution to the problem may in itself be of considerable value. This solution will be known and remembered by the pupil investigator, and probably by many of his classmates

2. The pupils carrying on such investigations may learn much of the desired factual material customarily taught in science classes

3. Retention of science facts so gained may be better

4. The pupils should learn how to carry on scientific investigations and perhaps be more critical in appraising other solutions found currently in newspapers, magazines, and bulletins.

So far, the evaluation of laboratory instruction centered around the real problems of pupils in the terms described above is scant. The difficulties lie in the relatively small amount of laboratory work organized around normal problems of pupils and in the lack of adequate testing devices for measuring outcomes other than the acquisition of factual material.

EXTENSION OF LABORATORY APPROACH. If the proposed distinction between the laboratory and the shop is accepted, it seems possible that there can be laboratories in other fields than the sciences. Perhaps the most obvious possibility in the extension of laboratory instruction is in the social sciences. It would seem that at least some of the work in history, geography, citizenship, economics, sociology, and government can be done under laboratory conditions.

For example, suppose that we try to visualize a laboratory for American history. The room used as a laboratory will be equipped as a workroom rather than as a place for recitation or discussion. Probably the furniture will consist of tables and chairs rather than school desks. There will be a classroom library for historical reference. In addition there will be available newspapers and magazines. The more commonly found references, the historical atlas, *The World Almanac, The Statesman's Yearbook,* the manual of state government, will be found on the tables. There will be maps and charts, and possibly a sound reproducer with a collection of records of significant historical speeches.

The output of this laboratory will consist of ideas, historical interpretations, and at least tentative solutions to political, social, and economic problems.

Many assignments will take the form of questions or queries for which verified answers will be sought. Some assignments will be in problem form, and workers in the laboratory will attempt to arrive at tenable solutions. Perhaps a common assignment will have the simple form of, "Let us see if we can get at the facts in the case."

During the class periods pupils will read, look up references, examine documents, consult charts and maps, write out summaries, construct charts and maps, make statistical tabulations, and formulate reports. There may be discussion but chiefly among groups working around a table upon a common project. The teacher will serve the group largely as a resource person and consultant.

As particular investigations are completed, there will be reports to the class group as a whole of findings, interpretations, or solutions. Each reporter will be expected to cite sustaining data, evidence, or source of authority.

There seems to be little doubt that pupils having worked a school year in such an history laboratory will learn much of the subject matter of American History. It is probable that they may learn qualities of delayed judgment, methods of historical investigation, and that they will be much less inclined to be gullible and hysterical when confronted with scarehead newspaper accounts or political chicanery. These latter possibilities present a challenge to the teacher who can invent appropriate means of evaluation for the concomitant learnings which may accrue from such laboratory experiences.

If the proposed American history laboratory is workable, teachers in other fields that are largely concerned with ideas, interpretations, verifications, and solutions to problems should be able to work out comparable laboratory situations.

CLASS EXCURSIONS. Another means of directing the learning of pupils through the use of direct and concrete experiences is found in the excursion, a modern version of Mohammed going to the mountain. There are many things in a community that are highly desirable for direct classroom use. Unfortunately, many of these cannot be moved into the classroom. Then, let's move the class to the source of the needed materials.

There are innumerable illustrations of the need for taking a group to the potential scene of learning. One of Shakespeare's plays is being presented at a local commercial theatre. The film is unavailable for school use. The whole English class that is studying Shakespeare may well attend the commercial presentation. A noted symphony orchestra is to present a concert. Probably the school orchestra should attend the concert as a group. A home economics class is studying attractive and convenient kitchen arrangements. It seems desirable to make appointments with a few selected homemakers who have well-planned kitchens for the girls in the class to visit their kitchens. Pupils in a citizenship class may attend a session of the city council or of the school board in order to see how such a body operates. The class in biology that is studying the ecological relationships of plants should spend at least an afternoon in the field observing the relationships of plants on a particular plot.

Everyone will recognize the management difficulties involved in the direction of a group outside the classroom. Under modern conditions these management difficulties are likely to be intensified by transportation problems. Therefore, excursions are not to be undertaken unless the experiences can be truly significant in relationship to the learning at hand.

Generally, it would seem ridiculous to take a high school group to a chain grocery. No new experiences are likely to be gained by any member of the class. If an interpretation of the operation and arrangement of the store seems desirable, it would be far simpler to assume the pupil-experiences with the grocery and invite the manager to come to the classroom to develop the interpretation.

On the face of things, it seems desirable for pupils in a class studying the physics of the automobile to adjourn to the school parking lot and observe a motor in operation. Actually, nothing is to be gained; time will be wasted and the morale be bad. All pupils will have seen an automobile in operation. Nothing much can be determined about the operation of the motor by looking at it. The whole thing is cased and enclosed. All that can be seen to move is the fan. Far better keep the group in the classroom and use a cut-away model or a motion picture diagram.

The teacher considering, a possible excursion needs a strong vein of common sense. Pupils are likely to set up a clamor for the excursion, sometimes merely to do something which differs from the usual school routine.

An excursion needs skillful planning and an assignment. The

assignment should be worked out with pupils in class before the trip is undertaken. Pupils will need either mimeographed direction sheets or assignment notes in notebooks which they are to carry with them. They need to be held responsible for answers to such questions as the following:

What are we expected to see?
What are we to look for?
How does the thing work?
Make a diagram to show what things?
What items are to be collected and brought back to school?

In addition there will be directions concerning the management of the excursion which involve such items as the following:

The time and place for assembling.
The arrangement for transportation facilities.
Clothing to be worn.
Equipment to be taken.
Directions for keeping the group together.
A signal for assembling and being attentive to direction.
The time for return to school.
Courtesy to be shown to people who own the property or aid with the excursion.

Such management details need to be worked out and clearly understood by pupils at the time of the assignment, usually on the day before the excursion.

If an excursion is to be meaningful, there must be class treatment of the ideas gained following the trip itself. This will involve in-class interpretation and organization, with possible summarization and reports.

For most effective use the excursion does not end with the post-treatment in class. There is also the stage of evaluation and testing. Usually it is an exceedingly wholesome thing for a class to have a quiz over what was learned on an excursion.

MOTION PICTURES. In the attempt to provide pupils with situations for direct and concrete experiencing it is often possible to get a motion picture which can be brought into the classroom instead of taking the class group out on an excursion.

There is a considerable accumulation of evidence to show that motion pictures do contribute to learning. There is also some evidence to indicate that the addition of sound and color add little to the learning values of pictures. It should be obvious that, to have learning value, a particular motion picture must contain the experiences and ideas that are pertinent and relevant to the situation at hand. There is also the element of timing. The picture must be shown at the point in the learning sequence where it can make the most telling contribution. If we are studying animals of Africa on Tuesday, we need the picture on lions on Tuesday, not on a week from Friday when we are studying plants of the Arctic tundra.

In the use of motion pictures it must be kept in mind that, for classroom purposes, the motion picture is not a substitute for the teacher but a means of providing experiences which the learners lack and which cannot be readily introduced into the classroom by more direct means. The motion picture offers one means of bringing the mountain to Mohammed.

It must be borne in mind also that motion pictures in the classroom are intended to contribute learning experiences and not merely for entertainment.

The evidence on the uses and values of motion pictures points clearly in the direction of certain techniques in the use of the films.

First, there needs to be developed a setting for the film to be shown. A motion picture is not just to be thrown at a group of pupils, as, "We shall have a movie on marketing for fresh foodstuffs tomorrow." Instead in a period previous to the showing of a film, as with the preparation for an excursion, pupils need to be briefed on what can be observed in the film, what particular things are to be looked for, what pupils are to be held responsible for, and what kind of summarization can be used for the ideas gained.

Secondly, there will be the showing of the film itself. In some cases intelligent and restrained teacher comment or a quiet insertion of a question or point of emphasis during the showing of the film may be useful. However, teacher comment during the showing needs to be kept to a minimum, to avoid annoyance at the interference with the film.

Thirdly, there should be a post-treatment of the content of the film. This may take the form of trying to state answers to the questions contained in the preshowing assignment. In other cases there will be attempts to summarize what was learned from the film. It is possible, also, to include suggestions of what the film failed to show, or of points that were not clear or well understood. The latter may result in some cases in a reshowing of parts of the film in an attempt to clarify obscure points. In other cases assignments to books or other sources may be used to throw light on issues raised but not clearly explained in the film.

The responsibility of pupils for being attentive during the showing of a motion picture may be enhanced by testing over the content of the picture. Such testing may be over the film only, or included as a part of a unit test to which the film content is assumed to have made a considerable contribution.

It is obvious that the teacher should have previewed for himself a film to be shown to his pupils. One way to do this previewing is to sit by the projector, slow the running of the film, and then with a pad and pencil note items of importance which can be utilized in framing a test over the film content. This will give the teacher both the needed preview and the material from which a film test can be made. In some cases the teacher will find that there is not enough material in a film out of which to construct a significant number of test items. This should suggest that, if the film has no important content, it may not be worth the showing. The preview procedure suggested here becomes at the same time a means of evaluation of the worth of a proposed film.

As everyone with some experience with classroom motion pictures knows, the bottleneck in the use of films is in film distribution. Few schools have film libraries adequate to service the needs of the various classes. Cost is a large factor here. A school system can tie up a considerable sum in a film to be shown to the biology class for fifteen minutes once each school year. Many schools depend upon central distributing libraries (city, state, or institutional) which service many schools. The difficulty here is to book a given film so that it is available for a particular class use at the point of maximum efficiency in furnishing certain needed experiences. Unless the film is available at this point, its showing may become comparatively useless. The situation is analogous to the need for a reference book in a school class which is not available in the library. The book must be ordered and cataloged. It arrives six weeks after the point at issue was raised. Probably no one in the class cares any longer to look up the information for which the book was ordered.

RECORDINGS, RADIO, AND TELEVISION.[1] The teaching principles established for the use of motion pictures in learning apply also to the use of other modern devices for bringing reproduced experiences into the classroom: recorded music, drama, and speeches of historical importance; radio programs; and television programs. The experiences provided by these media should *fit* the instructional program at hand. The materials should be available at the point in

---

[1] For more extensive treatment of problems arising from uses of these media see National Socity for the Study of Education, *53rd Yearbook. Part II, Mass Media and Education* (Chicago: University of Chicago Press, 1954).

learning when the experiences are most needed. Learning rather than entertainment is to be provided. The recording or the television program is not just to be thrown at the pupils. There should be stages of preview, showing or listening, and a postview. The learning resulting from such media should be tested. If there is nothing for which to test, the worth of the experience may be questioned. The bottleneck again is in having the record or the program available at the point of need for the indicated experience.

There is a considerable literature and a known history on the uses of motion pictures and radio programs in schools. There is developing a body of literature on educational television programs, and there are under way some large-scale pieces of experimentation with TV programs in schools.

A generation ago school people were as enthusiastic about school radio programs as present day people are about television. An illustration exists in the music appreciation programs done for N.B.C. by Walter Damrosch. Programs were graded for children, and teacher's manuals were avaliable. The difficulties which arose grew out of the relationship of radio programming and school schedules. It was difficult to insure that a tenth-grade music class in Crossroads High School would be in session at the time that the music appreciation program could be broadcast from New York. The final solution is to put the music programs of a great musician and teacher on records and sell the records to the school to be used as the local teacher will. Now it should be possible to make a tape recording of a radio program and repeat it as needed. This is what is done in the radio broadcasting industry with its own programs.

The same programming and scheduling difficulties arise with the use of television programs in schools. The solution being developed is to kinescope the programs and sell the kinescope films to the schools. Although these reproductions are at present high in cost, their use will probably increase. What is to be done with such reproduced programs is still at the discretion of the teacher in the local school.

At least some questions about the educational uses of television programs can now be answered. Young people can learn from television. The evidence can be gained in conversation with almost any child or adolescent who has access to a TV set at home or at the neighbor's. The use of a kinescope film would seem to resolve itself into the same treatment which teachers have learned in connection with any other motion picture film.

Manuals for teachers and work sheets for pupils to accompany the TV production should be a help. Teachers should see the performance before attempting to direct pupils in their experiences with it. A pretreatment or preview should prove effective. A post-treatment is to be recommended to insure effective learning. Evaluation of the results would seem imperative.

In institutions where the installation costs are not excessive, closed circuit television can extend the class size for a master teacher almost indefinitely. However, there must be a teacher for each section to insure that the further desirable learning experiences take place.

It does not seem probable that TV programs will replace any large number of teachers in school systems over the country at any time in the near future. The present tremendous costs of any kind of a TV operation are a factor that many school administrators have not thoroughly explored.

Methods stressing study and work processes

A third possible grouping of current methods includes those methods in which the primary feature is a change in the ways in which the pupils attack learnings. Of these four will be examined: extensive reading, directed study, group discussions, and group dynamics.

EXTENSIVE READING. An extensive reading approach can best be identified by considering it in contrast with intensive study or reading. With intensive study, assignment is made usually to a single text and a very limited number of references. Pupils are to be held responsible for the subject matter contained in the limited sources. In some cases, as was described under text-recitation, pupils are expected to be able to quote what is in the text. By contrast, extensive reading involves an assignment which requires a wide range of reading from a variety of sources. Reports from such sources are not to be quoted but organized by the pupils for interpretation.

Extensive reading procedures are adapted to those courses sometimes characterized as "content" courses, such as those in literature, the social studies, history, the natural sciences, home economics, and vocational agriculture. These are the courses in which ideas and interpretations are dominant and for which a considerable volume of available published material can be had.

Assignments are centered about a topic, theme, problem, or possibly a project. It is not necessary, or always desirable, that all pupils read the same references or from the same sources. In the process of introducing the unit, the themes or topics are presented and the available reading materials suggested to the pupils. Both a classroom collection and reserve books in a central library may be used. As pupils become accustomed to extensive reading on a particular theme or topic, they will profit by participating in building a list of pertinent readings. Ultimately, pupils may be expected to take a particular topic, theme, or problem and build a pertinent bibliography from which to work. The teacher will need to suggest the range of source materials available for class use.

During the class period, pupils will spend a considerable proportion of the time in reading from the various sources. Hence the needed books and newspapers, magazines, pamphlets, and references must be at hand in the room itself. There must be enough reading material to more than supply the members of the class at any one time. In many cases the best information can be found in a relatively few books or magazines, and the teacher must choose duplicates with care. Many school administrators object to duplication of reading materials. However, unless there are enough sources containing pertinent information, it will be impossible to keep all the members of the class profitably busy. Nothing will wreck an attempt at extensive reading more quickly than to have some pupils sitting idly with nothing to read, or waiting to be able to get at one of the books which contains the needed information.

Often pupils will make notes on reading. The teacher will need to help many pupils to learn to make notes which represent selected ideas rather than copying verbatim statements from the book or magazine at hand. The clue to the note-taking is obviously found in the question, problem, or topic accepted by the pupil in the assignment or unit introduction.

Certainly, as the work of a given unit develops, some class time will be taken in organizing the material gleaned from the reading. The organization may take a variety of forms: an oral report, a chart or map, a summary, a tentative solution to a problem with the supporting evidence, possibly a debate or panel discussion, or a demonstration.

Finally, class time is taken for the presentation of these organizations to the class group as a whole. If all the class has been working on a single topic, theme, or problem, the blackboard may be used to record, organize, and summarize the contributions of the different pupils into a whole. Either the teacher or one of the pupils may serve as the recorder. It should be the objective to have each pupil contribute something. Mere recitation as such is to be avoided. Contributions are to stay closely to the central theme. Here is a place for discussion, but circular arguments without evidence to support a point of view are to be avoided.

Generally, reading, organization, discussion, and reporting will not all go on in a day's class period. A whole period or perhaps several consecutive periods may be taken up with needed reading. Often the discussion and summarization will take one or more periods.

The use of extensive reading presents an excellent opportunity to provide reading materials suited to the reading levels and work rates of the different pupils. To take advantage of this opportunity, however, the teacher must try to find readings of differing levels and become expert in appraising the reading difficulties of the available materials.

While pupils are reading, the teacher should quietly observe the work operations of the various pupils. Often he can suggest to a pupil a book or a magazine article, sometimes a substitute for the one which he has chosen. Often the teacher can get a slow-starting pupil to begin work. Suggestions for organizing reports are also in order. It must be kept in mind that the teacher does not interfere with pupils who are self-directive and who are busily at work upon well-chosen reading.

To be effective in directing extensive reading, the teacher must be quite familiar with the possibilities for reading for the particular unit and also know well what is available within the school's recources. It is the teacher's responsibility to see that what is needed for reading is at hand and can be utilized by the pupils without unnecessary waste of time. The assistance of the school librarian will be essential. Posted reading lists and possibly work sheets with directive questions will be found helpful. The teacher himself must read widely enough to keep in touch with material which can be recommended to the pupils.

It becomes obvious that the possibility of utilizing extensive reading procedures in any given school is dependent upon the library resources of the school. A school with inadequate library facilities will at once set a limit upon what can be done with extensive reading. It is not intended here to digress into a discussion of the need for adequate school libraries. It is in point, however, to remind each teacher of his responsibilities in finding and recommending to the librarian and the school administration what is necessary to carry out a sound learning program within the courses which are assigned to him.

The evaluation of the results of a program of extensive reading can be made through the use of the customary devices for measurement. Pupils may be given tests covering the subject matter which centers around the themes covered by the reading, or possibly the reports to the class may be rated.

However, there is some evidence to support an approach to evaluation of extensive reading through an individualized check with each pupil. Early work with extensive reading was carried out by teachers of English in schools over the country. Generally, pupils read different pieces of literature. At first teachers tried to check on such reading by having pupils make written reports on each book or article read. This tended to artificiality and often led to wholesale cribbing of reports. Teachers tried then to evaluate each reading by oral reports made in class. These too were often artificial and certainly were difficult for the teacher to rate. Even the oral reports were often cribbed.

Some teachers tried a compromise scheme by having pupils make brief informal reports over each reading on 4-by-6-inch cards, written in class and kept as a running file for each pupil's reading. Often the card file was accompanied by a point system in which certain points were assigned to each of the books presented by the reading list. The cumulative points shown by the pupil's card file determined his final rating for the extensive reading program.

Finally, the English teachers arrived at a system of informal interviews with each pupil over his reading. These interviews could be made during the class period while the class as a whole was engaged in reading. Sometimes interviews could be made in a "free" period, or in the interval between classes. The interview approach can be combined with a simple card file of readings for purposes of record. With the interview any clever teacher can find out what a pupil has read and in general what he has gained by his reading. Most experienced teachers of English have now come to the interview scheme for the evaluation of extensive reading. Teachers in other fields may well profit by the experiences of the English teachers. If the reader is interested further, the history of this development can be traced through the files of *The English Journal* during the 1920's and early '30's.

The interview check on reading has two additional advantages. It is possible to use the interview to stimulate further reading and to suggest what might be read. It is possible, also, for the teacher to find out something about what a pupil can read with good interpretation and so by suggestion help adapt his further reading to his particular needs and capacities.

Evidence of the learning values of extensive reading has existed for some time in a variety of school subjects. The experimentation has consisted of comparing parallel groups of pupils, one group doing intensive study of limited sources and the other doing a wide range of reading in the same area. After the same teaching interval, the same tests were administered to the two groups.

Evidences of superior learning with extensive reading were found in early experiments in eleventh-grade literature, eleventh-grade American history, and junior high school science.

Since these early investigations, the evidence on the values of extensive reading has tended to pile up. Now a teacher working in a field which utilizes a considerable volume of printed matter, whose school has adequate library facilities, can expect to have his pupils profit by extensive reading experiences.

Before leaving our discussion of the use of extensive reading, it may be well to add that there are clearly other values inherent in experiences with a wide range of reading other than the subject-matter items learned. Among these are the formation of reading habits within the fields represented. *If some pupils develop a desire to continue reading literature, science, or history, this may in and of itself be more important than the particular facts retained.* In addition the extensive reading experiences should give pupils a knowledge of sources and their comparative worth. In a case of need for information the pupil should know where to look and whether or not the particular source is likely to be a relatively true one.

If we are to think of educative forces as continuing, that finally each individual must be responsible for the direction of his own education, the establishment of reading habits, a knowledge of what to read, and of the worth of reading materials becomes of extreme importance. Perhaps the need for such education is even greater with the widespread usage of other means of communication. There may be danger that for many people radio, television, and motion pictures tend to supplant reading. If much reading is not to become a lost art, perhaps more extensive reading programs should be carried on in the schools. This is not to say that we shall discourage the use of all kinds of modern means of communication. It is to say that reading will always remain important in the acquisition of ideas and their evaluation. In fact, reading may become the primary source for checking the accuracy of information presented by the other media.

DIRECTION OF STUDY. The second of the teaching procedures which imply changes in the ways in which pupils attack work is that of the direction of study. The attempt to direct the study of pupils in the classroom is by no means new. There is a considerable body of professional literature under the term "supervised study" which begins at least as early as 1909.

This early supervised study movement was without doubt a reaction against the memorizing processes of the text-recitation process. Under the text-recitation approach almost everyone—bright pupils, parents, neighbors—except the teacher, did the teaching. The teacher merely set the lesson and heard the pupils recite what they had been taught by others. Supervised study was supposed to remedy this situation by having the study done in the classroom under the guidance of the teacher rather than at home or in a study hall. A number of early experiments are available to show that the supervision of study could be made to improve learning, especially with those pupils at the lower end of a class. Often the brighter pupils did no better under supervised study than with independent home study.

In time the supervised study movement slowed down. The term itself became relatively unpopular with teachers, possibly for two reasons: (1) a number of the experiments with supervised study failed to show significant learning gains for superior pupils; (2) most teachers did not know how to direct work processes of pupils. Indeed, almost nothing was known about how to attack most types of learning. If the teacher could not tell the pupil how to read a history lesson, how to analyze a problem in algebra, or how to set up a paragraph for a piece of prose composition, the mere spending of class time on the part of the pupil in further struggles with not knowing how profited nothing.

DIRECTION OF THE WORK PROCESSES. The use of class time for the direction of the work of pupils and having pupils do school work in class are profitable to the extent that the teacher is successful in showing pupils *how* to attack the work at hand. As teachers have learned some things about how to attack work in their fields, interest in the supervision or direction of class work has increased. To avoid the connotations of the old movement, the term "the direction of study" is more often used than that of "supervised study." An even better term would be that of "direction of the work" of the pupils. This latter term could then be applied to the direction of learning activities in such fields as physical education, art, music, and the industrial arts shop. Too often the term study has applied to the use of books. But study can go on in the chemistry laboratory, the sewing room, the shop, or on the gymnasium floor. To be perfectly clear about this, the term "the direction of study" will be used for the direction of any kind of work or of learning activities.

In many cases general formulae for school procedures are undesirable because teachers interpret them as having a universal applicability. On finding that the formula does not work in some cases, the teacher loses faith and tends to discard the formula. With it are discarded any values it might have for the cases to which it can be applied. In spite of this, there is presented here a list of proposed essentials for the direction of the work of pupils that can be applied in many situations if the teacher will analyze the elements of the local situation in his attempts at application.

Essential Steps in the Direction of the Work
of Pupils During the Class Period

1. A clear statement of exactly what is to be accomplished by the work at hand.
2. A check back with the pupils on the statement of what is to be accomplished to determine the pupils' own interpretation of what is to be done.
3. A set of definite directions or suggestions for a plan of attack. This should include the sequence or order of the stages of the attack.
   a. Directions given by the teacher.
   b. Directions developed by teacher and pupils working cooperatively and perhaps outlined on the blackboard.
   c. Work processes suggested by the pupils.
4. A trial of the plan of attack, or at least basic parts of the plan, in the classroom with the teacher present.
5. Observation by the teacher of the difficulties of pupils in attempting to carry out the plan of attack.
6. Further suggestions on attack, especially for particular individuals. Probably, the freeing of alert and quick individuals to proceed on their own initiative.
7. Final assignment summary of items 1, 3, and 6 above.
8. Continued work on the part of the pupils. If pupils know quite clearly what is to be done and how it is to be done, some work from this point on may be done outside the classroom.
9. A check to determine what work has been done by the pupils and the extent of learning resulting from such work.

Importance of assignment. A scanning of the stages suggested above for the direction of the work of pupils in the classroom will show that the clue to successful operation is found in the assignment. Of course this notion of the assignment, for the unit, may be part of the unit introduction. The assignment technique must help pupils to see clearly what they are driving at. Pupils must understand why work is to be done and what they can hope to achieve as a result.

A bit of experience with the common reactions of pupils will show the value of the second step. Teachers take for granted that pupils are attentive and burning with zeal for the task at hand, or that their own language in presenting a goal is always clear and well understood. Suppose that the teacher pauses at this stage and asks the members of the class a few very simple questions. "Henry, just what

is it we are going to try to do? Tell the class in your own words."
"Harriet, I observed you making notes during the assignment.
Please read what you put down in your notes about what we are
going to do." "Polly, what would be the first thing to do with this
assignment?"

Several interesting details will be uncovered. Henry can repeat
what the teacher said, but make no interpretation in his own words.
His neighbor was busy making doodles in his note book and cannot repeat the statement of the goal for the unit. Harriet did make
notes but cannot now read parts of her own notes. Susan next to
her has no notes because she failed to bring a pen or pencil to class.
Polly seems to know what is to be done but has no suggestion whatever about what to do first. And so it goes around the class. Perhaps the original statement of purpose seems to be clear to approximately one-third of the class. Some classes are better. Some are
worse. The teacher who fails to make this simple checkback never
finds out until much time has been wasted in idling or inept approaches to the work at hand.

These two first steps are important, but the success or failure of
an attempt at the direction of the work of pupils is inherent in the
ability of the teacher to make pertinent suggestions about *how* to do
the work and *in what order*. Such directions must be worked out
to fit each particular case. The teacher must work continually at
such analyses and be observant of the work processes of pupils who
are successful. There is a caution here, too. Sometimes the successful procedures of superior pupils are not operable by the slower
learners. Special work approaches may need to be suggested for
some of the pupils in addition to the general directions for the class.

Observing pupils' work. Again, it is not enough to outline for
pupils the way in which a piece of work is to be done. The teacher
must know that pupils are able to carry out the work processes. The
only good way to find out is to see the pupils work. This means a
tryout of the attack in class. Several rules-of-thumb for the teacher
will apply here. All *new work* is to be tried in class with the teacher
present. All *new methods of work* are to be tried out in the classroom. All attempts at *written* work are to be begun in class. First
practices on *new skills* are to be tried out under the teacher's observation. Home work, or work to be done outside the class, is to be
done only on those things tried enough in class for the teacher to
be sure that each pupil knows how to do the work and is successful in the beginning stages. Superior and quick-learning pupils are
often to be let alone with their work as soon as it is evident that they
have seen how to do it. The reassignment stage, appearing in the

outline as step seven, should be carried out before pupils undertake out-of-class work.

Usually the statement of the thing to be accomplished, the check to see that pupils understand what is to be done, the plan of attack, and the trial of the plan of attack will take all of a class period. If time remains, it is to be used for continued work and the following class periods so used until results are achieved. It is possible that at the beginning of a new class period there needs to be a stock-taking to see where each pupil left off and that each one knows what he is to do next in the continuance of work. The general principle which applies to this stage is that class time and the classroom and its equipment are to be used for whatever needs to be done to further the work at hand.

If the reader will check back on what has gone before, he will see that many of the procedures previously treated can be classified under what is described here as directed study, or the direction of the work of pupils. Much that was said in chapter 6 concerning drill is in point. So also are the treatments of unit introductions, multiple assignments, committee report techniques, extensive reading, the laboratory and workshop approaches. All these sections emphasize the teacher's responsibility for direction and the use of the class situation for whatever work will further the needed learning.

Group discussion procedures

Group discussion procedures may be described simply as those which depend primarily for developing learning upon the give-and-take of pupil talk based upon experiences, observations, and reading. Here are considered two such procedures; group discussion and group dynamics.

DISCUSSION AND RECITATION. Group discussion is to be distinguished sharply from recitation. Recitation usually results from specific questioning. The pupil merely repeats what he was supposed to have learned before the recitation period. Since all pupils have had the same assignment, there is no feeling upon the part of the person reciting that he is making any contribution to what other members of the group know.

On the other hand, discussion results from the presentation of a general question or problem for the whole group. Differing experiences and knowledges of pupils are to be utilized. There is a place for differing opinions. Each pupil is to feel that what he has to say makes a contribution to the group.

Early use of discussion, without doubt, was a revolt against the formal recitation and lesson hearing. It was accompanied by a considerable movement for the socialization of classroom situations. The peculiar term, "the socialized recitation," frequently occurs in pedagogical literature.

Some schools attempted to implement socialization by using informal school furniture to permit the grouping of pupils for better discussion and more democratic procedures. Groupings around tables after the fashion of the graduate seminar became customary as did the arrangement of high school groups in the familiar kindergarten circle.

DEVELOPMENTAL DISCUSSION. Discussion was intended to *develop* a lesson. This took the form of the development of the details under a topic, the solution to a problem, or the answer to a question by means of oral contributions from class members. Effort was made to avoid having pupils talk to the teacher but to address remarks to members of the class. There is a considerable amount of literature on inductive and deductive development of lesson themes. Deductive discussion attempts to develop the details which can be grouped under a rule, principle, concept or topic, beginning with the generalization. In inductive discussion, details, experiences, and observations are gathered first and then summarized into some form of generalization.

Conduct of discussion. Often there is no formal assignment preceding a group discussion. In class, the assignment takes the form of a topic for discussion, a problem, a challenging question, or a proposed plan to be formulated. Sometimes the topic, question, or problem is presented to the pupils with a set of assigned readings on a previous day. Often the question or problem for discussion is written on the blackboard in an attempt to keep the central theme before the pupils.

During the class period the time is taken up by the oral contributions of the class members. Sometimes notes on these contributions are recorded on the blackboard.

If an assignment is made preceding the discussion, pupils may use out-of-class time in gathering ideas to contribute to the following discussion. Sometimes notes are taken and outlines made. Often the discussion depends largely upon the experiences, opinions, and observations of pupils. In such case the pupils may do nothing outside the class period.

The teacher must prepare the assignment and discussion questions or work these out in cooperation with the pupils. During the class period the teacher serves as chairman to keep the discussion on the points at issue and to keep the discussion moving. It is necessary for the teacher to keep a rein upon over-eager or over-talkative pupils and also to draw other pupils into the discussion.

The questions used to stimulate and direct discussion are important elements in the success of a class discussion. The usual simple factual and recitation questions are to be avoided. Generally the "what" questions are few and greater emphasis is placed upon "how" and "why" questions. A few questions for a single discussion are more effective than many. Vague "what happened then" or "what about so and so" are most often ineffective. The teacher's cleverness is shown in framing the discussion questions and keeping the pupils to the issues involved.

The measures used for evaluating discussion teaching can be the usual ones applied in most methods. Some teachers attempt to rate the oral contributions of the pupils, but this presents considerable difficulty and is beset with the pitfalls of fluctuating standards.

Limitations of discussion. The great dangers in the use of discussion methods are that pupils may wander from the point and that the discussion may be continued beyond the point where pupils have anything to contribute. Too often a discussion degenerates into a circular argument based upon biases or opinions of pupils. The teacher needs to stop such discussions with an assignment to look up the facts in the case, or to support a point of view with evidence. The great limitation on most discussion is that the amount of learning is limited to what is available in the experiences of the pupils as they come into the class. Little progress can be made until other sources are tapped. But experiences of some pupils can be extremely useful as sources—the child who has lived abroad, the one who knows what it is to be a refugee, etc.

Perhaps the discussion can best serve as an introductory medium for presenting a unit introduction, with other approaches supplanting the discussion as soon as the introduction is made, or as a summarizing device for use at the culmination of the unit. These techniques have been discussed elsewhere in connection with the development of units and along with the appropriate methods.

GROUP DYNAMICS. One of the values long claimed for group discussions lies in the socializing factor. The importance of this value has been revived since World War II by the proponents of group dynamics as a teaching procedure. These people have been most concerned with the use of group dynamics as a means for building democratic procedures with citizens, young and old.

Group dynamics procedures are similar to those which have just been described for group discussions in general. There seem to be the following two important differences.

1. There is less evident teacher direction and control; pupils seem to take a greater part in group leadership.
2. There is set a group machinery with certain designated participants who have the responsibility for keeping the discussion moving.

Machinery of group dynamics. Those charged with responsibility for a particular discussion are most often a *group leader,* a *recorder,* several *resource persons,* and an *evaluator* or summarizer. The person designated as leader serves as chairman and parliamentarian. With a typical group dynamics approach, the leader is always a pupil. The teacher becomes a resource person and sits in the group. The recorder takes down notes on the important contributions made by the group during discussion. Notes may be taken on paper or the blackboard may be used. For class purposes, it is probably better to have notes on the blackboard where all can see them. Two recorders may be used, one for the blackboard and one to make a record on paper from the blackboard. The resource people are persons with knowledge or preparation beyond that of most of the group. In a school class, outside resource people may be invited to sit with the class when certain special problems are under discussion. It is possible also to designate certain members of the class as resource people and ask them to do special reading or interviewing in preparation. The evaluator listens to the discussion and reviews the notes of the recorder. He then sums up for the group, "This seems to be what we have accomplished" or "This is what we have learned" or "This is what we have agreed upon." Under classroom conditions, the evaluator is a pupil not the teacher.

Limitations of group dynamics. It is evident that if this procedure is to develop training in democratic processes, the rotation of roles in operating the group machinery among the various members of the class is highly desirable.

As a means of learning, the use of group dynamics seems to have very much the same limits that was suggested for group discussions. It may work best as a means of unit introduction or of unit summarization. Obviously it has its values as a means of arriving at a group decision concerning some proposed action. However, there are some kinds of learning which seem impossible of attainment with a group dynamics approach, as for example, the formation of skills in composition, typewriting, garment construction, or basketball, or the acquisition of specific knowledge of chemistry or the structure of the human body. Although sometimes useful in such a fiield as American history, it may be doubted that adequate specific and accurate facts of history can be attained by a process of group dynamics. Enthusiasm for the democratic processes should not obscure the realities concerning much of the learning that should take place in schools.

The group dynamics approach would seem to have its greatest contribution to make in situations leading to group action. For example, a class in American Problems proposes the problem, "How can we get more desirable school publicity home to our parents?" A solution and plan of action may well be worked out through the group dynamics process as described. When the work is over, what the pupils have learned about group processes and group action may be far more important than the particular decision and plan which they have developed.

There is a caution, too, in the use of group dynamics as a developer of democratic attitudes and ways of action. In the hands of an autocrat or a small clique of leaders, the processes may be used to further a preconceived point of view or a plan of action which the leadership may wish to put over. All that is necessary is for the few leaders to plant the group functionaries, including the group leader and the resource people. If these are picked to represent a given point of view and not selected by the group as a whole the net result may be anything but democratic.

The measurement of the results of group dynamics is difficult. It involves the determination of changes in attitudes and of ways of behaving both on the part of individuals and on the part of a particular group as a whole. Perhaps the use of group dynamics will become more effective as improvement is made in tools for the measurement of its results.

Subunit implementation

SUBUNIT ORGANIZATION

1. The terms "teaching procedure" and "method of teaching" apply to the activities used by the teacher in stimulating and directing learning, rather than to teaching devices externally applied.

2. In similar situations, different pupils may learn as a result of the application of a variety of teaching procedures. Generally, there is no one best method.

3. Teaching procedures should be developed for the accomplishment of specific learning objectives.

4. There are no general methods applicable to the attainment of any number of objectives in a wide variety of teaching situations.

5. Teaching procedures must fit the needs and maturities of particular pupils and the psychological relationships of the particular phases of the subject matter used.

6. The modern idea of a good teaching procedure most often implies the devising of learning experiences for pupils which drive directly toward the learning to be achieved.

7. Mere exhortations to read, study, discuss, compare, trace, analyze, etc., are usually not sufficiently directive to produce learning.

8. The traditional recitation and similar "lesson hearing" devices do not provide sufficient individual activity to be useful in most learning situations.

9. Responsibility for the work involved in a learning situation should rest largely upon the pupil concerned after goals have been clarified and work processes defined.

10. Popular methods such as problem method, the project, contract assignments, three-level assignments, pupil participation in planning, have been in the beginning reform revolts against memoriter learning of stereotyped subject matter and mechanized general methods.

11. Ideal teaching procedures should provide for the development of initiative and self-direction in pupils.

12. Promising improvements in general methods, within the limits for all general methods, are found in the following: contract or block assignment; three- or four-level assignment; laboratory or workshop approach to classroom learning; lecture-demonstration; use of visual and auditory aids, especially motion pictures; committee assignments and reports; extensive reading; individual progress devices; pupil participation in planning; the direction of study, or the direction of the classwork of pupils.

13. In the past many teachers failed to accept the responsibility for helping pupils learn *how* to do school work.

Many pupils were never able to do the work assigned at school.

14. Typical supervised study devices have not worked well because often they have not included exact knowledge of work processes in specific situations in particular subjects.

15. The successful direction of the work of high school pupils depends upon the development of definite information concerning details of specific work processes for definite learning situations.

16. Assignments which challenge the interests and abilities of the pupils stimulate improved study techniques.

17. The term "adequate assignment directions" should include such immediate directions for work as those given on the gym floor, in the shop, in the clothing class, the kitchen, the music class, or in the typewriting workroom.

18. Improved assignments assume large-unit organization and planning.

19. Improved assignments should include the following:

a. Clear-cut objectives for the work of the pupils.

b. A checkback upon the pupils' interpretation of the direction for work.

c. Directions which include specific suggestions on *how* to go about doing the work at hand.

d. *New work* tried out under the direction and observation of the teacher.

20. Effective teaching method is to be interpreted in terms of a "direct attack" upon learning.

The direct attack implies a clearly defined learning objective and related pupil experiences so selected that, if pupils can be persuaded to go through them, learning will result.

21. A good method is one in which the learning experiences of pupils have been so selected that the desired learning is produced.

22. A poor method is one in which the selected learning experiences for pupils fail to produce the desired learning.

THINGS TO DO

1. Find and list all the definitely described methods of teaching contained in one of the older textbooks on methods of teaching.

Write in a few sentences a description or definition of each of these. Indicate for each one the following items: (a) the kind of assignment; (b) the things done by the pupils; (c) what is done during the class period; (d) what the teacher does.

2. Describe as indicated above in exercise 1 each of the following: contract or block assignment; workshop procedure; the project; visual education; committee-report technique; three-level assignment; problem method; laboratory instruction; lecture-demonstration teaching; extensive reading; individual progress reports; pupil planned units; group dynamics. (If some of the above have been described in exercise 1, do not repeat here.)

3. Select one high school course from your major field of interest. List in one column common teaching situations which are certain to occur as the course develops. For each of these, show the commonly accepted learning objective. For each of these objectives, indicate desirable learning experiences for pupils of a given maturity.

4. Select some one major unit of instruction from a high school course which interests you. Indicate definitely what you will expect pupils to learn in this unit.

Write out the exercises which might be expected reasonably to insure pupils mastering the objective of the unit. Write out exercises in the form of directions as you would expect to give them to high school pupils. Make directions specific. Do not indicate merely the general nature of possible exercises.

5. Repeat exercise 4 for some other unit or units in a selected high school course.

6. Collect a list of projects for high school pupils to be included in the activities of a selected course.

7. Outline a plan for the direction and control of an extensive reading program in some one high school course. List the reading materials to be recommended to the pupils.

8. Plan a contract assignment set for one unit of a selected high school course.

9. List the proposed exercises which might be used during workshop periods in a selected high school course.

10. Present evidence, accompanied by bibliographical references, to show that some one of the recently developed teaching procedures secures satisfactory learning within certain described situations in your field.

11. Select a particular bit of learning from one unit in your field upon which it seems desirable to have pupils work in the classroom under the teacher's direction.

State what you would say to the pupils in presenting to them the purpose of the work to be done.

Write out an interpretation of what you would say to pupils in explaining *how* to do the work at hand.

Try out your statement and directions with a group of fellow students to see how well they are able to follow what you have planned.

12. Select some desirable common out-of-school learning situation, such as carving a linoleum block, learning to knit, making a drive in golf, putting together a do-it-yourself gadget.

Plan a set of experiences which should produce the learning desired. Try out your direct attack upon some willing victim among your fellow students. How successfully can you predict the needed experiences?

HELPFUL READINGS

ANDERSON, VERNON E. *Principles and Procedures of Curriculum Improvement.* New York: The Ronald Press Co., 1956.

See chap. 3 for a treatment of group dynamics as a means of learning and development. Pp. 62–63 contain a bibliography of references to group dynamics procedures as applied to adult groups involved in curriculum reconstruction.

BILLETT, ROY O. *Fundamentals of Secondary School Teaching.* Boston: Houghton Mifflin Co., 1940. Chap. 19.

Chap. 19 contains an unusually good presentation of the classroom-laboratory. The treatment is that described as an extension of workshop and laboratory procedures to a variety of subjects. Includes a description of the use of extensive reading techniques and their relationship to the school library.

BOSSING, NELSON L. *Teaching in Secondary Schools.* 3d ed. Boston: Houghton Mifflin Co., 1952. Chaps. 4, 7, 11.

Chap. 4 is on problem method; chap. 7 on the direction of study; and chap. 11 on the use of assignments.

BURTON, WILLIAM H. *The Guidance of Learning Activities.* 2d ed. New York: Appleton-Century-Crofts, Inc., 1952. Chaps. 1, 5, 11, 16, 17.

A variety of teaching methods presented, but all from the essential point of view of the teacher as a director of the learning experiences of pupils.

CANTOR, NATHANIEL. *The Teaching–Learning Process.* New York: The Dryden Press, Inc., 1953.

A presentation of the operation of the group dynamics process in action. Teaching and learning are treated as an interrelated group process. The text is taken from tape recordings of a seminar in teacher education carried on through the group dynamics process.

CORYELL, NANCY G. *An Evaluation of Extensive and Intensive Teaching of Literature.* New York: Teachers College, Bureau of Publications, Columbia Univeristy, 1927.

In support of extensive reading in literature.

GRAMBS, JEAN D. and IVERSON, WILLIAM J. *Modern Methods in Secondary Education.* New York: William Sloane Assoc., Inc., 1953. Chaps. 5, and 12.

Chap. 5 on providing variety in learning and learning materials contains sections on audio-visual materials and on use of magazines and newspapers. Chap. 7 is on discussion techniques and the sociodrama. Chap. 12 treats the development of communication skills.

HALL-QUEST, ALFRED L. *Supervised Study.* New York: The Macmillan Co., 1923.

The one best source of collection of early literature and investigations on supervised study. Contains extensive bibliography.

HEISS, ELWOOD D., OBOURN, ELLSWORTH S., and HOFFMAN, CHARLES W. *Modern Science Teaching.* New York: The Macmillan Co., 1950.

Chap. 5 and 7 on methods of science teaching. Section 3 includes all kinds of means used for the objectification of science instruction.

KETTELKAMP, GILBERT C. *Teaching Adolescents.* Boston: D. C. Heath & Co., 1954. Chap. 6.

Chap. 6 is an effective chapter on the general problem of directing the learning activities of pupils.

MURSELL, JAMES L. *Successful Teaching.* 2d ed. New York: McGraw-Hill Book Co., Inc., 1954. Chap. 12.

Chap. 12 presents methods for the individualization of class instruction.

NATIONAL COUNCIL OF TEACHERS OF ENGLISH, THE COMMISSION ON THE ENGLISH CURRICULUM. *The English Language Arts in the Secondary School.* New York: Appleton-Century-Crofts, Inc., 1956. Chaps. 5–9.

Contains a sequence of chapters dealing with the teaching of the various phases of the modern English courses: literature; reading; speaking; listening; writing; and grammar, usage and spelling.

NATIONAL SOCIETY FOR THE STUDY OF EDUCATION. *46th Yearbook. Part I. Science Education in American Schools.* Bloomington, Ill.: Public School Publishing Co., 1947.

See chaps. 13 and 14 for evidence on the values of laboratory instruction and lecture demonstration in science teaching. Much more extensive experimental evidence on the values of laboratory instruction and on extensive reading in science can be found in the three volumes of F. D. Curtis, *A Digest of Investigations in the Teaching of Science, A Second Digest of Investigations in the Teaching of Science,* and *A Third Digest of Investigations in the Teaching of Science.* These digests of Curtis, published in 1926, 1931, and 1939, are out of print but should be available in many college libraries.

———. *47th Yearbook. Part II. Reading in High School and College.* Bloomington, Ill.: Public School Publishing Co., 1948.

See chaps. 7 and 8 for suggestions on teaching reading at high school level.

———. *48th Yearbook. Part I. Audio-Visual Materials of Instruction.* Bloomington, Ill.: Public School Publishing Co., 1949.

See especially chap. 12 on methods of using audio-visual materials.

———. *49th Yearbook. Part I. Learning and Instruction.* Chicago: University of Chicago Press, 1950. Chaps. 3, 4, 7, and 8.

Contains many suggestions for teaching procedures within a framework of principles of sound learning. Chapters stress especially the individualization of instruction.

———. *53rd Yearbook. Part II. Mass Media and Education.* Chicago: University of Chicago Press, 1954. Chaps. 7, 8, and 11.

Suggestions for the utilization of mass media in the schools. See for ideas on the use of radio and television programs.

OHIO STATE UNIVERSITY, CLASS OF 1938 OF THE UNIVERSITY HIGH SCHOOL. *Were We Guinea Pigs.* New York: Henry Holt & Co., Inc., 1938.

Included in reading suggestions as an illustration of large scale participation in planning and of evaluation in terms of descriptive testimonials of the learners. Supports the pupils' experiences as participators in planning.

RIVLIN, HARRY N. *Teaching Adolescents in Secondary Schools.* New York: Appleton-Century-Crofts, Inc., 1948. Chap. 9.

Chap. 9 is a very useful chapter on developing study and work procedures with adolescents.

RUEDIGER, WILLIAM CARL. *Teaching Procedures.* Boston: Houghton Mifflin Co., 1932. Chaps. 1, 17, 18, 20, 21, 22.

Chap. 1 presents the concept of the direct attack in teaching. Should be read by all students of teaching methods. The latter chapters deal with means of enrichment, classroom activities, assignments, work in the class period, and meeting individual differences.

SEENEY, JAMES A. *A Synthesis of Experimental Readiness Organizations in Secondary Schools.* Unpublished Doctoral Dissertation, Graduate School, University of Missouri, Columbia, 1955. Available on microfilm from University Microfilm Service, Ann Arbor, Michigan.

Microfilm copy should be made available in libraries equipped with microfilm reading devices. Contains a summation of experimental evidence on a variety of readiness organizations and methods in different subjects taught in junior high school, senior high school, and junior college. Useful here in connection with evidence on problem method, project teaching, extensive reading, use of audiovisual aids, and the structuring of subject matter in the ways in which pupils seem to learn best.

STILES, LINDLEY J. and DORSEY, MATTIE F. *Democratic Teaching in Secondary Schools.* Philadelphia: J. B. Lippincott Co., 1950. Chap. 15.

Group dynamics as providing experiences in the social process and growth in group relationships.

UMSTATTD, JAMES G. *Secondary School Teaching.* 3d ed. Boston: Ginn & Co., 1953. Chaps. 7, 8, 11, 12, and 13.

A series of chapters on teaching method. Chap. 12 is on visual aids and chap. 13 on radio.

WATERS, EUGENE. *A Study of the Application of An Education Theory to Science Instruction.* New York: Bureau of Publications, Teachers College, Columbia University, 1942.

A good illustration of a pioneer attempt at evaluation of pupil participation in planning. Describes the planning procedures used and attempts evaluation in terms of described learnings and pupil testimonials.

WESLEY, EDGAR B. *Teaching Social Studies in High School.* Boston: D. C. Heath & Co., 1950.

See for more specific application of teaching procedures in the social studies.

WITTICH, WALTER A. and FOWLKES, JOHN GUY. *Audio-Visual Paths to Learning.* New York: Harper & Bros., 1946.

Describes a whole series of experiments on the utilization of visual aids, chiefly motion pictures, directed from the University of Wisconsin. Summarizes the experimentation with definite recommendations for the presentation of motion pictures for most effective learning. Undoubtedly has many implications for the use of recordings and of TV programs in the schools.

Unit VI

How Can the Teacher
Determine What
Pupils Learn?

This unit is divided into two chapters, or subunits. The first subunit (chap. 13) centers about the problem of measurement, or evaluation, of the results of school and classroom experiences. The second subunit (chap. 14) has to do with the problem of marking, or of converting the results of the measurements and evaluations into some index of progress or achievement to be used in reporting to pupils and parents, and for purposes of record in the school files.

Both pupils and teachers are concerned with the extent of learning achieved within the limits of the school time devoted to various learning enterprises. Both are better satisfied with *evidence* of good learning. Teachers must become familiar with modern devices for the measurement of learning achievement and with the informal means of evaluation to be used in situations in which more exact instruments are so far unavailable.

School marks should be based upon the evidence obtained, upon the measurement and evaluation of achievement or progress. In general, a mark, or report, should help all those concerned to make a ready interpretation, or appraisal, of total achievement, or of relative progress in some class. Pupils themselves, parents, administrative officers, and sometimes prospective employers, are concerned with school marks as indices of achievement. School records and reports make necessary the conversion of the results of evaluation into school marks, or at least certain modern substitutes for marks which serve the same function. The teacher must be able to interpret the marks found in school records. The administrative or guidance officer must be able to recognize and avoid abuses. Then too, the teacher must be able to aid parents in making appropriate interpretation of marks or reports.

13

Evaluation of Learning

What to look for in this subunit

1. What kinds of tests and evaluation devices are now available for measuring the results of the work of high school pupils? Which of these are in fairly common use?

2. What is an objective test?

3. What is meant by the term standardized test?

4. What is a reliable test?

5. By what means can teachers insure reasonable reliability of tests?

6. What is meant by test validity?

7. By what means can the classroom teacher check the validity of test materials?

8. What uses can be made of standardized tests? Where can such tests be procured? What standardized tests can be found in your teaching field?

9. How much dependence can be placed on oral recitation as a means of measurement of achievement?

10. What difficulties arise in the use of prose examinations?

11. What are common useful types or forms of teacher-made, or informal, objective tests?

12. What is meant by the rating of pupil products?

13. How can a performance test be set up and the scoring safe-guarded?

14. At what stage in the progress of the development of an instructional unit should the unit test be constructed?

Whenever anyone engages in any enterprise, after a time there arises the need to know something of its outcome. The wage earner wants to know the size of his pay envelope. The player of a game wants to know the score. The actor wants to know the audience reaction. The child playing with blocks on the livingroom floor wishes the adult to admire what he has built. So with pupils in school, if they are to do school work, they wish to know what they have accomplished. In order to satisfy this need of pupils, the teacher must either measure the results of their efforts, or at least make some form of appraisal of what they have accomplished.

Teachers have always made an attempt to appraise the accomplishments of pupils. Even a casual "well done" is a form of evaluation. So also is "That isn't good enough. Better try it again."

School appraisal and measurement have always presented difficulties. There have always been some pupils who were disappointed or dissatisfied with the teacher's evaluation. Sometimes these dissatisfactions have led to a questioning of the validity of the measure or, for some pupils, a claim of favoritism on the part of the teacher. There exist, too, the problems of actually finding out what a pupil may have learned, at least how much he may have learned as a result of the school processes. These dissatisfactions and difficulties have led to a widespread movement to improve educational measurement.

Limitations of pencil-and-paper tests

This movement to improve educational measurement has, in the main, followed two lines: (1) to improve the measuring devices themselves; (2) to find ways to measure those factors which heretofore have been either unmeasured or very poorly measured. This latter phase of the testing movement has led to attempts to find ways to measure changes in attitudes, development of appreciations, problem-solving abilities, and the like. The earlier attempts at testing were largely attempts to improve the measurement of the acquisition and retention of knowledge and the extent of formation of skills. This kind of measurement has been represented by such tests as handwriting scales, typing tests, history tests, chemistry tests, grammar, spelling, and reading tests.

Almost all of the tests developed in the early stages of the testing movement were what may be characterized as paper-and-pencil tests. In other words, the test items were written out or printed, and the pupil recorded his response on paper. Perhaps the oldest form of pencil-and-paper test is the ordinary prose test, in which the teacher writes a few questions on the blackboard and the pupils write the answers on sheets of paper.

The pencil-and-paper test presents some obvious difficulties for some kinds of human qualities and behaviors. For example, if we accept a broad definition of citizenship as implying certain accepted kinds of civic behavior in dealing with people, then there is a serious question of whether such behavior can be measured by means of a paper-and-pencil response. If a pupil is asked to write down how he should behave in a given situation, he is likely to put down what he knows to be an acceptable kind of behavior. This is, however, no assurance that the pupil in question will actually behave in the way he has described. We can all quote, "Love thine enemies." But how many of us actually perform the act?

As schools have become more and more concerned with learnings other than knowledges and skills, there has been increasing awareness of need for other kinds of measures. Since the term "test" has come to mean some form of paper-and-pencil device, another term which could be applied to the determination of attitude changes, emotional responses, and actual behavior responses has seemed desirable. In later years the term "evaluation" has been used for attempts to get at behavioral and other somewhat intangible responses. Nowadays the term "evaluation" is often used to include all attempts at discovering what pupils have learned or what behavioral changes have taken place in them. In this sense the term includes the commoner pencil-and-paper tests also.

Evaluation devices available

If evaluation devices can be considered as tools to be placed in the hands of the teacher to be used in determining the progress or status of pupils, then it should be possible to make a practical working list of such tools as are now commonly available to teachers. Excluded from the proposed list will be evaluation devices used experimentally by measurement and guidance specialists that are not readily used and interpreted by most teachers in ordinary school situations. Below is a list of means of evaluation which most teachers can expect to learn to apply effectively. The list contains some that are in common use but which are not highly recommended as desirable tools.

A List of Possible Means of Evaluation
Now Commonly Available to Teachers

1. Uncontrolled teacher judgment
2. Oral recitation
3. Prose examinations
   a. Short and informal—the quiz
   b. Longer and formal—the examination
4. Standardized objective achievement tests
5. Informal, teacher-made, objective tests
6. The rating of samplings of products of pupils' work
7. Performance rating
8. Informal descriptive evaluations—case records, diaries, pupil testimonials, parental records and testimonials
9. Mechanical recording—photographs, motion pictures, tape recordings

In order to be sure of a common understanding of the terms used in the list above, there will be presented a brief definition or description of each of the types of evaluation included in it.

TEACHER JUDGMENT.   The expression of the teacher's judgment, or opinion, of the progress of a pupil or of his degree of accomplishment, is known as uncontrolled teacher judgment.   It is to be understood that the teacher will have worked with a pupil long enough to be thoroughly acquainted with him and with what he has been doing before attempting to express such a judgment. The term "uncontrolled" is used to indicate that the judgment is unsupported by other evidence gained by other kinds of testing. It is probable that this is the very oldest kind of evaluation and has existed since there were teachers and pupils. It is still widely used, especially in situations in which it is difficult to develop other forms of evaluation. Examples of use are found in such cases as that of the music teacher who says after some weeks, "You have made good progress with your violin," or "That was a good performance with your solo part" and that of the basketball coach who reports at the end of the season that some players are worthy of school letters and others only of numerals. Most citizenship ratings sent by modern schools to parents at the end of a term are based almost wholly upon the uncontrolled judgment of the teacher making the report.

ORAL RECITATION.   The term "oral recitation" is not likely to be misinterpreted.   However, at this point it is necessary to distinguish clearly between the recitation as a means of learning and the recitation as a measure of what a pupil has learned. It must be clear also that each pupil is evaluated upon the questions which *he receives and answers*. The recitation as a measure is not to be judged by the total questioning and the total class response. In these terms, on a given day there are some pupils who are not measured at all, some who are judged in terms of a response to one question, and some who are judged by responses to five or six questions.

Actually the oral recitation as a means of evaluation resolves itself into uncontrolled teacher judgment except that in the case of the recitation the judgment is often a snap judgment, in effect, expressed by the teacher on the run. Some teachers attempt to record judgments of recitations in a class book as the responses are made. This slows down the class performance, divides the teacher's attention, and usually results in less effective class management. It is probably wiser for the teacher to sit down in a calm moment after class and rate responses of pupils as they are remembered.

PROSE TESTS.   The prose examination consists of a set of questions or exercises developed by the teacher to which pupils write out responses during the class period. Typically the questions are relatively few, and rather elaborate answers are expected. Sometimes questions are written on the blackboard. In more modern practice, questions are run off on a duplicator, and each pupil has a set. Busy teachers often abuse the prose test by formulating the questions as they are written on the board. For a well-made test, questions should be carefully formulated in terms of the learning objectives before the test period. Duplication of questions for the pupils, since it must be done beforehand, tends to be some assurance of care in formulating questions.

School custom tends to distinguish between the written *quiz* and the prose *examination*. Both have the same form and are conducted in the same way. The quiz is relatively short and informal. Many quizzes use only a part of the class period. Sometimes quizzes are not previously announced to pupils. The examination tends to be longer and formally set. Most examinations take at least a full class period; some are specially set for a longer period. Pupils are always notified ahead of time of the coming of a formal examination.

OBJECTIVE TESTS. In our listing of evaluations we have included two general types of *objective* tests. First we shall attempt an interpretation of an objective test which will distinguish all objective tests from nonobjective ones.

Definition of objective tests. The dictionary contrasts *objective* with *subjective*. This distinction may lead to rather abstruse philosophical quibbling. For the teacher's purposes, it seems more desirable to present a practical interpretation of an objective test. An objective test, then, is a test that can be scored by means of a key in such fashion that the scoring does not fluctuate from one test paper to the next or when the scoring is done at different periods of time. With a properly keyed test, it is possible for different people to score the same set of tests and come out with the same scores for each test.

To be clearly objective, a test and the key must be so constructed that there is only one correct response for any given test item. There should be no debate concerning whether or not another response is an acceptable one.

The characteristics of an objective test may be seen more clearly by the use of contrasting negative illustrations of tests that are not keyed. Imagine a set of ordinary prose examination papers. There is no attempt to set up a single key for the questions to which the pupils have responded. Immediately the teacher is confronted with the problem of fluctuating scoring. It is impossible for two teachers to rate these test papers and come out with the same ratings for each paper. If a single teacher does the rating, it is probable that he cannot rerate the papers at the same values for each paper if the set is put aside for a few days between the scorings. Further, there is no assurance that the papers of different pupils are rated by the same standard as the teacher works through the set. Since there is no key, the standard exists only in the teacher's mind and may change with interruptions, with fatigue, or possibly with what the teacher remembers of the personalities of the pupils who wrote the responses. With a properly made keyed test, all these fluctuations are avoided.

The objective test has much in its favor. There is the essential element of fairness in dealing with the pupils. The teacher cannot be accused of favoritism or of prejudice in assigning scores to papers of different pupils. Perhaps more important is the scientific attitude involved. The objective test is an attempt to form an instrument to find out just what the pupil knows, or has learned, without having the teacher guess at an interpretation of what he may have said or written. Wherever the kind of learning lends itself to measurement with objective tests, every argument that can be mustered is in favor of their use.

Forms of objective tests. There are a good many forms of objective tests in use. Some ingenious test maker may devise a different one at any time. However, most of the objective tests in common use fall into a relatively few categories: completion, true-false, multiple-choice, matching, and identification.

The *completion test* form varies from the very brief sentence with a single recall item as a response, to the mutilation of a paragraph, or more, of text with blank spaces to be filled in.

The first president of the United States was —————. An ————— test is one that can be scored by means of a ————— in such fashion that the scoring does not ————— from one ————— to the next, or when the scoring is done at different ————— of —————. With a properly ————— test it is possible for different ————— to score the same set of tests and come out with the same ————— for each test.

Completion tests are chiefly measures of memory or retention. They are of value primarily in situations in which it seems desirable to find out what pupils remember of what they have been assigned.

The mutilated paragraph form presents difficulties in keying because different words can be supplied which give the text sensible meaning. The best way to avoid such keying difficulties is to place a list of acceptable words to be used in filling blanks on the sheet with the mutilated text. The directions require that words used in responding to the test be taken from this list. To avoid guessing by elimination, the list should contain more words than needed. Care must be taken not to include words among those used for filler that can be used appropriately in completing the text.

For some reason completion tests of the mutilated text type seem unusually difficult for most high school pupils. Unless the text is one for which pupils are to be held specifically responsible in detail, the use of such tests is not advised.

The *true-false test* consists of a series of statements, part of which are true and part of which are false. In the margin of the test is a set of symbols which the pupil marks to indicate whether each statement is true or false. A common device is to use T for true and F for false. Both symbols appear in the margin opposite each statement. The pupil draws a circle around what he believes to be the correct response.

There are a number of variants on the true-false form. A common one consists of a series of questions which are to be answered by yes or no. Again, the yes and no can appear in the margin opposite each question. The pupil draws a circle around the one which he believes to be the appropriate answer.

Great care needs to be exercised in building true-false tests to be sure that each statement is clearly true or clearly false. There should be no borderline or debatable items. Unless such care is taken, the test will not be entirely objective, and there will be endless arguments with pupils over the scoring. The number of true items should approximately balance the number of false items.

True-false tests tend to encourage guessing. Pupils respond whether or not they are sure of the answer. The chances are even that they may be able to mark some items correctly by simple guesswork. For this reason, early professional test makers proposed a penalized scoring involving the subtracting of the number of wrong responses from the number of correct responses. Pupils, in general, object to such scoring because it tends to lower the total value of scores and because they feel that they are being penalized for mistakes. Later test makers found that the same set of tests could be scored either by the rights-minus-wrong method or simply by counting the number of correct answers without significantly changing the ranks of pupils in the class group. Now most teachers score true-false tests by counting the number of correct responses.

A *multiple-choice test* consists essentially of a statement which may be completed by one of several choices from a group of words, phrases, or clauses which follow it. A variant consists of a question which may be answered by one of several answers which follow.

Usually the responses are keyed to the margin of the test, and the pupil uses a symbol which he transfers to the margin to indicate his choice of response. Some multiple-choice tests have special answer sheets to be marked with a carbon pencil, which can be machine scored.

The number of responses may vary from three to five. A two-response multiple-choice test resolves itself into the true-false form with all the difficulties involved in guessing. Increasing the number of choices increases the difficulties of test construction. A five-choice test is far more difficult to make than a three-choice one, because the choices must seem plausible to the person taking the test. With four or five choices, the test maker may run out of plausible items. All items in the same test should have the same number of choices.

The multiple-choice test has considerable flexibility in the types of learning for which it can be used. It can be used to check the pupil's retention of facts. It is adaptable to problem-solving and reasoning situations, and it has possibilities in checking attitudes and appreciations. For this reason it has come into quite widespread use. Many teachers seem to prefer the true-false form over the multiple-choice test, probably because a well-made multiple-choice test is quite time-consuming in construction.

Sample Multiple-Choice Test Items

In the following test exercises select the one expression which best completes the statement. Place the number of that expression in the parenthesis in the left-hand margin.

( ) 30. A floating object displaces an amount of water: (1) equal to the weight of the object; (2) equal to the volume of the object; (3) equal to the difference between the weight of the object and the weight of the water in which it floats; (4) greater than the weight of the object.

( ) 31. An object which sinks in water displaces an amount of water: (1) equal to weight of the object; (2) equal to the difference between the weight of the object in air and its weight in water; (3) greater than its weight; (4) equal to the weight of the amount of water necessary to make the object float.

( ) 32. The principle of buoyancy states that an object in water is buoyed up by a force equal to the weight of the: (1) object; (2) object in water; (3) water displaced by the object; (4) water the object will absorb.

A *matching test* can be applied to check the pupil's association of ideas. It is adaptable to situations in which it is desirable for pupils to fix the relationship between paired ideas. Illustrations are dates and events, events and people, people and dates, authors or composers and their works, pieces of literature and the characters, and so on.

The matching test consists of two columns of ideas which can be paired or matched. One column consists of a list of one set of the ideas to be matched. The other is a miscellaneous list of the ideas to be paired with those in the first list. Usually a bracket appears before the terms in the first list. Numbers are set before the items in the second list. The pupil is to transfer the number of the item in the second list to the bracket before the item in the first list with which it should be paired.

The lengths of the lists of items in any one matching exercise should be kept relatively short. If the list of items to be tested is long it can be broken into several exercises. This will avoid a considerable amount of lost motion on the pupil's part in merely hunting up and down a column of terms. One list should contain a few more items than the first. The filler items should not fit into the associations being tested. If this is not done pupils will be able to determine the matching of the last item or so by a mere process of elimination. Pupils should be warned that there are some filler items in the second list.

The matching test lends itself to use with the identification of parts on maps or diagrams. A diagram of a machine may have its parts numbered. Below will be a list of names for the parts which are numbered. The test consists of placing the number of each part in the bracket before its appropriate term. The same process can be used for map locations and anatomical diagrams.

A Sample Matching Test

Below at the left is a list of famous educators. In the list at the right is a list of books which these men have written. Place the number of each in the parenthesis before the name of the man who wrote it. There are more books than men. Use only one book for each author.

( ) W. C. Bagley　　　　1. The Psychology of Arithmetic
( ) Franklin Bobbitt　　　2. The Educative Process
( ) W. W. Charters　　　3. The Curriculum
( ) E. P. Cubberly　　　 4. Curriculum Construction
( ) John Dewey　　　　 5. The Principles of Secondary Education
( ) Alexander Inglis　　　6. A Brief History of Education
( ) W. H. Kilpatrick　　　7. Foundations of Method
( ) E. L. Thorndike　　　8. How We Think
　　　　　　　　　　　9. The Improvement of the Written Examination
　　　　　　　　　　　10. How to Experiment in Education

An *identification test* is one in which the pupil identifies the items in a given list which have some described characteristic, as for example distinguishing from a miscellaneous list those substances which are compounds and those which are mixtures. Another illustration would have to do with the separation from a list of names those men who were scientists and those who were statesmen, or those who were senators and those who were members of the House of Representatives. This form of test has rather limited usefulness. In general, both identification and enumeration tests can be reduced to either the multiple-choice or matching form.

STANDARDIZED OBJECTIVE TESTS. The leaders in the movement toward improved educational measurement of a generation ago developed the objective test and its various common forms. They were concerned with an attempt to make education a science. They were also concerned with an attempt to set standards of achievement for pupils of different school grades and different ages. In the process the educators began to apply statistical procedures and methods to the interpretation of psychological, sociological, and school data. Out of this total movement there developed the type of test which we know as the *standardized objective test.*

What is a standardized objective test? First of all it must be an objective test, having the characteristics which we have just described for such tests. Secondly, it has established norms or standards for pupils who have some common characteristic. Ordinarily this common characteristic is quite broad or general. For example, we wish to establish a standard of achievement in reading for all pupils in the eighth grade, or for all fourteen-year-olds, or for all fourteen-year-old boys, or for all rural pupils in the eighth grade.

The standard or norm is established by statistical procedures. In general the process is as follows: The test is constructed and tried experimentally with groups of pupils. A manufacturer would say that this trial run is to eliminate the "bugs" in the test. The test maker needs some assurance that the test measures what it proposes to measure, that it is a reliable measuring instrument, and that it can be readily administered. Next the test is administered to a relatively large total group of pupils that have the described characteristic for which it is desired to establish a standard. The tests are scored. The scores are arranged in a distribution in order of the size of the scores, the number of pupils having each score being shown in the distribution chart or table. Next by statistical procedures the central tendency, the mean score, or the midpoint of the distribution of scores, is determined for the large sample of pupils that has been measured. Further statistical refinements are applied to the data, such as determining the *probable error* of the test. Finally, however, the established midpoint of the distribution is indicated as the acceptable norm for the kind of pupils described.[1]

When the norm has been established, the test is published and distributed to school systems or teachers who wish to use it to determine the standing of their own pupils by comparison. It is necessary to insist that the standard is set by the midsegment of the originally measured group. This is considered the performance to be expected from a normal group of pupils. The standard is not at the top of the scale of the test but at the point about which the scores of an assumed normal group of pupils tend to cluster. The published norm is often given as a particular score on the test. But the teacher must not assume that a normal pupil in his group must make this score. There is a normal range of scores which fall on either side of the given norm. The teacher will expect to have pupils in his class who score considerably above the norm and some who fall below it.

An illustration can be taken from the common index used as an indication of intelligence. Intelligence measures for school pupils are most often reported as Intelligence Quotients, IQ's. An IQ of 100 is accepted as normal. This does not mean, however, that to be normal a pupil must have an IQ of exactly 100. IQ's in the 90's and up to 110 are considered normal. The teacher may well raise a question concerning a pupil with an IQ of 80 and ask for a further check on intelligence. On the other hand, he can expect to have some pupils with IQ's of 125, 130, and perhaps 140 and more.

The standardized objective test is of greatest service in comparing the achievements of *groups* of pupils. Teachers need to use extreme caution in interpreting the achievement or performance of a particular pupil in terms of the administration of a single standardized objective test. But it is often desirable to find out how a particular group of pupils compares with pupils in general or with other groups. A comparison of the scores of the pupils in the group in question with the published norm for the test will enable the teacher to make the interpretations needed. It is possible to find the "standard" for the group being measured and compare this with the norm for the test.

The norm or standard for a standardized test is as good as the

[1] For some tests the norms may be expressed as percentile rankings based upon the distribution of scores in the sample of the population measured to establish standards.

sample originally measured from which the standard was derived. If this group does not represent a true sampling of the pupils with the described characteristics, comparisons will be misleading. The teacher who uses standardized tests should always read carefully the literature which accompanies the tests to determine the kind of pupils measured in standardizing the test.

An illustration will serve to emphasize this point. In the early days of the testing movement a survey was made of the pupils in rural schools in a midwestern state. These pupils were all tested in arithmetic to determine their relative progress by grades in that subject. The test used had been standardized by administering it to pupils in the Detroit public schools. After the tests were given to the rural school pupils, it was found that in the various grades they were below the norms for the test. Since no rural school pupils had been included in the group upon which the test was standardized, the question arises as to whether the rural school pupils could be expected to achieve as well as the pupils who set the norm. For one thing, the rural school pupils had gone to one-room schools operating only eight months a year. The city pupils had gone to different types of schools operating nine or ten months per year.

Not all published objective tests are standardized. This is particularly true of many sets of objective tests sold to accompany workbooks. A package of standardized tests will be accompanied by a manual of directions which will show the norm and how to interpret the scores, as well as something about how the test was built and the standard derived.

Some standardized tests are furnished in two forms, usually known as A and B forms. Such tests have been scaled for the value or difficulty of each item included in the test. The two forms are then constructed to be of equivalent difficulty. Pupils who have been tested with one form may be tested with the other and the two sets of scores compared. Unless tests have been scaled for difficulty and equivalent forms constructed, no one knows whether the scores made on two different tests can be compared reliably.

INFORMAL OBJECTIVE TESTS. *Informal objective tests* are those constructed by the teacher in the local situation to use with his own pupils. They should have the characteristics of an objective test as described and may be of any of the common objective test forms. Practically, informal objective tests cannot be well administered unless the teacher has access to adequate school duplicating facilities so that a copy of the test can be placed in the hands of each pupil to be tested.

Test items and keys must be carefully constructed so that there is only one correct answer to each test item. If pupils can argue about the correctness of responses, the test loses in objectivity.

The number of test forms used in any one test should be few. Pupils are likely to be confused if it becomes necessary to "shift gears" too many times in responding to a single test. Such a form as the true-false has little reliability, if just a few items are thrown into a test which is otherwise in another form. All the responses to the test should be, if possible, in the same position on the page, as for example in the left-hand margin. A test of many forms with responses occurring here and there on the page is difficult to score and has a decidedly slovenly appearance. Such a test almost invariably labels the teacher as an amateur test maker.

PRODUCT RATINGS. The *rating of sample products of pupils' work* would seem self explanatory. It is applicable wherever the work of the pupils produces a tangible product which the teacher can examine. The rating of products of pupils' work is done on the assumption that the extent of learning of the pupils is in proportion to the quality of the products which they turn out. It is obvious that this assumption is not always valid. However, the world outside the school tends to judge in terms of the quality of work produced. Rating of products has the distinct advantage of putting into the hand of the teacher concrete and tangible objects which can be compared. After all, if pupils are to learn to write paragraphs of straightforward and simple English, the evidence of ability to do this lies in the writing of the pupils. It is possible, too, by comparing samples of the work of the same pupil taken at different times to get at least an approximation of the pupil's progress or improvement.

Situations in which the rating of products can be used are found in composition, drawing, the shop, typewriting, foods and clothing classes, and possibly certain phases of geometry.

It is possible for the teacher to collect samples to be rated and then arrange them in crude quality groupings in terms of a considered judgment of quality. This presents the difficulty that many pupils who receive relatively low ratings will want to know why, or what to do to improve the next piece of work. The teacher may be hard pressed to give a good suggestion. It does not help a pupil much to say, "Your work just wasn't quite as good as Joe's and Susan's."

Much of the difficulty inherent in rating in quality groups can be avoided by the use of a score card for the product to be rated. Such a score card consists of the items upon which judgment of the product is to be formed with an arbitrary point evaluation for each item. For convenience the total point evaluations should add up to some round number such as 50, 100, or 200.

The items included in the score card should be those upon which emphasis has been placed in the training preceding the evaluation. Those items which have been stressed particularly can be given higher weightings. After the rating of a given set of samples, if a pupil wants to know his strengths or weaknesses, these should be evident from the scoring. The teacher can go through the scoring of a particular sample with the pupil and point out wherein he was strong and where he needs to put forth greater effort in attempting to improve.

Score cards have long been used for rating agricultural products. Good illustrations can be found in the score cards for saddle horses, beef cattle, dairy cattle, poultry, and so on. In schools, score cards are readily made for pieces constructed in the shop, for garments made in clothing, for notebooks of various kinds, for posters, and prepared foods. Greater difficulties are found in devising score cards for composition, painting, and the like. Following is an experimental score card for rating unit plans of teachers which will serve as an illustration of score card making.

Score Card for Unit Plans

Course Layout
    Course introduction:
        Contains statement of course purposes   5
        Objectives clearly related to the field and not primarily
            disciplinary   5
        Addressed to pupils and plausible   5
                                ——
                                15

    Layout of course
        Definite unit organization   10
        Reasonable number of units   10
        Originality in selection and organization of unit pattern
            (not lifted from selected text)   10
        Headlining of unit titles   5
        Adequate adjustment of time schedule to unit program
            (*not day-to-day lesson scheme*)   15
                                  ——
                                50

Unit Plan   65

    Unit introduction:
        Statement of unit objectives to indicate clearly direction of unit   5

Indicates limits of accomplishment 5
Understandable by pupils 5

—
15
Unit outline:
Clearcut logical outline of subject matter to be included in unit 10
Subject-matter outline of reasonable length 10
Outlining in declarative sentence form 20

—
40
Unit learning exercises:
Exercises provide for accomplishment of stated objectives 20
Exercises set up as directions addressed to pupils 20
Exercises suited to maturity of high school pupils 10
Exercises maintain *unit* point-of-view (*not day-to-day assignments*) 10

—
60
Unit evaluation or test:
Valid (cf. unit introduction and outline) 10
Mechanics 5
Key 5

—
20

———
135
Total: 200

PERFORMANCE RATING. There are many school situations in which the learning is intended to produce skills which do not produce a permanent tangible product. The thing desired is some kind of performance which disappears as soon as the act is completed. Many illustrations will occur to the reader. Some of these are game performances in any of the common sports, formal speech situations, and the various kinds of musical performances. It is possible to evaluate the learning in such situations by *rating the performances* of the pupils.

Performance rating involves the same assumption as that involved in rating sample products, that is, that the learning is in proportion to the quality of the performance. Again, improvement of individuals may be estimated by performance ratings of the same individual taken at different times.

Performance rating presents greater difficulties than product rating for the simple reason that there is nothing which the teacher rater can get his hands on and re-examine if necessary. The performance must be caught at a given moment. Modern recording devices such as motion pictures and tape recorders are useful in overcoming this basic difficulty. At least, 'with such devices the original performance can be repeated as needed by the evaluator.

A teacher with experience in evaluation can learn to judge performances as a whole quite satisfactorily. But pupils will want to know why they rate as they do or how they may improve. To date, the best answer to this problem is the use of score cards for performance rating. The items included in the construction of the score card should be those stressed in the training. Pupils should be informed of the relative emphasis. Perhaps a copy of the score card can be posted on the classroom bulletin board as pupil practices begin. Scorings of individuals taken at different time intervals can be filed so that pupils and teacher can estimate the extent of improvement.

Certain existing devices are useful as a means of evaluation in performance rating. Official score cards for baseball and basketball which show the performances of individual performers are cases in point. The teacher should not overlook such available tools, which may be more effective than temporary teacher-made devices.

INFORMAL DESCRIPTIVE EVALUATIONS. Teachers in modern schools are attempting to use many evaluating devices to get at types of learning which do not seem readily measurable by means of the tools which we have described so far. For our purposes we have grouped these attempts under the heading of *informal descriptive evaluations*. Included in this grouping are such things as *case records, pupil diaries, pupil testimonials, parental records* and *testimonials*, and other comparable ways of describing behavior of pupils.

Such descriptive schemes are applicable to changes in appreciations of pupils and to the whole array of behavior changes which are often grouped as school citizenship. They may be useful, also, in appraisals of changes in attitudes and of developing ideals.

Case records. Case records are comparable to the case records kept by the physician for each of his continuing patients. The teacher keeps a file of data for each pupil. Included in each file are records of pertinent observations concerning changes in the behavior of the pupil concerned. Obviously it is necessary to date the observation records and keep them in order of the dates. Data derived from tests or supporting samples of a pupil's work may also be included. At certain specified intervals the teacher summarizes the data in the case record and makes an interpretation of any changes in pupil behavior. These interpretations can be used in reports to the school office or to parents. Data and interpretations from case records are often most useful in conferences with the pupils concerned.

Recorded observations and data included in a pupil's case record should not be hit-and-miss material. The record should be built around some planned analysis to indicate change in behavior in a given direction. For example, in a record which deals with a pupil's school citizenship, observations of the pupil's relationships with other members of his class groups are pertinent. These may include such items as evidences of leadership or lack of it, frictions with other pupils, tendencies to show off, quarrelsomeness, and so on. A record which deals with reading habits may include a reading list of materials actually read and some indications of pupil reaction to different types of reading. Such a record may also contain data derived from objective forms of reading tests which show rate of reading, comprehension, and vocabulary mastery.

Diaries and testimonials. The diary is an attempt to get each pupil to make observations concerning his own behavior. Generally the interpretations of such records will need to be made by the teacher after the diaries are completed. The reading list referred to in the last paragraph can be derived from a pupil's diary of his own personal reading and perhaps his own interpretation of his reactions to his reading. Diaries may be used for records of recreations of pupils, sports participation, music listening, and so on.

If pupils are to keep diaries for school purposes, the interval over which they are to be kept will need to be short. Items to be included in the diaries need to be made specifically clear, and the teacher will need to avoid being overcritical of the content. It may be necessary to set apart some part of certain class or homeroom periods for making the desired entries in diaries. It is doubtful if any large number of pupils can be persuaded to keep diaries consistently over any significant period of time if left to their own devices after a preliminary set of directions, or indoctrination.

The *testimonial* avoids the formal regular recording of the diary. The pupil is asked merely to state his own interpretation of what he thinks he has learned or of his own awareness of changes in his behavior. Perhaps testimonials are most useful as parts of case records in which they form only a portion of the record and are supported by other types of evidence. A rather famous illustrative case of a testimonial from a group of pupils is found in *Were We*

Guinea Pigs done by the first graduating class of the campus high school at Ohio State University.[2] In this case the pupil testimony is used as a means of evaluation of the whole program of a school.

Parental records and testimonials. Parental records and testimonials have the same characteristics as those obtained from the pupils. Of course there is the difference that the observation is made by an observer outside the learner himself and does not depend wholly upon introspective processes.

Statements from parents are used because much of the behavior of pupils *in schools* is controlled behavior and therefore likely to be somewhat artificial. If it seems desirable to find out how a pupil behaves *out of school,* then an out-of-school observer is needed. Presumably a parent of a pupil is the observer most concerned about the pupil's behavior and, therefore, most likely to respond to a request for help in completing the record.

The appraisal of out-of-school behavior becomes most important when we consider that the education acquired in school must operate in out-of-school situations, if schools are not to become completely ineffective. Much can be said for adding to the evaluative procedures the evidence collected by an out-of-school observer. There are many obvious difficulties in getting the cooperation of all kinds of parents in such an enterprise. Perhaps the most effective device is that of sending a report form for the parent indicating the information desired along with the regular monthly report of the school to the parent. Often the latter are carried home by pupils and must be returned to the school with the parent's signature. It is a simple matter to include an information form for the parent to fill out and return with the signed report. It is not so easy to get them actually filled out and returned.

All of the devices which we have grouped as informal evaluative devices are schemes for gathering observational and descriptive data concerning pupils. The differences lie in the observer, the pupil himself, parents, employers, or the teacher. The evaluation rests in the judgment of the desirability of the change in behavior as expressed by the teacher who makes the interpretation. These devices are not measurements in the usual acceptance of the term.

Perhaps the point can be made clearer by use of an analogy found in the physical growth of pupils. A teacher or a parent may say, "Johnnie has grown considerably during this school year," or "Susan is taller than she was last September," or again "Harry is a head taller than Frank, I think he is going to make a basketball

[2] Class of 1938, University High School, The Ohio State University, *Were We Guinea Pigs* (New York: Henry Holt & Co., Inc., 1938).

player." These observations may be true and valuable, but they are not measurements, at least in a quantitative sense. They do not indicate just how much growth even in the case of the "head taller." The statements also assume the desirability of being bigger and taller. Measurement would utilize quantitative devices such as scales, tapes, and yardsticks. Data would be gathered at specific time intervals and expressed in such quantitative units as pounds, feet, and inches. It would be possible to find out just how much growth had taken place in a given time. Note that the gathering of such quantitative data does not indicate the desirability of the growth. In general, we expect young people up to a certain age to continue to grow and assume that such growth is highly desirable. On the other hand, we sometimes say, "Mary weighs too much for her height and age" or "Frank weighs too little for his height and we should investigate his nutrition." Generally, crude descriptive devices are used in situations in which it is important to form judgments of changes, but in which the teacher is unable to devise more exact quantitative means of measurement.

Criteria for choosing evaluative devices

The kinds of evaluative tools that the teacher in service has available for common use in classroom situations have been described briefly. In considering these various types of tests the teacher must be able to decide which to use. In some cases he has an option between various types. For example, there is often a debate on the question of the desirability of using a prose test or one of the forms of teacher-made objective tests. How can such questions be decided?

Four criteria may be applied to all forms of tests in determining their relative merits, criteria which are commonly accepted by the test makers. These criteria are: ease and feasibility of administration, objectivity, reliability, and validity. Since abstract nouns representing concepts are sometimes difficult to comprehend, it may be well to express these criteria as questions. The questions may be expressed as follows:

1. Can the test under consideration be readily administered?
2. Is the test objective or, to what extent is the test objective?
3. Is the test reliable?
4. Is the test valid for the conditions under which it is to be used?

FEASIBILITY OF ADMINISTRATION. Feasibility of administration is determined by such factors as the time available for evaluation, the maturity of pupils, facilities available for test construction such as typing assistance and duplicating equipment, the time and difficulty involved in scoring, the extent of writing which the teacher needs to do in making a report on the evaluation, whether or not the test is to be administered to groups or must be applied individually, the mechanics of operation through which the pupil must go in taking the test, and others.

For example, if a test must be administered individually and requires at least thirty minutes to apply, a teacher with five sections of forty pupils each will need to spend one hundred hours to administer the test once. Obviously the test is impossible of administration on any large scale.

Again, many teachers fail to take into account the time needed to read a set of notebooks kept by pupils. Quite practically most notebooks to be used as a means of evaluation of the learning of pupils are not administratively feasible.

Suppose that we review quite briefly the types of tests which we have described in the preceding pages in terms of administrative feasibility.

Teacher judgment. Teacher judgment is easily exercised. This may be one of the reasons for its long-continued use in school evaluation. However, there are administrative complications which arise from claims of teacher favoritism or bias when the judgment is not supported by other evidence. The form in which the judgment is expressed for school records has been a long-continuing source of debate. There are problems which arise also from the lack of comparability of judgments as these are expressed about different pupils or for the same pupil at differing time intervals. Generally, however, teacher judgment is quite readily administered.

Oral recitation. Oral recitation as a means of evaluation seems easy of administration. This apparent ease is in part false. The recitation is readily carried out with a group as a whole. The difficulties lie in the attempt to get comparable and fair appraisal of responses from individual members of the group. There are administrative difficulties in getting an adequate record of oral recitations and maintaining the group morale at the same time. Then too, different pupils are evaluated upon responses to different questions, so that there is almost complete noncomparability of responses either between different pupils or with the same pupils during different parts of the same recitation period. In truth, the oral recitation is almost impossible of decent administration when it is considered as a means of measurement.

Prose tests. Prose tests are relatively easy to administer in that the time needed for preparation of questions is relatively short. There are administrative difficulties involved in the possibility that pupils may misinterpret questions. The prime administrative difficulty with prose tests lies in the time required for reading the responses of pupils. There are other difficulties inherent in the fact that pupils write at different rates and some cannot finish a test in the allotted time. It is difficult to convert evaluations of prose tests into quantitative terms. Perhaps the reason for the hold which the prose test has always had upon schools lies in the relative ease of preparation.

Some of the administrative difficulties with prose tests can be reduced by framing questions, problems, or directions that are readily interpreted and well understood by the pupils. This means additional time and care on the part of the teacher in preparing prose tests. It is also desirable to frame the questions so that they can be answered without elaborate and lengthy writing. One way to control the amount of writing on a prose test is to have the questions duplicated for the pupils. The questions are spaced on the pages so that the spacing limits the length of the responses. A basic direction for the whole test is that the pupil confine his response for each item to the space provided on the pages of the test. There are further administrative advantages in having a copy of the test placed in the hands of each pupil. It is probable that, if the teacher will take the time to work out a test with spacing for the responses and have the test duplicated, he will at the same time take greater care in framing the questions so that the total administration of the test will be improved.

Objective tests. The great majority of standardized objective tests are administratively feasible. Since most of them are published and commercially distributed, it is necessary that they be readily administered and take a minimum amount of class time in use. The teacher needs no time to prepare tests, although he does need to take time to study directions in the test manual. Since scoring is done with a key, the time for scoring is relatively brief. Difficulties of administration lie in misapplication of the tests and in misinterpretation of the scores by teachers, parents, and pupils.

Informal, or teacher-made, objective tests have the advantages over prose tests in that there is a minimum of writing on the part of the pupils and that since the tests are keyed the time for scoring is reduced. In general, teacher-made objective tests are not administratively feasible unless the school furnishes some means of getting tests typed and has good duplicating facilities. Objective tests written on a blackboard or dictated to pupils have presented so many administrative complications as to make the tests impractical.

The saving of time in the scoring of informal objective tests is in part deceptive. A well-made objective test and the key for it take considerable time in preparation. It is likely that a teacher will spend as much or more time in the preparation of a good objective test as would be expended in reading the papers gathered from pupils in a comparable prose examination.

Informal objective tests have the advantage that the scores either come out as quantitative expressions or are readily converted to such expressions. In general, administrative feasibility favors the informal objective test as compared with most of the other forms discussed with the possible exception of the commercially produced standardized objective test.

Product and performance rating. The rating of samplings of products of pupils' work is readily administered in those areas where products are the normal outgrowth of the classroom experiences. Fewer difficulties are encountered with the rating of samples if score cards are used. Such devices at the same time tend to solve the problems of reduction of judgments to quantitative terms for school records. Although the process of scoring products seems relatively time consuming, as the teacher becomes skillful in rating a particular type of product, speed of scoring is built up and actually such rating takes less time than the reading of most prose examinations. Product rating has the additional advantage of not taking additional class time for testing purposes, since the teacher can do the scoring at his convenience outside the class period. The sample work of the pupils will have been produced in the normal course of instruction and will not require a separate period for testing. It is desirable, however, to take class time to interpret scorings with the pupils.

Performance rating presents a number of administrative complications not found in product sampling. Again, administration is much more satisfactory if the rating is done by means of a score card. The difficulty with performance rating is that the ratings must be administered individually and generally must be carried out in the classroom situation during the class period, so that such evaluations are quite time-consuming. Otherwise the administrative factors are comparable to the rating of samplings. Because of the time factor, performance rating tends to be used in situations where performance is the primary goal and other means of evaluation are not applicable.

Informal descriptive evaluations. The various devices grouped under informal descriptive evaluations are all cumbersome in administration. Most of them must be applied individually. Much teacher time is consumed in writing up records and interpretations. There are numerous difficulties in reducing the interpretations to quantitative terms. Indeed, some proponents of the use of such means of evaluation protest any attempt to reduce the results to quantitative terms. This means that the records in the office tend to be lengthy, awkward, and cumbersome. There is the final difficulty of educating pupils and parents in understanding the school interpretation of such records. The informal descriptive evaluative devices have such difficulty in over-all administration that they are usable chiefly in situations where there seems to be no way to devise other means of measurement.

The possibility of using mechanical recording devices such as photography, motion pictures, and tape recordings, already suggested as a means of getting records to be used in the evaluation of performances, can also be used as a means of recording at least a part of case records used as informal evaluations. Administratively, mechanical recording devices are expensive to purchase and maintain, and they require special training for skillful operation. There is also the problem of individual rather than group measurement, which is both time-consuming and expensive. Storage of many records obtained by means of the mechanical devices is another administrative problem. Finally, there are the difficulties of interpretation and of converting judgments obtained into some quantitative form for the permanent school records. The use of evidence obtained by mechanical devices in dealing with pupils and parents can be quite telling and convincing. Undoubtedly, the use of these devices in schools will increase. At present they are largely valuable as means of supplementing the other means of evaluation found in the schools.

OBJECTIVITY OF EVALUATIVE DEVICES. In effect the criterion of *objectivity* has been defined in the description of objective tests on page 297. If this definition is used here, a particular means of evaluation can be considered as objective to the extent that it is possible to devise a key for it and the key applied so that the scoring can be done without fluctuating judgments from one pupil to the next or when scoring is carried out at different times or by different evaluators.

Teacher judgment. Uncontrolled teacher judgment appraised under this standard would seem to be at the opposite pole from objectivity. There is no key, no single standard of judgment to be constantly and consistently applied. Judgments do vary as they are applied to different pupils. The same teacher will vary in judgment of the learning of the same pupil, if the judgments are formed at different times. There is no assurance that two teachers observing the learning processes of the same pupils will arrive at the same or comparable judgments of them.

Oral recitation. The objectivity of the oral recitation as a means of evaluation is practically nil. It has all the bad points of uncontrolled teacher judgments. Further, evaluations of recitations by the teacher tend to be hurried judgments. Since different pupils are asked different questions during the recitation, there is no way to assure that all are judged on the same standard. There are, too, the traditions of the easygoing and the tough teachers, implying that different teachers render differing impressions of the same pupils.

Prose tests. If prose examinations are not keyed they are nonobjective. School tradition is full of stories of the noncomparability of judgments of teachers on the various written products of pupils. The same teacher cannot score a set of prose tests, lay them aside for a few days, and then rescore them and come out with the same scores allotted to the papers originally. Two or more teachers scoring the same set of prose tests will come out with all kinds of variations in the scoring of the tests for the same pupils.

But the objectivity of prose tests can be improved, and the road to improvement is inherent in the definition of objectivity. The test questions are to be carefully stated and then keyed for the essential responses which should occur in the answers, if the pupils have learned the proper responses. Pupils should not be expected to come up with the language of the key. Generally, such tests should not be tests of memory. Rather, pupils are expected to respond in terms of the ideas contained in the key. The tests are then scored in terms of the presence or absence of such ideas in the responses. Hence, the clever pupil who does not know the answer and writes a plausible response not representing the idea contained in the key will receive a zero score on that item. The key keeps the teacher from wandering from the issue with the straying pupil in forming his judgment. It also avoids the premium sometimes placed on the neatly written answer as contrasted with an answer which also contains the correct idea but is not neatly written.

Test mechanics are important in the improvement of the objectivity of prose tests. Tests should be duplicated so that each pupil has a copy. Spaces for responses should be provided in the mechanical make-up of the duplicated test. The amount of writing required of the pupil should be kept at a minimum needed for expressing the ideas expected in the responses. Such attention to test mechanics tends to insure comparability of rating responses as the teacher reads the papers.

All teachers should be able to use a typewriter. A good trick for keying a prose test is to place a copy of the duplicated test in a typewriter provided with a two-color ribbon. The key which indicates the ideas which should be present in the responses is typed in *red* in the spaces provided for answers. The teacher uses this as the guide and key in reading papers. Of course, the teacher probably will memorize the key after reading a few papers. However, it should be kept as a constant reference for deciding doubtful cases.

If a prose test is set in problem form and there are optional solutions for the problems, the key should contain all solutions acceptable as satisfactory. Credit should be given for any one of them presented by a pupil.

Some teachers defend the prose test as providing an opportunity for pupils to express themselves, to show originality, and to give evidence of creativeness. If these objectives are to be evaluated, it is more desirable that the test take the form of a "term paper," which gives the pupil time in which to express himself adequately. The paper should then be treated as a sample product of the pupil's and a suitable score card developed for rating it. The teacher will need to be analytic about the factors which should contribute to the kind of paper desired. The pupil should be informed of these factors before beginning to work and the score card contain these as items upon which the scoring is built.

Objective tests. The standardized objective test is objective by nature of its definition and the basis for its construction. All such tests are provided with keys. There are few difficulties found in the accuracy of items in such keys. Probably, standardized objective tests establish the basis for objectivity with which other forms of tests may be compared.

In the same way teacher-made objective tests are objective in terms of their basic construction and definition. Difficulties with the objectivity of such tests occur when test items may be interpreted in various ways or when there are correct responses not included in the key. Generally, there should be only one possible correct response for any one test item in an objective test. Almost all difficulties with informal objective tests are due to amateurish or careless test construction. In spite of such cases, informal objective tests have an advantage in objectivity over other forms of teacher-constructed evaluative devices.

Product and performance rating.   Since the rating of samplings of pupils' work involves elements of judgment which make it difficult to rate the same pieces of work at exactly the same values on two successive ratings, such rating can never be completely objective. Moreover, two teachers rating the same set of samples cannot come out with the same values for each sample.

The objectivity of sample rating can be improved by the use of well constructed score cards for rating. This device approximates a key in that it establishes the values upon which the judgments are based. It is true that an experienced teacher accustomed to judging the work of pupils can come fairly close to rating the same set of samples the same way on two successive ratings without the use of a score card. However, two different teachers cannot approach comparable ratings of the same set of samples unless they use a score card in judging. Even then, there will be differences which indicate that the scoring is not completely objective.

All these considerations apply equally to the problem of objectivity in performance rating. There are increased difficulties in attaining some degree of objectivity in performance rating because what is being rated does not hold still to be examined and cannot be readily re-examined.

The use of mechanical devices for recording performances can be used to increase objectivity. It is obvious that the evidence of a photograph, motion picture film, or tape recording is objective. Witness the use of the camera at the finish line in horse racing and that of motion picture films to settle disputes concerning close decisions in football games. The lack of objectivity comes at the point where the teacher makes a judgment of quality of performance based upon the recording. The tape recording of a pupil's violin performance is objective evidence. The teacher's judgment in rating the performance from the recording is not.

Informal descriptive evaluations.   One of the great drawbacks in the use of informal evaluative devices such as case records, diaries, pupil testimonials, and parental testimony and records is in the lack of objectivity. There is always a question of whether or not a person is an unprejudiced judge of his own behavior. Patent-medicine advertising based upon the patient's claims to cure as a result of the advertised nostrum is notoriously untrustworthy. In the same way a parent may be biased concerning the growth and behavior of his own children. To some parents, "My child can do no wrong." On the other hand, case records can contain objective evidence of pupil growth and behavior. A set of samples of a pupil's composition taken at different time intervals is a case in point. Possibly scores on an attitude test fall in this category. The non-objective element in the case record often enters at the point of interpretation. Some case records based wholly on teacher descriptions of pupil behavior obtained by observation lack objectivity.

RELIABILITY OF EVALUATIVE DEVICES. By the reliability of a test is meant the accuracy with which the test measures what it proposes to measure. Involved in the concept of reliability is the element of consistency of measurement. If a test is reliable, under application it will produce the same measurements when applied to the same people under the same conditions repeatedly. For example, a set of scales for determining weight will give the same weight in pounds and ounces for the same person if the person weighs ten or fifteen times, provided that conditions remain the same. The person being weighed wears the same clothing, eats or drinks nothing between weighings, adds or subtracts nothing from what he has in his pockets. The scales are not moved, and the temperature remains the same. If the scales give different weights for the same person under the conditions described, the scales are probably unreliable.

The question could be raised of the calibration and mechanical adjustment of the particular set of scales as compared with other scales or with a supposedly perfectly balanced and calibrated set of scales. On the other hand, the set of scales in question is reliable if, in comparison with its own performances, it always gives the same results under the same conditions.

The canon of reliability can be applied to any instrument of measurement. It is possible to measure the length of a room with a stick. The room may be thirty and a half sticks long. Can the room be measured several times and the same measurement results obtained? Probably not. The stick is not quite straight. There is some slipping when it is picked up and moved ahead. Since the stick is uncalibrated the definition of the half-stick is poorly delimited. Any random stick is a relatively unreliable measure of length.

If a yardstick is substituted for the stick, it should be a more reliable instrument because the yardstick does not need to be moved so often, and with care the cumulative error is less. The yardstick is a more reliable instrument than the stick.

If a cotton tape is used for measuring the room and the tape is longer than the distance to be measured, the moving of the instrument during the measuring is avoided. The tape should be a more reliable instrument than the yardstick. But a cotton tape will stretch when pulled tight. Errors will occur when the tape is stretched at different tensions.

A linen tape will stretch less than a cotton one. A steel tape has practically no stretch. If a reliable measurement of such lengths as that of an ordinary room is wanted, a steel tape is a reliable instrument of measurement, much more so than the other appliances suggested. But the steel tape is not completely reliable. The length of the tape will change somewhat with changes in temperature. Then too, there are always possibilities of error in the way in which an implement is handled. It takes two people to measure with the steel tape. If one is careless and lets an end slip, the measurement will not be reliable. For all practical purposes the steel tape is a reliable instrument of measurement, but it does not have absolute reliability.

The reliability of most of the tests and evaluative devices used by teachers is comparatively low. Some may be at the level of a foot rule for measuring distances. Most, probably many, are at the stage of the crooked stick, or possibly even less reliable.

It is possible to determine in quantitative terms the degree of reliability of an objective test. The procedure used is the statistical process of finding the correlation between two sets of scores for the same people. The figure with which the statistician represents correlation is known as the coefficient of correlation and is expressed by the letter r. When used to determine the reliability of a test the coefficient of correlation becomes a coefficient of reliability.

What is done is as follows. The test in question is administered twice to the same group of pupils. Usually there is an interval between the two administerings of the test so that pupils are less likely to remember the responses made on the first administration. Scores are tabulated and arranged in order of rank on the first testing. Scores on the second testing are paired with the first for each pupil. The coefficient of correlation between the two sets of scores is determined.[3] The test used should be fairly long and the group of pupils tested large enough to give a total number which lends itself to statistical treatment.

The coefficient of correlation, now a coefficient of reliability, will lie between 1.00 and −1.00. If the coefficient should turn out to be +1.00, there is perfect relationship between the two sets of scores, that is, the test is reliable. If the coefficient should turn out to be

[3] For a formula for determining coefficients of correlation and further elaboration of the process and its uses, see any standard textbook on educational statistics or on secondary school tests and measurements.

—1.00, there is a negative or opposing relationship. The test is entirely unreliable. Practically, coefficients of reliability run in decimals between 0 and +1.00. The higher the coefficient, the greater the reliability of the test. Tests with coefficients below +0.50 are commonly considered as having such low reliability as to have little value. Good tests have a reliability of +0.80 up to +0.95 and possibly higher.

It is not probable that an experimenter will find a test with a +1.00 coefficient of reliability. Practically no test is a perfect instrument. Perhaps more important is the fact of the extreme variability in human beings. Even such apparently simple characteristics as those of height and weight vary with the same individual at different times during the day. It is almost an absurdity to expect each individual in a group of one hundred pupils to make exactly the same score on a test on a second day that was made on the previous day. As a matter of fact, the learning factor enters into the situation so that scores on the second administration of a test tend to run higher than on the first application for the simple reason that the pupils have seen the test and have had experience with it. And yet the acceleration of scores on the second testing is not uniform; if ranks of pupils on the two testings are correlated, the correlation will not be +1.00.

The teacher who finds a report of a +1.00 reliability coefficient for a particular test can write it off as an accident, an exaggeration, or careless computation.

There is another frequently used means of determining the coefficient of reliability for an objective test that does not require retesting the pupils. This is known as the split-half method. If the test is long enough to split in two and still furnish a good sampling of test items in each half, the method can be used. Customarily the test is divided into random halves by taking scores for all even-numbered items in one part and scores in all odd-numbered items for the other. A correlation is then worked out for the two parts of of the test as described for two administrations of the same test. This procedure has the advantage that a statistically minded teacher can apply it to the determination of the reliability of his own informal objective tests without having to take another class period to retest his pupils with the same test.

There are other procedures for determining reliability used by statisticians, but these will not be considered here.

Suppose that now what has been said about reliability is applied to the various types of evaluations commonly available to teachers.

Teacher judgment. On the surface, uncontrolled teacher judgment would seem an unreliable form of evaluation. As a matter of fact, a teacher who has worked with a group of pupils for some time and has some experience with learning in his field can form quite reliable judgments of the extent of learning of the different pupils in his class. To do this, the teacher must make every attempt to avoid biases built up because of pupils' personal traits. It may be that a trouble maker is quick, bright, alert, and learns much. A phlegmatic, slow student may be a likeable person but just too lazy to accomplish much. Pupils from the wrong side of the tracks are often superior learners. Sometimes the socially elite are so spoiled that they put forth no real effort to learn for themselves. If the teacher can examine pupils in terms of the objectives set for the class and forget for the time being these other factors, he can learn to rate pupils satisfactorily in terms of his own judgment of their attainment of the objectives.

The best approach to rating pupils in terms of uncontrolled teacher judgment is that of ranking pupils in order of merit or of grouping into relatively rough quality groups, as excellent, good, satisfactory, ordinary, and failing. It is relatively easy to select the best three or four pupils out of a group of thirty. Often the one best pupil stands far ahead of the others. In the same way it is easy to pick out the slow learners. The difficulties arise in making distinctions between individuals. Teacher judgments should not be used to make fine quantitative distinctions between individual pupils. For example, the teacher should not, on the basis of his unsupported judgment, report that Joe has a mark of 80 and Josephine a mark of 81. Remember the analogy with the measurements of lengths; the teacher judgment is in the category of the uncalibrated stick. At best such judgments are estimates, but they can be relatively reliable estimates.

Oral recitation. There is no way of knowing the reliability of the typical oral recitation as a means of measurement. Probably it has almost zero reliability. Its reliability may be even of the negative order, if it were possible to compute a coefficient of reliability. Perhaps the best suggestion concerning recitations is that the teacher hear a succession of them and then, in a period of calm outside of class, rate the members of the class in terms of his judgments formed during the hearing of the series of recitations. This places the reliability in terms of what was just said about uncontrolled teacher judgments.

Prose tests. The reliability of most prose tests is questionable, also. At least the reliability of any particular prose quiz is unknown.

Almost never does the teacher go through the process of reapplication of a prose test and a correlation of the two sets of scores to determine reliability. Most prose tests in common usage are too short and have too few questions to permit of the use of the split-half technique of determining reliability. In spite of some reported hairsplitting decisions on small differences in scores based on a prose examination, the fact is that the teacher knows almost nothing concerning the reliability of the test. The reporting of small differences in scores between individuals is not justified in terms of the reliability of the testing instrument. To be specific, the teacher actually does not have any basis for defending one-point or fractional-point differences based on prose examinations.

Improvement of administration of prose examinations, such as eliminating vague questions and placing duplicated copies of the test in the hands of pupils, should improve reliability as should improving the objectivity of such tests as was suggested earlier. If the total length can be kept within the scope of the allotted time, an increase in the number of questions will tend to improve the reliability of prose tests.

Objective tests. The standardized objective test usually has high reliability. At least the reliability is known, and the coefficient of reliability for a given test will be found in the manual which accompanies it. Most published standardized objective tests have reliabilities which run from $+.80$ to $+.95$ and occasionally better.

The reliability of a well-made teacher-constructed objective test should be relatively high. However, most teachers have never checked the informal tests which they use, so that the reliability is unknown. If such an objective test is long enough to apply the split-halves method, the teacher can determine the reliability of his own test.

What was said about the improvement of the reliability of prose tests applies here also. Whatever can be done to improve the administration of a test should improve its reliability. It is imperative to clear up all ambiguous test items and directions. The lengthening of a test that is otherwise useful should improve its reliability. Beware of very short tests in the commonly used objective forms. A true-false test of twelve, fifteen, or twenty items has such low reliability that it is probably a waste of time to administer it to pupils.

Product and performance ratings. Generally, the teacher does not know the reliability of his rating of the samples of pupil work. A teacher who is experienced in rating a given type of product can learn to do quite reliable rating. What was said about the reliability of teacher judgment applies here. The rating of samples of work presents the possibility of re-examination and rerating. A teacher can rank the products in order of merit and then assign values for marks. It is possible then to rerank the same samples and, if the teacher desires, figure a coefficient of reliability on the two rankings.

The rating of sample products is reliable only for rough groupings into quality groups, not for fine distinctions between individual pieces of work. Since it is possible usually to rerate such samples, it is possible to make two or more ratings and then derive a final rating from a composite of the several. This procedure should give a more reliable evaluation than a single rating. It is probable that the use of score cards for rating increases reliability. With an expert teacher judge, this may be debatable. With less expert teachers, the score card will undoubtedly tend to increase reliability. Although an expert can arrive at reliable judgments without score card devices, they are urgently recommended for administrative reasons which were presented earlier.

Most performance rating probably has a lower reliability than that of product rating for the simple reason that the performance is fleeting and rerating not possible unless some form of mechanical recording device is available. What was said concerning rating of samples of pupils' work applies equally as well here. An expert and experienced teacher can make reliable ratings of performance. The use of score cards may add to the reliability of such rating. At least the use of score cards is advisable for administrative reasons.

The use of mechanical recording devices may add to the reliability of performance rating since they make possible rerating and even computation of reliability coefficients based on the rating.

In this connection the caution made for other relatively crude evaluative devices needs to be repeated. Performance rating may be reliable for distinguishing between a few quality groupings of performances. It is not reliable for making fine shades of distinction between the performances of individual pupils.

Informal descriptive evaluations. The reliability of informal descriptive evaluations is almost totally unknown. It is practically impossible to repeat any of these evaluations under the same conditions. They do not lend themselves to a split-halves approach to the computation of reliability. To the extent that these devices are nonobjective in the same ways, they fall short of reliability.

The informal descriptive evaluative devices may be said to have two phases of reliability. One has to do with the reliability of the record and the evidence contained in the record. The other has to do with the reliability of the judgments exercised by the teacher in the interpretation of the record.

The reliability of records based upon testimony of an observer or of introspection is always open to some question. Teachers' or parents' observation of a pupil's behavior and the testimony of observers are also of doubtful reliability. So also is the diary, which rests entirely upon introspection, observation of one's own behavior.

Reliability of the evidence in case records can be enhanced by the inclusion in them of scores derived from objective tests, concrete samples of pupil work, and recordings made with mechanical apparatus such as cameras and tape recordings. Indeed the primary value of the use of mechanical recordings lies in the increased objectivity and reliability of the evidence obtained with them.

The reliability of *interpretations* of informal descriptive evaluative devices, including those based upon mechanical recordings, is that of teacher judgment in general.

To summarize, there are some factors of reliability which apply to almost all forms of tests and evaluative devices. Reliability increases to the extent that objectivity can be attained. Improvement of administration tends to eliminate sources of error and, therefore, to increase reliability. Other factors remaining constant, increasing the length of a test tends to increase its reliability. Scientifically, the reliability of measurements of various human qualities and characteristics rests upon the same fundamental factors as does the reliability of other forms of measurement.

VALIDITY OF EVALUATIVE DEVICES. Imagine listening to groups of pupils coming out of a classroom just after they have had some tests. Opinions are likely to be divided concerning preferences for objective or prose tests. Some pupils prefer to be free to write what they feel they know. Others like the chance to work quickly with a minimum of writing and get the task over. To the latter, the objective test seems relatively painless. Almost never will the observer hear pupils raise any question concerning the reliability of the tests which they have had. It never seems to occur to pupils that there is any question of the reliability of tests used in school. Perhaps this is the attitude of the great majority of teachers also. But what the pupils do talk about is the innate "fairness" of the test which they have just experienced. Sometimes this is expressed as, "The teacher told us to study this, and we had something else on the test." Or, "Where did the teacher get that question? I never heard of it. We have never had that in class." These are the questions of *validity* with which pupils are immensely concerned.

The professional test maker will say that a given test is valid if it measures what it purports to measure. In most cases, he will add immediately that no one is entirely sure of just what any particular test does measure. This leaves the teacher who must attempt some form of evaluation in a quandary.

For practical purposes it can be said that a test is valid if it seems to measure what the pupils have been taught, or if it measures what pupils have been told to learn. Certainly, a test is valid if it measures in terms of the objectives set up for a given learning situation.

This statement immediately sets up the principle that it is possible to determine the validity of evaluation only if the objectives are known. There are various ways in which the principle can be stated. In order to construct a valid test, it is necessary to know the objectives of what has been done. The teacher must be able to state clearly objectives before any evaluation can be attempted. This is really the issue expressed by pupils who say they were told to work on one thing and then tested on something else. In other words, a valid test should *fit* the learning situation.

Teacher judgment. To review the prospective validity of the forms of evaluation commonly available to teachers, we shall begin again with uncontrolled teacher judgment. Teacher judgment is valid if expressed in terms of a clearly defined set of objectives. Added to this is the issue that these objectives should have been clarified with pupils for the judgment to be truly valid. The validity of a teacher judgment may be questioned if the basis for judgment is not defined or if expressed in terms of other factors than the present learning objectives.

The most common criticism of teacher judgment as a means of evaluation has to do with judgments apparently formed in terms of personality traits of pupils that may have little or nothing to do with the learning at hand. On the other hand, teacher judgments can be valid and in some situations seem defensible on the ground that no other more objective valid measures can be devised. For example, the art or music teacher has great difficulty in determining the extent of changes in appreciations of pupils except in terms of his judgment based upon continuing observations of their reactions to artistic and musical selections. In such case the teacher judgment may be the only valid measure presently available. Conversely, it is very foolish for a teacher to try to measure pupils' knowledge of history in terms of judgment when an objective test could be very readily devised.

Oral recitation. The oral recitation *seems to have validity* for bodies of knowledge assigned to pupils for learning. It is possible for the total number of questions presented to a class during a recitation to have a high degree of validity. It must be remembered, however, that any particular pupil is judged by a few questions which he receives and to which he has an opportunity to make responses. Judged in terms of the measurement of the reactions of individual pupils, the recitation offers such a limited sampling of what pupils are supposed to learn that it can have almost no validity. Certainly, wherever it is possible to substitute valid test forms which may cover a more adequate sampling of the learning involved for each pupil, the oral recitation should be avoided as a means of measurement.

Prose tests. The chief claim of the prose examination to continued use in schools lies in its assumed validity. Its objectivity is generally low and its reliability questionable. However, there seem to be test situations in which objective forms are not readily devised but prose forms do seem to fit. Many teachers claim that solutions to problem-solving situations can be presented only in prose form. The same claims are made for cases which involve interpretations. Expressions of appreciation in the fine arts are difficult to get into any kind of test form. Perhaps the prose test is more nearly valid than most objective forms used to get at such reactions.

Certainly, objective test forms can be valid for tests of knowledge and retention of information. Since the objective tests have the advantages of facility of administration, objectivity, and, generally, of reliability over prose forms, there is little argument for the continued use of prose tests for measurement of the extent and retention of knowledge. To stretch a point, it could be suggested that the continued use of prose forms to measure information is due to indolent teachers who will not take the time and effort needed to construct good objective tests.

There are many apparently valid attempts at the construction of objective tests to measure problem solving and some kinds of interpretation. Again, if these can be devised and are valid for established objectives they should be used to replace prose tests because of the advantages enumerated above.

Where prose tests are used to measure the pupil's abilities for self-expression, or expression of his own ideas in good language form, the teacher is to be reminded that these can be treated as samplings of products of the pupils' imagination, creativeness, and language facility. It is probable that validity in terms of selected objectives can be increased by setting term papers upon which pupils have time to approach truly the objectives described. The paper should be more nearly valid than production under the pressure of the ordinary test situation. It should be possible to devise score card devices for some papers of this kind in which the items for scoring are determined by analysis of the objectives. It can be seen quite readily that this should increase validity considerably.

Standardized objective tests. Standardized objective tests have great advantages over other forms in objectivity and known reliability. Most of them are readily administered. The serious question to raise concerning the use of standardized objective tests has to do with validity. Since these tests are made by someone other than the teacher and the standards obtained by application to pupils other than those to be immediately measured, there is always the question of whether the objectives upon which the tests were originally built are the same as those presented by the teacher to a particular class.

The use of standardized objective tests for application to all kinds of pupils in very different schools in many differing geographical regions assumes that all these pupils are working with common curricular content and, at a described stage of maturity, should arrive at a common range of achievement. The assumption of common curricular content is false in many cases.

Many of these tests have been built by professional test makers, not by classroom teachers, and some tests still in common usage are from five to ten years old. The possibility of differing content and of different goals for pupils in different geographic regions is obvious. As a matter of fact, objectives and content within the same subject area vary with pupils of differing economic and social status in the different schools of the same city system.

To illustrate the problem of validity with standardized objective tests consider the proposed application to an eighth-grade group of a standardized test in spelling. It is proposed to apply the spelling test at the end of a school quarter to determine the relative progress of these pupils in spelling. The test is based upon an assumed common spelling vocabulary for all eighth-grade pupils. However, with this particular class the teacher has been especially concerned with individual spelling needs. The "lessons" have been based upon lists of individual "demons" for each pupil derived from recent errors in composition. A list of these words for the class group as a whole does not contain many of the words that are in the standardized spelling test. In other words, a comparison of the words upon which the pupils have worked and the words in the test will show that the proposed test simply *does not fit.* If the test is given, the pupils may or may not be able to spell the words in it. If they can, it will not be due to the particular recent learning in spelling. If they cannot, they and the teacher will be criticized for failure to meet a standard for the eighth grade. Should they be so criticized?

These possibilities of error do not imply that a standardized objective test cannot be valid. They do mean, however, that before a supervisor or teacher uses such a test, it should be scrutinized for point of view, content, nature of the problems presented, and apparent or stated objectives or assumptions. When this is done, the findings should be compared with the objectives and content presented to the class to be measured. There needs to be assurance that the test is valid for the purpose for which it is to be used.

A standardized test is valid only when used with pupils who are comparable to those upon whom the test was standardized. A grade school test in reading is not valid for high school or college students. A college test in general chemistry is not likely to be valid for high school chemistry. Height-weight norms for boys are not applicable to girls. The illustrations are endless. To be sure that a test is valid for a particular group, it is imperative to have read the test manual far enough to find out the nature of the people in the sampling with which the test norms were established.

Informal objective tests. Informal objective tests should be made to fit the instruction of which the results are to be measured. If this is done, such tests should be valid. Some assurance of validity can be made if the test items are based upon subject matter utilized in the instruction and if the objectives are reviewed at the time the test items are constructed. If the test is to be a unit test, it is good practice to prepare a unit summary for the instructional outline used by the teacher. When the unit test is prepared, the teacher should use the unit introduction containing the objectives as stated for pupils and the unit summary to check the validity of the subject matter involved. A greater guarantee of validity is insured if the test is constructed as the instruction for the unit unfolds, rather than attempting to make a test hurriedly after the completion of the unit. Many unit tests fall short of desirable validity because the teacher overlooks items, or even adds items, of subject matter when tests are made as afterthoughts.

There should be no great difficulty in constructing valid objective tests for knowledge or retention of facts. Valid objective tests for many problem-solving situations and for interpretation are readily possible. Of the various test forms, the multiple choice form is more readily adaptable to problem solving and interpretation.

Valid objective tests for improvement in skills are difficult to construct. So are valid evaluations of changes in attitudes and appreciation. Difficulties in test construction for these several types of objectives are so great that most teachers will resort to other forms of tests to achieve validity. Valid objective tests of skills or of changes in attitudes are not impossible to construct if the teacher uses imagination. However, the majority of teachers for some time to come will depend upon other forms of evaluation of skills, appreciations, and attitudes.

Product and performance ratings. The rating of pupil products is a valid means of evaluation if the objectives of instruction are quality products. Pupils will need to have been told of these objectives and shown how to achieve the desired products. The quality standard set for the rating of the products needs to be appropriate for the maturity of the pupils. Often this standard can be set by the use of samples of work of the kind produced by other pupils of the same characteristics. The teacher should not expect to rate the letters written by ninth-grade pupils in terms of the letters of educated adults or of the masters of English prose. However, some ninth-grade pupils will produce letters that are better than those of most adults and some will have high literary merit. On the other hand, the group of ninth graders as a whole are to be measured in terms of a product that can be reasonably expected of ninth graders.

It will be remembered that in the original description of product rating it was pointed out, that for such rating, it is assumed that the extent of pupil learning is in proportion to the quality of the product rated. This assumption is not always valid for product rating on a scoring device applied once to the products of all members of a group. On the other hand, it is more nearly a valid assumption if several ratings of comparable products for the same individual are made and comparisons drawn between samples of work of the same person taken at different times.

School cases where the emphasis in objectives tends to be upon the products of pupil work and where rating of these products would seem to be a valid means of measurement are found in the following: various compositions from the English classes; articles made in the school shop; garments made in clothing classes; letters or manuscripts typed in the typewriting classes; letters transcribed and typed in stenography classes; drawings, paintings, and objects of art from art classes; food products or meals prepared in foods classes.

The validity of performance rating rests upon the same factors as does that of product rating. If the objectives are high-grade performances, the rating of the performances would seem the most valid approach. Again, there is the assumption that the learning of an individual is in proportion to the quality of his performance. This assumption may not be true if the rating is made once and covers the performances of the various members of the group. If several ratings are taken at intervals of the performance of each individual and comparisons made between performances of the same individual, the assumption may be held as valid.

An illustration of the validity of performance rating can be found in physical education classes. Often the physical education teacher seems anxious to use the apparently "respectable test devices" used by other teachers in the school. So he prepares an objective test covering the pupils' knowledge of basketball, including items on how to play the game, game strategy, and the rules. The test is administered to the class. It sometimes happens that the best basketball player in the group makes a low score on the pencil-and-paper test. A very bright, attentive, academic-minded lad who plays a miserable game will make a nearly perfect score on such a test. Immediately the issue rises, what were the pupils supposed to accomplish? Were they to *know about basketball?* Or, were they to be able to *play the game?* It is doubtful that any form of pencil-and-paper test device can measure the latter. For a valid test, some form of performance rating is indicated. Note that the best player in the group is probably a sand lot player who was a good performer when he came into the group. His rating will be high, perhaps with little improvement through the season. The bright bookworm may make a low score on a final performance rating and yet have improved his playing skills considerably. If improved skills are the goal, several ratings will need to be made and comparisons made between the ratings of the same player.

Other school situations in which performance ratings may be valid and in which pencil-and-paper tests have doubtful validity are in the school chorus, band, and orchestra, in dramatics, speech, and possibly certain leadership phases of citizenship.

The validity of records made with mechanical recording devices such as cameras and tape recorders involves the same issues which have just been presented for performance ratings.

Informal descriptive evaluations. The validity of the descriptive informal evaluations such as case records, diaries, testimonials, and so on, depends upon the extent to which descriptions can be obtained which fit the objectives of changed behavior set up at the beginning of the learning period. The difficulty with many of these is that both the objectives and the descriptions are expressed in generalities, usually in terms of abstract traits of character. To know anything about a pupil, it is necessary to know just what kinds of honest behavior reactions he makes in certain adequately described situations. It tells us little to have Silas write in his diary that he was a good sport. The teacher needs to know the situation which called for sportsmanship and a specific description of just what Si did which characterized his being a good sport. Such descriptions are extremely difficult to get into the record, partly because teachers are just as vague in defining objectives.

There is one other factor which affects the validity of informal evaluations, especially self-testimonials and diaries. If the objectives involve a judgment of behavior as formed by one's fellows, then a person's own reaction to his behavior may not be that of the others. In such a case self-judgment is nonvalid.

The various kinds of informal evaluations usually present difficulties in administration and certainly are often far from objective. Their chief value lies in the fact that they may be valid as approaches to measurement of pupil achievements that cannot be measured by any of the present forms of pencil-and-paper tests.

The values represented by objectives that seem not measurable by means of the commoner school devices are in many cases the most important of the human values. As an example, consider the group of values designated as good citizenship. If citizenship goals are defined in terms of the overt behavior of people toward one another and not in terms of abstract virtues or of knowledge about regulation of human conduct, then it is doubtful if any pencil-and-paper devices will get a true picture of a pupil's civic reactions. It is not enough to ask a pupil to choose between three or four possible ways to behave in a given situation. Neither is it enough to have him write down a description of how he ought to react to a given civic problem. What the teacher needs to know with considerable assurance is just how *he does act* when the situation arises. Some one of the informal approaches to evaluation is indicated. Perhaps a case record in which a teacher-observer records situations which arise in the group and an observation of just what the pupil did do under such situations is a way to make the evaluation of civic conduct. It need not be the only way.

In making a choice among various possible means of evaluation the prime criterion is that of validity. The measuring device chosen must *fit* the instructional situation, or there is no reason to attempt measurement at all. This is the standard by which pupils are inclined to judge the various school tests which they experience. This is the basis for much school criticism on the part of parents and patrons. The use of an invalid test by a teacher is professionally inexcusable.

Merits of various evaluative devices

A brief résumé of the application of the four standards to the various forms of evaluation is in order.

Uncontrolled teacher judgment is administratively feasible and often more reliable than would seem on the surface. It falls at the far end of the scale of objectivity. It can be valid if the teacher is careful to clarify objectives before exercising judgment. Because of frequent criticism based upon claims of bias due to nonobjectivity, teachers are advised to use it only in cases where more objective forms are not administratively feasible or seem not to be valid. When used it should be supplemented, wherever possible, with various forms of objective evidence such as samples of work of pupils or possibly with test scores.

Oral recitation as a means of evaluation has little to recommend it. If judged in terms of application to individual pupils, it is low in terms of all four of our basic criteria. Perhaps it has some use as a basis for forming teacher judgment of pupil growth. In such case, it is to be judged in terms of the merits of uncontrolled teacher judgment as a means of evaluation.

Prose tests have the merit of ease of administration in application. There are some difficulties of administration in scoring and interpretation. Objectivity and reliability are low. Prose tests may be valid for getting at the attainment of some objectives for which the construction of objective tests is difficult. Objectivity and reliability of prose tests can be improved by duplicating the questions for pupils, allotting the spaces for responses, and by keying the expected responses. If valid objective tests can be devised, they are to be recommended in place of prose tests because of superiority of administrative feasibility, objectivity, and most usually greater reliability.

Standardized objective tests have advantages in terms of all the proposed criteria except that of validity in the immediate local situation. If standardized tests are to be used with a particular group of pupils, the teacher needs to have scrutinized both the objectives of instruction for the particular group and the make-up of the proposed test to assure validity. A standardized objective test must *fit* the teaching situation to be of value. There are many learning objectives being attempted with pupils in schools for which no standardized objective tests exist.

Informal teacher-made objective tests are often more nearly valid than standardized tests. They are administratively feasible if the school has adequate typing and duplicating facilities. If well made, there should be no question of objectivity. Reliability is often unknown, but there is no good reason why teachers cannot learn to make reliable objective tests. Generally, teacher-made objective tests may be assumed to be more reliable than prose tests. The serious question is that of validity as compared to some prose tests, product rating, and performance rating. For testing knowledge, information, and retention of ideas, there should be no difficulty about the validity of informal objective tests. There will be difficulties in evaluating skills, changes in attitudes, interpretations, and appreciations.

The *rating of samples of pupil work* is administratively feasible. The rating is not clearly objective, although based upon concrete pieces of evidence. Reliability of ratings is variable. Objectivity and reliability can be increased by the use of appropriate score cards. Validity is high if the emphasis in learning is placed upon the production of the products specified. The analysis necessary in the construction of a score card should increase the validity of the ratings obtained by the use of the scoring device.

Performance rating is comparable to product rating when judged in terms of the basic criteria. Unless supported by evidence gained from records made with mechanical recording devices, performance rating is less objective. Probably performance rating is generally less reliable than product rating. The use of score cards should improve objectivity, reliability, and validity. Performance rating as applied to individual pupils presents great difficulties in administrative feasibility. The chief claim to value in performance rating lies in validity. Apparently there are some learning situations in which a rating of performance is certainly the only valid approach to evaluation.

The *informal evaluative devices* rank low in terms of all of the criteria except that of validity. They present great administrative difficulties, especially since most of them require individual application. They are nonobjective and of questionable reliability. They are to be recommended only in situations where other more reliable and objective forms that are more administratively feasible seem not to be valid. It must be kept in mind in considering this criticism of the informal evaluations that the objectives for which they are proposed are probably the most important undertaken in the schools. The shortcomings of the informal descriptive evaluations do not imply their abandonment but the limiting of their use to those situations where they are clearly indicated in terms of finding a valid measure.

Subunit implementation

SUBUNIT ORGANIZATION

1. Measures now available for the use of the classroom teacher are: uncontrolled teacher judgment; oral recitation; prose examinations; informal objective tests; standardized objective tests; rating of pupil products; performance rating; recordings done with mechanical devices; and certain informal descriptive means of evaluation such as case records, parental records, and pupil testimonials and diaries.

2. A test is *administratively feasible* if it can be applied readily to a whole group with a reasonable use of school time and with a minimum of interruptions of the school learning processes.

3. A test is *objective* if it can be scored by means of a key without fluctuations of scores due to variations in teacher judgment.

4. A test is *reliable* if, under the same conditons, it produces approximately the same results when repeated with the same group of pupils.

5. A test is *valid* when it measures what it purports to measure. From the teacher's point of view, a test is valid if it measures what the teacher has attempted to teach. Or, a test is valid if it measures what the pupils are told they should learn.

6. A *standardized* test is one that has statistically established norms of achievement for pupils that are alike in some respect.

7. Teacher judgment may be used as a means of evaluation of the results of school experiences. Teacher judgment can be quite reliable after the teacher has worked with a group of pupils over a considerable period of time.

8. Oral recitation is a generally unsatisfactory means of measurement. It is most often unreliable and frequently invalid.

9. Informal objective tests are satisfactory as a measure of those products of learning that can be measured with paper-and-pencil tests.

10. Standardized objective tests are not usually satisfactory measures for determining school marks for particular class groups in a local situation.

11. Wherever possible the teacher should use one or more standardized tests as a means of checking his own measures or standards. The standardized tests used must be valid for the situation in which they are used.

12. Where the end of training is ability to produce a good product, the rating of the product should be used as a measure.

13. Where the end of training is ability in skillful performance, performance rating should be used as a measure.

14. Longer tests tend to be more reliable than short ones.

15. Tests should be constructed as a part of the planning of instructional units rather than as afterthoughts.

16. Initial tests may be used as a means of diagnosing instructional needs and as a partial means of estimating progress of pupils.

17. Graphic representations of progress are useful in stimulating individual pupils.

18. Informal descriptive evaluation devices may be used in situations in which other forms of evaluation seem not to be valid for the objectives under consideration.

THINGS TO DO

1. Prepare an annotated bibliography of a few selected standardized tests for a course in your major field. Indicate classroom uses for each of these. Under what circumstances would each of these tests be valid? What is the coefficient of reliability shown in the test manual for each of these?

2. Make a list of publishers who publish a considerable volume of standardized tests. For each give the address. If these are branch offices, show the nearest branch office from which you would expect to receive service. Some educational institutions publish tests. Include these in your listing. As a class project make a collection of the latest test catalogs from the publishers in your list.

3. Set up a group of unit objectives for one unit of instruction from a course in your major field. Enumerate the items upon which the instructional unit and the test are to be built. Construct a test or set up a means of evaluation for this unit. Review the instructions for constructing teaching units in chapter 11. Use a unit which was prepared for an exercise with this chapter as the basis for your test, if you prefer.

4. Prepare a set of organizing problems for a class in one of the natural or social sciences to be used as a paper to take the place of a prose examination for pupils. State the problems as they should be stated for pupils and write out the pupil directions for assigning the paper.

5. Find an instructional unit in a school course for which a prose test would seem to be a valid instrument. Write out the questions for this test. Review your original questions and, if needed, increase the number by making the questions more definite and specific. Lay out the finished questions on sheets of paper providing spaces for pupils to write responses. Place an appropriate heading and set of test instructions at the top of the first page. When the test is properly spaced, key the test.

6. Make a score card for rating friendly letters written by pupils in a composition class. If you can find letters written by high school pupils, try scoring them with your scoring device.

7. Set up a score card for some type of musical performance. Try out your score card on some performance for which it seems valid.

8. Set up a score card for rating improvement of posture in a physical education class. Try out your rating device on members of the class. Are there any kinds of mechanical recording devices which could be used with your score card? If so, how are these be used?

9. Prepare two objective tests of differing forms for the same instructional unit. Key both tests. Which of the tests would you prefer to use? Why?

10. Make a score card for rating drawings, or posters, made in an art class. Try out your scoring device on some drawings or posters.

11. Work out a rating scale for a piece of clothing construction or an applied art project in home economics. Try out your device, if possible.

12. Work out a performance test in food preparation. How does this differ from a similar scoring device for finished food products? Under what circumstances would these devices be valid?

13. Prepare objective tests of three or four different types for the same instructional unit. How long do you believe each of these should be to insure reliability? How could you determine the reliability of each test?

14. Set up a committee for the class consisting of class members interested in speech instruction. Arrange with the teacher of a speech class in a nearby school to permit members of this committee to rate certain speech performances of pupils in the class. For example, suppose that pupils are to attempt introductions of speakers for the school assembly. Work out a rating card for this performance. Have members of the class committee rate the speeches with and without the score card. How do the two sets of ratings compare? If there is little difference in the two sets of ratings, can you defend the use of the score card? How?

15. Set up a case record scheme for evaluating the changes in school citizenship of a group of pupils. What items are to go into the record? Are recording forms needed? If so, what kind? What will a finished case record for a given pupil look like? Should you attempt to compare the records of different pupils? Why? If the results are to be reported to parents of the pupils, what is to be included in the report to parents? What kind of form is to be used in reporting to parents?

Helpful Readings

Bayles, E. E. *The Theory and Practice of Teaching.* New York: Harper & Bros., 1950. Chap. 15 and Appendix.

A philosophical approach to principles of measurement followed by an appendix showing sample test items emphasizing the measurement of understanding.

Garrett, Henry E. *Statistics in Psychology and Education.* 3d ed. New York: Longmans, Green & Co., Inc., 1947. Chap. 12.

A source book for the interpretation of educational statistics. Chap. 12 deals with the problems of test reliability.

Gerberich, J. R. *Specimen Objective Test Items.* New York: Longmans, Green & Co., Inc., 1956.

Title indicates content. Subtitle indicates use as a guide to achievement test construction.

Grambs, Jean D. and Iverson, William J. *Modern Methods in Secondary Education.* New York: William Sloane Assoc., Inc., 1952. Chap. 15.

Chap. 15 is on testing instruments. Includes some sample test items by way of illustration.

Greene, Harry A., Jorgensen, Albert N., and Gerberich, J. R. *Measurement and Evaluation in the Secondary School.* New York: Longmans, Green & Co., Inc., 1946. Chap. 2, pp. 10–26, Chap. 3, pp. 36–41, Chaps. 4–8, and Chaps. 14–23.

Use as a reference on educational measurements. Includes extensive treatment of criteria for judging tests and methods of statistical treatment of test data.

National Society for the Study of Education. *45th Yearbook. Part I. The Measurement of Understanding.* Bloomington, Ill.: Public School Publishing Co., 1946.

Title indicates content. Contains sample test items.

Ross, C. C. and Stanley, Julian C. *Measurement in Today's Schools.* Rev. ed. Englewood Cliffs, N.J.: Prentice-Hall, Inc., 1954.

Use as a reference. Readable and practical.

Ruch, Giles M. *The Improvement of the Written Examination.* Chicago: Scott, Foresman & Co., 1924. Chaps. 2, 4, and 5.

A source of evidence on the comparative reliability of various forms of objective tests.

STILES, LINDLEY J. and DORSEY, MATTIE F. *Democratic Teaching in Secondary Schools.* Philadelphia: J. B. Lippincott Co., 1950. Chap. 10.

Chap. 10 deals with ways to appraise the educational growth of pupils.

UMSTATTD, JAMES G. *Secondary School Teaching.* 3d ed. Boston: Ginn & Co., 1953. Chaps. 14 and 15.

Two effective chapters on measurement. Book emphasizes the statistical treatment of test data.

WRIGHTSTONE, J. WAYNE. *Appraisal of Experimental School Practices.* New York: Teachers College, Bureau of Publications, Columbia University, 1936. Chaps. 9–14.

For suggestions on descriptive approaches to appraisal of learning. Many devices of the non-objective type.

WRIGHTSTONE, J. WAYNE and JUSTMAN, JOSEPH. *Evaluation in Modern Education.* New York: American Book Co., 1956.

Includes much that is in the preceding plus a treatment of a wide variety of devices for evaluation.

Formulation of Marks, Records, and Reports

What to look for in this subunit

1. What is the difference between a test score, or evaluation rating, and a mark, or grade?

2. How many evaluations should be used in the process of determining a given mark?

3. Over what time intervals should marks be assigned?

4. Upon what "standards" should marks be based?

5. What is the difference between a *fine-step* and a *coarse-step* marking system?

6. What constitutes an ideal marking system?

7. What administrative difficulties are met in attempting to establish an ideal marking system?

8. What are the relative merits as systems of school marking of each of the following (a) an absolute percentage scale; (b) a five-step letter scale; (c) a letter scale based upon a normal distribution of marks; (d) a two-step, satisfactory or unsatisfactory, marking; (e) descriptive marking?

9. How may an adequate grade record sheet be set up?

10. What items should be included in the teacher's grade record sheet?

11. How are marks derived from test data and informal evaluations?

12. How do some schools attempt to set up record systems without formal marks?

13. What administrative difficulties are met in trying to establish a record system without formal marks?

14. Why do schools cling to relatively formal marking?

The teacher's relationship to the instructional process would seem to be complete at the point of evaluation. At least instruction seems complete at the point at which evaluation shows that a pupil has achieved satisfactorily in terms of the learning objectives originally set up. However, administratively the teacher's task is incomplete until the evaluations of the work of the pupils are summarized for the school records.

Need for records and reports

All schools keep records for individual pupils. As a matter of fact, school records form one of the fundamental bases for the approval of schools by all school accrediting agencies. The data used in formulating the record for each pupil are derived from the various evaluative devices. Invariably the transformation of evaluative data into such concise forms as may be needed for school records is a part of the task of the teacher.

In addition to the records needed, reports based upon the records are made periodically to those who are most concerned. Typically these reports go to the parents of the pupils. Of course pupils are informed, too, of the contents of the report which goes to the parents. Many teachers follow the policy of holding conferences with individual pupils on the basis of the reports shown by the school records. It is a typical school practice to send reports home to parents in the hands of the pupils.

It has been traditional school practice to base most of the content of the school record and of the report to parents upon achievement marks in the courses in which pupils are enrolled. Modern records and reports contain much other pertinent data concerning pupils such as health information, participation in activities of various kinds, social qualities of pupils such as group leadership, and any other pertinent evidences of pupil growth. In spite of this trend to broaden the scope of school records and reports, most are still built around achievement marks.

Typical conversations of high school pupils with one another and with most adults who come in contact with them include such questions as: "What are you taking this year?" "What kind of grades did you make last quarter?" "What did you make in English?" "How are you in mathematics?"

So, teachers have the perennial problem of school marks. It does not matter if the marks are expressed in prose statements rather than in symbols. It matters little whether the marks deal with the courses in the customary school subjects, or with experiences in the *core*, with school activities, or with citizenship, or just with evidences of growth. There is still the problem of marks derived by the teacher from whatever evidence may be gleaned from his evaluative devices. This chapter, or subunit, will deal with what the teacher can do to convert the various evaluations into suitable marks for school records and reports.

Definition of marks

Often some confusion exists in the minds of teachers between the result of a particular test, or evaluation, and a mark. It is obvious that a numerical score derived from an objective test is simply a test score. It is possible to rank pupils in the order of the scores on a particular test, but this ranking still results from the application of a single measure. Such a set of scores, or of rankings, on a single test do not constitute a mark as the term should be used.

Perhaps the actual confusion between evaluations and marks comes more often when, in the process of evaluation, the teacher groups the pupils of a class upon some relatively crude scale. For example, in rating the performance of members of a chorus the teacher may use such descriptive terms as excellent, good, fair, poor, and unsatisfactory. Pupils are actually ranked in relatively coarse groupings based upon the judgment formed during the test performance. The confusion arises if the school practice is to use these same terms as marks for reporting at the end of the month or quarter. Usually in such situations the symbol used for marking shortens the qualitative term into a single letter for convenience in reporting. The marks are E, G, F, P, U. The teacher accustomed to this marking scheme uses the same symbols in rating performance for a single evaluation. Nonetheless, the rating based upon performance during a single period is, properly speaking, an evaluation and not a mark to be reported at the end of an official marking interval.

A mark should be based upon a composite of evaluations and not upon a single measurement or judgment. What was said about reliability of measurements in the previous chapter is applicable here. A mark based upon a composite of several measurements or judgments should be far more reliable than a mark determined by any one of the devices used in forming the composite.

Marks, then, are what go into the school record to characterize the learning or growth of the pupils. In turn, marks are taken from the record to form the basis for reports made to pupils and parents.

Marks are formulated at periodical intervals as determined by the administrative policy of a school. Some schools use monthly marking and reporting. Quarterly marks are common. Colleges use either quarterly or semester marking, and some secondary schools do also. A few secondary schools formulate marks only at the end of the school year.

Often pupils, teachers, and parents refer to marks as "grades."

No distinction will be made between the terms, but the preferred term, marks, will be used in what follows.

Number of evaluations needed

The number of evaluations needed to formulate a particular mark will vary with the administrative policies of the local school. More evaluations are readily possible if marks are reported on a semester or a yearly basis than are feasible if marks are to be reported monthly or quarterly. If marks are reported relatively frequently, it may be possible to over-test. It is possible to use so much time in evaluative procedures that time for instruction is reduced. If frequent tests are used, they may become burdensome for the teacher, especially the teacher with a high pupil load. It may be unwise also to have pupils become too test conscious. Generally, it is desirable to have pupils work to attain the goals of learning rather than just to make grades. Too many tests have the effect of producing pupils who work largely for marks. This is especially likely to happen with bright pupils who rank near the top of a class. On the other hand, there needs to be enough measurement in formulating marks to insure that the marks assigned are not the result of chance, or errors in teacher judgment. It can be suggested that monthly marks should be derived from three or four evaluations and quarterly marks from five or six. This is purely an arbitrary rule of thumb. Certainly, the teacher should avoid marks assigned upon the basis of a single end-of-term test or rating.

Time intervals

There is no scientific way to determine how often marks should be reported. Administrative practices vary widely. It is undoubtedly true that pupils may work more consistently if marks are reported frequently. It is equally true that pupils are entitled to know of their own progress. The pupil who is achieving little should not be able to claim shock with an end-of-term report which he claims not to have expected.

The cooperation of parents in the attainment of the learning objectives of the school is imperative. There is, also, goodwill and public relations value in cooperating with parents who are fully informed of what is happening to pupils at school. This indicates relatively frequent reports. School administrators and teachers will need to strive to find a midpoint between a marking interval that is not so frequent as to become a burden to teachers and one which sets up desirable working relationships with pupils and parents. In secondary schools, marks and reports should be made at least quarterly. There are advantages in monthly reports. Probably schools cannot manage reports more frequently than once a month. With the younger pupils of junior high school age, the monthly report may be found desirable. For senior high school pupils, quarterly reports seem adequate.

Marking systems

The marking systems in common use in schools may be classified into one of the following: (a) an absolute scale reported numerically in percentages; (b) a five-step letter or symbol scale; (c) a five-step letter scale based upon a normal distribution of marks; (d) a two-step, satisfactory or unsatisfactory, marking; (e) a purported no-mark system expressed in prose descriptive terms.

Suppose that these marking systems are considered in terms of a set of qualities which effective marking systems should have.

1. A satisfactory marking system should be administratively feasible.
2. The standards set for the pupils implied in the marking system should be possible of definition.
3. The standards implicit in the marking system should be attainable by at least some of the pupils.
4. The steps between the intervals in the marking system should be relatively coarse.
5. Pupils and parents should be able to interpret the marking readily.
6. The marks should be obtained by summarizing the results of several measures or evaluations.

PERCENTAGE MARKING. The well-known system of marking in terms of figures expressed as percentages is administratively feasible. This is especially true since the symbols used are figures which can be readily manipulated and easily handled in records. However, the standard set in percentage marking, expressed as 100 per cent, represents an assumption of perfection which is almost impossible of definition. For most learnings there is no such thing as perfection, and it is doubtful if any teacher can identify the perfect learning indicated by the top score in this system. As examples of need for definition, try to apply percentage marking to citizenship, musical performance, letter writing, or drawings done in the art class. How is the teacher to recognize the 100 per cent mark in any of these?

STANDARD. In percentage marking, since the standard is set at the top in an assumed perfection, the established goal is unattainable. Or if some 100 per cent marks are assigned, they can be reached only by one or a very few pupils. The pupils who can possibly reach the top mark are known by the pupils before the marks are assigned, and as a consequence the great majority of the pupils cease to strive for high marks. The motivation set up by such a system operates only as competition among the select few.[1]

STEPS. The steps, or intervals between marks, in percentage marking are extremely fine. Theoretically the steps run from 0 to 100; that is, there are 100 steps. There are some teachers who go so far as to split these steps into half percents. The effect is to cut the number of steps of a too fine system into even smaller segments. Practically, there tend to be only about fifty steps in customary percentage marking. Most teachers will cut off all marking of 50 per cent or below as failure. This means that the scale operates from 50 upward towards 100.

The inherent difficulty with a fine-step marking system is that it leads to making distinctions between individual pupils unjustified in terms of the reliability of the measures used. There are almost no measures of any kind of human qualities that are accurate and reliable in making discriminations between human beings at the level of 2 per cent.

Imagine that a set of percentage marks reported at the end of a school quarter has been formulated in terms of evaluations which include the rating of a notebook, a teacher's performance rating, and scores on two prose examinations. Who knows the significance of the difference between two reported marks of 81 per cent and 82 per cent?

The newspapers recently carried a serial biography of a prominent American citizen. This biography included the marks made in the law school of a famous university. These marks include some of 79½ and 82½ per cent, as well as grade averages upon which scholarships were awarded reported in fractional percentages. Apparently the reading public, as well as some professors in law and other schools, are so naive as to believe that the judgments made were reliable enough to justify such distinctions. The best that can be said of such a situation is that apparently the marks were comparable to those made by other relatively bright young men of the time, and in comparison with other marks of such young men justified the renewal of a scholarship. Any school teacher, and any reader of a newspaper, ought to know that the small differences represented may have resulted from what some law professor may have had for lunch on a given day many years ago.

Interpretation. The percentage marking system does have the advantage of being readily interpreted by pupils and parents. This

[1] At this point it is suggested that the reader review what was said concerning competition as motivation in chap. 10.

ease of interpretation is open to abuse and misunderstanding due to the fineness of the steps in the system.

Percentage marking lends itself readily to arriving at marks that are summaries of several measures or evaluations, providing that other forms of evaluation upon which the marks are based can be expressed in quantitative terms.

Often in the summarizing of evaluations to arrive at a percentage mark the teacher is confronted with the problem of attempting to add measurements expressed in terms of differing scales. This raises the issue of the validity of the addition of ratings which may not be comparable. The usual approach to the settlement of this issue is that of reducing all measures and evaluations to a percentage scale before summarizing to arrive at a final mark. Administratively, this conversion of all evaluations to a percentage scale adds to the teacher's burden in that the arriving at final marks may involve a considerable volume of arithmetical calculation. Then too, the teacher must be aware that the assignment of such a percentage value as 80 to a C rating of a musical performance is a purely arbitrary judgment and may have no basic validity.

This factor of arbitrary judgment of the value of different percentages on a percentage scale involves also the decision concerning the demarcation between passing and failing. In some schools this dividing line is set at 75 per cent and in others at 60 per cent. If no statistical procedures are applied to the distribution of actual marks of pupils, this is a purely arbitrary decision and, like the 100 per cent at the top, defies rational definition.

This setting of an arbitrary passing line, in truth, leads back to the difficulties involved in a fine step marking system. If the line is drawn at 60 per cent, the pupil whose summarized measures come out at 59 per cent fails. Who knows the difference between the 59 per cent pupil and the 60 per cent pupil and is able to defend the difference by any tangible and satisfactory evidence? This problem is inherent in any such fine-step system, and the difficulty will occur no matter where the dividing line is set.

The use of the percentage system of marking persists largely because of tradition. Many older adults of this generation experienced it in schools. Teachers like it because it lends itself readily to arithmetical manipulation and demands a minimum of writing in record keeping and reports. Parents and pupils often like it because they believe they can readily understand what the marks mean. There is the added factor that it contributes to the competitive spirit. A pupil likes to boast that his mark is three points better than that of the pupil who sits next to him. The parent likes to display a school record that shows specifically that his boy has made consistently higher marks by a few points than the boy next door.

In spite of the preferences of many people for percentage marking and the fact that people in general believe that they know what its symbols mean, it is not to be generally recommended. The reasons are found in the inherent weakness of standards which cannot be defined and that are largely unattainable by most pupils and in the further limitation set by the abuses of the fine-step gradations in the system.

FIVE-STEP LETTER MARKING. The customary five-step letter system, with letters to serve as symbols for certain described qualities, has the advantage over percentage marking of coarse steps rather than fine steps. As an illustration use the letters A, B, C, D, and F. "A" is defined as a nearly perfect mark standing for the highest quality of achievement, perhaps most nearly approximated by the word *excellent*. "B" stands for *good* achievement but not that of the top quality which may be reached by only one or two pupils at the top of the group. "C" stands for ordinary, satisfactory achievement which may be expected of a large number of pupils, perhaps well represented by the word *fair*. "D" stands for achievement which is *just passable*, not quite failure. "F" stands for achievement which is not acceptable and therefore to be recorded as *failure*.

Standard. In practice the standard for ordinary letter marking is an arbitrary one set by each particular teacher in terms of his own ideals and judgment. Probably no two teachers will be in exact agreement concerning the kind of achievement to be marked "A." At least no two teachers confronted with the same group of pupils doing the same work are likely to agree on how many "A's" are to be assigned.

Often the "A" mark seems to be determined in the same fashion as the 100 per cent in percentage marking. It stands for perfect achievement, or for near perfect achievement in terms of standards set by educated adults. It is quite common practice for teachers first to mark in percentage and then convert to the symbols of the letter system. When this is done "A" often stands for achievement indicated by a percentage of 95 to 100. This means that the standard is the same as that for the percentage marking.

Steps. There is a distinct advantage in the five steps of the letter marking scheme. Pupils are grouped into five relatively crude categories, and it is unnecessary to make fine distinctions between the achievement or growth of most of the individuals. This is the merit of a coarse-step system over a fine-step one. The groupings are more nearly consistent with the reliabilities of the evaluations that may have been used in the composite for determining the mark.

The problem of distinction between individuals occurs in the use of letter marking with the borderline cases that seem to fall between letters or at the upper or lower edge of the group classified under one letter. As for example, the teacher may have trouble determining whether a given pupil should have a "high C" or a "low B." A similar situation can occur between "C" and "D" marks and between "D" and "F" and so on.

It is a common practice of teachers using letter marking to try to solve the border line cases by adding plus and minus signs to the letter symbols. This practice is encouraged, too, by the fact that normally the greatest number of pupils in a group will receive "C" marks. There is a considerable range of achievement between the best pupil receiving a "C" and the lowest receiving a "C." The use of the symbols "C+," "C," and "C−" seems to solve this particular difficulty.

The teacher who uses plus and minus marks as additions to the symbols of letter marking, in effect, tends to make a finer set of step gradations out of a system which is intended to have coarse steps. If plus and minus signs are used with all the letters, a five-step system is converted into a fifteen-step system. Practically, there is no point to "F+" and "F−." There is little significance to be attached to "D+" or "D−."

In the basic philosophy of letter marking "A" should stand for the highest achievement and should have honor and prestige attached to it. The assignment of "A+" tends to devalue the "A" for those pupils receiving it. The assignment of "A−" carries with it a feeling of disappointment at not receiving "A" for its recipients. For these reasons teachers using letter marking are urged not to assign "A+" or "A−" marks.

If the "A" is left alone and the use of plus and minus symbols restricted to "B" and "C" marks, there is still the effect of converting a five-step system into one of nine steps. This tends to lessen the chief value of letter marking found in the coarseness of the steps.

Administration and interpretation. Administratively, letter marking presents the problem of relatively awkward summarizing procedures. If it seems desirable to combine monthly or quarterly marks into a final mark for the year, it becomes necessary to assign numerical values to the various marks before the summary can be made. The same problem occurs in the formulation of the monthly or quarterly marks, if some of the evaluations used in arriving at them are expressed in the same symbols as those used for marks.

Many teachers in schools where letter marking is the officially recognized system follow the practice of first working out marks on a percentage system and then by arbitrary allotments of brackets on the percentage system assigning the letter marks to be reported. For example, such a teacher may assign letter marks according to the following table:

95 – 100%	A
85 – 94	B
75 – 84	C
60 – 74	D
below 60	F

Such practice is a confusion of two marking systems. The teacher who follows it is really thinking in terms of a percentage system and merely conforming to letter marking for administrative expediency. It does have the advantage that fine distinctions between pupils are *not reported*. However, many teachers spoil this advantage by telling pupils their percentage standings from which the letters were derived.

Letter marking has been employed so commonly in such a variety of schools that there are few difficulties of interpretation with parents, pupils, and the public in general. The chief difficulty of interpretation is the one mentioned above, the persistent confusion with percentage marking. There are, also, almost as many definitions of the different letter symbols as there are schools using the system.

Systems using descriptive word symbols rather than letters are almost invariably reduced to the letter system by teachers and may be so considered for all practical purposes.

When the letter system is used as a means of grouping pupils in terms of a summary of the evaluations used over a given time interval, it has a distinct advantage over percentage marking in spite of holding to approximately the same indefinable top standard. It is preferable that the number of groupings be kept to the basic five without increasing the number of steps in the system.

STATISTICAL DISTRIBUTION IN LETTER MARKING. A refinement of coarse-step letter marking is found in the continued use of letters as symbols but arriving at the grouping of summarized achievements represented by the letters through the application of statistical procedures to the evaluative data.

The teacher should keep in mind that the ideas about to be developed on a statistical treatment of marks can be applied to the data derived from each measurement or evaluation used, as well as to the summarization upon which the marks are based.

The statistical treatment of school marks grew out of the application of statistical procedures to measurements of the physical characteristics of various kinds of biological organisms. It was discovered by the biologists that if a refined measurement of a given characteristic was uniformly applied to all subjects in a sample of a plant or animal population large enough to be representative of the total population, the data from the measurement could be arranged so that when plotted a uniform curve resulted. This curve is now known as a curve of normal distribution. All such normal curves when plotted for different characteristics and different organisms have certain common characteristics and the areas contained within the curves also have certain common characteristics.

In the statistical treatment of biological data the measurements are first distributed in order, arranged from largest to smallest, or from highest to lowest. Where large numbers are to be handled a frequency table is made. This is done by grouping measurements into certain convenient even intervals and then tabulating the frequency of the measurements which fall within each particular interval. If the frequencies of occurrence of the scores are plotted against the value of the scores, a curve is formed. For most populations this will not give a true curve in the usual sense of the word but a somewhat jagged irregular line. Theoretically, if all of a large population can be measured on some common characteristic the curve will smooth out to approximate the symmetrical curve which is seen in illustrations of the normal curve of probability. If a perpendicular is erected at the midpoint of the base line and half the curve folded over on the other half, the two parts will fit exactly.

Range.   The distance on the base line from the lowest to the highest measurement is spoken of as the range. The measurements at the smallest and largest points represent the extremes for the measured characteristic in the population examined. For example, if the heights of all males between the ages of 20 and 40 years in the United States in a given year could be measured, the shortest man measured might be 3½ feet tall and the tallest 8 feet. The *range* for height of males in the population examined is then 3½ to 8 feet. Note that this tells something about the nature of the population examined. Nine footers are not to be expected. There is considerable variation in the heights of men in the United States.

Central tendency.   If the central measure in the population is found something more is known about the whole. There are two commonly used measures of the *central tendency* of a measured population. One is the *arithmetic mean* and the other the *median.*

The mean is found by adding all the individual measures and dividing by the number of cases in the population. There are statistical shortcuts for finding the mean when frequency distribution tables are used which will not be elaborated here.

The median is the midpoint in the distribution of measures. It can be found by locating the score, or measurement, which occurs at the point determined by taking half the cases in the population. For example, the teacher who wants to find the median for a set of scores on a test can do so by arranging the scores in order and then counting down halfway from the top. The score found at this midpoint is the median. It can be verified by counting up halfway from the bottom. The score should be the same, if the original calculation was correct. If the number of cases in the population is an odd number, the median will fall on the middle case. If the number of cases in the population is an even number the median will be halfway between the two middle cases and may have to be calculated. If the class group contains 41 pupils, the median will be the score of the 21st case. If the group contains 40 pupils the median will lie between the scores found for the 20th and 21st cases. If these scores are 72 and 73, the median lies between at 72½.

If there is a large sample population and a truly normal curve of distribution, the mean and the median will coincide. Practically, for the size groups with which most teachers work, there will be differences between the median and mean for scores of the same group. The reason for this can be seen quite readily. If one pupil makes a quite high score and this is separated from other scores by a considerable gap, the mean will be affected. The mean will be higher than the median of the same scores. In a similar fashion one or more very low scores separated from other scores will pull the mean down. The median is not affected by these extreme cases.

Since the median is unaffected by extreme measurements and is much more readily determined, in further application of simple statistics to marking in this chapter the median will be used as a measure of central tendency.

To return now to the illustration of the heights of adult males in the United States, the median height for men may be found as 5 feet 8 inches. This means that most of the men met on the street will be somewhere near five feet eight. An eight-footer will be rare. The dwarf of 3½ feet may never be encountered. Something else about the total population is now known. There is established a standard of expectancy for the height of men. The standard will be attained by a large number of men. Some will exceed it; others may fall short of the expectancy.

Quartile divisions. For the purposes of the typical classroom teacher, two other characteristics of a normal distribution are extremely useful. These are the *quartile* divisions. In the first place a quartile contains a fourth of the cases in the distribution. The first, or lower quartile, is found by counting up one-fourth of the way from the lower end of the distribution and is marked Q_1. The median marks the second quartile. The third is found either by counting down from the top of the distribution a fourth of the way or counting up from the lower end three-fourths of the way. The third, or upper quartile is marked Q_3. From this it will be seen that half the cases in the distribution lie on either side of the median and fall between the quartiles Q_1 and Q_3.

Often this intermediate range between the first and third quartiles is considered as normal for the population being measured. Returning to the illustration on the heights of men, the standard of expectancy is established by the median of 5 feet 8 inches. But deviations on either side of this within the interquartile range are common and are considered normal. More specifically, suppose that the lower quartile falls at 5 feet six inches and the upper quartile at 6 feet. Any man seen on the street between and including these heights is considered normal. A four-footer is looked at twice as being extremely short, and people stop to stare at the seven-footer as being unusually tall, perhaps thinking of him as a basketball center.

It will be noted that there are some cases just outside the interquartile range that do not seem unusual, for example, the man of five feet four or the one of six feet one or two inches.

Standard. In a statistical marking system, quantitative marks, arrived at by a summarization of measures, are distributed according to rank from highest to lowest. The median is found for the distribution of marks for the class. Quartiles for this distribution are also found. The marking standard is set by the achievement of the class group as measured. The primary mark stands for the achievement of those pupils in the two central quartiles found on either side of the median, the middle 50 per cent of the distribution. A letter mark is assigned as a symbol for this part of the distribution. A letter mark indicating higher achievement is assigned to pupils in the upper quartile, above Q_3, and a letter indicating lower achievement to pupils in the lower quartile, below Q_1. These marks are the ones clearly indicated by the statistical treatment of the marks.

Steps. However, most teachers and pupils are not entirely satisfied with a three-step marking system. Administratively, the three steps do not indicate the failures. These have been grouped in the letter symbol for the lower quartile. In practice, then, 2 to 3 per cent of the cases at the bottom of the lower quartile are cut off and arbitrarily assigned a mark of failure. In the same way 2 or 3 per cent of the cases at the top of the upper quartile are assigned a mark indicating outstanding work beyond that of the remainder of the group.

In the Missouri system [2] the letter "M" is used as the mark which represents achievement of the middle 50 per cent around the median. "S," or superior, is used for the upper quartile, and "E," or excellent, for the small percentage at the top. "I," or inferior, is used for achievement in the lower quartile and "F" for the small percentage of failures at the bottom of the lower quartile. An hypothetical class of 100 pupils would then have 50 "M" marks, 22 or 23 "S" marks, 2 or 3 "E's," 22 or 23 "I's," and 2 or 3 "F's."

The letters A, B, C, D, F, or others, can be used just as well. However, since A, B, C, D, F are often used for the common letter system of marking it may be well to use different symbols to distinguish a statistically based system.

Administration. Statistical letter marking can be readily administered if teachers are taught its significance and it is not confused with the other marking systems in traditional use.

The chief difficulty in administration is found in application of the system to small classes. If the number of pupils in a class is too small to make an adequate sampling for statistical manipulation, the system tends to break down.

By the laws of chance it is possible that all the members of a class of twelve or fifteen might fall within the upper quartile of a much larger sampling of comparable pupils. In the same way all of a small group might belong in a lower quartile or the middle of a larger sampling. Some teachers with several sections of the same class try to resolve this difficulty by combining evaluative data for pupils in all the sections in deriving marks. The data are treated as if all the pupils were members of one large group. There may be complaints when this is done since most of the "I" marks may fall to pupils in one section and most of the "S's" in another.

A further illustration of the difficulties found in the statistical derivation of marks in small classes occurs with groups of pupils in advanced courses in a particular subject-matter field. These

[2] So-called because the early application of statistical marking was established at the University of Missouri.

difficulties are exaggerated if the advanced courses are elective. At present even in large high schools the fourth-year language classes are quite small. If a school still offers Latin, there may be only six or eight pupils in fourth-year Latin. Fourth-year mathematics classes are often small, especially in moderate sized schools. The physics class for seniors is often small. In these situations all pupils who cannot do readily languages, mathematics, or sciences will have failed or received discouragingly low marks in the first two years. All pupils with little or no interest in these fields will have dropped out to elect other courses of greater appeal to them. There are left only those with interest and considerable ability in the advanced elective courses. From the point of view of many teachers the pupils left in these courses in the senior year are all upper quartile pupils and should all receive "S" or "E" marks. Almost any Latin teacher will take this point of view about the few pupils left in fourth-year Latin.

There is, of course, an opposing point of view. This is that if there were a large enough group of seniors with interest and some ability in Latin, they, too, would be distributed over a scale of normal distribution. Such pupils should be in competition with others of their kind and not with the unselected ability and interest group with which they started. The trouble remains that there are not enough of these people in any one school to form anything like a normal distribution.

There are some ways of meeting the small-class situation in statistical treatment of marks. One thing that can be done is to scrutinize the actual distribution of marks for the class as it stands. A compactness of the marks will indicate small differences among the individuals. Some dispersal with gaps between marks will indicate a lack of homogeneity.

The teacher always has impressions concerning the quality of a group of pupils as a whole. "This is a good class." "This is the best class that I have had." "These people are all poor." "This is the worst section that I have had in years." These impressions, if they are not unjustified biases, may be worth considering in determining what to do with the distribution of marks for a small class. Contrary to the belief of some teachers, there does not have to be a complete range of marks for the pupils in every class. Perhaps the marks in some class should begin with "M" and run down. In another the marks may begin with "E" and cut off at "M." No one has to fail in a particular class. No one must have an "E."

The impressions of the teacher concerning the quality of pupils in a class as a whole can be checked. Experienced teachers may make mental comparisons with previous classes attempting the same kind of work. The records of members of a class in previous school years can be checked from the school records. The intelligence quotients of pupils should be in the school records too. If a valid standardized test in the subject can be found, this can be administered to the group. The teacher's proposed distribution of marks can be compared with the distribution of the same pupils on scores made on the standardized test. The marks are to be assigned in terms of the teacher's own evaluative devices in the local situation, not in terms of the standardized test. But the scores of the pupils on the standardized test can be used to check the teacher's evaluations and the teacher's impression of the group as a whole.

The standardized test, in effect, enlarges the size of the sample to include the pupils upon which the test was standardized. The pupils in the small local class can then be located on the scale of this enlarged sample and the teacher's judgment checked.

A distinct advantage of statistical derivation of marks lies in the definition of the standard which is set. The standard is established by the actual accomplishment of the group being marked, not by some arbitrary assumption of perfection on the part of the teacher. The standard lies at the median of the summarized evaluations used in arriving at the marks. Even if top of the range is considered as the standard rather than the midpoint, this upper limit is set by the achievement of pupils in the group being marked. So also is the lower limit. With this system, marks are truly determined by what the pupils have accomplished rather than by what the teacher thinks they should accomplish.

It must be kept in mind that as soon as the teacher confuses statistical marking with either percentage marking or simple letter marking this advantage in definition of the standard is lost. An "E" is simply at the top of the range in the distribution and not 98 or 100 per cent; nor is it the "A" of simple letter marking.

The steps, or intervals, between letter symbols in statistical marking are coarse, customarily only five letters representing five groupings. The difficult points of decision lie at values near the upper and lower quartile divisions and in the determination of the few "E" and "F" marks. Further, the middle group is large, and no distinctions are made between pupils toward the lower edge of the middle 50 per cent and pupils toward the upper edge of this group. There are some advantages in this, but many teachers who use statistical markings are troubled by this lack of distinction between pupils in approximately half the class.

Interpretation. Teachers, pupils, and parents can learn to interpret a statistical approach to marking quite readily, but many of them have refused to do so. They have learned about marks in terms of either the percentage system or of simple letter marking and so persist in trying to interpret statistical marking in terms of these.

The most difficult concept to interpret in statistical marking is the change in standard involved. Over and over again a pupil who has been doing perfectly satisfactory work and has received an "M" mark has gone to his teacher to say that he is unhappy with a "mediocre" mark. Sometimes it is difficult to get him to understand that "M" does not stand for mediocrity but for normally satisfactory work on the part of the majority of the pupils in the class and that this standard is set by the very achievement of the pupils themselves. This point is difficult to establish too with parents who expect their son or daughter to bring home at least some "A's" or some "90's."

Another difficult point to establish about statistical marking is that some of the pupils are expected to achieve beyond the class norm and that the top achievement is not limited by any static goal, and that this, too, is established by the achievement of ambitious, talented, and willing performers in the class itself.

Perhaps a final item of interpretation to be established is that the responsibility for setting the standard of achievement lies with the pupils themselves—not with the teacher. Repeatedly teachers are saying, "I do not *give* grades, you *earn* them." With a statistical interpretation of marking, this becomes literally true, and the point must be well established with both pupils and parents.

In situations in which it can be administered and interpreted a letter marking scale based upon a statistical treatment of test and evaluative data is to be recommended because of its definition of the marking standards. No other marking system posseses this characteristic so clearly.

NONCOMPETITIVE MARKING. Another noteworthy shift of standards is found in two-step satisfactory-unsatisfactory marking. This change does away with competitive marking among members of the group and defines the mark in terms of progress or growth of each individual. The standard set is not in terms of comparison with the achievement of other pupils. Rather, the standard is set in terms of an answer to the question, "In comparison with his own beginning point, how much has this pupil improved?" When this standard is applied the marks of the different pupils are not comparable. What may be satisfactory progress for one pupil may be considered as unsatisfactory for his neighbor. The terms satisfactory and unsatisfactory are to be interpreted for each pupil in terms of his own potentialities.

The notion of an individualized interpretation of satisfactory and unsatisfactory progress can be illustrated by an actual case involving pupils in a ninth-grade general science class. The pupils in this class were given an objective test covering the items commonly found in ninth-grade general science textbooks. The maximum possible score for this test was 215 points. When administered to a class of twenty-three pupils in May the highest score was 180. The lowest score was 63. In normal competitive rating the boy with the highest score who was outstandingly at the top of the group would have made an "A" or "E." The boy with a score of 63 would have had an "F" mark.

But this same test had been administered to these pupils in September of the same school year. At that time the same boy had been at the top of the group with a score of 179. The same boy had been low with a score of 9. In terms of the test used, the boy at the top of the class, who remained at the top of the class all school year made no growth. The boy at the bottom of the class who remained at the bottom of the class grew markedly. He had improved his score by seven times the original. If marked in terms of satisfactory-unsatisfactory marking, the boy at the top of the class group would have been marked unsatisfactory and the boy at the bottom satisfactory, with perhaps added praise for his improvement.

There is no argument concerning the fact that the teacher of the illustrative science class failed in his obligation to stimulate a boy of apparently superior ability. This is the more evident since the teacher knew the high score this boy had made in September.

Standard. From the illustration it is evident that the standards for satisfactory-unsatisfactory marking can be defined, at least in part, if the status of each pupil at the beginning of the learning interval is known. The system is much more readily administered if the initial status of each pupil can be measured objectively, or at least identified by means of some tangible evidence such as samples of work or ratings of performance. There are likely to be administrative difficulties if the only evidence of initial status and of growth is anchored in unsupported judgments of the teacher. Case records lend themselves to the building up of the kind of cumulative evidence needed for satisfactory-unsatisfactory marking. It is entirely possible to use the system with the usual forms of objective tests and prose examinations if initial tests are administered at the beginning of the learning interval. But if initial and final tests are different tests, the scores may not be comparable for the same individual, and the evidence of growth, therefore, not reliable.

Steps. Satisfactory-unsatisfactory marking was defined as a two-step system. In reality it is a no-step system. There are no gradations of marking. There is then a distinct advantage to the teacher who does not have to worry about distinctions between individuals or the interpretation of such distinctions to pupils and parents.

In practice, teachers who have been indoctrinated in competitive marking schemes tend to break down the no-step lack of distinction between individuals. First, teachers for ease of record-keeping shorten the words to the letters "S" and "U." Next, some teacher proposes at a teacher's meeting that there should be some way to attach prestige to the mark of the pupil who has done outstanding work and has reached a high level of achievement. So the teachers vote to add a step such as "E" for excellent or "H" for honors. Now there is a three-step marking instead of a no-step one. The next stage is the addition of plus and minus signs to the letters. Finally, there are "H+," "H," "H−," "S+," "S," "S−," "U+," and "U." Now there is an eight-step letter marking system. The standard of individual growth is lost, and teachers have returned to competitive marking. All the advantages of the original satisfactory-unsatisfactory marking system have been lost.

In some schools, teachers will go through the negative evolution of lettermarking from the satisfactory-unsatisfactory marking without seeming to be aware of the confusion existing in mixing the philosophies underlying the two systems.

Satisfactory-unsatisfactory marking has an added advantage in that every pupil who is willing and tries to learn should be able to make some progress toward the attainment of the immediate objectives, provided of course that these goals are at all reasonable for the maturities of the pupils.

As a marking system in terms of potential stimulation to continued learning and one that is most consistent with the psychology of learning, the satisfactory-unsatisfactory scheme properly interpreted to the pupils most nearly approaches the ideal.

Administration. The fundamental difficulty with such an ideal system is that school people cannot deal with pupils wholly within the local school situation and entirely within an ideal learning environment. Although the pupil may be judged at school in terms of his own progress, outside of school he is judged by the standards of a highly competitive world. Even the parents are not entirely satisfied with a report of individual growth. They want to know, too, how Willie compares with others in his group or with others who may live in the same block.

At the secondary school level pupils are faced with the possibility of employment out of school hours, during the summer, or, for seniors, upon graduation. The potential employer of a young secretary does not want to know that she can type more rapidly than she could three months ago. He wants to know how well she can type. If the school recommends three possible secretaries for the same position, the employer wants to know which has the greatest speed and which is the most accurate in copying and transcription. For it is quite possible that a slow learning girl may have shown good recent progress and have been rated as satisfactory in terms of her own growth and yet be one of the poorest performers in her class, and quite unpromising as a candidate for a particular position.

School offices are asked continually by possible employers for recommendations or records of previous pupils, sometimes pupils who attended school ten to twenty-five years in the past. There may be no administrator or teacher on the present staff who knows a pupil in question. If the only thing which the school record shows is a series of satisfactory marks for work done over a period of four years and the mark is defined as adequate growth, no one knows whether the pupil can spell, solve algebraic equations, saw to a straight line, or operate a typewriter successfully. If several pupils are investigated for the same position, the records all look alike. No one can tell from the school records which pupil is to be preferred for a position. Some great corporations employing large numbers of people want the high school records of prospective employees. They prefer records which show comparative and competitive marking.

The demand for comparative or competitive marking does not lie wholly outside the school. The present population of our country is largely a migrant one. Families move, and pupils change schools. Seniors graduate, and a large proportion of them go on to colleges. When a pupil enters a new school, the principal wants to know more of his total achievement than that he had satisfactory marks in all that he did in terms of his own capacities. The principal wants to know where the new pupil belongs in relationship to the groups in which he may be placed. Colleges prefer not to admit pupils on just a record of satisfactory achievement in terms of individual capacities. Such a "satisfactory" pupil may not be able to do college work at all, as colleges are now organized. For a pupil entering college from a school using satisfactory-unsatisfactory marking, the principal will also need to furnish information concerning the pupil's *rank in his class group.* Such information cannot be obtained from the "satisfactory marks" on the pupil's record. Other data for the record becomes necessary.

For the reasons enumerated, the satisfactory-unsatisfactory marking scheme is administratively impractical unless it is accompanied by some other form of marking based upon comparisons of pupils in the school groups. Practically all schools who have tried such marking have kept dual records for administrative purposes. This means that teachers must mark pupils on two marking systems and report to the office in terms of both. Reports to pupils and parents are made only in terms of the "S-U" ratings.

"S-U" marking means that the teacher must derive individual growth marks rather than marks for a class group. It means that there must be some initial evaluation in order to establish a standard for the growth of individuals. It means that for purposes of the office records in dealing with other secondary schools, colleges, and employers, a second marking must be done in terms of the class group. It can be seen at once that from the teacher's point of view "S-U" marking is quite laborious and time consuming.

Interpretation. There are problems of interpretation of the growth, or lack of growth, of pupils with an "S-U" system involving the education of all concerned in appraisals in terms of individual rather than in terms of intergroup comparisons. These problems of interpretation are not necessarily insurmountable.

The interpretation of "S-U" marking really breaks down because of the necessity for keeping records in two marking systems. It is impossible to keep the existence of the second marking system a secret from pupils and parents. Ethically, the point can be argued that the pupil and his parents have a right to know the pupil's standing on both systems. Then, there is the situation of trying to explain why a pupil who has all "S" marks on his record cannot go to college because he *ranks in the lower third of his class* in terms of comparative achievement. This is only one illustration of an endless chain of difficulties of interpretation that grow out of the dual marking.

Most schools that have embarked enthusiastically into the idealism of satisfactory-unsatisfactory marking have broken down over the necessity for keeping other records in some other marking system and so have drifted back into a frankly competitive marking system of some kind. This is not to be interpreted as indicating that it is always impossible to administer and interpret "S-U" marking.

It is merely an attempt to point out some of the pitfalls in what seems to be an ideal approach to marking, if, in establishing this approach, teachers think only in terms of the learning effects of a marking system.

DESCRIPTIVE MARKING. The next step beyond "S-U" marking has been attempted in some schools. This involves an attempt to abandon all formal marking. Marking is replaced by brief prose descriptions of each pupil's growth and present status.

Administratively, descriptive marking means considerable writing on the part of the teacher and relatively bulky school records and reports to parents. In effect, the marking system tends to take the form of a case record. This has certain obviously desirable features, if the scheme can be effectively administered and interpreted.

Standards. It seems just to say of descriptive marking that it has no defined standards. Indeed, some teachers deny that there should be any marking standards. Henry and Susan are accepted as they are and the teacher attempts to make a factual description of their status at reporting time. This leaves the teacher without any idea of just where Henry should be or where Susan may stand in relationship to the achievement of other members of her group.

Steps. If there are no standards, the teacher has difficulty in determining the size of the steps or gradations between the descriptions used. There are either no such things as marking steps, or the number of possible gradations are infinite. Perhaps since this is a *no marking* system, the idea of steps does not apply to it at all.

Administration and interpretation. Most schools that have attempted descriptive marking have developed reporting and record forms to decrease the teacher and secretarial labor necessary in carrying out the marking. There is a tendency to use stereotyped descriptive terms which may be shortened to single words and possibly finally to a set of symbols comparable to letter marking. Such descriptions soon lose any significant meaning in the description of the status of a particular pupil at any given time. Perhaps letter marking would serve just as well when the attempt at description reaches this stage.

Descriptive marking has all the administrative and interpretative difficulties described under "S-U" marking. Often a more formal marking system is employed with it to meet the demands of other schools and prospective employers of youths. Almost invariably a conference with parents becomes necessary to interpret the report of a particular pupil. Such conferences are often desirable, but the necessity for many of them indicates that the descriptive terms used in the school reporting are, in general, meaningless to parents.

At present the best recommendation concerning descriptive marking would seem to be to use as a system one of the other recognized marking schemes and to supplement the marks on the periodic report for each pupil with a prose statement concerning his status and recent accomplishments. The descriptive material in the report may take the form of interpretation and elaboration of the marks assigned.

The descriptive matter may be in the form of a letter from the teacher to the parent. Note that if a pupil has five different high school teachers in a given term, his quarterly report will contain in addition to the customary marks, letters from the five teachers. In some schools such a report may include a note from the principal and the guidance official of the school as well. Teachers with heavy pupil loads will at once raise the question of how teachers are to find the time to write all these letters. Perhaps a partial answer to this can be made by suggesting that the school using the practice recommended above should have ample clerical help. Teachers might be able to dictate the letters needed to a school stenographer, or perhaps into a dictation machine for later transcription in the school offices.

If letters or descriptive material are sent to parents with the periodic reports of marks, copies of all such matter should go into the school files along with other records of the pupils concerned. It is a dangerous administrative practice to send any kind of reports concerning pupils out to parents and to fail to have in the school files a record of what was said. This means that permanent records for pupils may need to take the form of folders for each individual pupil in which, along with the usual school records, all matter of value in dealing with the pupil and his parents will be kept.

Considerable space has been devoted to the ideas inherent in different types of marking systems. In practice each teacher will have to follow the old adage of when in Rome behave as the Romans do. He will use the marking system officially adopted by the school in which he works. However, if he joins other teachers in a professional protest against the adopted system, he should understand the reasons for objecting and the potential headaches that may be involved in a proposed new scheme. Schools are continually trying to improve marking. In almost all cases the recommendations come from a committee of teachers and must be approved by members of the teaching staff before being put into effect. Again, the members of such a committee and the teachers voting on the adoption of recommendations for change need to know what is being proposed and in what ways the new proposals may be more effective.

Deriving marks from evaluative data

Here the steps through which the teacher should go in arriving at a set of marks for a class from the evidence gained from tests and evaluative devices are described. The marking system for the illustration is a statistically derived letter marking system. This system is chosen because it is the only marking system in which the standards used can be closely defined. The steps between marks are coarse and do not lead to fine discriminations between individuals. The application of statistical procedures also defines the various marks used and the distinctions between marks can be defended with little recourse to unsupported teacher judgment. The marks can be determined for a class group with a minimum of time-consuming mathematical manipulation. It is assumed that for administrative reasons most schools will continue to use some form of comparative and competitive marking and that the great majority of teachers will need to know how to derive marks from cumulative test and evaluative data.

GRADE RECORD SHEETS. The first requisite for summarizing data to arrive at marks is an adequate record of all the measures to be counted in establishing the marks for the reporting interval. In effect, what is proposed is a system of decent bookkeeping for evaluative data. In planning work, the teacher should decide which evaluations are to be used in formulating marks. The results of such evaluations should be properly recorded for each pupil at the time the evaluation takes place. The total record should be well organized, systematic, neat, and show all data from which grades are to be drawn. Teachers are not to trust to memory for judgments rendered three weeks before marks are to be established. Grade records are not to be kept on odd pieces of paper or original work sheets for taking off test scores.

In general, it is better not to record grades in the class book used for attendance records. Grade records should be kept as separate accounts. A looseleaf system is much more convenient than a tightly bound book. The pages can be removed for work. There is no reason to carry the grade records from one classroom to another as is done with attendance records. Grade records should be kept as far as possible at the teacher's work station. Since these records are highly important to everyone concerned they should be kept in the teacher's desk and in some situations it will be desirable to have them locked up. A pupil's record is his own affair, his parents', the teachers', and that of appropriate school officials, but not that of all his fellow pupils and the neighbors. Therefore, records are to be kept so that they are not open to the scrutiny of the curious.

ITEMS IN THE RECORD SHEET. The grade record sheet consists first of a class roll alphabetized according to last names of pupils. It should be appropriately headed to indicate the nature of the content and have spaces for headings to indicate the nature of the various recordings.

The heading for the grade record sheet should show the name of the school and indicate the nature of the work for which the mark is to be established, as, Aurora High School, English I, section 2. The date of the school year should be shown in the heading, and if the record is for a particular quarter or term, this should show too. There should be space, following the heading, for the name of the teacher responsible for the record. If the class is large enough to require more than one page of the record, each sheet should repeat the data given in the heading for the first. Second and third sheets can get separated from the record and are not always readily identified unless headings are repeated for each sheet.

The wider left-hand column of the record sheet contains the names of the pupils. The columns to the right of the name column provide spaces for entering the data for each test or evaluation for each of the pupils. These data columns should show in the heading at the top the following items: the nature of the test or evaluative device; the date of administration; an indication of the scope or content of the test; the maximum score of the test or the highest rating possible. There will need to be a column for each evaluation. The next column to the right of the data columns should be double or heavy ruled and headed "summary" with the date of summarization. The column following this is the column for recording marks derived from the summarization of evaluative data. It should be headed "final marks" and show the date when such marks were reported.

If the record sheet is ruled for more than one marking period, quarter, or school term, the entries in the summary and mark columns should be made in red to distinguish them from the entries in other columns. This will avoid the possibility of occasionally picking up an item from the first summary column and adding it to data for the following quarter.

Sample Section of Teacher's Grade Record Sheet

Aurora High School: English I, sec. 2, 1st quarter, 1960–61

Teacher: Otto Krank

Nature of Test	Quiz 1	Quiz 2	Teacher Rating	Notebook Rating	Quiz 3	Final Exam.	Summary Mark
Scope of Test	Parts of Speech	Sentence Structure	Composition	Reading	Verb Forms		
Date	9/30	10/15	11/1	11/15	11/30	12/10	
Maximum Score	100	100	E	E	110	150	Summary
Adair, Alice	75	80	50 M	60 M+	85	120	470
Botts, Calvin	90	95	100 E	90 S+	100	135	610
Culver, Ida	80	70	50 M	40 M−	80	115	435
Dugan, Donna	85	90	70 S−	80 S	90	130	545
Edwards, Clay	60	65	30 I	30 I	65	85	335
Fyfer, Cliff	70	80	50 M	50 M	85	110	445

Above is a sample section from a teacher's grade record sheet. It purports to be a record for section two of a ninth-grade English class in Aurora High School. The first entry is for a quiz administered September 30 which contained 100 points as a maximum score. The quiz contained items concerning the parts of speech. The second column shows scores on a second quiz administered October 15 on sentence structure. This quiz also contained 100 points. In the third column are letter ratings based upon the teacher's judgment of sample compositions of the pupils. This judgment was rendered on November 1 and the highest rating was "E" based upon a scale of "E," "S," "M," "I," and "F." The teacher has chosen to add plus and minus marks to "M" and "S" ratings. This practice is debatable, but the teacher in the sample has set up his record in this fashion. The next column shows teacher rating on the same scale. This is a rating of notebooks kept by pupils showing reviews or summaries of out-of-class reading. The teacher rated these notebooks on November 15. The following column shows scores on a third quiz administered November 30. This quiz contained 110 points and had to do with verb forms. Finally, the column dated December 12 shows scores on a final examination for the quarter which contained 150 points. Presumably this examination covered items selected from the work of the whole quarter. Again, school policies on such final examinations vary. But, in the school from which the sample was taken examinations were a part of school policy.

SUMMARIZING. It is to be noted from the sample record sheet that the scores recorded for the tests and examinations are raw scores and not percentage scores. It happens that since there were 100 points in each of the first two tests, these records are in percentages. It must be emphasized that tests may have any reasonable number of points. For example, this first test might have had a maximum number of 80 points rather than 100.

It is not necessary to convert test scores and ratings into percentages. It is proposed to summarize each pupil's record by a simple addition of the values shown across the page. Pupils are to be ranked upon the basis of the summary of raw scores and ratings. The conversion of each set of scores to percentages is unnecessary for summarizing. The time and energy expended in summarizing marks is to be kept at a minimum. The time required to convert all measures to a uniform percentage scale seems to be so much lost motion.

The only reason for converting various quiz scores to percentages is to enable the teacher to compare the achievement of the pupil on one quiz with his achievement on another. Such comparisons have both doubtful reliability and doubtful validity. As can be seen from the sample the quizzes deal with different bodies of content. Since the quizzes are teacher-made and have not been scaled for difficulty, the comparative difficulty of various quizzes is entirely unknown. It could be possible for the quarterly examination of 150 items to have been less difficult than quiz 3 with 110 items. If the teacher feels it desirable to make comparisons between the achievements of pupils on several tests, it is much more desirable to make these comparisons on the basis of the *ranks* of pupils on the different tests rather than on either raw scores or scores reduced to percentages. Space could be made for showing the rank of pupils on various measures on the record sheet. Since ranks are not to be used in summarizing, they are not shown.

CONVERSION OF LETTER RATINGS. The data of the sample are summarized for marks for the first quarter. Before scores can be added it is necessary to convert the letter ratings in the record into quantitative terms. To do this a simple conversion scheme for turning letter marks into figures is needed. Any arbitrary assignment of values which seems reasonable, is consistently applied, and can be explained to pupils will serve. To avoid confusion with percentage marking it is preferable not to use percentage values. Since the "M" in our marking system stands for midachievement, or performance, suppose that a value of 50 is assigned to "M." The teacher has used some plus and minus signs on letter marks. For purposes of illustration, suppose that these are retained. If values are assigned both ways from the "M" at even intervals a scale like the one shown below is formed.

E	100 points
S+	90
S	80
S−	70
M+	60
M	50
M−	40
I	30
F	0

Have in mind that other values could be assigned. The value of "M" could be made 75. All plus and minus signs could be ignored. As long as the values seem within reason and are consistently used, the actual values assigned are not of great consequence. It is more convenient for computation to stick to round whole numbers. The sample ratings cannot distinguish between small differences in pupils and were not intended to do so. Therefore, values assigned to letter marks within the order of 78 or 79 have no sig-nificance.

Using the values shown on the scale above, these have been interpolated above the letters as shown in the sample record sheet. This is probably just what the teacher would do in practice before beginning the summarizing task.

WEIGHTING OF MEASURES. There is a persistent tendency on the part of many teachers to weight such measures as a final exam-ination or the rating of a notebook at higher values than other tests and ratings. A common expression of the idea of weighting a measure is to tell the pupils that the final examination will make up one third of the quarter's mark. In the sample the notebook could also count for one third. This leaves the total of the remain-ing four evaluations at a value of one third of the final mark. Such weighting has little or no justification and should be avoided.

In the first place, no teacher knows the exact proportionate values of the various measures which he uses. Usually, he has no good notion of the comparative difficulty of his various tests or evaluative processes. Any attempt at weighting is merely a bold guess at what the teacher thinks may be relative values.

The high weighting of a final examination is especially ques-tionable. If there are enough other measures used, as is true in the sample record sheet, the high weighting of the final has prac-tically no justification. It ought not to be possible for a pupil who has established a good record on various measures throughout a quarter to spoil this record through some chance element which may affect only one measure such as a final examination.

As illustration of such an established good quarter's record note the case of Calvin or Donna in the sample. Donna could have a severe headache on the day of examination and do poorly. The final should not be so heavily weighted as to ruin her otherwise good record because of this circumstance, which may be unknown to the teacher.

The reverse case should also hold good. A pupil with an other-wise poor record for the quarter should not by temporary cram-ming procedures be able to raise himself by his own bootstraps on account of a highly weighted final test. As an illustration, note the case of Clay in the sample.

A highly weighted final places pupils under considerable ten-sion, all out of proportion to the worth of the measure. A given pupil may face failure as a result of the one test. Parents at home are often putting pressures on some of the pupils to either retain high marks or raise low ones. The tensions and pressures created by highly weighted final tests lead to cribbing and almost invariably to undesirable cramming. Cheating is not to be condoned, but certainly the teacher who creates pressures by the use of highly weighted final tests should share with the pupils the responsibility for the consequences.

The use of weighting in terms of fractional values of the total mark involves a continuing struggle with the mathematics of proportion on the part of the teacher. Accept, for the moment, the proposal for weighting in terms of thirds in the sample record. Work out the weightings for the six cases presented and see what confronts a teacher who might have to work out such problems for 100 to 200 pupils.

If a teacher believes that a particular measure because of the emphasis upon certain objectives with pupils is to be valued more highly than others, it becomes much simpler to weight such a measure in terms of a multiple. For example, in the sample record the teacher may believe that the notebook kept on outside reading is of great importance and that its rating should be weighted at greater value than the other measures used. A simple approach to weighting is to multiply all of the ratings in this column by two and add these in when the summary is made. If this is done, the heading at the top of the column should show an x2 and when the letter ratings are converted to figures the values doubled. If this should be done Alice's notebook rating would have a value of 100 in place of the 50 which the record now shows. The weighting can be further exaggerated by using an x3 as the multiple, therefore, tripling all of the original ratings. This method of weighting can be made to satisfy the teacher, who believes in it, with a minimum of mathematical calculation.

In spite of the fact that weighting can be accomplished with a minimum of difficulty, the teacher is advised against it for all of the reasons originally presented. If the sample record is examined, it will be seen that there is some natural weighting inherent in the fact that the test scores have different total values. The final is weighted somewhat in that it contains 150 points rather than the 100 to 110 of the quizzes and the maximum ratings of 100 points on the teacher ratings. When weighting is no greater than this it becomes of no great consequence, provided several measures are used in arriving at the summary. If the summaries are ranked, such incidental weighting will have relatively little effect upon the ranking of any individual pupil. It is simpler to let such measures and ratings as those shown in the sample record stand and to summarize without weighting.

TREATMENT OF EVALUATIVE DATA. Having come to a decision on the weighting issue the teacher is now ready to summarize the records of the pupils shown in the sample record sheet. The summary is to be made by the simple addition of the values shown across the page of the record for each pupil.

Another issue in marking arises at once. There are to be no *averages* of the measures. Averaging consists of adding all the measures and dividing by the number of measures. In the sample this would involve dividing all of the sums by six. The average has little significance unless all of the original scores and ratings are reduced to one base, for example a percentage score.

There are two reasons for skipping the averaging step. First, it adds much to the teacher's time in handling the data for marks. There is no particular point to having a teacher spend hours in doing simple short division problems. More important, perhaps, is the fact that pupils are to be ranked on the basis of summary. If ranking is done, the ranks of every pupil will be the same whether ranked on the raw sum or on the raw sum divided by six. The teacher who does not believe that this is true can spend an afternoon with a set of marks, ranking first on the basis of averages and then on the basis of raw sums and making a comparison of the results. The summary is to be made by the simplest mathematical calculations and pupils ranked on the basis of such summary. If the school office or commercial department has an adding machine, the summarizing process can be further speeded up.

Ranking of summary scores. The sample grade record sheet shows the names of only six pupils. Suppose that the whole class is a fairly large one for high school and consists of forty pupils. Assuming that the evaluative data for the whole class are summarized as demonstrated for the first six pupils, the summary ranked from the highest to the lowest total scores will appear as in the table shown on page 370.

Note that in the distribution of the summary scores some pupils have the same score. For example, two pupils have a summary score of 530 points. In this case the pupils with the same score must be assigned the same rank, and the pupil with the next lower score will have a rank lower by the number of pupils who have the tied score. In the example the two pupils with a score of 530 both have a rank of twelve. The pupil with the next lower score (525 points) has a rank of fourteen. If there had been three pupils with scores of 530, the pupil with a score of 525 would have had a rank of fifteen.

Finding range, median and quartiles. Having set up the distri-

Ranks on Raw Summary of Tests and Ratings

Aurora High School: English I, sec. 2, 1st quarter, 19xx–xx

Rank	Summary Score	Mark	Rank	Summary Score	Mark
1.	615	E	21.	475	M
2.	610	E	21.	475	M
3.	590	S	23.	465	M
4.	585	S	24.	460	M
5.	580	S	25.	455	M
5.	580	S	26.	450	M
7.	575	S	27.	445	M
8.	570	S	27.	445	M
9.	560	S	29.	440	M
10.	550	S	30.	435	M
		Q_3			Q_1
11.	545	S	31.	425	M
— — — — — — — — Adjusted Q_3			32.	415	M
12.	530	M	— — — — — — — Adjusted Q_1		
12.	530	M	33.	400	I
14.	525	M	34.	390	I
15.	520	M	35.	385	I
16.	510	M	36.	370	I
17.	500	M	37.	365	I
18.	490	M	38.	350	I
18.	490	M	39.	335	I
20.	480	M	40.	300	F

Median

bution of summary scores, the next step is to determine the median and quartiles for the distribution. These are indicated on the sample. Since there are forty cases the median falls between the twentieth and twenty-first cases. The summary scores on either side of the median are 480 and 475. The actual value of the median is halfway between, or 477.5.

In arriving at the marks for this particular class this median value has no great significance. However, if it seems desirable to compare the group of pupils in this section with other groups in other sections, measured on the same set of tests and ratings, the medians of the summary distributions are of value in making the comparisons.

The upper quartile, Q_3, falls between the tenth and eleventh cases and the lower, Q_1, between the thirtieth and thirty-first cases. From the earlier discussion of the application of simple statistical procedures to marking it will be recalled that the ten cases in the upper quartile should contain the "S" and "E" marks and the ten cases in the lower quartile the "I" and "F" marks. The twenty cases in the middle lying on either side of the median should be marked as "M's."

However, a class of forty may not be a large enough sample to expect a completely normal distribution of marks. We now propose to consider certain ways of dealing with such a situation.

Determining high and low marks. First, consider the problem of the total range of the distribution. The question to be determined becomes that of what is to be the highest mark assigned and what is to be the lowest mark assigned. In a given distribution for a particular class there do not have to be any "E" marks, nor any "F" marks. The marks assigned may begin with "S" and run down to "I" or "F," or possibly begin with "I" or "M" and run up to "E."

The possible range can be determined by an examination of the distribution as a whole. If the spread is small and the distribution fairly closely packed about the median with frequent tie scores, it may indicate that the range is narrow and that there should be few or no extreme marks. Usually in a class, such as in the sample, the marks at the extremes of the range will tend to stand out and be separated from the other scores by gaps in the distribution. If there are to be "E" marks these should stand out so that they can be seen from as far as the teacher is able to read the figures in the distribution. The same may be said concerning possible "F" marks.

When the distribution of summary scores for the sample class is examined, there are two scores at the top of the distribution which stand 20 and 25 points above any of the others. Therefore, it seems reasonable to assume that there are two "E" marks in the class. At the bottom of the distribution, there is one summary score 35 points below any of the others. This seems to indicate an "F" mark. The score just above this is low, too, and 15 points below the one just above it. However, if the mark of "F" is assigned to the second from the bottom of this distribution, what shall be done with the third from the bottom? The one lowest score seems clearly an "F" and so let this decision stand. The range of marks for the class will then cover the full range from "E" to "F."

Adjustment of Quartiles. It is necessary now to consider the quartile divisions that separate the "S" marks from the "M's" and the "I's" from the "M's" above them. The upper quartile falls between summary scores of 550 and 545. Five points separate the pupils ranking tenth and eleventh. There might be some difficulty in defending a decision to mark 550 as "S" and 545 as "M," if confronted by the two pupils concerned. Therefore, a principle for dealing with such situations is proposed. The principle is to adjust the quartile division to an artificial division occurring at the obvious break in the scores nearest to the true quartile.

In the sample there is a 10-point break between 550 and 560, but there is a larger 15-point break between 545 and 530. Therefore, it is proposed to set an artificial quartile at this latter point. This will mean a mark of "S" for the pupil with the summary score 545, and the "M" marks will begin with the 530 score.

The lower quartile falls between summary scores 435 and 425 at a ten point break, but there is a larger 15 point break between scores 415 and 400. Therefore, set the artificial quartile at this latter point and begin "I" marks with the 400 score and end the "M" marks at 415.

The assignment of all the remaining "S," "M," and "I" marks now becomes a very simple matter. Having determined the range and the dividing points near the quartile divisions, the other marks are set in the nature of the distribution. The sample summary sheet shows the final proposed assignment of all marks for the class.

Checking final marks against other evaluations. The teacher who uses the proposed approach for arriving at marks needs to be cautioned that the final marks assigned must be consistent with tentative marks that may have been previously reported to pupils in connection with the quizzes and ratings administered during the quarter. For example, suppose that the teacher of the class used for the sample has distributed the scores on the three quizzes and at the time of administering each quiz has reported tentative marks to pupils based upon these distributions. Assume also that pupils have been told of the teacher ratings on the notebooks and compositions. Now examine the record for Ida Culver on the sample sheet (see page 364). Without much doubt Ida would have received a report of "M" for each of the evaluations shown on the record sheet. Yet, her total on the summary score is 435, which is relatively low. The teacher will be in trouble with Ida and her parents if the adjustment of the quartile division for final marking is such that Ida should receive an "I" mark. The caution suggested needs to be operated in two directions. If marks are reported for single measures, the teacher will need to be relatively conservative in interpreting the distribution. It is always well to check what has been reported to pupils before releasing the marks based upon the distribution of the summary.

Merits of the marking system. First, here is a summary of the proposal made for arriving at marks by simple statistical treatment of data summarized from several evaluative devices.

1. Set up an adequate grade record sheet.
2. Determine measures or evaluations to be used.
3. Record scores in relatively large steps.
4. Devise a scheme for translating letters to figures.
5. Summarize scores in a summary column. Use sums rather than averages.
6. Avoid weighting as far as possible. If weighting is to be employed use simple multiples.
7. Rank the group on the basis of the summary of scores.
8. Find the median and the upper and lower fourths of the distribution.
9. Adjust divisions to the nearest normal breaks in the distribution.
10. Determine range of grades or marks to be assigned.
11. Assign marks.

This is not necessarily a perfect scheme for determining marks. It does have several distinct merits. It is simple. The number of steps in the process is few. There is a minimum of mathematical calculation. It is not time-consuming for the teacher. Fundamentally it is fair. If necessary, the process can be readily interpreted for a pupil or a parent. There will be few arguments with parents or pupils concerning the results. It is objective rather than wholly dependent upon teacher judgment. The responsibility for the final marks rests upon the pupils in their achievement and not upon whims or biases of the teacher. It does not put a high premium and great pressure upon one single evaluative device. It does put some degree of premium upon consistency of achievement of pupils.

There are, too, certain disadvantages. The scheme does not work well with very small classes. Note in passing that no marking system works too well with the quite small class. It is frankly a competitive marking system and has the objectionable features that grow out of competitive marking. Teachers must learn to use and not confuse the steps in it with other marking systems.

If teachers object to competitive marking, perhaps the only good solution is that of satisfactory-unsatisfactory descriptive marking with the standards set in terms of changes in achievement of individuals. There will follow all of the administrative difficulties which have been enumerated earlier.

Possibly a final argument in favor of the marking which has been illustrated here is that it can be administered with relatively few administrative headaches.

Subunit implementation

SUBUNIT ORGANIZATION

1. A *mark* differs from a test score or a pupil rating in that a mark is a composite of such scores or ratings.

2. A *mark* indicates the achievement or growth of pupils over some specified period of time such as a month, a school quarter, or semester.

3. A marking system is a means of determining, recording, and interpreting school marks.

4. A marking system should be administratively feasible.

5. The standards established for a marking system should be definable.

6. The standards set by a marking system should be as nearly as possible the same when applied by different teachers.

7. The standards set by a marking system should be attainable by at least some of the pupils for whom the system is used.

8. The steps or intervals between marks in a marking system should be relatively coarse.

9. It should be possible to defend the differences between individual pupils that are indicated by a particular marking system.

10. A marking system should not set fine-step differences in the achievement of individual pupils.

11. It should be possible for a teacher to arrive at the marks indicated by a marking system with a minimum of time and effort.

12. It should be possible for pupils and parents to interpret a marking system readily, with a minimum of assistance from members of the school staff.

13. There should be a large enough number of scores and ratings used in determining a set of marks so that marks do not depend unduly upon any one measure.

14. Marking systems frequently found in schools are: percentage marking; simple letter or symbol grouping; letter marking in terms of a statistical distribution; satisfactory–unsatisfactory marking in terms of individual pupil achievement or growth; and descriptive reports of growth.

15. In percentage marking and simple letter marking the standard is set at an hypothetical perfection which is practically unattainable by the pupils.

16. Percentage marking tends to make distinctions between individual pupils. These distinctions are not justifiable in terms of the reliability of the measures used.

17. Simple letter marking has the advantage of presenting coarse steps, or intervals, between marks.

18. The addition of plus and minus signs to marks in a letter marking system has the effect of increasing the steps in a coarse-step marking system.

19. In statistical letter marking the standard is set by the midpoint in the actual achievement of the pupils who are being evaluated.

20. The standard set in statistical marking can be attained by many pupils and surpassed by some.

21. There are difficulties in the application of statistical marking to small groups of pupils due to the fact that small groups may not represent a true sampling of a large number of comparable pupils.

22. In a distribution of marks or scores the *median* is the midpoint in the distribution.

23. In a distribution of marks or scores the *upper quartile*, Q_3, occurs one-fourth of the way down from the top.

24. In a distribution of marks or scores the *lower quartile*, Q_1, occurs one-fourth of the way up from the bottom.

25. In the summarization of test scores and pupil ratings to arrive at marks, the summary scores should be arranged by ranks in a statistical distribution.

26. If summary scores are arranged by ranks in a distribution, the summary can be derived by simple addition of test scores and pupil ratings.

27. There is little or no justification for the high weighting of any single measure used in the composite for determining final marks.

28. The range of marks in a summary distribution can be determined often by an inspection of the distribution. The extremes tend to be set off from other summary scores in the distribution.

29. If the quartile divisions in a summary distribution occur at points which make little or no discrimination between pupils, an artificial quartile adjustment should be made to the nearest break in the distribution.

30. In its psychological effects upon learning, a satisfactory—unsatisfactory marking system with no other discriminations between pupils is an ideal marking system.

31. The standard for satisfactory—unsatisfactory marking is determined for each pupil in terms of his own growth or increased achievement. The system is noncompetitive.

32. The administration of satisfactory—unsatisfactory marking tends to break down in dealing with people outside the school situation.

33. Teachers often destroy the merits of satisfactory—unsatisfactory marking by using symbols and by adding plus and minus marks to the symbols.

34. Descriptive marking presents great difficulties in interpretation with parents and others.

35. Descriptive marking tends to break down over its inherent interpretative and administrative difficulties.

THINGS TO DO

1. Lay out a grade record sheet for a quarter's work for one high school course in your major subject. Show the class roll and the appropriate headings for all the evaluative devices to be used in arriving at the marks for the quarter.

2. Fill in the test and rating data for the quarter's work on the record sheet indicated above. Determine the quarter's marks for the pupils shown on the class roll according to the directions outlined in this chapter.

3. Find in your class a student who has attended a high school using a descriptive marking scheme. Arrange for a report on the use of this system as experienced by the student. Set up a panel for a panel discussion of descriptive marking following the student report.

4. Examine a set of marks set up on a percentage basis. Distribute these marks in order of rank, if they are not so arranged. How many cases are there in the distribution in which one per cent discriminations are made between individual pupils. Suppose that two pupils who have marks in the order of 79 and 80 come to you as a teacher for an explanation of the difference. Write out a brief statement of what you would say to these pupils.

5. Find an actual set of English compositions done by a tenth-grade high school class. Select from these compositions a 100 per cent composition. If there is none, try making a statement of what a 100 per cent composition would be like for this class. If you mark a composition 100 per cent, what are its characteristics? Try having various members of the class rate the sample set of compositions without consultation with others. What variations are there in the markings of different individuals?

6. Arrange to get for the class a tape recording of a high school speech performance or a musical performance. A recording of an oratorical contest or a series of solo voice performances will serve. Present the recording to the class. What is an "A" performance? How is the "A" performance to be defined.

7. Try arranging the performers heard above in rough groupings beginning with a middle group of "about what you could expect." Make other groupings above and below this midgrouping. How would you propose to rate these groups?

8. Make a class collection of sample school reports to parents, "grade cards." Arrange these in a display on the classroom bulletin board or project them on a screen with an opaque projector. Arrange for a panel discussion of the relative merits of the different forms of reports in the collection.

9. Arrange for a panel of members of a high school PTA to come to your class to present the point of view of parents concerning school reports and "grade cards."

10. Write out a brief statement of what you would say to the parents of a pupil of relatively high achievement compared to other pupils who had been marked *unsatisfactory* because of little progress or growth in terms of his own capacity.

11. Make a poll of members of the class. Ask each person which system of school marks he prefers and which system he has had the most experience with in school. Can you gather any evidence to prove or disprove the notion that most people prefer the marking system with which they have the greatest familiarity?

Helpful Readings

ALEXANDER, WILLIAM M. and HALVERSON, PAUL M. *Effective Teaching in Secondary Schools.* New York: Rinehart & Co., Inc., 1956. Chap. 13.

Emphasizes the evaluation of pupil progress. Contains illustrations of descriptive forms and reports for the use of teachers. Includes a definition of marks and a description of satisfactory-unsatisfactory marking.

BOSSING, NELSON L. *Teaching in Secondary Schools.* 3d ed. Boston: Houghton Mifflin Co., 1952. Pp. 267–79.

Contains sample report forms and a description of different marking systems.

GARRETT, HENRY E. *Statistics in Psychology and Education.* 3d ed. New York: Longmans, Green & Co., Inc., 1947. Chaps. 4, 5, and 6.

Chapters on graphic representations of marks and the normal curve of distribution.

GARRISON, NOBLE LEE. *The Improvement of Teaching*. New York: The Dryden Press, Inc., 1955. Pp. 314–27.

Pages indicated are on reports to pupils and parents.

GRAMBS, JEAN D. and IVERSON, WILLIAM J. *Modern Methods in Secondary Education*. New York: William Sloane Assoc., Inc., 1952. Chap. 16.

Material on marks, marking systems, marking standards, the effects of marks on pupils, and on reports.

GREENE, HARRY A., JORGENSEN, ALBERT N., and GERBERICH, J. R. *Measurement and Evaluation in the Secondary School*. New York: Longmans, Green & Co., Inc., 1946. Chap. 25 and 26, pp. 589–606.

Chap. 25 deals with the statistical summarization of measurements; the latter part of chap. 26 with statistical interpretations.

JACOBSON, PAUL B., *et al.* *The American Secondary School*. Englewood Cliffs, N.J.: Prentice-Hall, Inc., 1952. Chap. 16.

Chap. 16 is on marking and reporting. Included are many sample report forms.

MURSELL, JAMES L. *Successful Teaching*. 2d ed. New York: McGraw-Hill Book Co., Inc., 1954. Chap. 16.

Read for an interpretation of marking systems.

ROSS, C. C. and STANLEY, JULIAN C. *Measurement in Today's Schools*. Rev. ed. Englewood Cliffs, N.J.: Prentice-Hall, Inc., 1954. Chaps. 8–10.

See for graphical representation and reporting of test data.

STILES, LINDLEY J. and DORSEY, MATTIE F. *Democratic Teaching in Secondary Schools*. Philadelphia: J. B. Lippincott Co., 1950. Pp. 423–30.

Pages indicated contain a short section on appraising and reporting progress of pupils followed by a section on the assignment of marks.

THORNDIKE, ROBERT L. and HAGEN, ELIZABETH P. *Measurement and Evaluation in Psychology and Education*. New York: John Wiley & Sons, Inc., 1955.

See section on various means of evaluation and on reporting and interpretation.

UMSTATTD, JAMES G. *Secondary School Teaching*. 3d ed. Boston: Ginn & Co., 1953. Pp. 416–42.

Includes sections on reporting pupil progress and on informal descriptive evaluations.

WILLIAMS, L. A. *Secondary Schools for American Youth*. New York: American Book Co., 1948. Chap. 10.

See sections on pupil appraisal and the assignment of marks.

WOODRING, PAUL. *Let's Talk Sense About Our Schools*. New York: McGraw-Hill Book Co., Inc., 1953. Chap. 2.

Chap. 2 is on the reactions of parents and patrons to the changes taking place in school marks. Raises the problem of interpreting marks and reports to the people who support the schools.

Index